Understanding People
in Context
The Ecological Perspective
in Counseling

Edited by
Ellen P. Cook

AMERICAN COUNSELING
ASSOCIATION
5999 Stevenson Avenue
Alexandria, VA 22304
www.counseling.org

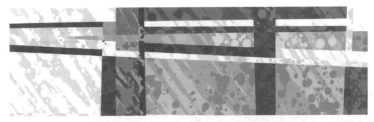

Understanding People
in Context
The Ecological Perspective
in Counseling

10 9 8 7 6 5 4 3 2 1

American Counseling Association
5999 Stevenson Avenue
Alexandria, VA 22304

Director of Publications   Carolyn C. Baker

Production Manager   Bonny E. Gaston

Editorial Assistant   Catherine A. Brumley

Copy Editor   Beth Ciha

Cover and text design by Bonny E. Gaston

Library of Congress Cataloging-in-Publication Data
Understanding people in context : the ecological perspective in counseling /
edited by Ellen P. Cook.
    p. cm.
    Includes bibliographical references and index.
    ISBN 978-1-55620-287-2 (alk. paper)
    1. Counseling.   2. Environmental psychology.   I. Cook, Ellen Piel, 1952–
BF636.6U533   2012
158.3—dc23   2011047055

For David, Jenny, and Laura

Chaps 8, 11, +12

Other chaps as interested

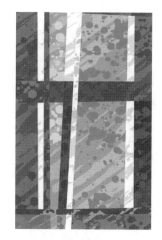

Table of Contents

Part I   **Understanding the Ecological Perspective**

1

2

3

4

5

6

Acknowledgments

Any project with a gestation period as long as this one owes its completion to many people, all doing their thing very, very well. Carolyn Baker, the Director of Publications of the American Counseling Association, was patient, precise in her commentary, and supportive as always. She does her work so well that it makes mine as an author go much more smoothly. I am grateful to Bob Conyne, who helped me birth an early version of the perspective. Other colleagues at the University of Cincinnati contributed thought-provoking chapters and tolerated my endless complaints about how long my own writing was taking. Counseling students over the past decade helped to develop these ideas and contributed time, energy, and enthusiasm to the various projects noted in this book.

People in the other contexts of my life contributed as well. Friends really did believe that I would finish someday. Loved ones at St. Timothy's Episcopal Church reminded me every week what is genuinely important in life. The ever-cheerful baristas at Starbucks remembered my customary order and regularly asked how I was doing on the project. My pets fought for the best position at my feet throughout the process. At the heart of it all is my family. You know how much I love and appreciate you.

About the Editor

The Rev. Ellen P. Cook, PhD, is a professor in the counseling program at the University of Cincinnati. She earned her bachelor's degree (*summa cum laude*) from the University of Toledo and her doctorate in counseling psychology from the University of Iowa in 1977. She has spent virtually her whole career at the University of Cincinnati, training graduate students in the ecological perspective, counseling theory and research, professional ethics, internship, and prevention. An accomplished author and editor, she has served on numerous editorial boards in counseling and psychology, one as national journal editor, and has published many articles in professional journals. This is her fourth book. She holds the status of Fellow of the American Psychological Association, which recognizes her contributions to the professional literature in gender issues, and was awarded the national Association for Counselor Education and Supervision Counseling Vision and Innovation Award. She is also an ordained vocational deacon in the Episcopal Church, Diocese of Southern Ohio.

About the Contributors

Huma Bashir, MS, is a child and family counselor at Rocking Horse Community Health Center in Springfield, Ohio.

Michael D. Brubaker, PhD, is an assistant professor and academic coordinator of the Substance Abuse Counseling Program at the University of Cincinnati in Ohio.

Susannah C. Coaston, MA, is a counselor at LifePoint Solutions, Inc., in Amelia, Ohio.

Jeri Crowell, EdD, is an assistant professor in Capella University's counselor education program.

Nzingha Dalila, MS, LPC-S, is a clinical counselor at the University of Cincinnati's Counseling Center.

Jill Gomez, MSW, LISW-S, LICDC, is an instructor and area coordinator for social work, human services, and addiction studies at University of Cincinnati Clermont College and serves as a Commission for Accreditation for Rehabilitation Facilities Surveyor.

Michelle Flaum Hall, EdD, is an assistant professor of counseling at Xavier University in Cincinnati and maintains a private practice, the Highlander Group, in Kettering, Ohio.

Greta Hochstetler Mayer, MA, is Assistant Director of Programs and Communications at the Mental Health & Recovery Board of Clark, Greene, and Madison Counties in Ohio.

Wairimu Wanjau Mutai, PhD, is a counselor educator and counselor who has experience working in faith-based counseling organizations in the United States and Kenya.

Steven W. Patrick, MA, PC, is an adjunct faculty member in the School of Professional Counseling at Lindsey Wilson College in Columbia, Kentucky, and a counselor in private practice.

Kerry E. Sebera, PhD, is an assistant professor of counseling at Northern Kentucky University in Highland Heights.

Joseph A. Stewart-Sicking, EdD, is an assistant professor in the Department of Pastoral Counseling at Loyola University Maryland in Baltimore and an Episcopal priest.

Mei Tang, PhD, is a professor and the Program Coordinator of the Counseling Program at the University of Cincinnati.

Albert L. Watson, PhD, is an associate professor of counseling at the University of Cincinnati.

F. Robert Wilson, PhD, is a professor emeritus of counseling at the University of Cincinnati and a mental health counselor and supervisor in the Health Resource Center of Cincinnati.

Geoffrey G. Yager, PhD, is a professor in the Counseling Program at the University of Cincinnati and maintains a private practice, Holistic Counseling Care of Cincinnati.

Part I

Understanding the Ecological Perspective

Introduction

Ellen P. Cook

What are human beings, and why do they behave as they do? This question is more than a provocative opener for a philosophy class. It is actually a quite practical question that people ask in various forms throughout their lives: Why do teenagers behave in such maddening ways? Does reading your horoscope every day help you prepare for what's ahead? Just how much control do we have over our lives anyway?

I don't have a definitive answer to any of these questions, but I do believe it is safe to say two things in response. First, if you are reading this book you have likely chosen a career in human services, and so you are probably as fascinated by these questions as I am. Second, how we answer these questions influences our work with people—how we conceptualize our clients' problems, desirable goals for them, and the interventions that we hope will make a difference in their lives.

This book is about both the basic questions we humans all ask about life and the specific answers we human services professionals use as cornerstones for our work helping people rebuild their lives. Based on what professionals have already learned about human behavior, what frameworks can serve as useful guides for our clients and ourselves? What interventions seem most consistent with our current knowledge base and the values that animate our profession?

Problems With Individual Explanations for Behavior

Since their inception, human services professions have envisioned human behavior as a sometimes uneasy reconciliation between individual motivations and social imperatives, although the variables and values embodied in these

3

could vary quite dramatically. Until quite recently, individuals were viewed as solely responsible for their problems, often unintentionally so. Freud and his contemporaries launched a cultural revolution with their groundbreaking ideas about the causes and remedies for human behavior problems. In their view, psychic misery was not caused solely by biological dysfunction or spiritual turpitude but was meaningful in its own right as a coded message about unseen but very real internal conflicts. Each individual stood at a crossroads between individual needs and societal mores and customs. Since the turn of the 20th century, theories about human behavior have proliferated, embracing the brilliant observations of clinicians and the newly developing social sciences, broadly shared philosophical/theological premises about the good life, and transformations in the broader sociocultural context.

Over recent decades counseling/psychotherapy schools of thought mushroomed into the dozens. Although any student in a graduate-level theories class could testify about the mind-numbing diversity in theories *du jour*, theories generally varied more in terminology than in real substance. Theorists typically agreed that individual characteristics—drives, traumas, beliefs, and so on—caused problems that could be resolved through verbal exploration and emotional expression. This change process was directed by an expert whose professional education equipped him or her to intuit the problem expressed by the client in disguise and then conduct the painstaking excavation needed to unearth and correct it. As theories increased in number, precision, and depth, the precise nature of the individual's problem assumed different shapes and sizes but the birthplace remained the same: the individual and his or her tragedies, deficits, poor choices, and so on.

This focus on the identification of individual causes of problems continues today and certainly has proven its value in ameliorating human misery. In recent decades, however, human services professionals have increasingly spoken about how an exclusive personal focus is limited in the phenomena it can address. This perspective can be insufficient for many reasons we discuss in this book. For example, by its very nature, human behavior is often more accurately described as interactional rather than personal. The power of individual variables on their own to predict behavior is often surprisingly poor. And to blame certain categories of human misery (e.g., sequelae of horrific abuse) on the survivor's individual deficiencies seems not only inadequate but unjust.

For many reasons, then, individual models of human behavior have increasingly been viewed as ultimately limited in their explanatory value. One alternative model that recognizes individual factors as providing necessary but insufficient answers to questions about human behavior is the ecological perspective.

The Metaphor of Ecology

The ecological perspective is based on a metaphor of ecology within the physical world, which humans have cohabited with all creation since the beginning of the species. Life on our planet consists of interlocking systems of living creatures, each depending on other living and nonliving features of the environment for sustenance. Despite human illusions of omnipotence, we cannot exist without sunlight, minerals from the ground, and nourishment from green plants and other organisms. Our greed in using natural resources has left our home depleted and perhaps irreversibly changed; our greed has also caused species of living creatures we may never even have seen to become extinct. And yet in the spirit of the creation stories told by ancient religions, we also nurture barren spaces and suffering species back to life through our loving care.

All humans share in common certain requirements for life: We all procreate by the same physiological process, and we all care for our young for years. Through evolution, our physical beings have adapted to demands imposed by the physical context (e.g., changes to skin color in peoples living close to the equator). Other variability is attributable to choices rooted in our intellectual capacities instead of external imperatives (e.g., whether we ingest fluids in the form of water, tea, or beer). Regardless of which beverage they reach for, humans rely on the fruits of the surrounding contexts to sustain their lives.

Living beings of one species share certain requirements for life unique from those of other species—for example, some species of plants require abundant moisture, whereas others can endure prolonged drought conditions. However, within every species exist many shades of variation, whether predictable or seemingly random. Animal breeders know that the runts of a litter may need to be separated from their siblings in order to survive. Crops planted in a field ruined by flooding may require special farming techniques to be coaxed into fruition once again. In recent years, deer have been found nibbling designer landscaping plants because their habitats are shrinking. In innumerable ways, small groups or individual creatures may face unusual demands (or opportunities) because of environmental factors outside their control.

The ecology of everyday human life follows similar natural laws. Each of us is part of a constantly changing dynamic with other living and nonliving things. The term *ecosystem* refers to the sum total of interactive influences operating within an individual's life in varying degrees of proximity, ranging from his or her biologically determined characteristics to the broader sociocultural context structuring human interactions. Every human life is influenced by factors and processes common to all humans (e.g., the need for food and water), unique to the members of a particular context or group (e.g., weather conditions experienced in the Congo vs. Greenland, dietary customs of orthodox Jews vs. observant Muslims), or idiosyncratic to that individual (e.g., the sum total of life experiences as a biracial, gay, devout Catholic man). What happens to an individual rarely occurs in a vacuum but rather is shaped by the confluence of events, propensities, relationships, memories, and other features of a life elaborated over time and across settings.

In certain ways, humans rely on the sustenance provided by the context around them as unconsciously as fish rely on water to sustain them. What makes humans human, however, is their capacity to *think* about their lives. Trees do not consciously choose how much water they ingest, but humans can develop and voluntarily recover from obesity, anorexia, or alcoholism. A palm tree does not decide to try living off the coast of Maine, but humans

5

do choose to uproot and replant themselves in environments just as alien. And plants engage only in the unselfconscious sharing that all members of an interdependent ecosystem have evolved over the centuries; a human may hoard or give away all personal resources for more reasons than a tree has leaves. It is this capacity to perceive and make sense out of one's makeup, relationships, contexts, and potentialities that makes human ecology qualitatively different from the ecologies of any other living beings. It is the complexity of this human ecology that makes counseling as helpful to human growth as fertilizer is to plants.

As is discussed in this book, the ecological perspective is a model for understanding human behavior that is based on the guiding vision (or basic assumption) that *human life is fundamentally connected with the world around us.* The ecological perspective is consistent with a well-known formula for representing human behavior (Lewin, 1935), B = f(P × E), or behavior is a function of a person interacting within his or her environment. From this guiding schematic flow three propositions:

1. Human behavior is influenced by characteristics of both the individual and life contexts.
2. Human behavior is the product of an individual interacting with his or her life contexts, or environments.
3. Human behavior is shaped by meaning making.

In the next section I sketch the substance of each of these propositions.

The Ecological Perspective: Fundamental Propositions

The ecological perspective is not a theory per se but a way of thinking about behavior across theories. The ecological perspective attempts to embrace diverse counseling theories under a single conceptual umbrella by assisting counselors in deciding when, where, and how to use various change strategies. Ecological principles have been widely embraced in counseling, psychology, and social work. Three aspects of human behavior—its personal and contextual nature, its interactional nature, and the importance of meaning making—serve as conceptual building blocks in the ecological perspective.

Behavior Is Both Personal and Contextual

As noted before, counselors are accustomed to attributing their clients' problems to some combination of personal characteristics—traits, learned behaviors, poor self-esteem, and so on. As we see in Chapter 2, there is nothing wrong with this focus on personal characteristics. Yet the ecological perspective recognizes that this focus is only part of the answer to the puzzle of human behavior and only half of the first proposition described in this section.

The fundamental precept in the ecological perspective is a restatement of Kurt Lewin's (1935) famous formula: All human behavior must be understood as the outcome of a human being's interaction with his or her environment. Behavior always occurs within a set of contexts whose differentiation is commonly represented as concentric or nested circles (Bronfenbrenner, 1979). The individual with his or her unique biological, psychological, and social makeup functions at the center of these interpenetrating contexts, influenced most directly by interpersonal relationships within everyday life. The next level of proximity is the groups of which the individual is a member, followed by neighborhoods, communities, large organizations, and broader social institutions. Encompassing all other levels are macrolevel influences, which represent the broader sociocultural mores, patterns of behavior, values, and so on that effectively structure life implicitly or explicitly for members of the society. The nature of the person, interactions within social groups, and models of human action in a variety of settings all embody coherent frameworks of meaning implicit across a culture. Counselors also need to remember that the physical environment, whether natural (e.g., topography) or human made (e.g., architecture), exerts an often subtle but undeniable influence on behavior.

Behavior Is Interactional

Individuals are not passive placeholders within these environments but actively interact with them. Individuals are influenced by, and in turn influence, the contexts of their lives. Individuals do have some genetically based propensities for behavior, but whether and how these propensities are actualized within an individual life is likely to be moderated by the individual's interactions with his or her life contexts. It is crucial to understand how a particular individual reacts to salient events within the immediate life context. Individuals with similar genetic constitutions or social histories may react to certain events similarly—or very differently.

Culture is a multidimensional construct representing person–environment interactions at myriad levels. In essence, culturally related behavior is affected by the interaction of both individual and contextual variability. Ecologically minded counselors routinely remind themselves to look for within-group diversity among groups of people they predict will behave similarly.

Behavior Is Meaningful

The ecological perspective emphasizes *meaning making:* A person responds to events as he or she perceives and understands them. The ecological perspective elaborates how differences in meaning making can occur because of influences at each contextual level (e.g., individual spiritual development, family values that prompt certain career choices, organizational mission statements that shape on-the-job behavior). Biological sex, physical markers of race, and other culturally meaningful differences activate complex systems of meaning that in turn structure social roles, political rights, career opportunities, and other powerful determinants of possibilities within the fabric of social life. Yet there is also incredible variability across individuals within the same category because of the interaction between person and context. A counselor and client can determine which meanings implicit within the client's life may contribute to his or her distress and which of these meanings are possible or even desirable to change.

Goals of Ecological Counseling

A common purpose of counseling using the ecological perspective is to help individuals develop more satisfying, productive, and meaningful lives through understanding how their lives are rooted in diverse contexts, interactions with the world around them, and their meaning-making processes. In an earlier book on ecological counseling, Robert Conyne and I emphasized helping people to maximize *concordance* within their lives, defined as "mutually beneficial interaction between person and environment" involving a "harmonious balance between challenge and support" (Conyne & Cook, 2004, p. 24). The sense of *discordance* is universal at times and common among clients: Something essential in life is missing or is present but toxic; a person does not fit in roles, relationships, or life paths. Individuals experience discordance according to their meaning making.

In this sequel, *Understanding People in Context: The Ecological Perspective in Counseling*, I view ecological counseling somewhat more broadly than before. The concordance/discordance distinction does not quite fit many possible goals and strategies in ecological counseling. A counselor using the ecological perspective may discern just how a person may experience the self, the interpersonal/cultural/physical environment, or the interaction between person and environment as a source of pain. Past life events, present-day conflicts across relationships, and future hopes and dreams may all be the focus. From among the wealth of connections making up each person's life, the counselor considers which life resources lend strength (nutrients) and which challenges from within and outside the client complicate his or her quest to make a life worth living.

Counselors utilizing the ecological perspective appreciate that there are many ways to facilitate change. Counselors can work within a person's unique ecosystem or address less immediate contexts (e.g., groups, neighborhood) for remedial, developmental, or preventive interventions. The ecological perspective can expand a counselor's ability to image the complexities of human behavior and how the counseling profession can work collaboratively with clients and systems to change lives.

These propositions and their corollaries as discussed throughout this book are simple but far from simplistic in nature. There is little specialized jargon to master, no mathematical equations to unravel. Counselors learning about the ecological perspective are not called to master yet another set of arcane techniques; rather, they typically discover that they can continue using tried and true strategies, albeit sometimes with different purposes in mind. Yet in my experience (and the experience of my coauthors), these deceptively simple ideas have the power to integrate research data across disciplines, open lines of communication across helping professionals, and empower clients to take action within their lives with dignity and self-respect. These ideas are far from reductionist in intent. Instead the intent behind using the ecological perspective is to assist counselors in appreciating the complexity of clients' lives and, in so doing, to generate strategies for interventions that honor the interconnectedness of human lives across situations and over time.

If you are already familiar with ecological principles in counseling, you might find my focus on individuals and the interconnecting contexts of their personal lives to be somewhat different than other ecological discussions that typically place greater emphasis on systemic, macrolevel influences. As you will see, my coauthors and I indeed discuss these broader dynamics; we firmly believe that the helping professions must recognize the significance of social power, economic resources, politics, and other dynamics often invisible to people trying to live their lives day to day. We will also try to coax you into considering how you might try to change our world to offer individuals and groups differential access to resources, opportunities, and rewards. In these chapters, however, we generally maintain our focus on the clientele we try to serve through our daily work. How can we better understand the contexts, interactions, and meanings influencing the concerns of, for example, Juan and Shoshanna, the Kwan family, and Jamie's classroom? We hope to demonstrate that some ecological ideas that might seem abstract at first—for example, ecosystems, meaning making, sociocultural dynamics—are actually very useful in understanding the complexities of human life today.

Organization of the Book

This book contains two major sections. In Part I, I describe the major propositions of the ecological perspective in some detail, citing theory and research in support of these propositions. One important thing to keep in mind is that the ecological perspective is grand in design, embracing a wealth of ideas across diverse theoretical points of view. The perspective recognizes that there are a great many ways of understanding human behavior and that we as counselors can benefit from casting our nets wide in gathering information to support our work with clients. Genetics, community psychology, and cultural anthropology represent a tiny sampling of the fields that can teach us how behavior is a function of individuals interacting within life contexts, trying to make sense of their lives.

In my enthusiasm to see just how broad in scope these ideas are, I managed to cover a mind-numbing range of the recent professional literature. In addition to sampling the counseling literature, early in the project I decided to concentrate on various fields of psychology that, in my experience, are relatively unfamiliar to counselors in training and practice. This review convinced me that these ideas are compatible with topics and points of view explored in a broad range of disciplines today. An unforeseen outcome is that this book just might be useful in updating and filling out your own education, whether you are preparing for comps, an upcoming presentation or article, or the next client of the day.

The chapters in Part II of this book were written by experts who have applied the ecological perspective in their own field of practice. Many of these experts are connected with the counseling program at the University of Cincinnati, which has adopted the ecological perspective as its official vision for teaching, research, and counseling practice. In these chapters, the authors discuss their own unique version of ecological counseling and how they have used it in their work. I firmly believe that any topic in counseling can be discussed using the ecological ideas in this book. The specific chapters included in this book were designed to reflect my coauthors' own areas of expertise and to cover topics not addressed in other ecological resources (e.g., Conyne & Cook, 2004), such as faith-based communities. Tang and Bashir assert that cultural identity is fluid and multifaceted, a changeable product of people interacting with people different from themselves. Counselors need to explore the individualized meaning of clients' diverse identities in order to be helpful to them. Wilson demonstrates how clinical processes of assessment, diagnosis, and treatment fit well within the ecological perspective. The concepts of ecological niche, interactions within life contexts, and coconstructed meaning in the counseling process all play central roles in his discussion. Crowell, Sebera, and Coaston discuss the ecological challenges school counselors face daily in their efforts to encourage students' development. Myriad problems facing young people at home, in the community, and within schools can be addressed with the combination of realism, hope, and dedication possessed by school counselors in these settings today. Substance abuse and addiction are issues endemic throughout society—indeed, they are global issues. Watson and his associates argue that the ecological approach to counseling may be a comprehensive and effective model for addressing the systemic causes and consequences of substance abuse and addiction. In their chapter on faith-based communities, Stewart-Sicking and Mutai explain how these communities function as social institutions that differ in size, structure, and purpose as well as theology. Counselors share with these communities an interest in enhancing people's wisdom and development; they can work together to provide social, emotional, and material resources to community members. Finally, in their chapter on counselor training, Hall and Yager explain how to build ecological sensitivity in counseling skills through self-assessment and case illustrations. Counselors are people in context too and need intellectual, emotional, and behavioral elasticity to provide the best possible care. I have encouraged all of these authors to use examples to help their discussion come alive for you.

I close the book by integrating the ideas discussed across the chapters and suggesting some next steps for developing the ecological perspective in counseling today and tomorrow.

And now: the ecological perspective in detail!

References

Bronfenbrenner, U. (1979). *The ecology of human development: Experiments by nature and design.* Cambridge, MA: Harvard University Press.

Conyne, R. K., & Cook, E. P. (Eds.). (2004). *Ecological counseling: An innovative approach to conceptualizing person–environment interaction.* Alexandria, VA: American Counseling Association.

Lewin, K. (1935). *A dynamic theory of personality.* New York, NY: McGraw-Hill.

Behavior Is Personal

Ellen P. Cook

We as individuals bring a broad range of personal characteristics to our interactions in the world around us. These characteristics—whether innate, learned, or both—function as predispositions influencing the nature of our behavior. The combination of our personhood and our lifelong interactions make us the unique individuals we are.

In Chapter 1 I established that the E in the P × E paradigm refers to the various environments or contexts that make up a person's life. The P, in turn, refers to you or me—the person living within the life contexts. In the ecological perspective behavior is the result of ongoing interaction between P and E. A counselor using the ecological perspective to understand an individual client's presenting problem thinks about the person, the pertinent life contexts, and how person and context interact. This information provides ideas for how the counselor and client can work together to help the client make changes in his or her life. This task is easier said than done: Considering how complicated people's lives can be, which aspects of P and E must we as counselors consider in our work with a particular client?

Thinking about P, or the person, is probably more natural for counselors than thinking about context, regardless of their theoretical point of view. Most people, counselors included, are predisposed to view characteristics of individuals as the source of their problems. Folk wisdom asserts that we behave as we do because that is our nature; in other words, we are what we are born to be. Shy people will be wallflowers; natural born leaders will take over any crowd; and artistic people can arrange anything beautifully, whether flowers or bulletin boards. We follow what we were born to become.

There is some truth to this point of view, but it is usually more complicated than we might first think. Consider the life story of Jay-Z, a musician and producer. Jay-Z grew up in the most rugged of urban settings, surrounded by drugs, violence, and desperation. He was selling drugs by his teens and barely escaped the early death so often the fate of his companions. Instead he managed to become a potent force in the music business, fabulously wealthy, the husband of a multitalented star in her own right (Beyoncé).

What caused Jay-Z's problems and his eventual salvation? Innate resilience? Abandonment by his father? The drug culture of his neighborhood? His mother's prayers? Lack of stimulating education and positive role models? His intelligence? Perhaps all these factors, and many more. Who Jay-Z was as a person certainly shaped his life choices, and the same neighborhood contributed to both the early death of his friends and his own remarkable success. It is the unique combination of "Jay-Z-ness," the life contexts he inhabited with others, and countless other life events he uniquely experienced that made him what he is today.

In this chapter I consider what a person brings to the interactions with the world that make up his or her life. Some of what we refer to as P, or personal factors, is innate, whereas other aspects are learned over time. Much of what makes us unique as people is "both/and" rather than "either/or": both our personhood *and* our lifelong interactions with the world around us. We know with certainty little about the ultimate origins of our uniqueness; from our earliest days and throughout our lives, who we are as people is modeled and modified through our life experiences. These life experiences in turn are openly and invisibly shaped by the cultural contexts that make us a certain flavor of person: one primarily oriented to individual accomplishment, for example, or one committed to the welfare of family and community above all else. All of this learning happens through relationships with others. To know for sure whether a given characteristic is innate or learned, researchers would need to be able to compare typical humans with people who develop without the human interactions we experience from our first moments outside the womb. This is an experiment not likely to happen!

Luckily, in the ecological perspective answering questions about the ultimate origins of behaviors is not crucial. The ecological perspective emphasizes the fact that even apparently simple behaviors may be affected by interactional chains that we will never be able to unravel. No matter: Our job as counselors using the ecological perspective is to help clients change their lives not by ferreting out ultimate causes of problems but by making changes today that are effective, feasible, and meaningful for them.

In this chapter I review some of what is known today about the predispositions that people bring to situations. Every counselor reading this book can list a staggering array of personal characteristics worth considering: self-esteem, self-concept, or self-efficacy; social and coping skills; spiritual orientation and religious practices; intelligence of various kinds and learning styles; and on and on. This chapter should be considered an introduction to a way of thinking about individuality based on the recent professional literature rather than a comprehensive review of its components. I begin by reviewing the position of P in the famous P × E formula: What is it, and what does it contribute to behavior?

Background: Just How Personal Is Behavior?

The mission of counselors is to help individuals, often one person at a time, behave more effectively and satisfyingly. In the earliest days of the helping professions, people in emotional distress sought help from highly educated professionals who listened intently for clues to the person's dysfunction. The problem was presumably linked to a mysterious, often hidden deficit or trauma responsible for the person's inability to cope effectively as most healthy people did. The public believed that psychological experts possessed extraordinary skills in discernment and, akin to Sherlock Holmes, knew where to look for solutions to the most perplexing behavioral puzzles. Once the offending ultimate cause was uncovered, the expert could perform the equivalent of psychic surgery to excise or reconstruct the offending component part and thereby return the psychic machine to smooth functioning.

As noted elsewhere (Conyne & Cook, 2004), counselors then and now typically base their work on a person-centered paradigm, displayed schematically as B = f(P). Behavior is a function of personal characteristics such as genetic heritage, emotions, or previously learned behavior. The environment may indeed influence behavior as well, but in this person-centered paradigm it is believed to be a secondary role at best, perhaps modifying how or where the personal characteristic is expressed. The focus remains on the person and what he or she does to effect what happens in life.

P characteristics are at the very center of counselors' professional training. From our first day in class we learn to think about, assess, and make plans to change the characteristics that get people into psychological trouble. Here's a quick exercise to illustrate: A new client complains of feeling down, overly emotional, and hopeless to change things for the better. What types of factors come to mind to explore in counseling? Perhaps low self-esteem, disordered thinking processes, inept social skills, past trauma, malfunctioning neurotransmitters, or physical illness? All of these factors are P factors, factors that are hypothesized to be enduring client characteristics that regularly contribute to clients' personal discomfort and dysfunction. Innumerable clients have been helped by counseling focused on such P factors. The ecological perspective reminds us, however, that other factors might be present instead of or in interaction with P factors: caring for a family member with disabilities, perhaps, or harassment and attacks from others because of the client's sexual orientation. We may also need to look more broadly for answers: an economy that offers city dwellers little hope for the future or efforts to accommodate to a new cultural context in a community where everyone else looks the same. P characteristics are a good place to start, but they are often not enough to get the full picture of a client's situation.

For decades researchers, too, assumed that person-based determinism was where psychological truths could be found. In recounting his life's work as a researcher in the field of personality, Walter Mischel (2004) noted how distressing it was to researchers to discover time and again that simple trait measures did not predict behavior very well by themselves. In light of these unexpected findings, researchers first did what people usually do when faced with information that contradicts something essential they had assumed was true: They simply looked harder in the same place for the truths that were eluding them!

The popularity of person-oriented explanations in everyday settings suggests that people generally find such explanations plausible. Quizzes in popular magazines are ubiquitous because readers take for granted that the best choices for everything from fragrances to romantic partners depend on what type of person you are. Behavior is blamed on everything from one's astrological sign to qualities that run in the family and, more ominously, to flaws passed down in one's religious tradition or ethnicity (witness the Nazis' preoccupation with tiny percentages of "Jewish blood" in one's ancestry). It simply seems plausible and easier to attribute other people's problems to character flaws rather than to a confluence of factors rooted in the interaction of person and context.

This tendency to automatically attribute others' behavior to personal dispositions is consistent with what Morton, Postmes, Haslam, and Horney (2009) labeled *essentialist* lay theories: explanations for behavior that rely on stable, inherent, and unchangeable causes, often invoking biological roots. It is habitual for us, including counselors in their work, to overlook factors outside a person. Our behavior at any given time certainly may be correctly attributed to personal factors and personal factors alone—or maybe not. Today I chose a certain breakfast cereal because I prefer it over the other options (personal). Tomorrow I may not have a choice of cereals because the other cereals are all gone (situational). Or perhaps I am traveling in a culture that customarily offers either soup or fish for breakfast (a different type of choice situation indeed). There are certainly many ways in which personal characteristics may influence a person's life, but it is a mistake to think that P factors alone determine behavior. It is also a mistake to dismiss these personal tendencies as inconsequential.

One plausible version of personal explanations for behavior is genetics: Perhaps people behave the way they do because their genetic makeup dictates that they do so. People tend to believe in genetic determinism, assuming that genes determine one's behavior and future (Sankar, cited in Moffitt, Caspi, & Rutter, 2006). Moffitt et al. (2006) further suggested that this belief in genetic determinism is related to publicity about rare disorders caused by chromosomal or single-gene defects (e.g., Huntington's chorea). If we learn that some genetic propensities for illness exist, then it is a short step to wondering whether other aspects of behavior are also linked to genetic makeup—our resilience in the face of chronic stress, for example.

Moffitt et al. (2006) labeled the public's general understanding about the link between genetics and psychological problems as "naively deterministic" (p. 19). To state it simply, this belief is probably just a little bit true. Research suggests that behavior is determined by an interaction between personal predispositions and environmental influences, with the precise combination of interactions subject to a vast range of influences. The effects of genes on behavior are probably the result of complex interactions. For instance, genes may affect how individuals respond to environmental challenges (Bronfenbrenner & Ceci, 1994; Moffitt et al., 2006). In some cases interactions occur among a variety of genes in a particular combination or sequence; for other outcomes a specific environment might be necessary (Caspi, Roberts, & Shiner, 2005). Behavior is determined not by genetics or the environment alone but by how people in their genetic glory both create and respond to what happens to them. Genes alone may determine whether we have blue or brown eyes, but for the types of behaviors of interest to counselors, any genetic contribution is likely to be indirect, through influencing how a person interacts with the environment. We come to know who we are, and realize our potential, only through our interaction with the world around us (Gottfredson, 2005).

In the ecological perspective we do recognize the validity of genetic factors, but we regard them as only one part of the picture. Consistent with present research, in the ecological perspective our genetic makeup functions as predispositions, making it easier to behave in a certain way. Our makeup does probably prompt us to try certain things, such as athletic pursuits, in the first place (cf. Gottfredson, 2005). Even for the strongest predispositions, our life experiences make a big difference in uncovering and developing them, as the movie *The Blind Side* dramatized. We can develop our genetic potential only when our life environments provide the necessary opportunities to do so over time (Bronfenbrenner & Ceci, 1994). The role of biologically based predispositions that do not require physically based skills is even harder to determine: Is the ability to debug a computer, teach a class, or empathically respond genetically based? We may never be able to answer these questions with a definitive yes or no.

In summary, in the ecological perspective simple answers to complex questions about the origins of behavior are rare. Our understanding of causes depends on where we are looking and how we understand what we are seeing. An individual's life always occurs in context, influenced by possibly thousands of factors both trivial and monumental in importance. People are always people in relationship with the world in which they live. And for people whose immediate environments lack stimulation and encouragement for them to try out various possibilities, an unknown quantity of their potential will remain hidden.

I have discussed these ideas at some length because they are central to understanding the ecological perspective; we will return to them time and again in the course of this book. We now consider some ways we can think about P in the context of the world around a person, beginning with the idea of personality and the importance of traits.

Personality and Traits

The study of personality has generated thousands of experiments and academic arguments over the years. In everyday life, we think of personality as the bundle of characteristics that people carry with them from place to place that define their uniqueness and prompt them to behave in ways that others regard as distinctive to them. When we define others, we think of their friendliness, intelligence, life interests—whatever makes them distinctive.

One useful way for counselors to think about personality is in terms of categories suggested by McAdams and Pals (2006): traits and characteristic adaptations. The first category within personality is *traits,* or the personal predispositions that identify a person's uniqueness across situations. Traits are probably the best known aspect of personality. If personality is a grand portrait of a person's being within the world as she experiences and understands it, traits are the separate items in the portrait: the dress, the dog sitting on her lap, her smile. How these items are portrayed and integrated into the portrait make all the difference (imagine how Norman Rockwell's and Picasso's portraits of the same person might compare). McAdams and Pals stated that people are also characterized by the way they typically adapt to life situations, the integrative life stories they develop to make meaning in their lives, and the effect of culture on their everyday lives. I consider McAdams and Pals's second feature of personality, personal adaptations, later in this chapter and discuss meaning making (life stories) and culture in Chapter 5.

The Nature of Traits

McAdams and Pals (2006) defined *personality traits* as markers of individuality, "broad, nonconditional, decontextualized, generally linear and bipolar, and implicitly comparative dimensions of human individuality . . . accounting for interindividual consistency and continuity in behavior, thought, and feeling across situations and over time" (p. 207). Two features of this technical and detailed definition are worth underscoring here. First, personality traits describe individuals in a manner that is expected to be essentially true about them: a person is friendly, outgoing, or moody not just occasionally but characteristically so. Second, the definition includes how people tend to respond to situations. A person labeled as *friendly* behaves toward others in a certain manner at ages 15 and 30, on the job and at home. The first part of McAdams and Pals's definition highlights the enduring, consistent nature of traits over the course of one's life; the latter part reminds us that traits are inferred from a person's behavior in situations. By their very nature traits exist in interaction with the environment.

In reviewing research on personality traits, McAdams (1995) concluded that trait measures do seem to be consistently linked to actual differences in individuals' behavior across situations and over long periods of time. Early in life, a nucleus of early temperamental leanings takes the form of stable predispositions, such as activity level, irritability, and ability to be soothed. These early temperaments are often linked to neurobiological functioning, influenced by the external environment (Roberts & DelVecchio, 2000). Eventually, through the course of childhood development, these early leanings are transformed into traits that continue in some form throughout life if the environment stimulates and sustains their expression (Kagan, 2003). Individual differences in traits seem to become settled in adolescence (Klimstra, Hale, Raaijmakers, Branje, & Meeus, 2009).

The consistency between temperament and subsequent traits is likely to be affected by a number of processes both internal (e.g., ability to cognitively process life events) and external (e.g., expectations of caregivers) to the person. Roberts and DelVecchio's (2000) integrative statistical analyses indicated that personality traits are quite consistent through adulthood, peaking sometime around age 50. In adulthood, five personality traits, commonly labeled the *Big Five,* consistently contribute to behavior across settings and over time: the traits of extraversion, neuroticism/negative emotionality, conscientiousness, agreeableness, and openness to experience (Caspi et al., 2005).

Research has supported the validity of the Big Five traits across individuals in diverse settings, including across cultures (Church, 2000; G. T. Smith, Spillane, & Annus, 2006; but see also Triandis & Suh, 2002). Church (2000) found it plausible that traits may affect how individuals respond to the expectations of the cultural setting in which they are born. These traits also influence which life partner is chosen and which kinds of relationship events may occur thereafter (Caspi et al., 2005). There are also some consistent but subtle sex differences across cultures on aspects of these dimensions (cf. Costa, Terracciano, & McCrae, 2001). Furthermore, when researchers have developed from scratch their own inventories of personality traits for cultures other than American, their results have been fairly comparable to those of American inventories (Church, 2000). Church noted that other cultures do have some specific traits that do not appear in American analyses, a finding that suggests that traits are influenced by one's culture of origin. Traits tend to change most in early adulthood, perhaps because people typically undergo life-altering role changes then (e.g., beginning a career and/or family).

In summary, experts generally agree today about the nature of some core traits that describe individuals. Unfortunately for counselors looking for precise tools to use to understand their clients, however, experts cannot say with certainty how individuals who possess these traits will behave in a given situation. Behavior is an interactional matter.

How Traits Interact With Environments

Traits are important but not on their own. Traits affect how we interact, and the nature of our interactions eventually creates the individuals we become and the personal worlds we inhabit. Our genetic makeup is transformed over time into stable traits through our life experiences (Gottfredson, 2005). This person–environment interaction process is exquisitely unique to every person. In Gottfredson's (2005) words, "Even if we were all provided identical parents, classrooms, and neighborhoods, our personal proclivities would constantly incline us to perceive, provoke, and exploit them differently. As a result, we would eventually come to inhabit different worlds"

(p. 75). Gottfredson would view each of us reading this book as living in a different world created through the unique interaction of what we have brought to the events and settings of our lives and how we have shaped the development of our potential and, in turn, our life contexts themselves. We may not be able to choose all of our life contexts, but we might influence them to some extent by how we choose to interact with them.

Caspi and his associates (2005) concluded that personality traits can influence our lifelong learning, career choices and achievement, susceptibility to illness and reactions to it, and even longevity because of the types of choices we make. Traits in themselves do not make us happy or unhappy, but we might feel happier when our life activities and broader life goals are consistent with our traits. McGregor, McAdams, and Little (2005) even suggested that "knowing oneself should include knowing what one's personality traits are, and that being true to oneself should perhaps involve construction of goals and identities that are supported by one's personality traits" (p. 569). When should we focus on developing our natural predispositions, as they recommended, and when should we try to compensate for them instead? That is an interesting but difficult question to answer. We do have some ability to allow our traits to affect our choices in life, and our choices eventually compose the pattern of our lives over time.

People do appear to become more themselves over time and for a simple reason: It is easier and more comfortable to behave in ways consistent with our predispositions, and with practice behaviors become routine. Caspi and his associates (2005) called this capacity to seek out or create environments compatible with internal predispositions *niche building*. Individuals prefer to be in situations that, psychologically speaking, feel like home. Niche building occurs every day, carried out in our choice of bowling leagues, Alcoholics Anonymous meetings, lunch tables in the school cafeteria, and neighborhoods. These niches may support personal predispositions by making it easier for people to engage in harmonious person–environment interactions over time.

Depending on the compatibility of people within a given setting, repeated interactions over time may strengthen both parties' initial predispositions. Compatibility is not always a good thing, though. Counselors know that some degree of mismatch can encourage people to grow beyond their comfort zone, whether in a campus dorm or within a marriage. Conyne and Cook (2004) described this growth-stimulating degree of mismatch as "a harmonious balance between challenge and support . . . an 'optimal misfit'" (p. 24). When we are very comfortable, we may not feel much like changing.

It is clear that personality traits may make development over time somewhat predictable. People seek out compatible settings (including people) and respond in ways that can make these settings even more compatible over time. Not always, however. G. T. Smith (2009) described some of the difficulties in predicting precisely just how people will develop over time. Different people can perceive and respond to similar life circumstances quite differently. People can draw markedly divergent conclusions from the same life events. Cultural contexts can affect how people try to express and develop universal human characteristics, how well certain characteristics resonate with others within a certain context, and whether behavior that is adaptive in one setting is adaptive in another setting. If we were to try to guess the eventual pattern that a person's life will take, knowledge of his or her traits may narrow down the possible options to some extent, but the final outcome may still surprise us. Traits help us form hypotheses about a person, but we may very well be wrong if we draw conclusions on the basis of trait information alone.

It also appears that some types of people are, by their very nature, likely to be more consistent over time than others. For example, people who experience more consistent environments, who are resilient, who are in environments that match their predispositions, and who have a strong sense of personal identity are more likely to be consistent in personality and behavior over time (Roberts & DelVecchio, 2000; see also Bleidorn, Kandler, Riemann, Angleitner, & Spinath, 2009). These observations apply to consistency from childhood into adulthood and to consistency that is achieved over the course of adulthood. Is consistency good? It depends on the challenges of life one has experienced. As we will soon see, what *is* undoubtedly good is the ability to adapt to what life presents, whether it is a progression of reassuringly familiar circumstances or a roller coaster of changes that continuously test a person.

We should remember also that some types of environments are generally more conducive to ongoing development than others. The most advantageous jobs in terms of positive growth are those that permit self-direction, intellectual flexibility, and a variety of novel tasks (Kohn, 1995). Exercising one's problem-solving capacities and learning to appreciate the diverse needs and perspectives of other people will be more likely to encourage lifelong development than performing routine, repetitive tasks. Counselors who perceive that they are fortunate to be learning every day from their professional work may find themselves growing in wisdom and skills each decade.

We can conclude from this discussion that traits, especially the Big Five, may predispose us to act in certain ways and that the sum total of these actions over time can shape our lives to a considerable extent. Personality traits interact with other characteristics to influence how people interact within their particular life contexts (e.g., Kieffer, Schinka, & Curtiss, 2004).

We now turn to some of the tools that people use to transform their life possibilities into their future realities: what McAdams and Pals (2006) called *characteristic adaptations.*

Characteristic Adaptations

Counselors might be interested in traits to highlight predispositions within an individual, but in their work they are more likely to attend to aspects of personality that McAdams and Pals (2006) described as *characteristic adaptations* of a person, a term they credited to Costa and McCrae (1994). Under this broad term McAdams and Pals classified "motives, goals, plans, strivings, strategies, values, virtues, schemas, self-images, mental representations of significant others, developmental tasks, and many other aspects of human individuality that speak to motivational, social-cognitive, and developmental concerns" (p. 208). Compared with traits, characteristic adaptations have more to do with motivation and cognition, environmental and cultural influences, everyday and situational dynamics, and the features of a person that are changeable in counseling. McAdams and Pals noted that these characteristic adaptations are "contextualized in time, place, and/or social role" (p. 208); this level of personality refers to how people make a place for themselves in the world as they experience it, through what they choose to do over time.

Characteristic adaptations are basically end products of previously lived life that shape present and future behavior. These adaptations have to do with how we view ourselves and our possibilities in the world as we have come to perceive them. These characteristic adaptations may be affected by traits and other enduring characteristics, but they may also be unrelated to them. A discussion of these adaptations belongs in this chapter because they tend to be enduring across situations and over time. They affect how we live within diverse life contexts and tend not to change easily, although every counselor would recognize these adaptations as common topics of discussion during the counseling process.

As mentioned earlier, the range of characteristics classifiable as characteristic adaptations is vast, and full coverage is outside the scope of this chapter. Instead let's discuss a sample of characteristics likely to be familiar to counselors.

Happiness and Psychological Wellness

If you ask people what they most want for loved ones and themselves, they are likely to answer "to be happy and feel good." A desire to enhance these states of well-being prompts major life transitions, new relationships, and decisions to enter counseling. Taking this desire seriously has prompted mental health professionals to reexamine their focus in their work; however, it is challenging to define what people actually mean when they say this.

Living a good life should be more than simply avoiding a life that feels bad. According to Keyes (2007), this is precisely the common view of mental health today: Mental health is the absence of mental illness. If people are free from obvious psychological symptoms, they are assumed by default to be mentally healthy. Keyes argued, however, that genuine mental health is greater than this. Research suggests that people Keyes termed as completely mentally healthy or *flourishing* were lowest in perceived helplessness; were highest in goal setting about life, self-reported resilience, and intimacy; and had the least number of chronic physical conditions. The opposite of flourishing was labeled *languishing*. People labeled as *languishing* may not necessarily have an identified mental health problem, but they do not enjoy life in the same way that flourishing people do. Keyes concluded that less than 20% of U.S. adults can be categorized as flourishing with no diagnosed mental health problem. How can we help the remaining 80% who are currently falling through the cracks?

In recent years, mental health practitioners have increasingly turned their attention away from remedying problems toward building character strengths and preventing future problems. Seligman, Rashid, and Parks (2006) recommended that rather than focusing on what clients are doing wrong, counselors should work with them to be more successful in doing what is right. People need to develop character strengths, use their unique personal qualities to meet the challenges inherent in everyday life, and be involved in pursuits larger than their own concerns (Duckworth, Steen, & Seligman, 2005). In other words, "a 'build what's strong' approach to therapy may usefully supplement the traditional 'fix what's wrong' approach" (Duckworth et al., 2005, p. 631).

E. J. Smith (2006) defined a *strength* as "that which helps a person to cope with life or that which makes life more fulfilling for oneself and others" (p. 25). On the basis of cross-cultural research, Seligman, Steen, Park, and Peterson (2005) identified six universal human virtues: wisdom, courage, humanity, justice, temperance, and transcendence. Strengths commonly endorsed with these virtues are kindness, fairness, authenticity, gratitude, and open-mindedness. Developing these positive characteristics will help people to be resilient, to be positive in attitude, and to build and maintain satisfying relationships with others.

Ideally people develop these strengths and virtues through early life experiences so that they have the capacity to cope with life challenges as they occur. Counselors can also help people develop these strengths and virtues in numerous ways, for example by identifying existing strengths evident in clients' lives; relabeling weaknesses in terms of strengths whenever feasible; and encouraging clients to practice expressing them in everyday life, developing gratitude and forgiveness, and exploring spirituality (e.g., Harris, Thoresen, & Lopez, 2007; Seligman et al., 2005; E. J. Smith, 2006).

How individuals evaluate their lives tends to be fairly stable over time (Diener, Oishi, & Lucas, 2003). Most people consider themselves happy most of the time; the stability of these impressions and the reasons for fluctuations may differ across people and according to the domain being evaluated (Diener, Lucas, & Scollon, 2006). The criteria for these evaluations are rooted in culture (Christopher, 1999). Satisfaction with oneself is important to well-being in highly industrialized, individualist Western nations, whereas people from more collectivist cultures may value more how they are contributing to their group's welfare (G. T. Smith et al., 2006). There are also differences across cultures in how important it is to describe oneself as "happy" (Diener et al., 2003) and in which values and practices contribute to well-being (Constantine & Sue, 2006).

Another means of defining psychological health is provided by the wellness model. Myers, Sweeney, and Witmer (2000) defined *wellness* as an optimum state of well-being available to everyone, a state that integrates body, mind, and spirit. Their "wheel of wellness" depicts spirituality at the hub as the most important element with 12 spokes (e.g., exercise, sense of worth, problem solving, creativity) relevant to the life task of self-direction radiating from it. After analyzing an extensive database using their Wellness Evaluation of Lifestyle, they formulated another model (The Indivisible Self) specifying numerous wellness factors (e.g., thinking, leisure, gender identity, nutrition) and four contexts (local, institutional, global, chronometrical). Detailed definitions of the model's components and a review of relevant research are available in Myers and Sweeney (2008). Wellness requires attention to each area within their model, and each area interacts with the others to constitute a person's overall wellness. Myers and Sweeney's body of work is both unusually integrative and applicable to a variety of counseling clients, formats, and settings (see the counseling practice discussion in Myers et al., 2000).

One important feature of the wellness model is the recognition that healthy functioning does not mean the same thing for everyone. All well people have some degree of balance across aspects of wellness, but there is no guaranteed wellness formula (e.g., two units of leisure, three of exercise, and so forth). The precise nature of wellness can differ across individuals. Physical wellness will mean something different for a teenage surfer and a middle-aged person reliant on a wheelchair; spiritual wellness will mean something different for an Orthodox Jew and a person without any formal religious tradition. Being well means optimizing the available possibilities across all dimensions.

Ultimately the characteristics a person deems essential for a happy life are determined through meaning making on multiple levels, as I discuss in Chapter 5. The American culture values certain qualities (e.g., independence, goal-directedness) over others; some quite different qualities (e.g., some degree of concern about others' feelings) are needed to thrive in today's interpersonal world. These basic parameters allow plenty of room for individual discretion, for example being devoted to the pursuit of fun versus being committed to helping others. The choices we make over time will reward the pursuit of some values over others; the particular contexts of our lives can influence our well-being; and because of who we are as individuals, we may have to wrestle with conflicting values. Clients may find it illuminating to consider whether their life choices thus far have permitted them to actualize key values and how future choices can permit them to experience more fulfillment and satisfaction.

Resilience

Regardless of the nature of the life choices we make, everyone at some time will encounter rough spells when customary coping abilities are taxed. Resilience is the ability to bounce back after the stresses and strains of life. Lightsey (2006) provided an ecologically friendly definition of *resilience* as "an awareness of one's strengths or capacities that allows one to better cope with future stressors and to use available resources" (p. 101). Resilience is the difference between merely surviving and thriving in the face of life's difficulties. Resilient people possess crucial attitudes and skills applicable across situations: a positive view of themselves, an ability to avoid repetitive negative thoughts about adversity, and a desire and ability to maintain interpersonal relationships. Resilient individuals are often concerned with finding a meaningful purpose in life and believe that they can both learn from and at least partially influence events in their lives (Bonanno, 2004; Maddi, 2008).

Based on their unparalleled 30-year longitudinal study, Block and Block (2006) identified *ego resiliency* as resourceful adaptiveness, or an ability to change in response to the demands of life over time. Moen and Erickson's (1995) view of resilience is more interactional than the Blocks', recognizing the need for interpersonal as well as personal resources. Two sets of resources are needed: social resources (which are related to connectedness to others) and personal resources (which draw on a sense of personal mastery). Parents' contribution to their children's resilience can be twofold: Resilient parents not only possess high levels of resources themselves but also model how to cope with life's challenges. To develop resilience, people need experience in confronting and successfully managing stressful situations (Fleig-Palmer, Luthans, & Mandernach, 2009). Also recognizing the value of personal resources, E. J. Smith (2006) advocated looking for risks and protective factors across ecological levels, ranging from the individual, family, and close friends to the neighborhood. It seems clear that individual resilience is simultaneously defined and challenged by connections with the environment, particularly those relationships on which the person's daily life depends.

A concept related to resilience is the old-fashioned quality of *grit*. Grit enables a person to stay on the road to success despite its potholes. In the words of Duckworth, Peterson, Matthews, and Kelly (2007), "Grit entails working strenuously toward challenges, maintaining effort and interest over years despite failure, adversity, and plateaus in progress" (pp. 1087–1088). Grit appears to be related to self-control but not to intelligence, to effort but not to extraordinary talent. They concluded by wondering "whether follow-through or, as we prefer to call it, grit, may in fact matter more than IQ to eventual success in life" (p. 1099). Grit is learnable, and its implications apply to the highly talented as well as the more modestly blessed: Stamina counts.

Resilience is an important concern in the counseling process. Does the person have the stamina, the attitudes, and the resources to cope with what is confronting her? Do his resources fit and either match or exceed the stresses of his life? Ideally resilience is a legacy of a childhood supervised by loving caregivers who could provide the child the support, skills, and sense of hope needed to face the ups and downs of life with some measure of equanimity. When this legacy is missing—or when the events of life cruelly overpower a person's ability to cope—a counselor can help a person to develop resilience crucial for the remainder of his or her life.

It is important to note that this discussion of resilience is culturally based; it is consistent with a Western view of individual human beings and the resources they need to thrive in the world. Grit, personal strength, individual coping—all of these are personal attributes of the individual that are carried from place to place and available for use like a debit card. Many people in the world, however, might find this description at best limited or at worst sadly selfish and immature. For them, fundamental strength lies in the invisible army of support (e.g., family both living and departed, community members and mores) that accompanies them daily through life. What description resonates for you, and where did this grounding come from?

The Self, Identity, and Self-Esteem

One of the characteristic adaptations most familiar to counselors is *the self*. The idea of the self has been around since the beginning of modern psychology. Savickas (2002) noted that "a self consists of symbolic representations that are personally constructed, interpersonally conditioned, and linguistically communicated" (p. 161). According to Bohan (2002), although some early theorists recognized the importance of relationships to one's sense of self, most adopted the early 20th-century cultural emphasis on the individual as an independent, self-contained being. What eventually emerged is a Western sense of self as

> the "I" that persists over time, acting as the agent of behavior, the referent of experience, the owner and operator of the body . . . at the core of each self-contained individual resides an identity, a persistent self that transcends particular contexts and comprises the essence of the person. (Bohan, 2002, p. 80)

As I discuss in Chapter 5, this view of the self is familiar to Westerners but does not reflect the way that much of the world defines personhood.

Renowned researcher Albert Bandura (2006) defined *personal identity* as "self-characterizations of what one is" (p. 170). This is not as simple as it first sounds in that "a sense of selfhood is the product of a complex interplay of personal construal processes and the social reality in which one lives" (p. 170). In Bandura's view, people are "agents of experiences, not just undergoers of experiences" (p. 168). Our lives are the expression of a triadic interaction between our own choices and actions, the influences of others, and the broader environment. Each of us is the product of interaction with the environment as we have experienced it.

How a person views self varies across persons; how I describe myself as a person is probably different in some important respects from how you would describe me. Yet what is interesting is that some common patterns of "self-construals" (Guimond et al., 2007) are discernible for people who share a common culture or gender. There also appear to be some cultural differences in the manner in which self-concepts are consistent across situations. Americans' cultural prizing of authenticity as involving consistency *across* situations may seem strange to East Asians, who typically prize consistency *within* relationships (e.g., consistency among family members vs. another self required at work; English & Chen, 2007). It is not the case that one culture values consistency and the other does not; instead the type of consistency that is valued appears to be different.

Swann, Chang-Schneider, and McClarty (2007) used *self-views* to refer to thoughts and feelings people have about themselves. According to Swann and his associates, self-views, behavior, and the environment interact in a cyclical manner so that each element affects the other (does this sound eco-logical?). Self-views that are highly important to the person and are held with certainty—for example, that I am a person concerned about the feelings of others—are more likely to influence that person's behavior as a consequence. However, global self-views do not predict specific behaviors very well be-cause, as Swann and his associates noted, specific behaviors are influenced by many factors. My self-view about caring for people's feelings might not predict whether I give in to my child's temper tantrums, because I know that being a good parent sometimes requires me to stand firm. (Okay, I am indeed a softie too often!) Thus, to predict behaviors such as school performance it is more useful to look at specific related self-view criteria (e.g., one's ability to succeed in certain subjects) rather than global self-views.

In general, identity is a "linking" concept that indicates a relationship be-tween individual and sociocultural processes (Stewart & McDermott, 2004). How we view ourselves as individuals—in terms of both context and its value—is linked to the human contexts in which we live our lives. Identities tend to be stable across situations and over time, but for all of us they are subject to change. On an ongoing basis people negotiate who they are and how others may see them, especially as they attempt to manage demand-ing roles in their lives. Kreiner, Hollensbe, and Sheep (2006) described the challenging processes by which Episcopal priests balance their private lives with the demands of the priesthood. The paid work of these priests is more than just a job: For most of them it is a vocation, a response to a calling from God. Church members and the general public carry extraordinary demands for their behavior throughout the week as they also attempt to be parents, partners, and friends. Wearing a clerical collar while running family errands can provoke some downright bizarre conversations, as I know from personal experience! For priests and other clergy members, identity negotiation is a conscious process of balancing how they experience themselves as individu-als with demands from the external world.

The ideas pertaining to the self discussed thus far refer to how people see themselves as unique beings. A slightly different concept is *self-esteem*, broadly defined as a liking or a valuing of oneself. Swann and his colleagues (2007) criticized the "extravagant claims of the self-esteem movement" in which "thousands of laypersons across America were smitten with the hope that in self-esteem they had a found a modern-day Holy Grail" (p. 84) protecting them from psychological ills galore. The common expectation is that if people had better self-esteem, they would not be overweight, irritable with their families, tolerant of unfulfilling jobs and relationships, and so on. The research literature compiled by Swann et al. shows the effects of self-esteem as generally inconsequential in size. In short, self-esteem by itself does not seem to have much power. What they advocated instead are programs that "cultivate behaviors that produce self-views that are both realistic (i.e., based on objective evidence) and adaptive (i.e., emphasizing activities that are predictive of long-term adjustment in society)" (p. 90). In other words, what is valuable for young people is not programs that encourage them to say "I am awesome" whenever they catch a glimpse of themselves in the mirror but ones that encourage them to say "I have some marketable skills" after completing a challenging educational or job-training program.

The bases of self-esteem may differ by sex to the extent that people try to measure up to standards specific to their own sex (Josephs, Markus, & Tafarodi, 1992). Men's self-esteem may be more related to individual accomplishments and women's to connections with others. Both sexes, however, live in a cultural context that values independent, goal-directed activity, so that self-esteem for both sexes requires this type of success to some extent. A massive analysis of self-esteem studies indicated that men tend to score a bit higher than women on global self-esteem measures (Kling, Hyde, Showers, & Buswell, 1999). This finding is consistent with the idea that men as a group are rewarded for doing what the independent, achievement-oriented U.S. culture most values. Of course, individuals may consciously choose to ignore these sex-based standards and to use other standards (e.g., religious values) to judge their own value. The standards people use to evaluate their self-esteem, sex based or otherwise, may vary according to a host of factors (ethnicity, developmental stage, social class, and so on) so that any person's self-esteem is likely to be the product of a unique, complicated valuation process.

Finally, self-esteem is commonly misunderstood as equivalent to *self-efficacy*. Both terms refer to assessments people make about themselves, but these assessments occur at different levels of specificity. Self-esteem tends to be global, whereas self-efficacy is much more specific. As Lent and Brown (2006) explained, "Self-efficacy refers to personal beliefs about one's capability to perform particular behaviors necessary to achieve valued school and work goals or, more generally, to perform tasks requisite to success in one's work or school context" (p. 239). Thus, a person completing a challenging training program develops self-efficacy beliefs regarding specific job tasks, such as debugging a computer program. Such self-efficacy beliefs appear to be important to one's success in tasks associated with the relevant domain (e.g., the domain of technology applications and one's self-efficacy regarding debugging).

In summary, numerous terms have been used to refer to the thoughts and feelings people have regarding themselves as unique human beings. Experts agree that how people view themselves is likely to be multifaceted, in some respects global and in other respects specific to particular aspects of themselves. Although these self-relevant thoughts and feelings have some continuity, they do change over time as people engage in an ongoing process of interacting with the world around them. This most private part of ourselves is the product of our engagement with the challenging world of people, ideas, and possibilities around us.

Sociocultural Identity

Sociocultural identity is used here as a generic category to refer to views about themselves that people develop because they are categorized as belonging to a group particularly important in their sociocultural context. That is, people in the United States differ in terms of shoe size, but that matters little in terms of the stereotypes, opportunities, and expectations placed on them by others. In contrast, biological sex, sexual orientation, ethnicity, and race do matter a great deal, and people develop views about themselves as a consequence (e.g., I am male/gay/Latino and all that that means to others and to me).

Sociocultural identity is discussed separately here because of its importance in the counseling literature. Ponterotto and Park-Taylor (2007) noted that there are at least 22 models of racial, ethnic, feminist, and gay/lesbian identity. (Their article is an invaluable reference for researchers interested in the topic, as is Chapter 7 of this book.) These models differ somewhat in their specifics but have in common the idea that identity is formed through an individual's negotiation with the sociocultural expectations and opportunities afforded him or her as a consequence of being identified with a certain group. A range of identity statuses is possible depending on the person's degree of identification with the group, his or her positive or negative experiences, the importance of this identification vis-à-vis other self-definitions, and so on. Issues of identity are particularly complex for the growing number of multiracial individuals, whose development and experiences do not fit neatly into any one category (see Miville, Constantine, Baysden, & So-Lloyd, 2005; Rockquemore, Brunsma, & Delgado, 2009).

It is natural to view whatever is portrayed as the highest, most evolved, most complex status as the best for everyone, but the reality for a given individual may be different. After reviewing relevant research on racial identity, Quintana (2007) concluded that "there appears to be no single racial ideology that [has] provided adaptive advantages over other ideologies in all contexts—clearly, different ecological contexts require different racial identity ideologies and orientations" (p. 267).

Finally, it is worth remembering that a component of people's identity today is related to their position as a citizen of the world. Arnett (2002) argued that the nature of people's identities everywhere has changed because of the rapid globalization of our world. Economies are increasingly interdependent, communication via complex technologies is more fluent and informative, and knowledge about alternative ways to live is more widespread and sophisticated. Consequently, many people develop an identity as part of the global culture as well as their culture of birth (i.e., they become bicultural), whereas others become confused about who and what they are. Still others choose to identify with a dissident, self-selected culture, often a religious one, that appears more meaningful to them than the consumer-oriented, secular global culture. For people throughout the world who have some degree of freedom about their lives, globalization offers new opportunities and challenges for self-definition beyond the parameters of their birth cultures.

The Gendered Self

It is a common cultural belief that male/female differences are rooted in biological differentiation that begins in the womb and then manifests in all sorts of delightful and exasperating ways throughout life. There is little doubt that gender differences continue to exist despite the far-reaching cultural changes of the past several decades. However, in this book gender differences are viewed as the result of person–environment interaction, not predestined by chromosomal activity in utero. Why?

Gilbert and Rader (2001) defined *gender* as follows: "Gender pertains to what we assume is true or will be true of someone who is born biologically female or male. Thus, gender concerns personal and societal beliefs, stereotypes, and ingrained views about the fundamental nature of women and men" (p. 167). Citing the work of Hare-Mustin and Marecek, Bohan (2002) stated that "gender [is] the enactment of a social arrangement rather than . . . a set of sex-related traits . . . a universe of enactments that reside in social transactions and are not intrinsically connected to individuals or their sex" (p. 77). In essence, gender is linked not to biological determinants but to "forms of social organization" (p. 77). Gender studies can examine differences between men and women; variability among one or the other sex on certain criteria; the sociocultural power dynamics regarding the sexes that shape individual, group, and societal interactions; or a combination of all of these (Stewart & McDermott, 2004).

As this book discusses in more detail later, the gender differences obvious in choices of career and family involvement, hobbies, clothing preferences, and so on are not our biological destiny but are the product of millions of interactions with others, whether face to face or indirectly through our observational learning capacities. This perspective makes the topic of gender even more interesting: If male/female differences are not a matter of dimorphic (either/or) biological differentiation as is commonly assumed, how can there be so much consistency in the pattern of differences across settings and over time? This question is definitely worth asking, especially if one research-based conclusion is kept in mind: There are more differences among members of one sex, and more commonalities across the sexes, than a simple model of genetic destiny would suggest.

An example of how researchers have contradicted everyday wisdom is in the body of work on masculine (M) versus feminine (F) personality traits. F refers to the broad set of physical features, interests, preferences, social behaviors, and so on typical for women, and M for men. Members of a particular culture are in remarkable agreement about what characteristics should be categorized M versus F. For example, in the present U.S. culture the color pink is considered F and blue is M; women prefer chick flicks, whereas their presumably hapless male dates are expected to prefer violent action films instead. For decades experts assumed that there was a psychological core of personality differentiation underlying these sex differences corresponding to an independent, assertive, goal-directed orientation for masculinity (and men) and an emotionally expressive, interpersonally focused orientation for femininity (and women; see the review in Constantinople, 1973).

For decades researchers tried to prove that the sexes are as different psychologically as they are physically, but they were in for a surprise. Many women and men, in a wide variety of age groups and settings and using different personality measures, describe themselves to some extent using *both* masculine and feminine characteristics: for example, both independent and interested in relationships, sometimes emotionally expressive and other times goal directed. A balance between positive masculine and feminine personality characteristics—a pattern labeled *psychologically androgynous*—may in fact be the healthiest pattern for both women and men (see Cook, 1985; see also Lippa, 1995, for comparisons between F, M, and the Big Five traits).

Research has indicated that there are indeed some fairly consistent sex differences in behavior, but not as many as people typically believe. Comprehensive analyses across research studies have shown far more similarities than differences between the sexes in psychological variables such as memory and abilities (Hyde, 2005). Sex differences in variables such as types of intelligence, personality, and thinking patterns tend to be quite small, with extensive overlapping between women and men. Differences can appear and disappear depending on the particular domain studied, age, and context. Yet there are indeed well-known differences in *learned* life patterns and preferences: career choices, household roles, hobbies, clothing styles, and so on. The degree of the difference can vary depending on the characteristic under consideration: Men are more likely to go to chick flicks willingly than they are to wear skirts outside a Scottish cultural festival. The sex differences that matter appear to be learned after birth rather than preordained because of one's chromosomes.

The study of gender has provided some thought-provoking insights into the relationship between traits and behavior. Levels of masculine and feminine characteristics expressed by individual women seem to vary according to the life roles that these women assume (Kasen, Chen, Sneed, Crawford, & Cohen, 2006). This suggests that what we do in life affects the personality characteristics we develop over time, not just the reverse (i.e., traits affect role behaviors). In Twenge's (2001) study, changing endorsement of some traits (e.g., assertiveness) may be related to changes in women's social status and roles over time that are then expressed in the form of increased assertiveness for women as a group. Twenge argued that because women's educational and career accomplishments changed over time, these trends essentially created differences in women's role performance and attitudes toward women's roles. These social psychological changes eventually became part of women's psychological functioning. What is interesting is that men's scores did *not* change in a comparable manner, a finding consistent with the absence of a similar social transformation in men's roles. The same social changes can be perceived and understood differently by men and women, a fundamental interactional difference affecting the sexes' lives all over the world (Yoder & Kahn, 2003).

One important gender difference for counselors to keep in mind is that men of diverse ages, nationalities, ethnicities, or races are less likely than their female counterparts to seek counseling for mental health problems (Addis & Mahalik, 2003). It is important that counselors explore the reasons for this well-documented discrepancy in their own client populations, because the pattern can be attributed to numerous factors (e.g., how men perceive other men as seeing them, whether they see their problem as typical for men).

I close this brief discussion of gender by noting that there are indeed some crucial, biologically determined male/female differences—those related to reproduction and lactation. Differences in patterns of physical health and disease also exist, some that are indubitably linked to biology (e.g., women cannot have prostate cancer, although men can develop breast cancer) and some whose origins are less immediately obvious to any armchair anatomy student (e.g., incidence of coronary disease). One step removed from these simple biological determinants lie disorders that are certainly influenced by gender-based physiology but whose origins are more complicated (e.g., only women can have premenstrual difficulties, but these problems are not universally common across groups of women worldwide).

In counselors' field of study—human behavior rather than biology—it can be important to be aware of possible biological determinants of some clients' problems (e.g., depression). In the case of most client puzzles we encounter, biology does indeed contribute some crucial pieces to the finished picture. Yet our work requires us to assemble a puzzle of 5,000 pieces, some sturdy and oversized, some smaller than the naked eye can see, and many missing altogether. Whenever we engage in counseling, we simply try to do the best we can with the pieces we have in front of us. For now, many questions about biological determinants of behavior are missing parts of the overall picture. Frameworks like the ecological perspective are intended to provide a sketch of the finished puzzle to guide us in assembling the puzzles presented by our clients' lives.

Summary

In any interactions with the world around them, individuals' behavior is influenced by a broad range of personal characteristics. These characteristics define the P in the ecological equation of behavior: $B = f(P \times E)$. Some of these P characteristics are innate, others are learned, and most are a combination of nature and nurture. We will never be able to tell for sure the ultimate origins of our uniqueness, because who we are as people is modeled and modified through our life experiences.

P characteristics do share some qualities in common. They can vary in intensity or type across persons. For example, one person may score as very introverted on a personality measure, whereas another may exhibit much less of this quality. P characteristics rarely cause certain behaviors on their own. People behave in introverted ways not simply because they report having this trait to some degree. Instead P characteristics should be thought of as predisposing people to behave in some manner. People who score as introverted on personality measures behave consistently with this trait's descriptions not only because the trait forces them to act in this way but because their life experiences have taught them certain ways of behaving, have rewarded (or at least not punished) them for doing so, and so on. People may also exhibit this trait in some situations (e.g., at home) but not in others (e.g., at work or with friends) for a variety of reasons. Certain characteristics may predominate during some periods of life and not others depending on the demands of a person's life at any particular time.

Rarely do traits determine behaviors in the simple, straightforward way that people are prone to believe: People generally don't behave in a certain way simply because they were made that way. The plasticity of human life accounts for jaw-dropping surprises at the high school reunion, such as when we discover that the student voted most likely to end up in a penitentiary became a priest. Even a privileged genetic heritage (e.g., having two Olympic athletes for parents) requires extraordinary motivation, financial support, nurturing teachers, and other resources to blossom—and the recipe for success may vary across individuals. What a person brings to life is a set of building blocks rather than a prefabricated kit awaiting assembly. We need to look around us to get assembly instructions to build a life worth living. Counselors can help people identify the nature of their gifts, the array of possibilities that have yet to be set in stone, and the tools they need to transform these possibilities into reality.

As I discuss more in the next chapters, we need to remember that although all people share an essential humanity—an integration of mind, body, and spirit—how we develop and express this humanity is not universally the same. As Arnett (2008) pointed out about behavior research, we rely on "the assumption—rarely stated, and rarely actually tested—that people anywhere can be taken to represent people everywhere and that the cultural context of their lives can be safely ignored" (p. 610). Counselors tend to do their assuming about human nature in an office rather than a research setting. We need to remember to explore the individual person or group rather than jump to conclusions based on our own a priori conclusions about human nature. Once we realize that our view of the world depends on us wearing a certain set of eyeglasses, we are freed to try on other ways of appreciating human life.

Discussion Questions

- Write down a list 5–10 words describing you as a person. Ask yourself: Where did these characteristics come from? Have I always been this way, or have some of them changed over time? If possible, share the list with someone who knows you very well and ask him or her these same questions.
- Remember an event in your life that you found very stressful: having a flat tire on the highway, for example, or going to the hospital to visit a dear one who had become very ill. What characteristic adaptations helped you to cope with the situation?
- Think of something about yourself you would like to change: perhaps a way of interacting with others (e.g., nervousness when going to parties) or a habit that causes you trouble (e.g., I refer to myself as "the Late Ellen Cook"). Discuss with someone else what you might do to change this personal characteristic, and implement this plan for a while. What does your degree of success in making this change tell you about yourself as a person?

References

Addis, M. B., & Mahalik, J. R. (2003). Men, masculinity, and the contexts of help seeking. *American Psychologist, 58*, 5–14.

Arnett, J. J. (2002). The psychology of globalization. *American Psychologist, 57*, 774–783.

Arnett, J. J. (2008). The neglected 95%: Why American psychology needs to become less American. *American Psychologist, 63*, 602–614.

Bandura, A. (2006). Toward a psychology of human agency. *Perspectives on Psychological Science, 1*, 164–178.

Bleidorn, W., Kandler, C., Riemann, R., Angleitner, A., & Spinath, F. M. (2009). Patterns and sources of adult personality development: Growth curve analyses of the NEO PI-R scales in a longitudinal twin study. *Journal of Personality and Social Psychology, 97*, 142–155.

Block, J., & Block, J. H. (2006). Venturing a 30-year longitudinal study. *American Psychologist, 61*, 315–327.

Bohan, J. S. (2002). Sex differences and/in the self: Classic themes, feminist variations, postmodern challenges. *Psychology of Women Quarterly, 26*, 74–88.

Bonanno, G. A. (2004). Loss, trauma, and human resilience: Have we underestimated the human capacity to thrive after extremely aversive events? *American Psychologist, 59*, 20–28.

Bronfenbrenner, U., & Ceci, S. J. (1994). Nature–nurture reconceptualized in developmental perspective: A bioecological model. *Psychological Review, 101*, 568–586.

Caspi, A., Roberts, B. W., & Shiner, R. L. (2005). Personality development: Stability and change. *Annual Review of Psychology, 56*, 453–484.

Christopher, J. C. (1999). Situating psychological well-being: Exploring the cultural roots of its theory and research. *Journal of Counseling & Development, 77*, 141–152.

Church, A. T. (2000). Culture and personality: Toward an integrated cultural trait psychology. *Journal of Personality, 68*, 651–703.

Constantine, M. G., & Sue, D. W. (2006). Factors contributing to optimal human functioning in people of color in the United States. *The Counseling Psychologist, 34*, 228–244.

Constantinople, A. (1973). Masculinity–femininity: An exception to a famous dictum? *Psychological Bulletin, 80*, 389–407.

Conyne, R. K., & Cook, E. P. (Eds.). (2004). *Ecological counseling: An innovative approach to conceptualizing person–environment interaction.* Alexandria, VA: American Counseling Association.

Cook, E. P. (1985). *Psychological androgyny.* New York, NY: Pergamon.

Costa, P. T., Jr., & McCrae, R. R. (1994). Set like plaster? Evidence for the stability of adult personality. In T. F. Heatherton & J. L. Weinberger (Eds.), *Can personality change?* (pp. 21–40). Washington, DC: American Psychological Association.

Costa, P. T., Jr., Terracciano, A., & McCrae, R. K. (2001). Gender differences in personality traits across cultures: Robust and surprising findings. *Journal of Personality and Social Psychology, 81*, 322–331.

Diener, E. L., Lucas, R. E., & Scollon, C. N. (2006). Beyond the hedonic treadmill: Revising the adaptation theory of well-being. *American Psychologist, 61*, 305–314.

Diener, E., Oishi, S., & Lucas, R. E. (2003). Personality, culture, and subjective well-being: Emotional and cognitive evaluations of life. *Annual Review of Psychology, 54*, 403–425.

Duckworth, A. L., Peterson, C., Matthews, M. D., & Kelly, D. R. (2007). Grit, perseverance and passion for long-term goals. *Journal of Personality and Social Psychology, 92*, 1087–1101.

Duckworth, A. L., Steen, T. A., & Seligman, M. E. P. (2005). Positive psychology in clinical practice. *Annual Review of Clinical Psychology, 1*, 629–651.

English, T., & Chen, S. (2007). Culture and self-concept stability: Consistency across and within contexts among Asian Americans and European Americans. *Journal of Personality and Social Psychology, 93*, 478–490.

Fleig-Palmer, M. M., Luthans, K. W., & Mandernach, B. J. (2009). Successful reemployment through resiliency development. *Journal of Career Development, 35*, 228–247.

Gilbert, L. A., & Rader, J. (2001). Current perspectives on women's adult roles: Work, family, and life. In R. K. Unger (Ed.), *Handbook of the psychology of women and gender* (pp. 156–169). Hoboken, NJ: Wiley.

Gottfredson, L. S. (2005). Applying Gottfredson's theory of circumscription and compromise in career guidance and counseling. In S. D. Brown & R. W. Lent (Eds.), *Career development and counseling: Putting theory and research to work* (pp. 71–100). Hoboken, NJ: Wiley.

Guimond, S., Branscombe, N. R., Brunot, S., Buunk, A. P., Chatard, A., Désert, M., . . . Yzerbyt, V. (2007). Culture, gender, and the self: Variations and impact of social comparison processes. *Journal of Personality and Social Psychology, 92*, 1118–1134.

Harris, A. H. S., Thoresen, C. E., & Lopez, S. J. (2007). Integrating positive psychology into counseling: Why and (when appropriate) how. *Journal of Counseling & Development, 85*, 3–13.

Hyde, J. S. (2005). The gender similarities hypothesis. *American Psychologist, 60*, 581–592.

Josephs, R. A., Markus, H. R., & Tafarodi, R. W. (1992). Gender and self-esteem. *Journal of Personality and Social Psychology, 63*, 391–402.

Kagan, J. (2003). Biology, context, and developmental inquiry. *Annual Review of Psychology, 54*, 1–23.

Kasen, S., Chen, H., Sneed, J., Crawford, T., & Cohen, P. (2006). Social role and birth cohort influences on gender-linked personality traits in women: A 20-year longitudinal analysis. *Journal of Personality and Social Psychology, 91*, 944–958.

Keyes, C. L. M. (2007). Promoting and protecting mental health as flourishing: A complementary strategy for improving national mental health. *American Psychologist, 62*, 95–108.

Kieffer, K. M., Schinka, J. A., & Curtiss, G. (2004). Person–environment congruence and personality domains in the prediction of job performance and work quality. *Journal of Counseling Psychology, 51*, 168–177.

Klimstra, T. A., Hale, W. W., III, Raaijmakers, Q. A. W., Branje, S. J. T., & Meeus, W. H. J. (2009). Maturation of personality in adolescence. *Journal of Personality and Social Psychology, 96,* 898–912.

Kling, K. C., Hyde, J. S., Showers, C. J., & Buswell, B. N. (1999). Gender differences in self-esteem: A meta-analysis. *Psychological Bulletin, 125,* 470–500.

Kohn, M. L. (1995). Social structure and personality through time and space. In P. Moen, G. H. Elder, Jr., & K. Luscher (Eds.), *Examining lives in context: Perspectives on the ecology of human development* (pp. 141–168). Washington, DC: American Psychological Association.

Kreiner, G. E., Hollensbe, E. C., & Sheep, M. L. (2006). Where is the "me" among the "we"? Identity work and the search for optimal balance. *Academy of Management Journal, 49,* 1031–1057.

Lent, R. W., & Brown, S. D. (2006). Integrating person and situation perspectives on work satisfaction: A social-cognitive view. *Journal of Vocational Behavior, 69,* 236–247.

Lightsey, O. R. (2006). Resilience, meaning, and well-being. *The Counseling Psychologist, 34,* 96–107.

Lippa, P. (1995). Gender-related individual differences and psychological adjustment in terms of the Big Five and Circumplex models. *Journal of Personality and Social Psychology, 69,* 1184–1202.

Maddi, S. R. (2008). The courage and strategies of hardiness as helpful in growing despite major, disruptive stresses. *American Psychologist, 63,* 563–564.

McAdams, D. P. (1995). What do we know when we know a person? *Journal of Personality, 63,* 365–396.

McAdams, D. P., & Pals, J. L. (2006). A new Big Five: Fundamental principles for an integrative science of personality. *American Psychologist, 61,* 204–217.

McGregor, I., McAdams, D. P., & Little, B. R. (2005). Personal projects, life stories, and happiness: On being true to traits. *Journal of Research in Personality, 40,* 551–572.

Mischel, W. (2004). Toward an integrative science of the person. *Annual Review of Psychology, 55,* 1–22.

Miville, M. L., Constantine, M. G., Baysden, M. F., & So-Lloyd, G. (2005). Chameleon changes: An exploration of racial identity themes of multiracial people. *Journal of Counseling Psychology, 52,* 507–516.

Moen, P., & Erickson, M. (1995). Linked lives: A transgenerational approach to resilience. In P. Moen, G. H. Elder, Jr., & K. Luscher (Eds.). *Examining lives in context: Perspectives on the ecology of human development* (pp. 169–210). Washington, DC: American Psychological Association.

Moffitt, T. E., Caspi, A., & Rutter, M. (2006). Measured gene–environment interactions in psychopathology: Concepts, research strategies, and implications for research, intervention, and public understanding of genetics. *Perspectives on Psychological Science, 1,* 5–27.

Morton, T. A., Postmes, T., Haslam, S. A., & Horney, M. J. (2009). Theorizing gender in the face of social change: Is there anything essential about essentialism? *Journal of Personality and Social Psychology, 96,* 653–664.

Myers, J. E., & Sweeney, T. J. (2008). Wellness counseling: The evidence base for practice. *Journal of Counseling & Development, 86,* 482–493.

Myers, J. E., Sweeney, T. J., & Witmer, J. M. (2000). The wheel of wellness counseling for wellness: A holistic model for treatment planning. *Journal of Counseling and Development, 78,* 251–267.

Ponterotto, J. G., & Park-Taylor, J. (2007). Racial and ethnic identity theory, measurement, and research in counseling psychology: Present status and future directions. *Journal of Counseling Psychology, 54,* 282–294.

Quintana, S. M. (2007). Racial and ethnic identity: Developmental perspectives and research. *Journal of Counseling Psychology, 54,* 259–270.

Roberts, B. W., & DelVecchio, W. F. (2000). The rank-order consistency of personality traits from childhood to old age: A quantitative review of longitudinal studies. *Psychological Bulletin, 126,* 3–25.

Rockquemore, K. A., Brunsma, D. L., & Delgado, D. J. (2009). Racing to theory or retheorizing race? Understanding the struggle to build a multiracial identity theory. *Journal of Social Issues, 65,* 13–34.

Savickas, M. (2002). Career construction: A developmental theory of vocational behavior. In D. Brown & Associates (Eds.), *Career choice and development* (4th ed., pp. 149–205). San Francisco, CA: Jossey-Bass.

Seligman, M. E. P., Rashid, T., & Parks, A. C. (2006). Positive psychotherapy. *American Psychologist, 61,* 774–788.

Seligman, M. E. P., Steen, T. A., Park, N., & Peterson, C. (2005). Positive psychology progress: Empirical validation of interventions. *American Psychologist, 60,* 410–421.

Smith, E. J. (2006). The strength-based counseling model. *The Counseling Psychologist, 34,* 13–79.

Smith, G. T. (2009). Why do different individuals progress along different life trajectories? *Perspectives on Psychological Science, 4,* 415–421.

Smith, G. T., Spillane, N. S., & Annus, A. M. (2006). Implications of an emerging integration of universal and culturally specific psychologies. *Perspectives on Psychological Science, 1,* 211–233.

Stewart, A. J., & McDermott, C. (2004). Gender in psychology. *Annual Review of Psychology, 55,* 519–544.

Swann, W. B., Jr., Chang-Schneider, C., & McClarty, K. L. (2007). Do people's self-views matter? Self-concept and self-esteem in everyday life. *American Psychologist, 62,* 84–94.

Triandis, H. C., & Suh, E. M. (2002). Cultural influences on personality. *Annual Review of Psychology, 53,* 133–160.

Twenge, J. M. (2001). Changes in women's assertiveness in response to status and roles: A cross-temporal meta-analysis, 1931–1993. *Journal of Personality and Social Psychology, 81,* 133–143.

Yoder, J. D., & Kahn, A. S. (2003). Making gender comparisons more meaningful: A call for more attention to social context. *Psychology of Women Quarterly, 27,* 281–290.

Behavior Is Contextual

Ellen P. Cook

Behavior is influenced by a range of human and nonhuman (physical) contexts. Key features of these contexts are proximity, salience, and embeddedness. The power of these contexts depends in part on the nature of interaction with individuals.

Elsewhere (Conyne & Cook, 2004) I described a behavior problem exhibited by a 9-year-old girl named Jamie. Jamie's behavior on the school bus had become increasingly disruptive, distracting and frustrating the driver. The driver and school personnel concluded that Jamie's developmental disabilities were to blame and that she may need to take other transportation. As a last-ditch effort, the school agreed to allow a behavior specialist to ride the bus for a few days in order to observe Jamie's behavior. The specialist quickly noted how Jamie's behavior was influenced by lax disciplinary procedures on the bus, other riders' encouragement for Jamie to misbehave, and Jamie's loneliness and boredom on the bus because she always sat alone. Jamie's disruptive behavior was quickly extinguished by changes in seat assignments, better enforcement of bus rules for all riders, and an ingenious game Jamie could play in her notebook to amuse herself and attract other riders' positive attention. Jamie subsequently rode the bus throughout high school with only a few minor setbacks, and she now loves to ride the metro bus for special outings. Her behavior skills will permit her to ride the bus to work someday.

The school personnel were not exactly biased against Jamie but, like many counselors, had a limited understanding of her behavior. They framed Jamie's problems solely in terms of her limitations. So would many of us readers: Consistent with the Western cultural emphasis on the individual as creator of his or her own destiny, human services professionals in the United States (and others sharing our worldview) tend to focus on the individual's own strengths or weaknesses as explanations for his or her fate.

In the ecological perspective this individual focus is only part of the picture. A primary assumption in the ecological perspective is that *human behavior is contextual.* Even simple, routinized behavior (e.g., brushing one's teeth) is influenced by the context in which this behavior occurs. In this chapter I explore how these contexts vary in proximity and complexity and how they can be either human or nonhuman in nature (e.g., family members vs. climate). Finally, I discuss how these contexts are interconnected and together can exert a powerful, unacknowledged influence on behavior.

Overview: The Nature of Contexts

The Merriam-Webster Online Dictionary defines *context* as "the parts of a discourse that surround a word or passage and can throw light on its meaning" or "the interrelated conditions in which something exists or occurs." The term *context* conveys a sense of the weaving together of words or conditions in a way that provides coherence. A closely related term is *environment,* or "the circumstances, objects, or conditions by which one is surrounded" or "the aggregate of social and cultural conditions that influence the life of an individual or community." Both terms refer to a collection of conditions that sustain life and provide meaningfulness, and both are used interchangeably in this book.

We are prone to think of context or environment as a backdrop against which the drama of human life plays out. It may be more accurate to view it as a member of the cast with few lines whose role is often underappreciated because it is present in every scene. When we pay attention to the context of our life at any given moment, we may be surprised to discover the degree to which our presumably free choices are constrained by the conditions enveloping our lives.

Consider, for example, your reading of this chapter. How successful are you at concentrating at this moment? Certainly your intelligence, reading ability, motivation to learn these ideas, and background academic preparation—all personal factors—influence your concentration. How about interruptions from family or friends? The temperature of the room: too warm, too cold, or just right? The comfort of your reading chair? Are you reading for pleasure or for a required class assignment? Certainly personal characteristics are important to consider, but they occur in context. Context defines and supports our lives, much like a skeleton we take for granted.

In the course of this chapter I discuss how contexts vary in terms of their proximity, complexity, and human versus nonhuman nature. First let's consider how counselors over the years have typically considered the role of contexts in determining people's behavior.

Origins of the Ecological Perspective

In part reacting against psychology's preoccupation with intrapsychic factors, other experts over the years have championed an exclusively environmental focus when analyzing influences on behavior. This paradigm can be schematized as $B = f(E)$, or behavior is a function of a person's environment (cf. Conyne & Cook, 2004). Human services providers have never widely accepted this environmental paradigm, which totally excludes person factors, but it is worth considering this paradigm as a possible model of human behavior.

In this paradigm, behavior is shaped by a plethora of environmental factors, many of them beyond a person's awareness or control. One group that champions the environmental paradigm is human rights advocates. This perspective illuminates the often tragic effects of prejudice and discrimination against certain categories of persons (e.g., older adults, people of color, immigrants). As discussed in Chapter 5, targets of prejudice and discrimination on the basis of race, ethnicity, or gender become targets primarily because they are classified as members of a group devalued by those in power.

Counselors typically find the environmental paradigm insufficient in itself: What happened to the individual with his or her unique psyche and experiences? Experiences do occur in environments, but isn't it also important to consider how individuals respond to what happens to them? Yes indeed. Environmental variables cannot replace person-centered ones, and vice versa (see Wapner & Demick, 2000). Individuals exposed to the same environmental circumstances may react in very different ways. Some individuals subjected to increasingly restrictive airport security measures respond with good-natured humor; others view the same search process as an unconscionable infringement on their rights to privacy. Some individuals may transcend life tragedies with grace and courage; others subject to much less daunting circumstances may psychically disintegrate under the stress.

It seems clear that person-centered and environmental factors work hand in hand to determine human behavior. The synergistic—and ecological—paradigm symbolizes this interaction as $B = f(P \times E)$, or behavior is a function of persons interacting within their environments. This paradigm at the heart of the ecological perspective is more fully discussed in Chapter 4. For now let's consider different aspects of contexts that influence people's lives every day, beginning with an important distinction between physical and interpersonal (human) contexts of behavior.

Physical Contexts of Human Behavior

The simplest distinction among types of contexts is physical versus human. Physical contexts reflect factors that can be apprehended by the senses and that would exist whether or not people were present. A house's square footage, its furniture arrangement, and its temperature will continue to exist when its inhabitants are away (unless, of course, the owner arranges for home repair, furniture delivery, or a programmable thermostat!).

Examples of how the physical context affects human life every day are not hard to find. Consider the following:

- Neighborhoods in the greater Cincinnati area are subject to cicada infestations on a periodic basis, when these noisy and fulsome creatures make driving and walking unpleasant for several weeks. Cicadas get caught in one's hair and mouth, divebomb into windshields, and litter the sidewalks with their corpses. Businesses report a dramatic decrease in outdoor dining during these summer periods.
- A more serious consequence of living in Cincinnati is the prevalence of respiratory problems related to seasonal allergies. Allergy specialists report that for reasons linked to the topography, adults often develop allergy problems after moving to Cincinnati, or the symptoms of long-term sufferers worsen.
- Global warming has potentially catastrophic consequences for the whole planet Earth. Human behavior has contributed to it and could eventually arrest it, but it will affect every living being for years to come.

As I suggested earlier, counselors tend to underestimate the potential impact of the physical context on their clients. Now consider the following:

- A new counselor is assigned an office that is too small to accommodate three chairs. There is no source of light other than fluorescent bulbs overhead, and the room's cinderblock walls are shedding their paint. The client's chair is a bit wobbly, with a stained seat cushion.
- A single mother living in the inner city with her four small children learns that for the sake of her high blood pressure, she should minimize life stress and get more exercise. Her two-bedroom apartment is far too small, especially considering that several of her children exhibit signs of attention-deficit/hyperactivity problems. She is afraid of walking outside because of how dangerous her neighborhood seems, even during the day.
- Workers in Antarctic research stations are afforded physical protection from the elements but experience stressors related to their isolation from the outside world, their confinement and lack of isolation within the research station, and the extreme physical environment (e.g., high altitude, extreme light/dark cycles). Psychological distress is common even though workers are carefully screened before being admitted to the research program. Some individuals adapt surprisingly well, though, suggesting a unique person–environment congruence (Palinkas, 2003).

Elements of the physical environment can contribute to people's well-being and development in countless ways, some of which are applicable to human beings in general (e.g., living near a toxic waste dump) and others of which depend on personal sensitivities and/or perceptions (e.g., noise levels, architectural features of buildings; see Evans, 1999). Entomologists may eagerly anticipate cicada mating season. An administrator with a coveted corner office surrounded by windows may assert that physical environment does not really affect the counseling process because *his* work is never affected by negative environmental features. A researcher working in Antarctica who spends little time outdoors even during the comparatively balmy summer season may be less affected by the outside temperature than her family members coping with a 40-degree temperature fluctuation back home.

Many aspects of the physical environment are beyond humans' control, and humans must either change their location or adjust to it. Residents of the Hawaiian Islands cannot change the fact that their lives are geographically bounded by the Pacific Ocean. For native-born Hawaiians, these boundaries are home; some new residents find that what is rhapsodized as paradise feels too small for them, and they return to the mainland. (Perhaps this choice is hard to believe, but I have known two such persons myself.)

Relocation requires resources: resources to identify alternatives, negotiate terms of the move (e.g., terminating a lease, making a down payment), make the move, and adjust to the new surroundings. It may be difficult for counselors to remember that for many people, especially low-income individuals, relocation is beset with too many challenges to make it a viable solution. Saving for the costs of a move is not possible. People rely on urban bus transportation to get to work and school. Social services programs are easier to access in a city. One's social resources—help with child or elder care, one's church and friends—may not be transportable and would disappear from everyday life. A hidden cost of urban renewal projects that offer new housing in exchange for demolishing low-income neighborhoods is that the human networks that provide free child care, barbeque on the corner, and talks on the front stoop are also demolished.

It is clear that the physical context is not simply an interchangeable backdrop for human life; it is part of life itself. A deeply felt sense of place can develop nearly everywhere people live. Stokols, Clitheroe, and Zmuidzinas (2000) used the term *place identity* to reflect the psychological significance certain places can have in our lives, to the point of becoming a part of our overall sense of self. We humans connect with one another in an ecology firmly rooted in the physical world embracing all our lives.

Because counselors' focus of attention is on the personal rather than the physical features of life contexts, in my experience counselors rarely spend much time exploring the features of clients' physical life context with them. Depending on how clients perceive and react to it, the physical context can influence life for better or worse. Fish are probably not aware of living in water, as the maxim states, and humans may not be aware of how the physical context of their lives affects them as well.

An awareness of physical context can suggest some new possibilities for changing lives. A can of paint can be a counseling intervention when it changes how comfortable group members feel about their surroundings (Conyne & Cook, 2004). What impact might some inexpensive redecoration of the cinderblock office have on the clients who cannot afford to vote with their feet by choosing to attend a more attractive office? How might the inner-city mother respond to a counselor who seems to appreciate the limitations of her life settings?

Unlike other living creatures, humans have the capacity to change the impact of their physical context by evaluating where and how they live out their lives. We also have the unique ability to intervene in others' lives, understanding that we can redistribute physical resources and advantages. By attending to where and how a person's life is situated, we can much better appreciate what it means to be living the life the client tries to share with us.

Interpersonal Contexts of Human Behavior

Early in their training counselors learn to be attuned to the interpersonal contexts of life. Humans are dependent on other humans for survival. We are social animals whose personalities, behaviors, memories, and dreams for the future are the products of life lived with others. Especially in our complex societies, we implicitly depend on others to provide for our various needs. We identify ourselves by the human contexts in which we elaborate our lives; we connect ourselves across space and over time with invisible lifelines to those who mean the most to us. The course of life is a large arc, in that we begin in infancy and end in old age typically dependent on a small number of people in our immediate lives. In the most active years of life many of us could describe ourselves as surrounded by layers upon thickly embedded layers of interpersonal contexts that vary in proximity and immediacy. Spiritual individuals perceive individuals as connected with the creative and sustaining force of the universe itself.

Each individual's life may be thought of as composed of multiple life settings, each a mini-world with its own set of people, location, rules governing interaction, and so on (cf. Swindle & Moos, 1992; Wapner & Demick, 2000). Depending on the individual person, these life contexts may be experienced as overlapping or separate, compatible or conflicting, easy or difficult to move from one setting to another. One woman I know manages a computer-based business out of her own home, working with her husband and daughter. She and her family members joke about what an unreasonable boss they have (her!). She experiences few boundaries between home and work life as her grandchildren clamber on her lap during phone calls, and her work day starts and stops numerous times between 5 a.m. and 6 p.m. each day. In contrast, another woman works weekdays at a job hundreds of miles away from her family and commutes back home every weekend. She rarely brings work home on weekends, preferring to focus exclusively on her family life for a precious few days. She describes her work and family lives as entirely separate and strives to enhance that separation however possible. Each woman asserts that her own manner of combining work and family is best for her; our personal reaction to each life pattern says volumes about our needs and preferences and those of the people with whom we share our lives.

One of the significant contributions of ecological experts to the understanding of human behavior is the discussion of subsystems of human behavior. These subsystems interact with one another, yet each level uniquely contributes to understanding the complexities of human life in interaction.

Overview: Subsystems or Levels of Interpersonal Contexts

Human development is typically most influenced by those human life contexts closest to our everyday life, called *proximal* contexts. Urie Bronfenbrenner (1977) organized human life contexts as a series of concentric circles with the individual nestled at the heart. Each concentric circle represents a level of *system* less immediate and more abstract to the individual. In Bronfenbrenner's earliest work, the smallest unit was dyadic relationships representing the most intimate system influencing human development. He added the focus on the individual in later work.

Bronfenbrenner (1977) defined the systems that influence human development as follows:

- The *microsystem* refers to developmental structures and processes that occur in an immediate setting containing the person (e.g., home, school). The physical features of the setting, the activities, and the roles of the people all affect the relationships involved.
- The *mesosystem* involves linkages and processes between two or more microsystems (each containing the person). For example, the term *mesosystem* might refer to developmental implications of connections between the relationships a child has at home and at school: How well do the child's parents and teacher work together?
- The *exosystem*, like the mesosystem, refers to linkages between two or more subsystems, but at least one of these linked subsystems does not directly contain the person (and by inference at least one does contain him or her). An example of an exosystem might be the relationship between a child's home and a parent's work site. Like the more proximal subsystems, exosystems in Bronfenbrenner's model involve specific settings of a person's life.
- The *macrosystem* is defined as "the overarching institutional patterns of the culture or subculture . . . carriers of information and ideology that, both explicitly and implicitly, endow meaning and motivation" to people's lives (Bronfenbrenner, 1977, p. 515). The macrosystem contains the broader ideals, meanings, values, and other invisible yet meaningful features that characterize a culture in general. For example, the American ideal of rugged individualism, the self-made man, and success guaranteed by hard work and personal goals is an influential macrosystemic feature of the U.S. cultural heritage. We recognize this ideal as American even though many Americans might view this ideal as more of a dream than a reality for them and others might view it as not very desirable at all.

43

Bronfenbrenner's schematic model of systems that influence human development has been cited repeatedly since the 1970s as a thought-provoking way to describe contextual influences on human development (see Moen, Elder, & Luscher, 1995, for a rich tribute to Bronfenbrenner's legacy). In my experience, however, counselors are typically more comfortable thinking about the sites (e.g., home, school, neighborhood) involved in someone's life than about abstract connections among systems that can be difficult to translate into the particulars of a person's life. (In 10 seconds or less, try to think of an example of an exosystem influence in your early childhood.) There are other ways to think ecologically about behavior while remaining faithful to Bronfenbrenner's insightful schema. In our ecological perspective, then, we will refer to contexts differently than Bronfenbrenner did while retaining several of his key assumptions about the nature of contexts. These key assumptions about contexts concern proximity, salience, and embeddedness.

First, as Bronfenbrenner noted, contexts vary in terms of their nearness or *proximity* to an individual. Those contexts that play a starring role in a person's everyday life—home, workplace, membership on an athletic team—tend to have the strongest influence on a person. These up-close and personal contexts are called *proximal* contexts. Conversely, those contexts that are less intimately involved in a person's everyday life are *distal* contexts.

Second, the same contexts can have different *salience* to different people. Consider my own neighborhood, which is prototypically suburban: quiet cul-de-sacs, self-contained, no outside traffic. For my own family with teenagers, the neighborhood has little impact on our daily lives, although we do appreciate that it is safe and quiet. In contrast, families with young children tend to play outside and take walks with babies in strollers. I would expect that these young families consider the suburban neighborhood to be a prominent context for their everyday activities, whereas my family is seldom aware of the same neighborhood surrounding us.

Third, in the ecological perspective contexts are seen as *embedded* within one another, progressing from the most proximal contexts (e.g., home) to those that are less direct but nevertheless influential in a person's everyday life (e.g., the national economy). Much as the iconic Russian dolls hold a series of progressively smaller duplicates, the larger, less personal contexts effectively hold and surround the smaller, more personal contexts. My suburban home is nestled within my neighborhood, a part of the township, located in one corner of a state in the Midwest, and so on. Bronfenbrenner (1999) proposed that because of how contextual systems may be nested or situated within one another, "the power of developmental forces operating at any one systems level of the environment depends on the nature of the environmental structures at the same and at all higher systems levels" (p. 11). In other words, individuals rarely effect changes in the functioning of the national economy (unless one is elected president, perhaps). Consider, by contrast, the impact that the national economy can have on national industries situated in geographic regions, providing local employment and distributing individual paychecks. Thus, in analyzing any behavior, it can be informative to recall that every broader level of context is always involved in some manner, however subtle and indirect (cf. Wapner & Demick, 2000).

In applying these concepts to behavior, I (e.g., Conyne & Cook, 2004) have found it more useful as a counselor and educator to think in terms of *levels of relational contexts* rather than to use Bronfenbrenner's reliance on systems terminology. Relevant contextual levels can be organized as follows:

- The individual as the major reference point—the center—of his or her life
- Important personal relationships as the contextual level closest to the individual (proximal) and thus the most influential
- Groups, referring to membership in "an open, complex, and interactive social system that is embedded within physical, temporal, sociocultural, and organizational contexts" (Arrow, McGrath, & Berdahl, as cited in Conyne & Cook, 2004, pp. 126–127)
- Organizations, referring to membership in structured dynamic social systems such as school, the church, or the workplace. Relationships are present, but their purpose is to advance some broader, shared purpose (e.g., to worship or to earn money)
- Communities, referring to people connected through geography who share common ties and communication (based on Hutchison, 2008)
- Institutions, defined by Hutchison (2008) as "patterned ways of solving the problems and meeting the requirements of a particular society" (p. 299). Key social institutions include the government, the economy, education, health care, and the media.
- Macrolevel contexts, which provide the abstract, sociocultural blueprints of roles, policies, and practices regulating and maintaining the more proximal contextual levels

Let's consider some aspects of these levels in more detail.

Near and Dear Influences: Microlevel Relationships

According to *Real Simple* magazine, the writer Tennessee Williams reportedly said that "life is partly what we make it, and partly what is made by the friends we choose." How right he was: The quality of the friendships that make up our lives contributes mightily to our lives as a whole. Microlevel relationships are those that make up our everyday lives: the relationships that define us, mean home for us, provide support and company. These are the people we think about calling in the face of triumphs or disasters. These relationships shape how we develop over time, beginning in but continuing well past early childhood (R. H. Bradley, 1999).

Generally speaking, the family offers the most important set of relationships for an individual. The family can be nuclear, extended, defined by blood ties, covenant, or simply chosen by the person. Especially when family ties have been strained or dissolved because of death, geographic distance, or irreconcilable differences (e.g., political or religious disputes, announcement of a gay or lesbian identity), alternative families may be established through choice.

Some individuals might define relationships established through marriage (e.g., in-laws) as more supportive and loving than those provided by their families of origin. Also within this family contextual level are close friendships and/or other relationships that the person labels as important to him or her (e.g., lifelong coworkers or best friends of siblings). The precise nature of the relationships considered as important can vary considerably. Within one family I know, the grandparents consider their (grown) children their family, with spouses and grandchildren occupying a second tier of importance. In contrast, one of their daughters considers her extended family through marriage and an assortment of younger people affiliated with her children all part of her family.

In contrast to the Western culture's emphasis on nuclear families, many other cultures define families and the obligations accompanying them much more broadly. Extended families, and obligations to care for them financially and emotionally, are common. For example, decisions about education and career are commonly made after consulting with other family members.

These differences do not mean that the quality of relationships is superior in one form than another but that counselors need to be aware of how particular individuals define their own families. Crucial family relationships can also include people who are geographically separated or who have died; they are physically absent but very present in spirit. For a microlevel relationship to be influential, the individual needs to maintain some sense of reciprocal interaction with the other person (e.g., communicating with a dead parent through prayer).

Bronfenbrenner (1999) recognized that people may also interact with objects and symbols, for example fantasy play, hobbies, or reading. Small children commonly have blankets or toys that provide considerable comfort; adolescents appear totally devoted to cell phones or iPods. Such objects may be considered part of the person's intimate world if they are valued and may serve an important function for the person.

Another type of microlevel influence is group interaction. Most groups classified here involve face-to-face interaction (e.g., athletic teams, religious groups, reading clubs). Yet Internet groups can play an important role in someone's life as well, although it is not clear whether these technologically based groups provide the same interpersonal benefits for people as face-to-face groups. Experts in group interaction have noted that the nature and quality of the group interaction as a whole—what one student once called the "groupiness" of the group—influences each member too.

Just what do these microlevel relationships provide to people? Bronfenbrenner (1999) defined a crucial proposition in his interactive model of development as follows:

> Especially in its early phases, and to a great extent throughout the life course, human development takes place through processes of progressively more complex reciprocal interaction between an active, evolving biopsychological human organism and the persons, objects, and symbols in its immediate external environment. To be effective, the interaction must occur on a fairly regular basis over extended periods of *time.* Such enduring forms of interaction in the immediate environment are referred to as *proximal processes.* (p. 5, italics in the original)

Attachment to caregivers is a crucial feature of early life that affects people's development well into adulthood (cf. Wright & Perrone, 2008). Theorists have argued that intimate, mutual relationships are crucial in the development of one's sense of self, capacity for engaging in relationships, and resilience throughout life (Liang et al., 2002). The ability to affiliate and empathically connect with others is crucial to lifelong personality and social development (see relational-cultural theory as discussed in Comstock et al., 2008).

These relationships obviously define the parameters of our world early in life. Love may arguably be the most important nutrient that caregivers provide young ones, but caregivers also provide much more through early socialization practices. According to Super and Harkness (1999), culturally defined child-rearing practices affect how and when young children develop essential human capacities such as walking and talking. The beliefs, practices, and contexts characteristic of a particular cultural setting support and stimulate children's development of basic motor skills. Children in rural Kenya could indeed learn how to walk if their caregivers failed to engage in certain training practices, but what parent would be willing to take that chance?

Our relationships provide an essential nutrient of human life: social support. Social support communicates to recipients that they are loved, valued, and not alone (H. S. Kim, Sherman, & Taylor, 2008). Relationships offer crucial support to career planning and establishment, particularly in adolescence and early adulthood for young people of color, when crucial initial decisions are made (Diemer, 2007; Kenny & Bledsoe, 2005; Kenny et al., 2007; Schultheiss, 2003; Wright & Perrone, 2008).

People who have more types of relationships live longer and tend to be healthier (Cohen & Janicki-Deverts, 2009). The degree to which people believe that support will be available to them if needed (perceived support) is more important to good health than the support they have reported actually receiving, usually during times of need (received support; Haber, Cohen, Lucas, & Baltes, 2007). If the form of support does not match what the person needs, or if the support reduces the recipient's self-esteem, the overall effect of the received support may be negative (Uchino, 2009). Cultural factors also play a role in what type of social support is most helpful, for example, whether others typically listen to people talk about their difficulties or whether they communicate support nonverbally simply by their presence (H. S. Kim et al., 2008). Extended family systems can help poor families thrive despite the cycle of stresses facing them (e.g., American Psychological Association, 2007). However, these same support networks of family and friends can also bring distress, even outweighing the positive resources they supply (Belle & Doucet, 2003).

Finding balance between personal concerns (e.g., pursuing personal goals) and relational concerns (e.g., providing support to others) is not easy but is important to a person's sense of well-being (Kumashiro, Rusbult, & Finkel, 2008). Satisfaction with intimate connections can wax and wane according to changes in role responsibilities, such as after a child is born (Doss, Rhoades, Stanley, & Markman, 2009). The emotional and physical stresses of raising young children coincide with the job challenges commonly faced by young couples. If the stress is compounded by infertility or adoption challenges, unique needs of the child (e.g., physical or psychological concerns), financial difficulties, or a host of other possible stressors (e.g., caring for an elderly parent), the parental relationship may be strained beyond repair.

To appreciate the psychological complexities of social settings, one must take into account numerous factors, including the nature of the ongoing transactions, personal roles within the settings, the nature of resources (e.g., financial), and how these resources are allocated (see Tseng & Seidman, 2007; Tseng & Seidman's article also contains a fascinating comparison of Asian and American classroom practices). Researchers have developed rather precise ways of analyzing relationships among people. Comprehensive checklists concerning relationships and needs are used in many behavior programs (e.g., Munger, 2000) and types of research (e.g., Liang et al., 2002). Most counselors have been introduced to genograms, which portray the nature of a family system. Ecomaps can diagram connections between a family and other groups or institutions (Horton & Bucy, 2000). Social network analysis (Koehly & Shivy, 2000) is a still more complex coding of social systems. Counselors have much to learn from other disciplines.

It is easy for counselors to understand that immediate, interpersonal life contexts influence the nature, quality, and satisfaction of a client's life. However, counselors need to look in other corners of the person's worlds for clues to his or her concerns. Might a child's hostile negativity about school be related to factors beyond his parents—for example, an emotionally abusive teacher or the child's perceptiveness about daily microaggressions from the community because of his ethnicity (Sue et al., 2007)? Exploring less obvious possibilities may help counselors become more effective in helping clients deal with the realities of their everyday lives.

The Ecological Niche

A unique and especially useful concept in the ecological perspective is that of the *ecological niche,* which is adapted from the broader developmental concept of the developmental niche. The developmental niche (e.g., Super & Harkness, 1999) refers to features of a shared cultural community (physical and social settings, child care and child-rearing customs, beliefs and orientations of caregivers) that contribute to human development. The ecological niche is more easily described: features of the person's ecosystem that make up his or her daily life (e.g., home, family, workplace, where he or she goes and with whom he or she interacts on a daily basis; Conyne & Cook, 2004). The ecological niche encompasses the personal and impersonal settings of a person's life, and many elements can be described quite accurately by outsiders. It includes friends and family, favorite places to stop for coffee, the friendly parking attendant who always has welcoming words, the fallback option for dinner on the run, a favorite radio station or iPod playlist for background music. As a concept it spans both the interpersonal and the material worlds, emotionally significant relationships as well as the more transient ones that color the backdrops of our everyday roles and functions.

By definition, the ecological niche emphasizes proximal influences, those physically present in a person's daily routine. These influences can vary in importance across people. (My teenager's cell phone is a treasured part of her ecological niche; I don't feel much attached to mine.) A niche may also include people or places regularly present in spirit only (e.g., a dead parent with whom a person regularly converses) or spiritual practices that involve communing with a divine presence, nonetheless real to a person even though not physically present.

The concept of the ecological niche is elaborated through reference to biological ecology, which discusses an organism's place within the broader ecosystem. All organisms, humans included, need to be safe and nourished. Each organism requires specific types of environmental resources and protection to survive and in turn carries out subtle but invaluable functions for other organisms within the ecosystem. In Willi's (1999) words, we use our ecological niches as "a functional structure that shapes the interactions between what [people] have to offer and the structural conditions and interests of their environment" (p. 8). The ecological niche represents our daily lifeline to the world around us. Although nonhuman organisms may not be able to survive the destruction of their niches due to environmental changes, humans are uniquely capable of adapting to changes in their niches, choosing where and how they live out their lives.

Certain aspects of the ecological niche carry no particular significance; they are simply there (e.g., the typical route a person's car seems to navigate by autopilot). Within the nature of the ecological niche, however, are important clues about the quality of the person's life. When the ecological niche radically changes (such as happens with a geographic move), the person can feel disconnected. People who lack regular, affirming interactions with others, however fleeting, can feel lonely. In contrast, simply having a barista at a coffeehouse remember your favorite coffee order can be consoling; retired persons eating breakfast every day at the same restaurant can find discussions about the weather and bantering with servers downright life giving.

Because the ecological niche is where people live out their daily lives, niche-based interactions are crucial instruments of psychological development throughout life (cf. Willi, 1999). People grow through evolving relationships with others, and the ecological niche is an important player in past experiences and future plans. An ambitious person may network with others throughout the day with the possibility of future business transactions in the back of her mind; an anxious person may choose certain types of friends or intimate partners who will both protect him and avoid challenging him psychologically (see the case examples in Willi, 1999).

Because the ecological niche is as much part of our everyday life as breathing, we may not be aware of how ostensibly simple changes can substantially alter our daily experience. A person's life may have too few contacts to nurture feelings of connection to the world or so many that he or she feels depleted. The physical space may be cluttered or otherwise unappealing but changeable with some attention. When the process of making life changes feels overwhelming, identifying small, practical changes in the ecological niche can be encouraging and surprisingly effective.

For example, Sylvia reluctantly agreed to support her husband's latest job promotion, even though it required her to move to another state with their three young children. She sank into a depression over the loss of her beautiful home, circle of friends, part-time job, and volunteer activities at her children's school. She felt it was immature and selfish of her to miss these things. The counselor helped her explore her complicated feelings about the move. Sylvia recognized that she certainly did have a home, but her loss was real: She felt unprotected in a unknown world. She soon identified lifelong strategies of accommodating to new locations as strengths she could use now. She intentionally fostered her feeling of having a new home, locating some small local grocers and coffeehouses where people soon began to greet her by name. In settling her family's belongings, she made it a priority to establish her own corner for meditating. As she felt she had reestablished a comfortable niche for herself, she and the counselor explored how it could help her develop an increasingly meaningful life for herself and what contextual resources she could draw on in her new life directions. How she viewed her new life context became a launching pad for a richer life.

Counselors need to be careful not to make assumptions about the personal meaningfulness of a person's ecological niche; a given aspect might have a different importance than we might expect. A particularly poignant example is provided by the women participants in R. G. Bradley and Davino's (2002) research. For some of these inhabitants of a medium-security prison, prison was perceived as a safe place lacking in the often severe violence they had experienced as children and/or adults. Bradley and Davino recommended that "treatment approaches should help women find ways to increase the safety and support of their future environments" (p. 357), which requires attention to issues of poverty and substance abuse. The counseling relationship itself can serve as a model of supportive relationships that might be possible in the future.

Neighborhoods and Public Community Settings

Most humans live in neighborhoods, but defining them is no simple matter. According to Nicotera's (2007) detailed review, definitions can be based on social composition (which demographic groups live there), economic composition (e.g., income levels, economic class), social processes (e.g., crime, neighboring), or physical composition/resources (e.g., condition of the housing, presence of community resources). Scientific measures of neighborhoods run into the dozens, yet without them parents everywhere still make judgments about what makes a good neighborhood setting for their children.

Counselors are commonly concerned with what they see as the impact of bad neighborhoods on the children they serve, but Shinn and Toohey's (2003) review demonstrates how we need to be careful not to make snap judgments. Economically poor neighborhoods frequently but do not always lead to bad outcomes for children. It also appears to be true that exposure to violence and crime, what Shinn and Toohey called "incivilities" (e.g., public drunkenness, litter), and neighbors' perceptions of the presence of social problems are associated with distress, but a sense of community and working together for the common good can make a positive difference. Shinn and Toohey also pointed out that community settings created for a particular function, whether economic (e.g., stores, businesses that provide jobs) or service (e.g., medical offices, churches), can encourage a sense of identity and roles, enhance a sense of community, provide resources to the community, and establish norms that affect behavior (e.g., schools' formal and informal norms about aggressive behaviors can generalize).

Shinn and Toohey's analysis emphasizes the fact that simple generalizations about the impact of these settings are likely to be inaccurate at least part of the time. The same settings are likely to be affirming to some and negative to others (e.g., because of someone's minority status or individual temperament). People often develop what Brodsky and Marx (2001) defined as a "psychological sense of community": "a feeling of belonging to, importance of, and identification with a community" (p. 161). This sense is very similar to what Nicotera (2007) called "place" as opposed to "environment": what characterizes an environment can be seen by outsiders, but place fits one's sense of self. What individuals define as *their* neighborhood or community setting may vary quite dramatically and for a variety of reasons (e.g., the age of the respondent). In Shinn and Toohey's (2003) words, "Family members residing at the same address might have different functional neighborhoods" (p. 449). People may have different degrees or sources of a sense of community across diverse communities (neighborhood, work) or with subcommunities within a broader community (e.g., a group of members at an Alcoholics Anonymous chapter; cf. Brodsky & Marx, 2001). It may be important to understand these complex patterns of psychological affiliations with communities to obtain a full picture of the role of communities within a person's life.

Ross and Jang (2000) emphasized the importance of visible cues that inhabitants interpret as indicators of order versus disorder. Cues of neighborhood disorder include people hanging out on streets and vandalized, abandoned buildings. Ross and Jang's research indicates that people living in neighborhoods they perceive as disordered also report more fear and distrust of others. However, if inhabitants of neighborhoods with high levels of perceived disorder have informal alliances with other neighbors, then levels of fear and distrust are reduced. Ross and Jang suggested that efforts to improve the neighborhood itself (e.g., by tearing down abandoned buildings) may also help reduce the fear and distrust that are magnified by these cues.

It seems clear that supportive relationships among neighbors can have a significant impact on the well-being of the community's members (Farrell, Aubry, & Coulombe, 2004). This finding applies to wealthier communities as well. Members of wealthy suburbs can suffer from alienation, as can people who live in neighborhoods stressed by poverty and its correlates. Counselors may be able to assist community organizations (e.g., schools, churches) in exploring ways to foster neighborliness within a range of communities, particularly efforts that enhance relationships among the members.

In considering complex social settings I have focused on neighborhoods because this literature is relatively unfamiliar to counselors. The community psychology literature is a rich source of information for thinking about social settings in general. Tseng and Seidman (2007) provided a thoughtful analysis of social settings intended to help experts plan change interventions. School counselors will particularly appreciate their analysis of school settings, particularly their comparison of elementary school classes in the United States with those in Japan and Taiwan.

Institutions: Invisible Yet Powerful Social Structures

This level of subsystem presents an uncomfortable paradox for people: It is clear that these huge organizations affect all of our lives to some extent, but we cannot see them. We can observe more proximal, up-close levels of human systems—family relationships, and neighborhoods, for example—but we cannot "see" our government or the Internet. These complex systems were developed to meet a need experienced by many people and are maintained by intersecting networks of roles and relationships. These structures do not rely on the leadership of any one person and are typically self-maintaining, although they may be funded by external sources (e.g., the educational system is funded by government dollars).

Examples of these institutions abound: the government, the legal system, the media, education, health care, the world of work. Adult life typically carries expectations that individuals engage in these systems (e.g., vote, pay taxes, work to support themselves and their dependents, enroll their children in schools). Some involvement might be required (e.g., paying taxes), whereas other involvement is strongly encouraged via cultural mandate (e.g., responsible people vote in every election, people should regularly consult the media for news).

These institutions serve as the skeleton for our way of life, providing form, function, and support for challenges humans face in attempting to live together peaceably. They carry enormous power—imagine life without any one of them. Inevitably, and unfortunately, institutions also reflect the inequities endemic in a culture and through their functioning maintain policies and procedures that can appear wrong and unchangeable to its members. Some people believe that "lazy" people get support from public welfare programs; others believe that these programs are insufficient to meet the level of need experienced by people. Media images glorify a certain physique and type of face as ideal. Are these images harmless means to the end of selling products? Perhaps so, but they also can present a standard for attractiveness impossible for most of the population to emulate.

There may be little that individuals can do to change the powerful institutions that affect their lives, but people working together can move these invisible mountains. Consider the success of the Civil Rights movement in the United States and government upheavals all over the world. Some counselors value working toward various forms of institutional change as part and parcel of their commitment to transforming people's lives (see the discussion of social justice in Chapter 6). We can also help some clients consider how these institutions might contribute to life problems that they regard as entirely their fault and help others explore how to respond creatively to the demands of these institutions. For example, we all need to pay taxes, but some clients coping with financial crises might not know that tax debts might be paid on a payment plan over time and in a few cases even dramatically reduced. We can help clients explore such alternatives and develop the skills necessary to ask institutional representatives for these solutions and to carry them out.

The Macrosystem: Culture and Human Behavior

Perhaps because of their interest in clients' personal relationships (microsystems), counselors typically do not give much attention to the role of culture in clients' lives. However, culture is the invisible macrolevel blueprint (to use Bronfenbrenner's evocative term) that shapes every human interaction across every ecosystem level. Lehman, Chiu, and Schaller (2004) suggested that culture

> represents a coalescence of discrete behavioral norms and cognitions shared by individuals within some definable population that are distinct from those shared within other populations. These normative beliefs and behaviors provide resources for realizing individual and collective goals, and so are often institutionalized in a variety of formal and informal ways. Moreover, there exist means for transmitting beliefs and behaviors to new members of the cultural population, so that the norms defining a culture may persist over a very long period of time. (pp. 690–691)

Culture includes norms, tools, values, and what Triandis and Suh (2002) called "shared standard operating procedures" and "unstated assumptions" (p. 136). Triandis and Suh asserted that cultures differ from one another in terms of complexity (e.g., hunter/gatherer cultures vs. modern technological cultures) and tolerance for deviation from norms. Culture includes both shared activity and meaning that accumulate over time (Greenfield, Keller, Fuligni, & Maynard, 2003). It offers a system of symbols (language) and their meanings crucial to making sense of the world (Lehman et al., 2004). In essence then, culture encompasses what a defined population believes and does as a people and distinctive beliefs and behaviors that are maintained now and for future generations.

McAdams and Pals (2006) suggested that culture has a complicated effect on our individual lives. It has little to do with the size and strength of inborn traits, but it does affect how and where we express them. It also strongly affects the meaning we derive for our lives as a whole and how we see ourselves as human beings in this time and place. If genetic parameters for the human species are represented by pen and ink, providing a common outline shared by all of us, culture is the watercolor shadings that make human life so colorful.

One significant distinction between cultures is collectivism versus individualism (see Markus & Kitayama, 1998, for an influential article discussing this infrastructure of cultural differences). The distinction between collectivist and individualist cultures as summarized here rests on a large body of scholarship that has explored differences in cultural cognitions, values, goals, emotions, and experiences.

Cultures characterized as individualist (or independent) typically value developing self-reliance and individual uniqueness, having many choices, making important life decisions independently, actualizing one's inner potential, and pursuing one's individual goals. Social obligations are selected and managed individually. Personal excellence and individual development are paramount. In contrast, collectivist (or interdependent) cultures value maintaining relationships, fulfilling obligations to others, transcending narrow self-interests in favor of collective pursuits, and enhancing the welfare and social standing of the group. Collectivist individuals are more likely than individualist culture members to actively consider others' behaviors and thoughts and underplay their own strengths; they may even see people from individualist cultures as socially immature because of their focus on the self. The United States and other European or Western cultures exemplify individualist cultures; Asian or Eastern cultures typify collectivist cultures. There also appear to be other more subtle differences in emotional experiences, degree of ambiguity in conversation, cognitive processing styles, flexibility of the self-concept across situations, and so on between these types of cultures (see English & Chen, 2007; Greenfield et al., 2003; Lehman et al., 2004; Triandis & Suh, 2002, for research on these and other differences).

Through the process of human development over time, what Greenfield and her colleagues (2003) called the "deep cultural meaning" represented by these dimensions is encoded in myriad ways: mothers' handling of infants and parents' parenting practices, patterns of language development and emotional sensitivity, and the importance placed on familial duty, among other differences. The precise nature of these differences is less important to our discussion here than is Greenfield and her associates' basic observation: Deep cultural meanings structuring our sense of self, our relationship with others, and our basic life values are taught to us from an early age and are maintained in how we carry out the business of daily life each day (see also Super & Harkness, 1999).

In the Western culture that characterizes the United States as a whole, evidence of this individualist cultural orientation is not hard to find. We encourage young children to be independent in their play and adolescents to choose careers based on personal interests, capacities, and life goals. We value assertive communication in our relationships and expect our loved ones to help us to "become our best selves" (check popular magazine headings for examples). When our adult children move back into our homes after college, we worry about them being immature and too dependent on us. We believe that hard times call for hard (individual) work to get out of them, and we celebrate people who can do the impossible through sheer gumption. (One example is a person who had lost both legs and most of his arms yet succeeded in swimming the English Channel.) Television reality

54

shows that reward fierce competition and individual initiative can be seen most nights of the week.

Does each of us support these values unreservedly? Few of us probably do. Within daily life, cultural values are communicated through particular institutions, communities, schools, and families, each of which filter them through their own lens (e.g., Green, Deschamps, & Paez, 2005; Lehman et al., 2004). Did your client grow up in the Deep South or Alaska, was he or she exposed to liberal or conservative political messages, did he or she become a devout Muslim or an avowed atheist? Many of us have lived within two or more cultures, whether from birth (e.g., having bicultural parents) or through major life changes (e.g., moving to a different country). How we have adapted to these contrasting cultural contexts through the process of acculturation may result in a unique cultural way of being: part new, part old, part a synthesis of the two (cf. B. S. K. Kim, Atkinson, & Umemoto, 2001). Some of us may even shift from one cultural way of being to another consistent with the demands of the situation (Lehman et al., 2004).

In short, each of us has experienced broader cultural influences reinforcing a particular way of life. What contributes to our sense of well-being is deeply influenced by the culture that surrounds us (see the review in Diener, Oishi, & Lucas, 2003). It is plausible that cultural values—the deep meanings—have shaped our lives in ways that we do not recognize.

I have discussed culture at some length because it is easy to overlook, except when clients are obviously different from us. It is easy to forget that we, too, live in a cultural context, one that shapes who we are and how we see the world. We also live in a culture that has enormous global power, one that is emulated throughout the world because of the economic and social privileges we enjoy. It is easy—but not necessarily accurate—to assume that a way of life that offers televisions to virtually everyone is culturally superior in every respect. What is a good way to live, and why? These are issues of meaning not answered by one's economic prosperity. I discuss issues of meaning more later.

The Context of Poverty

One consequence of our economic system is that personal wealth grants a person the ability to choose the most desirable, attractive, and safe living spaces. The obvious corollary is that people with few financial resources do not have much choice in where they live. People in this disadvantaged category include disproportionate numbers of people from racial or ethnic minority groups, people in low-income jobs, immigrants, older adults, and individuals with physical and/or psychological disabilities.

Consider the observations my doctoral seminar class made a few years ago when we worked on planning a community center for local women, predominantly African American or Appalachian women. The women lived in public housing, with minimal public assistance as their primary income. These public housing units were built on the side of a steep hill and were very difficult to navigate during bad weather because of crumbling steps. There were no trees and no places to congregate or walk outside. Their children's school was literally falling down in spots, overcrowded, with no money for extras (e.g., sports). Regarding recreational centers, there was a YMCA with a basketball court and little else. The only community health or counseling center was just a few miles away but required two buses with a transfer some miles away in the opposite direction. No child care was available either, unless a trustworthy relative was nearby. Most women preferred to care for their children themselves so that they could have some control over what happened to them. There were no job opportunities in the area. Pursuing employment elsewhere was not considered an option because of the lack of transportation, child care, and money for clothing. Fortunately, a local church community provided occasional meals, festivals, some food and clothing, and a place to go.

People living in poverty are more likely than others to live in housing no one else wants: overcrowded; badly maintained; near waste dumps; and contaminated by pests, allergens, and lead. Municipal services, schools, and access to transit services are poor. Inhabitants cannot simply choose to move, either; it takes financial and interpersonal resources to manage voluntary moves, and the involuntary moves common in these neighborhoods keep personal relationships fragmented (Saegert & Evans, 2003). Saegert and Evans (2003) pointed out that all of these contextual features work together to pose a cumulative risk to people's welfare—things get worse for them over time.

The effects of these contexts on people's lives are simultaneously dramatic and difficult to disentangle (cf. McLoyd, 1998). Physical health is influenced by the environmental toxicity (particularly if health is already compromised by poor diet, inadequate health care, and so on) and the few opportunities for physical activity. Financially strapped organizations offer children less constructive activity, especially during summers. Children living in poverty are prone to developing negative changes in personality and resilience over time (Hart, Atkins, & Matsuba, 2008; see Wandersman & Nation, 1998, for a discussion of social factors contributing to resilience for children living in poverty). Research (cf. Jackson & Nutini, 2002) suggests that by early adolescence young people already understand the connections between their poverty, education, and their diminished chances for future achievement. It is not surprising that teens are likely to have a pragmatic view of work—as a means to obtain money rather than the personal fulfillment prized by their wealthier peers (Chaves et al., 2004). School achievement tends to decrease as the length of time living in poverty increases (McLoyd, 1998). Parents' chronic economic difficulties stress parenting and marital interactions, and children's mental health problems can make it more difficult to parent them effectively (Conger & Donnellan, 2007; Solantaus, Leinonen, & Punamaki, 2004). Parents get the most blame if their children turn to crime, but excessive as well as too little parental monitoring appears to be related to young people's behavior problems. Peer relationships, in particular gang membership, are strong determinants of delinquency. Parents need to connect with others in the neighborhood as well (Tolan, Gorman-Smith, & Henry, 2003). Data from a variety of studies prompted one researcher (Brooks-Gunn, 1995) to note that poor families with few resources (e.g., parental education) have a very difficult time managing daily life as they struggle to survive (see also Pakman, 2007; Rojano, 2007). Poverty and its associated stressors are strongly related to depression in women (American Psychological Association, 2007). Poor women are likely to experience events they cannot escape, to be confronted with choices inconsistent with basic moral values, and to face the scorn of their children when they cannot provide the material goods the children may yearn for (Belle & Doucet, 2003). And yet not all individuals living in poverty suffer adverse psychological outcomes (e.g., hopelessness) as a result (see Bolland, Lian, & Formichella, 2005). The impact of poverty on family interactions is likely to depend on a combination of factors (e.g., parents' personality; Kochanska, Aksan, Penney, & Boldt, 2007). Extended family systems can provide considerable support to family members coping with the multiple stresses associated with poverty (American Psychological Association, 2007).

It is indeed true that parents' personal characteristics can influence their ability to obtain a decent education. However, these characteristics merely initiate a lifelong vicious circle: Poor parents commonly received substandard education in childhood that did little to motivate them to change the life options they saw around them, and thus they dropped out of school early for a variety of reasons (e.g., learning challenges, peer influence, early pregnancy). Their own children were exposed to family stress prompted by poor living conditions, their parents' personal characteristics, their parents' child-rearing skills (which in turn were affected by their education and exposure to parenting models), and their own responses to their poverty (Conger & Donnellan, 2007). No single factor prompted the cycle; although there are no simple ways to discontinue this cycle for good, there are indeed multiple points at which the cycle can be disrupted for an individual family or community.

People living in poverty have few of the resources needed to move up and out of their life situations, such as good education, contacts, and experience navigating educational or occupational systems. Integrated community and institutional interventions could make a big difference (e.g., Black & Krishnakumar, 1998) but require a seismic shift in our cultural belief that individuals construct their own destiny through motivation and hard work. Counselors who understand the ecological connections between systemic functioning and personal welfare must ponder challenging questions: Is child care and health care for the families of people in the workforce their personal responsibility? What if affordable care is simply unavailable? What constitutes a minimally adequate education, and who should pay for it? How about housing and other basic needs for elderly people and those with disabilities who cannot provide for themselves? Should we penalize clients who do not show up for their appointments because their only source of child care or transportation fell through? Our answers to these and similar questions reflect the deep cultural meanings that guide our priorities as a people today.

Unfortunately, many counselors lack the experience and training needed to understand the realities of people living in poverty. People who are not poor commonly distance, exclude, and devalue poor people (Lott, 2002). There exist widespread negative attitudes about low-income people, beliefs that they are lazy, not intelligent, unattractive, apathetic about their children's lives, and so on (see Lott, 2001, 2002). Many counselors do engage in programs to help the poor, but Lott (2002) made the sobering assertion that "help is too often accompanied by beliefs in the dysfunctionality of poor families and the discounting of strengths, skills and wisdom" (p. 108). Counselors know little about the personal strengths developed over time from living in ecological contexts they personally know very little about (cf. Herr, 2004). The partnership between counselors and clients essential for change is often derailed from the start by counselors' own limitations.

The Reality of Power in Our Social World

This discussion of economic realities leads us to a crucial but uncomfortable discussion about context: the presence of differences in economic, social, and political power among individuals in society. Lott (2002) defined *power* as "access to resources [that] enables the group with greatest access to set the rules, frame the discourse, and name and describe those with less power" (p. 101). People with less power are seen as expendable and undeserving of better treatment (moral exclusion) and thereby worthy of treatment as outsiders. Poor people are consequently seen as deserving their social standing because of their negligence and laziness, an attitude that perhaps explains why welfare recipients often experience humiliation, denigration, and shame (Belle & Doucet, 2003). Lott's (2002) harsh yet documented conclusion is that "a dominant response to the poor by the nonpoor is that of distancing, and examples of such distancing in the form of exclusion, separation, devaluing, and discounting, which operationalize classist discrimination" (p. 108).

The multicultural literature has made it clear that life is easier in certain respects if one is born American, White, male, middle or upper class, and of a Judeo-Christian religious tradition. These parameters continue to describe the majority of political, corporate, and professional leaders today. What these people and their families might view as givens in everyday life (e.g., having someone else to cook and clean for you, the freedom to shop without suspicion of being a shoplifter) are privileges not available to others (Almeida, Dolan-DelVecchio, & Parker, 2007).

The breadth and persistence of this differentiation is not a topic I can adequately explore here. However, every counselor must decide what responsibility he or she bears for dealing with this reality. Is it fair that children born in poor neighborhoods are more likely than other children to receive substandard education? How do we as counselors react when Muslims in our local community are the targets of hate crimes? Do we wonder why few people of color apply to our counselor education programs? These questions require us to wrestle with issues about justice that compromise the well-being of so many people we strive to serve.

Global Transformative Changes in Our World?

The contexts of our small personal lives change continually (e.g., as a result of marriage or divorce, or the success or failure of our small business venture). Humans as a species also continually evolve over time in ways that we cannot perceive at present. At times, however, rapid, transformative environmental changes alter the foundations of our human world at large. Stokols, Misra, Runnerstrom, and Hipp (2009) argued that we are in a transformative period now.

The global source of these changes is manifold. Within the past two decades, the rapid development and dissemination of sophisticated communication technologies has permitted environments to be used for a variety of purposes (e.g., we can work from our homes or from a coffee shop). Others can contact us virtually anywhere, leaving us more connected and distracted than ever before. Global changes in our physical world (e.g., global warming, pollution) leave us more concerned about our own safety and that of our planet at large. Widening disparities occur among different groups of people at every level of proximity to us, prompting concerns for safety (e.g., from terrorism) in diverse settings. Stokols and his associates (2009) indicated that these categories of global change are synergistic, multiplying the personal effects of these changes (e.g., technology provides startling images of natural and human-made disasters).

What impact have these changes had on modern life? Stokols and his associates (2009) focused on the impact of technological changes on people's relationship to their life contexts. Our favorite behavior settings (e.g., home, coffeehouse) frequently become polyfunctional environments such that we can do our work in parks or in restaurants or connect with loved ones in the same places via the Internet. Although there are enormous benefits to having access to information and communication technologies, the cost is substantial:

> fragmentation of people's activities resulting from continued multitasking, greater vulnerability to psychological stress and physical strains generated by chronic exposure to information overload, and heightened anxieties and feelings of helplessness arising from frequent media reports of ecological and sociopolitical dangers in local as well as distant regions. (p. 189)

People's daily lives are often fragmented with multiple interruptions, overstimulation from the constant flow of information, and attentional fatigue from multimedia exposure to global degradation and human conflict that they feel helpless to address.

Stokols and his associates (2009) admitted that we know little about how people respond in the face of such unprecedented change and how to help them accommodate to this new world. This revolution has happened within the span of one generation: Parents who still remember mimeograph machines have children who have never been without access to the Internet. We counselors can begin by exploring with our clients the impact of these sweeping technological changes in their lives and where familiar

59

identities, relationships, and connections to places have been transformed or disrupted. Although the ground may have shifted beneath clients' feet, we can help them firmly plant themselves in new soil.

Summary

Our Western conception of ourselves as individuals is that we are at the center of our own unique universe that we control through our will and skills. The ecological perspective recognizes an antidote to this inflated self-importance: Each of us represents a potentiality dependent on the environment around us for growth and sustenance. Without nourishment from the environment we would wither away. We may need different nutrients than the person next to us; we are more different still from the nonhuman organisms sharing our life space with us. Unlike these other organisms, we as a species have the capacity to choose where we will grow and what and who will nourish us. We have the capacity to either enhance or stunt our own development and that of the others around us.

We humans share the physical world with all creatures. Many of our species tend to assume that earth is not only our habitat but our personal property to dispense with as we wish. The global implications of this vanity have been catastrophic. On a daily basis our lives are influenced by the physical world in innumerable ways: climate affects crops across the world and our personal plans for the afternoon, topography influences some humans' ability to drive certain days of the year and other humans' ability to ward off starvation. We also create physical contexts as locations for human endeavors. Their practicality, comfort, safety, and physical and psychological healthiness are crucial features of everyday life.

We also live in deliberate community with others as a result of our ability to engage in symbolic communication. We communicate our own needs to others and respond to theirs in return; we aspire to communally shared values, try to regulate our habits of living together, and teach our young to live in community as well.

It should be no surprise that it seems sensible to conceptualize human life as a nested series of contexts representing relationships that vary systematically in terms of proximity to an individual: from the important relationships with others that define everyday life and offer us self-definition, personal and material resources, and courage to less intimate groups, neighborhoods and communities, and institutions. The least personal yet broadest and most universally influential level of context is the macrosystem: the blueprint for our human behavior in all other interpersonal contexts. The macrosystem structures our perceptions, goals, rules for interacting with others, and other features of our shared human life in ways so pervasive, so implicit that we can view such blueprints as inherent to the nature of reality rather than human made.

As we shall see in future chapters, thinking ecologically can dramatically alter how we view life as a process. Humans are not isolated creatures, but beings-in-relationships, not only with people they know but also with strangers, groups, impersonal institutions, and the physical world. What do experts today believe to be true about the nature and quality of these interactions? How can the range of interactions that characterize a life enhance the person's potential functioning and ability to contribute to others? In particular, we will explore Bussey and Bandura's (1999) assertion that "human development is influenced by the construed environment rather than mechanistically by the actual environment" (p. 699). I consider these and other questions in the next chapters.

Discussion Questions

- Describe the physical contexts of your life: the rooms, natural habitat, transportation, noise levels, and so on. Where do you feel the most comfortable, and why? For the next month, try making one small change every week (e.g., put air freshener in your car, check e-mails while sitting on your front porch, play soft music in your office). How do these small changes affect how you feel in that context?
- For the next few days, while you are listening to or reading the news, try to imagine the contexts in which news stories occur (e.g., the location of a celebrity's multimillion-dollar wedding, the chaos following a natural disaster). How might these contextual features have affected participants' experience of the news events?
- Describe your ecological niche (or if you prefer, sketch it). How do you react to seeing your niche described in words or on paper? Does it seem satisfying to you? During the next week, try changing something in it (e.g., get your coffee only at your favorite place, even if it's a bit out of your way). What effect does this change have in your life?
- Meditate about the many people who contribute to the quality of your everyday life: family and friends, of course, but also the kindly maintenance person at work or the old friend who faithfully sends good wishes every holiday season. Silently thank all of these people for enriching your life. Promise yourself that you will do better at thanking them personally as well.
- Commit yourself to doing something to change the context of other people's lives.

References

Almeida, R., Dolan-DelVecchio, K., & Parker, L. (2007). Foundation concepts for social justice-based therapy: Critical consciousness, accountability, and empowerment. In E. Aldarondo (Ed.), *Advancing social justice through clinical practice* (pp. 175–206). Mahwah, NJ: Erlbaum.

American Psychological Association. (2007). Guidelines for psychological practice with girls and women. *American Psychologist, 62,* 949–979.

Belle, D., & Doucet, J. (2003). Poverty, inequality, and discrimination as sources of depression among U.S. women. *Psychology of Women Quarterly, 27,* 101–113.

Black, M. M., & Krishnakumar, A. (1998). Children in low-income, urban settings: Interventions to promote mental health and well-being. *American Psychologist, 53,* 635–646.

Bolland, J. M., Lian, B. E., & Formichella, C. M. (2005). The origins of hopelessness among inner-city African-American adolescents. *American Journal of Community Psychology, 36,* 293–305.

Bradley, R. G., & Davino, K. M. (2002). Women's perceptions of the prison environment: When prison is "the safest place I've ever been." *Psychology of Women's Quarterly, 26,* 351–359.

Bradley, R. H. (1999). The home environment. In S. L. Friedman & T. D. Wachs (Eds.), *Measuring environment across the life span: Emerging methods and concepts* (pp. 31–58). Washington, DC: American Psychological Association.

Brodsky, A. E., & Marx, C. M. (2001). Layers of identity: Multiple psychological senses of community within a community setting. *Journal of Community Psychology, 29,* 161–178.

Bronfenbrenner, U. (1977). Toward an experimental ecology of human development. *American Psychologist, 32,* 515–531.

Bronfenbrenner, U. (1999). Environments in developmental perspective: Theoretical and operational models. In S. Friedman & T. Wachs (Eds.), *Measuring environment across the life span: Emerging methods and concepts* (pp. 3–28). Washington, DC: American Psychological Association.

Brooks-Gunn, J. (1995). Children in families in communities: Risk and intervention in the Bronfenbrenner tradition. In P. Moen, G. H. Elder, Jr., & K. Luscher (Eds.), *Examining lives in context: Perspectives on the ecology of human development* (pp. 467–519). Washington, DC: American Psychological Association.

Bussey, K., & Bandura, A. (1999). Social cognitive theory of gender development and differentiation. *Psychological Review, 106,* 676–713.

Chaves, A. P., Diener, M. A., Blustein, D. L., Gallagher, L. A., DeVoy, J. E., Casares, M. T., & Perry, J. C. (2004). Conceptions of work: The view from urban youth. *Journal of Counseling Psychology, 51,* 275–286.

Cohen, S., & Janicki-Deverts, D. (2009). Can we improve our physical health by altering our social networks? *Perspectives on Psychological Science, 4,* 375–378.

Comstock, D. L., Hammer, T. R., Strentzsch, J., Cannon, K., Parsons, J., & Salazar, G., II. (2008). Relational-cultural theory: A framework for bridging relational, multicultural, and social justice competencies. *Journal of Counseling & Development, 86,* 279–287.

Conger, R. D., & Donnellan, M. B. (2007). An interactionist perspective on the socioeconomic context of human development. *Annual Review of Psychology, 58,* 175–199.

Conyne, R. K., & Cook, E. P. (Eds.). (2004). *Ecological counseling: An innovative approach to conceptualizing person–environment interaction.* Alexandria, VA: American Counseling Association.

Diemer, M. A. (2007). Parental and school influences upon the career development of poor youth of color. *Journal of Vocational Behavior, 70,* 502–524.

Diener, E., Oishi, S., & Lucas, R. E. (2003). Personality, culture, and subjective well-being: Emotional and cognitive evaluations of life. *Annual Review of Psychology, 54,* 403–425.

Doss, B. D., Rhoades, G. K., Stanley, S. M., & Markman, H. J. (2009). The effect of the transition to parenthood on relationship quality: An 8-year prospective study. *Journal of Personality and Social Psychology, 96,* 601–619.

English, T., & Chen, S. (2007). Culture and self-concept stability: Consistency across and within contexts among Asian Americans and European Americans. *Journal of Personality and Social Psychology, 93,* 478–490.

Evans, G. W. (1999). Measurement of the physical environment as a stressor. In S. L. Friedman & T. D. Wachs (Eds.), *Measuring environment across the life span: Emerging methods and concepts* (pp. 249–277). Washington, DC: American Psychological Association.

Farrell, S. J., Aubry, T., & Coulombe, D. (2004). Neighborhoods and neighbors: Do they contribute to personal well-being? *Journal of Community Psychology, 32,* 9–25.

Green, E. G. T., Deschamps, J., & Paez, D. (2005). Variation of individualism and collectivism within and between 20 countries: A typological analysis. *Journal of Cross-Cultural Psychology, 36,* 321–339.

Greenfield, P. M., Keller, H., Fuligni, A., & Maynard, A. (2003). Cultural pathways through universal development. *Annual Review of Psychology, 54,* 461–490.

Haber, M. G., Cohen, J. L., Lucas, T., & Baltes, B. B. (2007). The relationship between self-reported received and perceived social support: A meta-analytic review. *American Journal of Community Psychology, 39,* 133–144.

Hart, D., Atkins, R., & Matsuba, M. K. (2008). The association of neighborhood poverty with personality change in childhood. *Journal of Personality and Social Psychology, 94,* 1048–1061.

Herr, E. L. (2004). The context of American life today. In R. K. Conyne & E. P. Cook (Eds.), *Ecological counseling: An innovative approach to conceptualizing person–environment interaction* (pp. 37–66). Alexandria, VA: American Counseling Association

Horton, C. B., & Bucy, J. E. (2000). Assessing adolescents: Ecological and person–environment fit perspectives. In W. E. Martin & J. L. Swartz-Kulstad (Eds.), *Person–environment psychology and mental health: Assessment and intervention* (pp. 39–57). Mahwah, NJ: Erlbaum.

Hutchison, E. D. (2008). *Dimensions of human behavior.* Los Angeles, CA: Sage.

Jackson, M. A., & Nutini, C. D. (2002). Hidden resources and barriers in career learning assessment with adolescents vulnerable to discrimination. *The Career Development Quarterly, 51,* 56–73.

Kenny, M. E., & Bledsoe, M. (2005). Contributions of the relational context to career adaptability among urban adolescents. *Journal of Vocational Behavior, 66,* 257–272.

Kenny, M. E., Gualdron, L., Scanlon, D., Sparks, E., Blustein, D. J., & Jernigan, M. (2007). Urban adolescents' constructions of supports and barriers to educational and career attainment. *Journal of Counseling Psychology, 54*, 336–343.

Kim, B. S. K., Atkinson, D. R., & Umemoto, D. (2001). Asian cultural values and the counseling process: Current knowledge and directions for future research. *The Counseling Psychologist, 29*, 570–603.

Kim, H. S., Sherman, D. K., & Taylor, S. E. (2008). Culture and social support. *American Psychologist, 63*, 518–526.

Kochanska, G., Aksan, N., Penney, S. J., & Boldt, L. J. (2007). Parental personality as an inner resource that moderates the impact of ecological adversity on parenting. *Journal of Personality and Social Psychology, 92*, 136–150.

Koehly, L. M., & Shivy, V. A. (2000). Social environments and social contexts: Social network applications in person–environment psychology. In W. E. Martin, Jr., & J. L. Swartz-Kulstad (Eds.), *Person–environment psychology and mental health: Assessment and intervention* (pp. 59–87). Mahwah, NJ: Erlbaum.

Kumashiro, M., Rusbult, C. E., & Finkel, E. J. (2008). Navigating personal and relational concerns: The quest for equilibrium. *Journal of Personal and Social Psychology, 95*, 94–110.

Lehman, D. R., Chiu, C., & Schaller, M. (2004). Psychology and culture. *Annual Review of Psychology, 55*, 689–714.

Liang, B., Tracey, A., Taylor, C. A., Williams, L. M., Jordan, J. V., & Miller, J. B. (2002). The Relational Health Indices: A study of women's relationships. *Psychology of Women Quarterly, 26*, 25–35.

Lott, B. (2001). Low-income parents and the public schools. *Journal of Social Issues, 57*, 247–259.

Lott, B. (2002). Cognitive and behavioral distancing from the poor. *American Psychologist, 57*, 100–110.

Markus, H. R., & Kitayama, S. (1998). The cultural psychology of personality. *Journal of Cross-Cultural Psychology, 29*, 63–87.

McAdams, D. P., & Pals, J. L. (2006). A new Big Five: Fundamental principles for an integrative science of personality. *American Psychologist, 61*, 204–217.

McLoyd, V. C. (1998). Socioeconomic disadvantage and child development. *American Psychologist, 53*, 185–204.

Moen, P., Elder, G. H., Jr., & Luscher, K. (Eds.). (1995). *Examining lives in context: Perspectives on the ecology of human development.* Washington, DC: American Psychological Association.

Munger, R. L. (2000). Comprehensive needs-based assessment with adolescents. In W. E. Martin & J. L. Swartz-Kulstad (Eds.), *Person–environment psychology and mental health: Assessment and intervention* (pp. 11–37). Mahwah, NJ: Erlbaum.

Nicotera, N. (2007). Measuring neighborhood: A conundrum for human services researchers and practitioners. *American Journal of Community Psychology, 40*, 26–51.

Pakman, M. G. (2007). Risk reduction and the micropolitics of social justice. In E. Aldarondo (Ed.), *Advancing social justice through clinical practice* (pp. 151–173). Mahwah, NJ: Erlbaum.

Palinkas, L. A. (2003). The psychology of isolated and confined environments: Understanding human behavior in Antarctica. *American Psychologist, 58,* 353–363.

Rojano, R. (2007). The practice of community family therapy. In E. Aldarondo (Ed.), *Advancing social justice through clinical practice* (pp. 245–263). Mahwah, NJ: Erlbaum.

Ross, C. E., & Jang, S. J. (2000). Neighborhood disorder, fear and mistrust: The buffering role of social ties with neighbors. *American Journal of Community Psychology, 28,* 401–420.

Saegert, S., & Evans, G. W. (2003). Poverty, housing niches, and health in the United States. *Journal of Social Issues, 59,* 569–589.

Schultheiss, D. E. P. (2003). A relational approach to career counseling: Theoretical integration and practical application. *Journal of Counseling & Development, 81,* 301–310.

Shinn, M., & Toohey, S. M. (2003). Community contexts of human welfare. *Annual Review of Psychology, 54,* 427–459.

Solantaus, T., Leinonen, J., & Punamaki, R. (2004). Children's mental health in times of economic recession: Replication and extension of the family economic stress model in Finland. *Developmental Psychology, 40,* 412–429.

Stokols, D., Clitheroe, H. C., Jr., & Zmuidzinas, M. (2000). Modeling and managing change in people–environment transactions. In W. B. Walsh, K. H. Craik, & R. H. Price (Eds.), *Person–environment psychology: New directions and perspectives* (2nd ed., pp. 267–296). Mahwah, NJ: Erlbaum.

Stokols, D., Misra, S., Runnerstrom, M. G., & Hipp, J. A. (2009). Psychology in an age of ecological crisis: From personal angst to collective action. *American Psychologist, 64,* 181–193.

Sue, D. W., Capodilupo, C. M., Torino, G. C., Bucceri, J. M., Holder, A. M. B., Nadal, K. L., & Esquilin, M. (2007). Racial microaggressions in everyday life: Implications for clinical practice. *American Psychologist, 62,* 271–286.

Super, C. M., & Harkness, S. (1999). The environment as culture in developmental research. In S. L. Friedman & T. D. Wachs (Eds.), *Measuring environment across the life span: Emerging methods and concepts* (pp. 249–277). Washington, DC: American Psychological Association.

Swindle, R. W., & Moos, R. H. (1992). Life domains in stressors, coping, and adjustment. In W. B. Walsh, K. H. Craik, & R. H. Price (Eds.), *Person–environment psychology: Models and perspectives* (pp. 1–33). Hillsdale, NJ: Erlbaum.

Tolan, P. H., Gorman-Smith, D., & Henry, D. B. (2003). The developmental ecology of urban males' youth violence. *Developmental Psychology, 39,* 274–291.

Triandis, H. C., & Suh, E. M. (2002). Cultural influences on personality. *Annual Review of Psychology, 53,* 133–160.

Tseng, V., & Seidman, E. (2007). A systems framework for understanding social settings. *American Journal of Community Psychology, 39,* 217–228.

Uchino, B. N. (2009). Understanding the links between social support and physical health. *Perspectives on Psychological Science, 4,* 236–255.

Wandersman, A., & Nation, M. (1998). Urban neighborhoods and mental health: Psychological contributions to understanding toxicity, resilience, and interventions. *American Psychologist, 53,* 647–656.

Wapner, S., & Demick, J. (2000). Person-in-environment psychology: A holistic developmental, systems-oriented perspective. In W. B. Walsh, K. H. Craik, & R. H. Price (Eds.), *Person–environment psychology: New directions and perspectives* (2nd ed., pp. 25–60). Mahwah, NJ: Erlbaum.

Willi, J. (1999). *Ecological psychotherapy: Developing by shaping the personal niche.* Seattle, WA: Hogrefe & Huber.

Wright, S. L., & Perrone, K. M. (2008). The impact of attachment on career-related variables: A review of the literature and proposed theoretical framework to guide future research. *Journal of Career Development, 35,* 87–106.

Behavior Is Interactional

Ellen P. Cook

Behavior is the consequence of unique individuals leading complicated lives in diverse settings shaped by a plethora of animate and inanimate influences. Both contexts and people living within them are changed by their interaction. Human life is a process of elaborating complex person–environment interactional patterns across situations and over time.

In Chapter 3 I discussed how human behavior is influenced by a multitude of contexts, both human and physical, differentiated by complexity and proximity to the individual. This idea is a fundamental assumption underlying the ecological perspective. Without contexts we cannot orient behavior in any meaningful way. A context is more than a backdrop in a play about human life; it is part of the story itself. Consider the following examples:

- Five unrelated children grow up in an impoverished inner-city neighborhood. Each child (and his or her siblings) is raised by a different single mother through the help of public assistance and charity programs. All five children attend the same public schools; one graduates, one later earns a general equivalency diploma. Two of the children eventually become single heads of households like their mothers. The third child dies of a drug overdose at 15, and the fourth supports his family by working two jobs in the fast food industry and volunteers in a teen fathers program. The fifth child becomes an emergency room physician.
- The 2001 terrorist attack on the World Trade Center killed thousands of Americans and had a profound impact on millions more. People all over the country called loved ones as soon as they heard the news. Many flocked to their houses of worship

67

for spontaneous prayer services. Some feared that the end of the world had come and stocked up on supplies; others went to New York City to assist in relief efforts however they could.

These two examples—one played out daily in various forms throughout the world, another an extraordinary crisis in U.S. history—indicate a basic insight about behavior: Different people respond to the same environment in very different ways. One child seems stuck in a dead-end situation; another is inspired to transcend it. In the face of tragedy and threat, people can respond with denial, anxiety, or sacrificial heroism—or all three at once. In the ecological perspective these puzzling variations occur because $B = f(P \times E)$, or behavior is a function of a person interacting in the environment. The existence of variability in responses across individuals can be expected; the outcome of a person–environment interaction depends on how participating individuals respond to the situation. In particular, the behavior of other human beings involved in the same situation has a determining impact on others.

Whenever people engage with each other, each person becomes part of the immediate environment influencing the other. The ecological perspective encourages counselors to think about what dynamic person–environment interactions constitute a client's evolving life on a moment-to-moment basis. By being aware of these ongoing interactions, a counselor can be more appreciative of the uniqueness of a client's concerns. Through becoming part of the client's life on a temporary basis, a counselor assists the client in developing a more satisfying life over time.

This interactional perspective applies to families, groups, and larger organizations too. A corporation's financial success depends on its interactions with its own constituent divisions and government agencies and the vagaries of the global economy. A neighborhood's history and future are closely linked with changes in the larger metropolis it inhabits. And the corporation and the neighborhood can also affect the functioning of the larger groups in which they are nested.

Understanding this interactional focus should allay a concern you might have about the ecological perspective: If behavior is influenced by life contexts, does this imply that humans are determined by outside forces? Are we helpless puppets whose actions are manipulated outside our control? Yes and no. More than we like to admit, our lives are outside of our control. On any given day, we could die or win the lottery. This does not mean that we are completely helpless in the face of implacable fate: Our life also takes shape over time because of how we manage to condition, evoke, or influence what happens to us and how we respond to life events once they occur. As an old German saying I learned years ago states, "We have to take life as it happens, but we should try to make it happen the way we want to take it." Through understanding the nature of person–environment interactions, we can learn ways to make life happen closer to how we want to take it.

In Chapter 5 I address the final important element in the ecological perspective: the importance of how we perceive and understand our lives.

For now, I explore facets of the person–environment interaction useful in helping counselors understand the unfolding of a client's life across situations and over time. I focus on the nature of person–environment interaction rather than interactions between groups of varying sizes and complexity, because counselors typically work with individuals or with individuals interacting within small groups. A complete discussion of communities, organizations, institutions, and so on requires grounding in a literature base that is enlightening but outside the modest focus of this book.

The Nature of Person–Environment Interactions

From the earliest days of psychology as a discipline, thinkers recognized that interactions with the environment make humans who and what they are. Freud's controversial ideas about the primacy of sexual drives rarely sustain much attention these days, but many counselors take another psychodynamic idea for granted: A child's interactions with his or her caregivers in infancy create a template for psychological functioning throughout life. Theorists ever since Freud's day have routinely considered the processes by which important people and events in the person's life contribute to daily psychological functioning and lifelong satisfaction.

The theme of person–environment interaction shaped the emergence of counseling as a profession. From early in the 20th century experts have pondered how to help people whose lives were buffeted by the stresses of poverty, war, immigration, and broad-based economic transformations in the nature of work and urban life. Over the years the question has not been *whether* person–environment interactions cause human suffering; the question is *how* these problems can be addressed when the natural resources provided by home, neighborhood, and the natural world are insufficient to address people's needs.

Career counselors in particular recognized the usefulness of P × E interactional models early in the counseling profession (see the overview in Swanson & Chu, 2000). Career counseling instructors have taught for decades that people yearn to find a place in the workplace where they can exercise their talents, interests, and values. The most satisfying, long-lasting career choices are likely to be ones in which people can do congenial tasks in the company of people like them (cf. Holland, 1997) so that their work is satisfying both to them and to their employers (cf. Dawis & Lofquist, 1984). Correspondingly, career counselors commonly try to identify the most accurate profile of abilities and traits useful in prescribing the best fit between person and occupation.

As we will see in this chapter, models of goodness of fit between person and environment certainly have a place in the ecological perspective. Yet the goal is not to describe simplistic categories of persons and context that fit together like hand and glove. Our work as counselors would indeed be much easier if we could assume that when type A person enters type B situation, type C behavior will be the result. Real life person–environment interactions are rarely that predictable at home or on the job. If that were so, hiring a matchmaker in early adulthood would be as routine as getting childhood vaccinations: Do them both, and avoid diphtheria and divorce! Counselors know that there are no inoculations against relationship strife regardless of how well matched the couple seems to be.

Instead the focus of interactional models is better described as looking for *patterns of possibilities:* Which combinations of persons and life contexts are *more likely* to result in certain outcomes? What do people bring to life situations, what do others expect and demand of us, which rewards are possible, which skills do we need to thrive? Simply speaking, there are no guaranteed ways to make a person thrive in certain circumstances. It is likely that many factors contribute to and modify life problems. A behavior is influenced by how a person perceives and understands it, and even when two people share the same problem (e.g., substance abuse), there are likely to be as many contributing differences as similarities in their lives. What the ecological perspective provides is not simple cause–effect rules but insight into patterns of interactions that can then be transformed into more satisfying and meaningful ways to connect with the world around us.

In the ecological perspective we recognize that in every single moment of our lives we interact with the world. This is true even when we sleep: We breathe in the air around us and can incorporate sounds into our dreams. Who we are, what we have experienced, and what we hope will happen all influence how we respond to routine life contexts. We can think about what a person does in terms of an observable behavior, processes internal to the person involved (e.g., feelings), or the social meaning attached to the behavior (e.g., its ultimate consequences), but all of these aspects are simultaneously involved in any human action (Young, Valach, & Collin, 1996).

In earlier chapters I considered some of the unique individual characteristics that people bring into even the most mundane daily interaction and features of the context—especially other people—that influence people's lives. In this chapter I consider what happens when humans and their environments connect. What are qualities of good person–environment interaction? What do people try to make happen in their interactions? I begin by presenting some theorists' descriptions of person–environment interactions.

General Descriptions of Person–Environment Interactions

The challenge of describing person–environment interactions has interested counselors for decades, and such descriptions have moved from descriptions of occupational choices to discussions of matching and assessment strategies and eventually toward the recognition of the systemic, ever-changing nature of the interactional process (see the review in Dawis, 2000). Walsh, Craik, and Price (2000) suggested four basic propositions about the interaction between a person and the environment. First, individuals act within an environment to meet a need or pursue a goal. The environment is the place in which this goal-directed action occurs. Second, the individual responds to demands emanating from the environment. How we perceive this environment will affect how we then respond within it. Third, the nature of the match between the person and the environment is crucial. The degree of compatibility of characteristics of the person and the environment has certain implications for the behavior that results. Fourth, how people interpret the present situation and past events will influence how they choose to behave.

Consider, for example, the routine chore of going to the grocery store. I usually go to the same store because I am familiar with the store's layout and it generally has the items I need (I act to meet a need within a certain environment). I like how the store displays its merchandise, and occasionally I am enticed to try new products not on my list (perceptions of the environment affect my shopping). One reason I am a faithful customer is that this store meets a variety of my needs, for example, a coffeehouse, a bank, and a pharmacy are in the same store (compatibility means that I return regularly). Finally, if I feel good about my purchases and find the store employees to be pleasant and helpful, I will decide, as usual, that the store is a good place to shop (interpretations affect present and future choices). This everyday process is repeated throughout my life and your life, often with much more complicated interactions of needs, perceptions, and outcomes.

Although Walsh and his colleagues (2000) did not use the word, their perspective is certainly ecological in tone. People's behavior occurs in life contexts. Behavior is not simply random but is meaningful to the person—the person attempts to accomplish something by what he or she does. Meaning making involves how people perceive the environment and why they make life choices in the present. Finally, whether a match is a good match or a bad one ($P \times E$ fit) affects the nature of the behavior resulting from it.

Neufeld and his associates (2006) described the processes by which an individual engages in the environments composing his or her life in terms of three constructs: *negotiation,* referring to how P and E accommodate each other through an ongoing adjustment process; *participation,* or positive interactions between P and E in physical, emotional, and psychological domains; and *evaluation,* or an ongoing two-way process conducted by both P and E. The end product is goal attainment at both the personal and contextual levels.

Car sales and dating rituals both exemplify this process of engagement. A possibility for a consummation of sorts appears on the radar. The pursuer draws closer and begins to woo the target, looking for clues about how to please and negotiating the sales pitch accordingly. The target either makes a hasty exit or begins to participate by coming in to hear the sales pitch, asking questions, coming closer, and moving away. Eventually comes a test drive around the block or on Friday night. If the test drive is evaluated as successful and the target decides to go for it, both go home feeling that they've made a great deal. If not, the salesperson tries again on Saturday morning, and the jilted would-be lover croons to another prospect, "Another Saturday night and I ain't got nobody" (with apologies to singer Sam Cooke).

This process of $P \times E$ interaction occurs throughout our lifetime. Who we are and what we become is influenced by a succession of interactions with the physical and interpersonal contexts in which we live. We in turn influence the contexts within which we live, sometimes by our simple

71

presence and more significantly by how we understand them and how we choose to behave within them. Each moment then is not exactly the same as those we have experienced before; each person and situation we encounter is somehow changed by us. We are connected to the past and the future by how we live in the present each and every day.

Contexts shape the type of people we become over time. Any time we choose to enter a new environment based on our preferences—what we hope to gain, what is comfortable for us—we look for ways to function effectively in it. If we stay and learn what we need to know in order to thrive in this setting, we generally develop skills consistent with our original preferences and with others in the context. Choosing contexts consistent with our personal characteristics thus helps us become more the persons we potentially could be and helps us integrate the diverse parts of ourselves into more consistent sets of traits, skills, and interests (cf. Armstrong, Day, McVay, & Rounds, 2008). Counselors interested in helping clients construct a plan for their future should look closely at how clients have interacted with various environments constituting life thus far: "the environments from the past and the present, the interaction of the person with these environments, and the way the environments were observed and interpreted by the individual" (Savickas et al., 2009, p. 244).

In the ecological perspective then, life is not a matter of internal psychology facing external influences. Life is a fluid interplay in which we become beings-in-relationship with our world, both inside and outside our skins. We meet even our simplest physiological needs (e.g., thirst) using behavioral alternatives (well water? beer? juice?) developed over years of lessons learned through interacting within our life contexts (cf. Mayer, 2005). The challenge for counselors is to help clients determine what is a good fit between their characteristics and what the environment offers or requires from them in a world that is changing under their feet.

Defining a Good Fit in P × E Interactions

The concept of fit is commonplace in everyday life. Teens agonize over whether they will ever truly belong in a group of friends. We search for jobs that will be a comfortable match for our personal characteristics. Internet dating services, horoscopes in magazines, and the ancient art of personal matchmaking each in their own way proposes the best match for our romantic needs and desires, thereby helping us avoid the unpleasant fireworks that accompany a less than optimal match. (Despite dire predictions to the contrary, my husband and I have been able to negotiate conflicts between our Capricorn and Libra natures for more than 30 years now.)

Using more elegant language, Schneider, Smith, and Goldstein (2000) described person–environment fit as referring to "some index of the degree of similarity, overlap, or convergence between a particular set of person-related attributes and a set of environment-related attributes" (pp. 63–64). P × E proponents agree that the nature of the fit between the person and environment can range from optimal to poor. Wapner and Demick (2000) saw adaptation as "a congruent person-in-environment system state consisting of optimal relationships between the person and his or her environment" (p. 45). A poor fit is the consequence of trying to fit a square peg (person) into a round hole (environment). You may be able to force the peg into the hole, but it is not likely to be a comfortable process for either the person or the environment! Models about P × E fit are popular in personality theory and research and help to explain some common consequences of the diversity we are apt to see in a group of people (see the review in Roberts & Robins, 2004).

P × E fit has been an especially popular idea in career development. Blustein (2008) stated that the common assumption in these models is that "people are best suited for a circumscribed array of occupations that are consistent with their interests, abilities, personal attributes, and values" (p. 232). The version of P × E fit most familiar to counselors is Holland's (1997) theory of vocational choice, which classifies people and work environments using the same six-way typology. Congruence is operationalized as the degree of similarity, or fit, between an individual's personality type and that of the work environment and is hypothesized to contribute to job stability, success, and satisfaction.

Nauta's (2010) excellent review of Holland's theory and related research concisely describes how Holland first developed and eventually modified the theory and discusses the associated instruments and classification materials familiar to many counselors. Nauta concluded that the theory has been "unsurpassed" and "resoundingly successful" (p. 17) in its contribution to experts' understanding of careers and counseling practice in general. Research indicates that congruence between personality type and environment may indeed be an important factor in academic or occupational choice, persistence, performance, and satisfaction, but the modest size of the relationship indicates that other factors (e.g., schedule flexibility, values) are also important (Allen & Robbins, 2010; Donohue, 2006; Hoffman & Woehr, 2006; Nauta, 2010; Spokane & Cruza-Guet, 2005; Tinsley, 2000). In other words, if your work is a good match for your personality, you *might* be happy in that job, but you may also be happy (perhaps for other reasons) even if the personality–work environment match is not so strong. Other factors such as gender deserve close examination too (cf. Kieffer, Schinka, & Curtiss, 2004).

This matching process sounds objective and precise, and to some extent it is. However, one crucial factor that influences the outcome of P × E fit is the individual's perceptions about the nature and consequences of the matching. In their review of organizational settings, Piasentin and Chapman (2006) reminded researchers to look beyond issues of fit based on objective criteria (*objective* measures of fit) to explore how people feel they fit in a given setting (*subjective* measures). In other words, what appears to observers to be a good match may not be so good after all from the view of the person involved in the interaction. Persons and environments can be linked in a manner that is uniquely personal and deeply felt. Little (2000) used the evocative term "habitats of the heart" (p. 111) to describe the special places in which we feel most ourselves, communicate who we really are, and pursue activities that are the most meaningful to us.

People's perceptions about what might be a good match for them can severely limit the range of possible choices open to them. According to Gottfredson (2005), people eliminate possible career alternatives that conflict with their self-concepts. People designate a zone of acceptable alternatives using a compromise process that can eliminate some desirable options in favor of ones that may be less compatible but apparently more appropriate for them. It can be tragic when individuals eliminate potentially fulfilling options they consider not to be possible because of their gender, race or ethnicity, social class, or other delimiting statuses. Counselors can encourage people to explore the reasons behind their abandoning some possibilities and consider whether they might indeed gain the resources and support they need to move outside their familiar comfort zones in making life choices.

Counselors interested in further exploring the P × E fit process from an ecologically rich perspective might refer to social-cognitive theory (e.g., Lent & Brown, 2006). This model suggests that a range of P × E factors, including personal traits and skills, self-efficacy (personal beliefs about one's ability to perform specific behaviors), work conditions and outcomes, and environmental supports and obstacles, influence a person's ability to meet his or her goals. Lent (2004) has applied these ideas to the general concept of well-being, recognizing the complicated interactions between personal traits, perceptions, social and environmental resources, and personal life goals.

In summary, for decades counselors have used the idea of person–environment fit to discuss the everyday reality of people relating to the world around them. Interest in this ongoing relationship is the central defining feature of the ecological perspective. Even when we appear the most alone, we human beings are connected via a web of relationships sustained over time and across ecological levels. These connections sustain and challenge us, define who we are and are not, and at their most profound give our lives meaning that may outlive us. Counselors who use the ecological perspective focus on which aspects of their clients' person–environment interactions can be changed in substance or in meaning to enrich their present and future lives.

Ecological Definitions of P × E Interactions

Within the ecological perspective are two concepts that describe how well persons interact within a given environment: *concordance* and *synergy*. Bob Conyne and I favored the term *concordance* in an earlier book (Conyne & Cook, 2004); as my thinking has continued to develop, I have increasingly preferred the term *synergy*.

According to Conyne and Cook (2004), *concordance* is a dynamic term referring to

> a constantly recalibrated balancing of elements central to the person–environment interaction. The environmental context provides the nutrients essential to human survival—notable examples include food and shelter or safety and love—while catalyzing change and growth crucial to long-term development. (p. 24)

74

Concordance is consistent with Holland's (1997) idea of congruence, a fit between a personality type and a work environment. The converse of concordance is *discordance*, in which a person does not receive the necessary conditions for growth.

Note the references in the definition to recalibration and change. Humans need both support and challenge for ongoing development. Without challenge, growth becomes stagnant; too much challenge without accompanying support exhausts a person's resources. When both support and challenge are present, an optimal misfit can exist in that the conditions for both security and growth are present. Optimal misfit is not a matter of finding a perfect fit, as one might want for a close-fitting dress glove, but more like finding a mitten for a child that provides warmth and protection while allowing room for growth and play (Conyne & Cook, 2004). Concordance does not always feel easy, but it feels right: A person feels a general sense of having a good place within his or her life context, one that both validates and stimulates him or her.

Another description for good P × E fit is *synergy*. Conyne and Cook (2004) noted that synergy "refers to combined or connected action between elements" and "exists when the elements of an ecosystem work smoothly to sustain and enhance the connected life they share" (p. 24). When synergy is present, people feel that they are a part of the larger environment in which they live and that they contribute to its smooth functioning. In the case of synergy, the essential quality is not match but enhancement between each participating element. For example, when synergy is present between a person and the workplace, the person feels that his presence and actions enhance the well-being of his workplace as a consequence of the interaction, and vice versa.

The ideals represented by the ideas of concordance versus synergy are valuable in different respects. *Concordance* captures the familiar connotation of hand-in-glove fit and can be easier to define (as when Holland's, 1997, career theory and instruments are used). *Synergy* refers to the dynamic nature of P × E interaction. Both terms permit one to discuss P × E interaction as continuously changing and responsive to individual perceptions; *synergy* evokes these meanings more readily, the reason for my preference for this term.

Whichever term you use, it is important to remember that P × E fit in real life is often a slippery thing, changing form quickly. For example, a teen moving from an urban to a rural high school may feel discordance between her urban style and what she interprets as a distinctively inferior small-town sensibility. Her father, accustomed to the fast pace of a large financial company, may find a higher degree of synergy with a small-town bank in that his habit of chatting with every customer is now seen as a contribution to the family of employees and he feels more appreciated in return. The teen feels more and more out of place until the school play, when her exposure to Broadway plays brings some new ideas for staging. Suddenly her differences are seen as creative rather than freaky and she gains satisfaction from her new status. Her father finds fulfillment in customer relations but is bored by the smaller range of work challenges he experiences daily. Because his daughter is happy, the father's job is good enough, at least for now . . . Everyday life makes it difficult for experts to come up with simple models that explain everything!

To summarize briefly, the concept of fit is useful in thinking about the nature of the interaction between person and environment (or context). It is consistent with how people discuss their lives every day, and in the professional literature counselors have at their disposal a variety of ways to assess person and context. The power of P × E fit as a predictive tool is modest for numerous reasons: the range of variables and processes often needed to portray an apparently simple P × E interaction in all its everyday glory, the hidden nature of some variables to observers (and to the persons themselves), and the propensity of people to invest the most ordinary of events with deeply personal meaning.

Person–environment fit may provide a starting point for discussing the manner in which clients interact with the various contexts that make up their lives. We all want to find a place in this complicated world where we feel we belong and contribute to those around us. Counseling tools help professionals to translate the often bewildering mass of data regarding our clients and their life possibilities into specific options that we can explore with them. Whether these proposed matches will actually work for clients depends on both how they perceive these options and what the particular environment will ask of them. The uncertainties of these outcomes reminds counselors that we must make sure our clients have the skills they need to adapt to life as it unfolds for them over time.

When Fit Is Not Enough: The Example of Work

Notions about the desirability of person–career environment fit rely on assumptions about the nature of work that no longer seem tenable today. One significant change is the nature of work itself: Jobs are changing rapidly enough that the work environment is no longer predictable. The nature of work has changed dramatically from stable, well-defined tasks to jobs that require responsiveness to massive influxes of information, rapid technological changes, and globalization. Workers must develop flexible patterns of problem solving and a dynamic view of the self interacting meaningfully within a changing world. Successful workers today and tomorrow contrast dramatically with those of previous generations who could assume that they would serve as a piece of an organizational puzzle that would remain after being put in place (see Savickas et al., 2009).

Recent research also indicates that actual work performance is much more complicated to predict than a simple matching model permits (cf. Hoffman & Woehr, 2006; Kieffer et al., 2004). A variety of personal characteristics (e.g., self-esteem) may influence how individuals evaluate the quality of their fit with the work environment (e.g., Piasentin & Chapman, 2006).

The fit of an individual within a complex organization may vary depending on when and where you look. As a newcomer gradually transitions to being comfortable on the job, the fit may seem to improve as she gains confidence and familiarity with coworkers; conversely, an initially challenging set of work tasks may become repetitive and unrewarding. As a worker's personal life changes, what he needs from a job also can change (e.g., a flexible schedule with limited travel after baby makes three). The nature of the fit may also differ depending on where you look: for example, the nature of work tasks may be congenial but the relationship with the supervisor a bit strained and the person's fit with the organization's mission only so-so (see Piasentin & Chapman, 2006). People whose gender or race/ethnicity is not typical for a work setting may find that although the work tasks fit them well, the organizational climate is not comfortable or facilitative for them. From the perspective of the employer, similarity of viewpoints, values, and goals may assist growth in the early stages, but later such homogeneity may stifle shared problem solving and adaptation to new situations (Schneider et al., 2000).

In general then, research suggests that matching can partly explain people's satisfaction within certain situations, but its value as a stand-alone construct is probably more limited than some counselors might believe (Donohue, 2006; Hoffman & Woehr, 2006). In the ecological perspective we believe that people have an array of good life choices to consider. As counselors we can help our clients explore various "life trajectories" through which they can "progressively design and build their own lives" (Savickas et al., 2009, p. 241) and teach them the skills they will need as their lives unfold over time. These tasks are developmental in nature.

P × E Interactions and Development

The ecological perspective has been prominent in recent theory and research about human development. The work of one of its best known proponents, Urie Bronfenbrenner, was influential enough to inspire a book devoted to honoring its impact (Moen, Elder, & Luscher, 1995). Bronfenbrenner enabled developmentalists to see past timeworn concepts of ages and stages to appreciate human development as the unpredictable but not random work in progress of an individual formed by, yet also influencing, contexts patterned by geography, social structure, time, choice, meaning making, and bonds of mutual support and affection. In this section I sample some developmental topics likely to interest counselors. The topics are likely to be familiar; what might be novel is where the emphasis is placed. A brief overview of the ecological perspective in development is followed by a closer look at the element of time, a variable that attracted Bronfenbrenner's attention late in his career.

The Ecology of Human Development: General Statements

Bronfenbrenner (1999) described the process of development as follows:

> Especially in its early phases, and to a great extent throughout the life course, human development takes place through processes of progressively more complex reciprocal interaction between an active, evolving biopsychological human organism and the persons, objects, and symbols in its immediate external environment . . . The form, power, content, and direction of the proximal processes affecting development vary systematically as a joint function of the characteristics of the *developing*

person, the *environment*—both immediate and more remote—in which the processes are taking place, the nature of *developmental outcomes* under consideration, and the social continuities and changes occurring over time during the historical period through which the person has lived. (p. 5, italics in the original)

This statement represented a change from his earlier work, which focused on the developmental contributions of multiply faceted environmental systems. Today the individual is placed front and center to indicate what all the developing is about.

Magnusson (1995) described the impact of P × E interaction on human development as follows:

Current individual functioning is the result of a life history of a person–environment interaction, which environmental and inherited factors participate in a process for which it is not possible to disentangle their relative role at the individual level. The outcome of the process, at a certain stage of development, depends on the potential resources and limitations of the individual from the start and the properties of the environment with which the individual interacts during the life course. (pp. 32–33)

Lerner (2002) proposed that "a changing configuration of relationships constitutes the basis of human life" (p. 195). People actually produce their own development in how they engage in bidirectional, dynamic interactions with multiple life contexts throughout life. How individuals perceive and understand their environments is crucial to lifelong development (Bussey & Bandura, 1999). The line between internal processes and the environment becomes blurred as environmental standards become internal criteria for how we privately evaluate ourselves (cf. Bussey & Bandura, 1999; Twenge, 2001). In short, a normal feature of development is that the outside environment becomes a part of us.

People are likely to differ in the rate of change they undergo over time (cf. Bleidorn, Kandler, Riemann, Angleitner, & Spinath, 2009). Some characteristics may be more influenced by contextual variation than others; some people may continue to change in important respects throughout life, whereas others change little. Once developmental challenges early in life have succeeded in promoting certain adaptive resources, there is no one right way to develop throughout life; rather, there are many possible right ways depending on the characteristics of the person and the life contexts encountered that can promote satisfying, meaningful lives.

P × E Interaction and Development Occurs Over Time

The ecological perspective explicitly recognizes a truism of everyday life: People change over time. Indigenous experts at beauty salons and bars are full of wisdom about stages of life: the terrible twos, rebellious adolescence, the honeymoon period after marriage, the midlife crisis. These developmental stages persist in popular wisdom because they carry more than a grain of truth: People often do seem to behave similarly during these times. Development does follow a universal human blueprint in some respects; for example, infants usually begin to walk around 1 year of age, and sexuality emerges strongly during adolescence. In general, however, developmental changes are less predestined according to age and stage than we might think (e.g., Steenbarger, 1991). The process of development is more fluid than predetermined, more a matter of unique people confronting the changing challenges of their lives than following a path laid out for everyone to follow.

The course of development is a progression of increasingly complex interactions between the person and the physical, social, and cultural world around him or her. It depends on many things that affect the person, the context, and how they interact at any given point in historical time. The determinants of the process also vary depending on which types of developmental changes are being considered: Peer relationships may influence certain aspects of a child's social but not academic development, or vice versa.

As children mature, demands placed on them also change. Common developmental tasks are "sociocultural constructions" (Roisman, Masten, Coatsworth, & Tellegen, 2004, p. 130) consistent with what the developing person is expected to be able to do at a given time. Six-year-old children are expected to be able to separate from caregivers and attend to tasks for 7 or more hours a day. American high schools grant students some choices in coursework in preparation for the adult choices around the corner. In the United States 15-year-olds are considered too immature to marry and have children; people in their 60s are considered ready to retire. Variations in the timing of these developmental transitions across cultures and over time (e.g., the retirement age varies during recessions) indicate just how relative they can be.

From birth throughout life an individual actively participates in how development ensues over time. Consider two infants, both born healthy and full term. One infant is irritable, highly sensitive to environmental changes, and fearful of new situations. The other infant is placid, seems to ignore many environmental stressors, and adapts quickly to new situations and caregivers. Which child is more likely to earn the label of being a good baby? Now imagine that one child is born to parents with marital distress and time-consuming careers, and the other is born to parents who are happily married and value family time above all commitments. How might the interaction between the baby's temperament and the parents' behavior influence each child's development? Finally, imagine that when the parents are not at home, one child has access to high-quality child care whereas the other infant is cared for by an unimaginative and overburdened nursery attendant. Which combinations of factors will potentiate the children's natural characters? Which factors will compensate for, or additionally challenge, the stresses posed by these possibilities?

A similar interaction between person and life context is apparent during adolescence. We assume that adolescence is an emotional rollercoaster of trials for beleaguered parents. Yet research suggests that the emotional tenor of these years varies dramatically by the adolescent, interactional dynamics (e.g., cultural background, parenting styles, sibling and peer relationships), and how adolescents make meaning of their social contexts (Smetana, Campione-Barr, & Metzger, 2006). Wise adults can help teens develop social-emotional skills and ways of understanding adolescent social dynamics at a level of complexity that challenges but does not mystify the young person. This process requires ongoing nonjudgmental, empathic listening that needs to be in place before crises occur.

The process of lifelong development is the outcome of a set of circumstances, some chosen by us and others out of our control, interacting with our individuality. Some aspects are influenced by genetic makeup and others are shaped over time by life events and cultural influences often too numerous to count and too complex to unravel. Regardless of the origins of our life situations, the best we can do is often circumscribed by where and who we are at the time.

Development sometimes occurs as a consequence of situations we would avoid if given a choice in the matter. Many life events can be time consuming, exasperating, and difficult to manage—a plumbing malfunction that causes a flood of dirty water in one's basement, for example. Such trials are not usually associated with personal development, unless the process of coping prompts enduring changes in one's life—the flood being the last straw in a struggling marriage, for example. Resilience as we commonly understand it develops through a process of struggling with adversity, much like muscles develop from exercise.

Conceptions of Time as a Variable in P × E Interactions

Time as we know it is a product of P × E interactions. Many centuries ago humans agreed to structure their experience of life according to the interrelationship between the majestic movements of the Earth and its moon and the center of our planet's universe, the sun. Before sophisticated measuring devices were conceived, scientists painstakingly mapped these movements and labeled the progression of humans' experiences according to these patterns. The labels applied to these demarcations (e.g., Janvier vs. January, numbers denoting years vs. animals) and decisions about when each year began and ended (e.g., January 1 vs. early spring) varied across groups of people. Time as we measure it was based on observations of the physical world, but how it structures everyday life is a product of human meaning making at its most elegant and influential.

Time is a silent partner in person–environment interactions. Life is a succession of immediate moments, each moment subject to conditions and possibilities altered by the passage of time. What happens to you today is constrained in some ways by what has happened to you in the past. Previous life experiences may permit the development of certain skills (e.g., former education makes it easy to learn new job skills); for some skills, real competence is possible only if the skills are developed at a certain time in life (e.g., try learning gymnastics during midlife rather than early childhood). Other choices are more common during a certain phase of life than others (e.g., marrying in early adulthood) so that individuals following a different timetable (e.g., those marrying for the first time in midlife) may feel out of step. For the rest of this section I consider some of the ways that time influences human life and how it changes.

Biological Age

Physically healthy human beings are capable of successfully managing a multitude of challenges throughout life. Certain skills or life tasks require a specific level of maturity before they can be mastered (e.g., walking in infancy, fertility in adolescence and beyond), and achieving them is much harder after a peak period has passed. Although the march of time can be slowed, things do change with age. Very young children can learn languages with less effort than their parents require. It is hard to accept limitations posed by an aging body, as shown by the prevalence of sports-related injuries later in life. Relatively few human behaviors are subject to strict biological determinism, however. Although few middle-aged people can handle the rigors of basic training in the armed services, it is possible to remain vital decades past midlife. People can manage health risks and maintain a youthful appearance through wellness practices not known even a few generations earlier.

One of the wonders of the aging process is how young people can feel themselves to be, despite their chronological age. (I have been 35 years old for a long time now.) Even if we ban the use of mirrors after a certain point, other people will remind us how old we really are, and others' reactions embody powerful social attitudes about the connection between youth and beauty. Negative expectations about older adults' capabilities are at the root of pervasive ageism expressed in doubts about performance despite evidence about a person's current abilities.

Coming to terms with the joys and losses of growing older is part and parcel of development later in life. For those who relied on youthful attractiveness as a significant personal resource, aging can provoke real despair about the perceived loss of one's personal value. Aging people ideally gauge their self-worth using values that are often fully realized only with advancing age: service to others, generativity, and a pattern of accomplishments and relationships sustained over time.

Social Age

U.S. culture maintains expectations and norms about when life events or transitions should occur in life, called *social age* (Elder, 1995). For example, around the age of 18 young people in the United States typically complete compulsory education and make their first personal decisions pertaining to their adult life roles, and within the next decade they usually marry and start their families. Because of people's planfulness about their lives, there is some degree of loose coupling (Elder & Rand, cited in Elder, 1995) between life stage and when people actually complete life tasks. The timing of when and how important events actually take place can make a difference in the stress associated with these events. Events that occur on time in terms of social age carry a sense of predictability and rightness about

81

them, whereas individuals whose life events occur on a different timetable may feel that they are not fitting in as expected.

This sense of social timing is evident in starting a family, especially by giving birth. Fertility decreases dramatically in a woman's mid-30s and beyond. The phrase *ticking of the biological clock* refers to women's awareness that the peak time for bearing children may soon be past them. Women's ability to choose the timing of pregnancy is a social consequence of contraception, a significant contributor to changing gender roles in past few decades. This control over conception has been especially welcomed by women and couples who choose to schedule child bearing after the intensive career building characteristic of early adulthood. Yet unfortunately this control proves illusory for many women, who find their fertility dramatically compromised at the very time they are psychologically ready to start a family.

This delayed onset of family building, through giving birth or otherwise, has ripple effects throughout the life span because of how people's lives are interdependent (Elder, 1995). Adults may find themselves caring for aged relatives and young children simultaneously and having fewer years after the children leave home to prepare financially and psychologically for retirement. I myself was tenured and established in my career before I became a parent, so I believe it was much easier for me to juggle home and career tasks than it was for those who were simultaneously nurturing professorial careers and toddlers. However, having teenagers at an age when other people become grandparents has posed unexpected challenges for my husband and me!

My husband's and my contemporaries do share one time-related, life-defining characteristic: We are part of the generation known as the Baby Boomers, born in the years following World War II. I now consider the phenomenon of generational effects.

Generational Effects

When a person was born, in terms of historical time, may have a marked impact on his or her perceptions, values, and life choices. People born within the same span of years form a *cohort*. The idea of generational effects refers to the possibility that cohorts experience certain historical conditions in common and that these conditions result in some shared characteristics (e.g., values or life goals) as a consequence.

A familiar (and arbitrary) way to delineate cohorts is by decade—for example, children born during the 1960s presumably constitute one cohort, and those born during the 1970s fall within another. This delineation is generally not very meaningful, developmentally speaking. The critical determinant of a generation is whether young people during a given time period experienced "cataclysmic historical events, periods of tumultuous religious revitalization, or abrupt secular change" (Rogler, 2002, p. 1015). Children brought up during the Great Depression and World War II were influenced by the fears and sacrifices of their time and developed a shared ethos of social interdependence. In contrast, Baby Boomers, who came of age during the 1950s and 1960s, experienced a very different economy, sense of optimism, and global politics.

Historical eras can pose distinctive opportunities and challenges to citizens; each member of that generation will perceive and react to the current ethos to constitute his or her unique life course. It appears likely that young Americans of this past decade will be united in some as yet undefined manner because of 9/11, the terrorist attacks that changed America's illusions about its invulnerability and status as a world power. Such historical events can interrupt the normal processes of skills development and decisions involved in life transitions for people across multiple generations yet can also enhance psychological growth in unexpected ways (Bronfenbrenner, 1995).

Families typically span several generations, and the same social change can have very different effects on members of the same family (Elder, 1995). In a recent discussion group populated with midlifers, we acknowledged how we Baby Boomers have very different attitudes toward the American flag as a patriotic symbol than did the previous generation with its legacy of World War II. Burning a flag in protest was a shocking act during the 1960s. What made it shocking then was the flag's extraordinary power as a symbol of home and national pride to a country that had been at war a few short decades earlier. Today we hear not about flag burning but about the burning of sacred texts (e.g., the Koran by a Christian pastor). Present symbolic acts and subsequent dissension may center on ethnic/religious tolerance rather than patriotism, a shift understandable in light of today's blending of formerly disparate global cultures.

The ecological perspective applied to human development reminds us just how fluid and creative each human life is: a process crafted over time by a person with unique capacities from multiple encounters with personal and impersonal contexts. Development is never a project of assembling a random series of events; it is planful, intentional yet serendipitous, and expressive of a person's ongoing mission to live with meaning.

P × E Interaction in Everyday Life

The previous section examined human life using a broad lens, looking at how P × E interaction plays a role in producing changes that occur and persist over time. In this section I focus on the immediacy of everyday life in which, in the words of an ancient religious text, we live and move and have our being. Here I sample some ways that P × E interaction is implicated each day, often without our awareness.

The Coping Process

References to the coping process crop up time and again in these chapters, and no wonder: Counselors' work often aims to help clients cope with life more happily and successfully. For example, people recently diagnosed with cancer may cope with the help of prayer (a personal resource), a sympathetic friend (an interpersonal resource), and generous health insurance (a material resource). A crucial determinant of coping is how the person evaluates the situation and the adequacy of the available resources (meaning making).

Previous developmental experiences have ideally granted a person the resources needed to cope with garden-variety life stressors: a romantic breakup, a poor evaluation at school or work, a domestic crisis (my young children once happily tested their colored markers on an expanse of brand new carpeting). There is no simple formula for successful coping, because the person's appraisal of the situation, the available resources, the ability to engage certain specific strategies now, the effect of the situation on significant others, and many other interactional issues can affect what works and why. Recently former presidential candidate John Edwards was in legal hot water as a result of allegedly using campaign funds to cover up a personal scandal. The nature of the scandal (the pregnancy of a girlfriend), the availability of the funds, and the latitude campaign staff had for using the funds made this action seem like a good way to cope with the situation at the time. Yet features of this situation—including an innovative interpretation of the law and the public's sympathy for Edwards's terminally ill wife—made the use of the funds appear to be an unsavory act on the part of someone whose moral compass could no longer find true north. (I am reporting some commentary in the media rather than passing judgment myself.) Successful coping depends on a combination of resources and challenges: how people perceive the situation, their ability to cope with similar situations and with life stresses in general, and their likelihood of succeeding; the resources that are needed, available, and attainable; and challenges obtaining cooperation and support, among other factors—in other words, factors rooted in P × E interaction.

Conyne (2010) proposed that as a general rule of thumb a person's strengths or resources in the form of protective factors should exceed deficits or challenges that occur as environmental risks and stressors. Examples of strengths include resilience, engagement with others, group-based social support, and advocacy skills. Deficits include stressors in the natural environment, stressors in social relations, and oppression that originates in the culture. Counselors interested in reducing the incidence of problems could focus on increasing strengths, decreasing deficits, or both.

Conyne's (2010) recommendation appeared in the context of preventive counseling designed to reduce the incidence of specific problems in identified groups of people. Yet the balance between resources and challenges applies to individuals coping with unique life concerns too. There is no magic coping recipe to follow (you need a cup of money, a tablespoon of self-efficacy . . .). Does a person have the knowledge, behavior skills, support, and personal qualities needed to cope with a situation at hand? (Chapter 2 offers suggestions for strengths to explore.) What features of the problem situation will make it particularly challenging to cope?

For example, we might speculate that during the recent economic recession, individuals who successfully coped with losing their jobs had some combination of minimal outstanding debt and some savings and/or a partner with some economic security (financial resources), job-hunting skills and networks of contacts (career resources), supportive friends and family to help them weather the stressful times (interpersonal resources), and a faith tradition that granted their struggles some meaning and dignity (meaning making).

Yet the full story behind any successful coping process is bound to be more complicated than this general picture. A job seeker can use networking possibilities only if she knows how to ask for career assistance from others. Prevailing conditions, such as a chronic illness that reduces one's fortitude, may make it more difficult than usual to cope. Rarely are life challenges simply additive (e.g., the presence of one illness plus one troubled teenage child plus one terminated job equals three separate problems); rather, they are often experienced as multiplicative in effect (e.g., it can be much harder to cope with a teenager in trouble when one is out of work and undergoing chemotherapy!). A life stressor can also be a crucial life resource (e.g., a loving marriage with a temperamental partner). Previous experience with a category of life stressor can make it easier—or more difficult—to deal with it (e.g., having a second child diagnosed with autism). And the degree to which a person believes that he or she has the necessary resources to cope with life's challenges in general or in this particular situation can make all the difference in how successfully he or she can manage the situation. Meaning making is, once again, at the heart of how people live out their lives.

Roles in Everyday Life

Roles provide ways for people to connect meaningfully to the broader sociocultural context surrounding them (cf. McAdams, 1995). Roles represent situations affiliated with a common set of expectations and behaviors. Roberts (2007) pointed out that life roles have about the same level of abstraction with respect to situations as traits do with respect to personality: "Social roles organize situations into thematically consistent categories that are similar in breadth to personality traits" (p. 1073). Traits help to explain why one person responds to different situations in the same way; roles do so as well but focus on shared expectations for different people in the same situation. People are commonly expected to enact certain roles because of characteristics such as sex, race, and age (cf. Savickas, 2002).

Some roles (e.g., how often you see friends) can be adjusted by the parties involved, although certain expectations for their structure and function hold across situations (e.g., in U.S. culture, friends rarely support us financially). Some roles are considered optional; others carry strong expectations because of a person's age, gender, and other variables. Young women dedicated to career development (work role) often lament the pressure exerted by older relatives for them to marry and have babies (partner and mother roles) because it is time for them to do so (age-related expectations). People abandoned alone on a desert island can decide on a moment-to-moment basis how they will spend their time, a freedom commonly envied by overburdened young adults. This "web of life roles that connects the individual to society" has the function of giving "meaning and focus to their lives" (Savickas, 2002, p. 157).

85

On a macrolevel, the nature of roles can evolve over time. Our previous experience with familiar roles guides our everyday behavior so that we may be surprised when things change. In the mid-20th century, women's magazines prescribed a cheerful domesticity for homemakers intended to make home a refuge for men struggling with the stresses of the working world. A clean apron, a casserole in the oven, slippers by the armchair, and the freshly washed faces of children were features of a stress-free homecoming worthy of the hard-working man. Magazines today may still feature casserole recipes, but this post–World War II cultural ideal for homemakers has changed dramatically.

It can be difficult to appreciate how our role engagement today is culturally influenced. We may mistakenly assume that we have invented the particulars of our lives, when in reality our sociocultural context has shaped our values, preferences, and behaviors. For example, in my university work I assume the role of teacher and others assume the role of students. Because we share a common understanding about these roles, my students and I implicitly agree that I will provide class activities and grading and they will do the assignments as I structure them. Details about how to carry out the student–teacher role vary according to the particular context or type of class, however, so that new doctoral students accustomed to lecture-style classes need to learn how to participate as learners in small seminars. Some students feel that faculty who do not lecture in every class session are not really teaching; their expectations about faculty role performance, and their own role as learners, inevitably color their evaluations.

As a faculty member in an American institution I am not officially expected to help students resolve life issues outside the classroom, although I do try to listen empathically to their concerns. These role expectations for teachers do not hold everywhere. A Taiwanese instructor recounted how as an academic advisor she was expected to help out if her students had a flat tire or to make hospital visits to ailing students—even making them nourishing porridge and feeding them by hand if family members were not available. And how would American students react to the expectation that they visit faculty in their homes on New Year's Eve as a sign of respect, as they traditionally do in China? Role expectations we fulfill without questioning them are less set in stone than we might think.

Roles also help us develop over time. Roberts (2007) pointed out that roles help us organize and adapt our behavior to situations over time because they are accompanied by expectations and consequences for behavior. If children do not behave in the classroom (the role of students), they may be sent to the principal's office. According to Roberts, social role relationships in which the associated expectations do not match one's personality can be a powerful socializing agent: Being sent to the principal's office enough (or experiencing another, more powerful consequence) may change children's behavior. This process happens throughout life: Marriage can teach us how to adapt to others, parenthood can teach patience, and so on. Adapting to role demands over time can change our personalities.

Career development theorist and researcher Donald Super (1980) is commonly credited with officially recognizing how the life roles adopted by a person affect one another (e.g., work and family roles) and vary over the life span in terms of their importance within the person's life. The combination of roles adopted by an individual and where these roles are enacted (e.g., very young children are often cared for at home) comprise the *life space* of an individual (Savickas, 2002). Savickas (2002) further defined the several roles considered central to a person's identity and life satisfaction at a given time as *core roles*. For example, because of their age young adults are typically expected to assume the social roles of worker, life partner, and parent. For an adult pursuing a demanding career, work is likely to be a core role; for another, waiting tables to earn money for education may be time consuming but not a core role. Core roles combined with other, peripheral roles (e.g., part-time student? citizen?) make a person's life space unique.

The nature of role expectations, their performance, and their importance within a life can take a variety of forms. The parent role can be very important to a person who has no children (consider an infertile couple undergoing treatment or a person who has mentored countless adolescents). People may choose remarkably different paths to actualize their commitments (compare a person who defines good citizenship as voting in each national election with a person who never misses local government meetings). Whatever the form or importance of our roles, our private lives are connected with others by which roles we choose and how we perform them.

To summarize, roles connect us with the human world around us, provide us with meaningful and crucial tasks to perform, and help us discern how we are expected to behave. Our core roles help to define us both in our own eyes and as others see us. As a pattern for P × E interaction, roles help us acquire the opportunities, skills, and values that form the basis of our future life choices. Because of how interconnected our roles are by nature, a problem that appears rooted in one role (e.g., work) may actually be "spun in another strand of the web" (Savickas, 2002, p. 157). Interconnections between home and career roles can cause people years of stress, as I explore next.

Home–Career Conflicts

Experts have devoted considerable attention to exploring the issue of conflict among roles, particularly between work and home/family responsibilities. Across a few short generations, the nature of the connection between home and work roles has changed dramatically, especially for women (Putney & Bengtson, 2005). More women (particularly mothers of young children) work full time, and greater numbers work in positions that require extensive training and commitment (e.g., business management, medicine). Some of this change in participation is by choice, some out of financial necessity. For whatever reason, change in women's paid work involvement has transformed countless households because of how life roles are intricately connected with one another.

Although men's and women's responsibilities for home and family are more balanced than in previous generations, women continue to assume more of these duties than men, whether by choice or out of necessity (Putney & Bengtson, 2005). Career commitments and decisions among women today are more similar to those of men than in previous years (e.g., Gutek, 2001), but standards for mothering have changed little: Mothers are supposed to be self-sacrificing and completely available to their children, and paid work is seen as detracting from the labor intensive commitment of mothering (Medina & Magnuson, 2009). Women can perceive role expectations as complicated and contradictory, in some cases leading to considerable conflict (Stroink, 2004). These day-to-day accommodations have been linked with lower salaries and more modest career accomplishment over time for women compared with men with similar training and initial job placements (e.g., Bowles, Babcock, & McGinn, 2005; Halpern, 2005), even when the women are very talented and gifted (Ferriman, Lubinski, & Benbow, 2009). Some of these gender-based discrepancies can be attributed to women choosing different careers, positions within a career, and day-to-day scheduling. Even when a woman's choices are indistinguishable from those of her male counterparts, her employers may still assume that she has made such compromises (Kirschmeyer, 2006)!

Although research suggests that maternal employment per se is not harmful to children, the inadequacy of institutional resources in the United States for caring for and educating children poses extra challenges (Halpern, 2005). For example, it is up to each parent to locate and maintain affordable child care (there is little on-the-job or nationally subsidized child care), and family leaves are less generous than in other affluent countries. In particular, poor female heads of households experience enormous stress from working at jobs with insufficient pay and erratic schedules, no scheduling flexibility or absences to care for sick children or attend school functions, and inadequate or unreliable child care. For them, work–family conflicts are an inescapable fact of life.

Several points warrant emphasis here. First, home–career conflicts are particularly acute when individuals are raising children, but such conflicts can occur for other reasons as well. Caring for family members with disabilities or illness, or caring for elderly family members, can also lead to considerable conflict for extended periods of time. Aging homes can also drive people to distraction with one repair after another. (My favorite example is a house whose back wall oozed honey because of the thousands of hard-working bees living there, hidden from view.)

Second, both sexes may well benefit from a redistribution of home and family responsibilities. Just as women, like men, often thrive in paid work positions, men can find more involvement in home/child duties to be fulfilling. Men, too, often experience a struggle defining themselves as fathers and men in general (Silverstein, Auerbach, & Levant, 2002). More men today, out of choice or necessity, devote more of their waking hours to caring for the home and their dependents. Depending on how they view such involvement (e.g., "I am making important contributions to those I love" vs. "I am a hapless schmuck doing women's work"), this change can be very rewarding.

Finally, the negotiation of duties among couples can be surprisingly painful. One or both of the partners may feel that a previous pattern of sharing had a certain rightness to it consistent with core role preferences or may resent the expectation of additional responsibilities when they feel that their current duties are already more than demanding. A counselor can help couples to find resolutions that feel fair even if they would not appeal to other couples (e.g., "I will cook dinner if you clean out the litter box").

P × E Interaction: Another Look at Diversity

I have already considered diversity from different angles in previous chapters. Race, ethnicity, gender, and other similar variables commonly serve as definers of social value. People possess different opportunities, rewards, and even geographic locations for their homes as a function of who and what they are in the broad sociocultural context. Individual people also bring to the contexts of their lives a way of being in the world evolved from a combination of their genetic makeup, family life, and innumerable learning experiences. Essentially, people learn who and what they are and how they are to behave in the world as a consequence. Human nature is not a matter of either nature or nurture; every life is a one-of-a-kind product created in interaction with personal and impersonal contexts.

Experts typically acknowledge the fact that diversity as we experience it is an interactional phenomenon. For example, West and Zimmerman (1987) described the process of "doing gender": The way we present ourselves as women or men in everyday life is multifaceted, changeable, and influential in shaping how people react to us in turn. We do gender without thinking, relying on subtle cues to speak for us without words. (What different messages do wing-tip leather shoes and well-worn athletic shoes convey?) Unfortunately, what we do to present ourselves as a gendered being may communicate something incongruent with other ways we wish to be perceived (e.g., revealing cleavage may peg a young woman as receptionist material rather than the law school graduate she really is). Another common example of doing gender is related to speech, such that our choice of words, topics, and inflections and even our frequency of interruptions all illustrate how communication patterns send messages, both deliberate and unintended, about our gender (see Crawford, 2001, for a fascinating analysis).

It is important to remember that the interactional dynamics that underlie diversity apply to parties that benefit from the dynamics as well as those whose position is less advantageous. White, middle- or upper class, well-educated Judeo-Christian men have advantages in accessing social resources, but there may be some disadvantages as well. For example, the rapidly expanding literature on men and masculinity documents "the negative consequences of conforming to, deviating from, or violating the gender role norms of masculinity ideology" (O'Neil, 2008, p. 363), norms that prescribe rules for success in the occupational and political worlds. Robinson-Wood (2009) noted how Euro-Americans unaware of their privileges may suffer various consequences (e.g., limited empathy; see also Spanierman, Todd, & Anderson, 2009). There is an unacknowledged burden in being expected to achieve without limit, being limited only by one's efforts (the American myth of success). No one is truly free from externally imposed limitations,

89

and the belief that one's achievements are never quite good enough is a heavy burden.

There is no justification to equate the costs of privilege with the suffering of people struggling to live in a world in which they are invisible or actively oppressed. The world's great religious traditions teach that human beings are one family and that oppression hurts us all because of our interconnectedness. Ultimate fulfillment for any member requires recognizing the spiritual costs of privilege and the imperative of caring for others with a full heart and open wallet.

One recent contribution to the diversity literature is the concept of intersectionality. *Intersectionality* refers to "analytic approaches that consider the meaning and consequences of multiple categories of social group membership" (Cole, 2009, p. 170). This concept encourages counselors to take seriously the heterogeneity within a group of people accruing from their multiple statuses. It makes a difference, for example, whether one is not only a middle-class single parent but also of Asian descent and bisexual. The consequences of these complex statuses also vary according to context: one's small-town, religiously conservative family of origin, for example, versus one's eclectic neighborhood in New York City. The implications of intersectionality are not additive (e.g., you face the combination of a little bit of prejudice from several sources) but frequently unpredictable. In short, recognizing intersectionality requires us to think deeply about the consequences of having a complex position within current social structures, consequences that are influenced by interactions with others and how people perceive themselves as unique social beings (Stewart & McDermott, 2004).

Finally, counselors should remember that interactional patterns associated with diversity may not transfer across settings; the parameters and consequences of our relationships with the world surrounding us can suddenly change. A tall, blond young woman may be essentially invisible in Scandinavia but exotic in Japan; her physical presence could become invisible for very different reasons in a Muslim culture that requires her to wear tent-like clothing. When our social standing as defined by our social categorization vis-à-vis others suddenly changes, the consequences can be unsettling indeed. Biracial individuals have recounted startling stories about how their social standing has altered dramatically when others put them in a different category than they have customarily been perceived as being in.

The ecological perspective facilitates the integration of diversity issues into counseling because of how it places intrapsychic issues typically favored by counselors firmly into context where they belong. How have others responded to this unique person because of her gender, or to that one because of his physical disability? What public schools has this child attended, and how has the quality of his education affected his career self-efficacy? Which microaggressions has this person experienced day after day on the basis of race, and how have these traumas affected her identity and relationships? My decision to phrase these issues as questions was deliberate, because as counselors we don't automatically know the answers for any given client. One gay man may have lived his life in an urban environment accepting of his sexual orientation, whereas another one in the same environment may have experienced rejection from his religiously orthodox family members. Exploring diversity from the richness of clients' own lives permits us to help them cope with the unique circumstances of their lives in the complexity of how they perceive them.

Summary

Experts who adopt a P × E model believe that an interactional view of behavior is more accurate in explaining subtleties than approaches that advocate attention to either personal characteristics or environmental features in isolation. Real life is not easily captured in simple cause–effect descriptions. The ecological perspective thus leads us to several important conclusions about human behavior. First, behavior is rarely if ever caused by a single factor, whether a personal characteristic or an environmental one. Behavior is the end result of people leading complicated lives in settings that are shaped by a host of animate and inanimate factors. The context itself changes as a consequence of the people acting within it. Simple cause–effect statements proposed to explain why something happens—bad values, parental apathy, poverty, you name it—are generalizations that are virtually guaranteed to do an inadequate job of capturing the complexities of human behavior. We should be especially alert to explanations that attribute complex sociostructural problems (the increase in drug abuse, problems of violence in urban settings) to simplistic forms of moral turpitude (laziness, broken families, lack of motivation, and on and on). These explanations communicate much more about the meaning making of the speaker than any effective causes of problems that have resisted intervention.

This insight is important to remember when applying the results of research studies to an individual or a group of individuals. Research-based conclusions are at best hypotheses that have some generally undefinable degree of validity when applied to similar individuals or groups. Even within the research itself, participants generally respond with some degree of variability. It is the responsibility of the researcher, and later those reading the article, to suggest how confidently we might predict that other people will respond in a comparable manner. It is worthwhile to remember famed ecological psychologist Urie Bronfenbrenner's maxim about research in general: The main effect is usually in the interaction. Simple statements that are applicable to everyone rarely hold water because everyone encompasses a host of person–environment interactions worth teasing apart.

This insight is scarcely new but is worth repeating: Research studies provide counselors with invaluable insights about human behavior, but any single individual may or may not behave in a way that is predictable from a study's findings. A client's situation may be different; the combination of factors influencing his or her behavior may be unique enough to suggest a whole other possibility. Wise counselors utilize conclusions based on others' lives as possibilities for understanding their own clients but remain open to new insights based on their clients' uniqueness.

Second, counselors look for ways to alter person–environment interactions that may or may not involve addressing the cause of the problem. Counselors are apt to ask why a person has a particular problem, but that question is often unanswerable and perhaps even irrelevant to changes in present behavior. The cause may have originated in a psychological dynamic present years ago, there may be no simple causes but instead chains of causative factors, the factors maintaining the behavior today may be very different than those at its origin yesterday, or the cause may be rooted in the environment and out of the control of the counselor and client.

What counselors *can* do successfully is to look for feasible, meaningful ways to change the person–environment interaction by addressing the person, the context, and how the two intersect in the client's life. The counselor and client together can determine where and how the client's life can change. Examples of interventions are discussed in Chapter 6.

Finally, in ecological counseling the target of the change process may be the environment as well as the client. Because of prevailing understandings about the nature of behavior, counselors working with individual clients are apt to think first about changing the dysfunctional individual. When we also think about the strength of person–environment interactions, we can recognize that the problem might lie in an environment that disempowers, abuses, stresses, drains, poisons, crowds, enervates, fails to validate, ignores, torments, infantilizes, disrespects, and so on, the person. In counseling we can help a person make changes in the environment itself or in how he or she interacts within the environment. The recognition of environmental culpability can transform how a person sees his or her life and the possibilities for renewal. In Chapter 6 I discuss some of the ways this transformation can occur.

Individual counseling rarely occurs simply between two persons in one room. The client brings in representations of all of the important relationships in his or her life. Descriptions of life events are shorthand summaries of complex two-way interactions that are in turn influenced by other people, other settings, and other needs and perceptions beyond those activated in the particular interaction in question. The counselor's task is to help the client envision new ways of being in the world that enhance meaningful connection with others and are consistent with core life values. We want to help the person become the person he or she yearns to be, building on the resources at his or her disposal. By understanding the full range of interactions making up his or her life, we are better able to appreciate its regularities and inconsistencies and help the client elaborate a life that fits who and what he or she wants to become.

Discussion Questions

- Choose a recent human interest story in the news (e.g., a celebrity sex scandal) and gather as much information from the media that you can about the participants: their roles and apparent motivations, how they reacted over time, what factors may have made them vulnerable to what happened. What does this media coverage suggest about why this event occurred as it did? Considering that the public knows only a portion of the truth about the interactions that made up this event, what other explanations are plausible?

- Young people today live in a technological world in which they can be in constant contact with friends; their grandparents relied on less immediate and less frequent face-to-face interactions. If possible, interview a teenager and an elderly person about how they maintain(ed) relationships during adolescence. What impact might the technological revolution have had on this important developmental period? What advantages and disadvantages correspond with each style of social interaction?
- Describe the nature of your career development thus far, especially your crucial decision points. What factors or people influenced these decisions at these transitions? How has your career developed as a consequence of these decisions?
- Many counselors are familiar with the Serenity Prayer, popular in 12-step programs that address addictions: "God, grant me the serenity to accept the things I cannot change, the courage to change the things I can, and the wisdom to know the difference." Discuss the wisdom of this perspective by using ideas about person–environment interaction covered in this chapter.

References

Allen, J., & Robbins, S. (2010). Effects of interest-major congruence, motivation, and academic performance on timely degree attainment. *Journal of Counseling Psychology, 57,* 23–35.

Armstrong, P. I., Day, D. X., McVay, J. P., & Rounds, J. (2008). Holland's RIASEC model as an integrative framework for individual differences. *Journal of Counseling Psychology, 55,* 1–18.

Bleidorn, W., Kandler, C., Riemann, Angleitner, A., & Spinath, F. M. (2009). Patterns and sources of adult personality development: Growth curve analyses of the NEO PI-R scales in a longitudinal twin study. *Journal of Personality and Social Psychology, 97,* 142–155.

Blustein, D. L. (2008). The role of work in psychological health and well-being: A conceptual, historical, and public policy perspective. *American Psychologist, 63,* 228–240.

Bowles, H. R., Babcock, L., & McGinn, K. L. (2005). Constraints and triggers: Situational mechanics of gender in negotiation. *Journal of Personality and Social Psychology, 89,* 951–965.

Bronfenbrenner, U. (1995). Developmental ecology through space and time: A future perspective. In P. Moen, G. H. Elder, Jr., & K. Luscher (Eds.), *Examining lives in context: Perspectives on the ecology of human development* (pp. 619–647). Washington, DC: American Psychological Association.

Bronfenbrenner, U. (1999). Environments in developmental perspective: Theoretical and operational models. In S. Friedman & T. Wachs (Eds.), *Measuring environment across the life span: Emerging methods and concepts* (pp. 3–28). Washington, DC: American Psychological Association.

Bussey, K., & Bandura, A. (1999). Social cognitive theory of gender development and differentiation. *Psychological Review, 106,* 676–713.

Cole, E. R. (2009). Intersectionality and research in psychology. *American Psychologist, 64,* 170–180.

Conyne, R. K. (2010). *Prevention program development and evaluation: An incidence reduction, culturally relevant approach.* Los Angeles, CA: Sage.

Conyne, R. K., & Cook, E. P. (Eds.). (2004). *Ecological counseling: An innovative approach to conceptualizing person–environment interaction.* Alexandria, VA: American Counseling Association.

Crawford, M. (2001). Gender and language. In R. K. Unger (Ed.), *Handbook of the psychology of women and gender* (pp. 228–244). Hoboken, NJ: Wiley.

Dawis, R. (2000). The person–environment tradition in counseling psychology. In W. E. Martin, Jr., & J. L. Swartz-Kulstad (Eds.), *Person–environment psychology and mental health: Assessment and intervention* (pp. 91–111). Mahwah, NJ: Erlbaum.

Dawis, R., & Lofquist, L. H. (1984). *A psychological theory of work adjustment.* Minneapolis: University of Minnesota.

Donohue, R. (2006). Person–environment congruence in relation to career change and career persistence. *Journal of Vocational Behavior, 68,* 504–515.

Elder, G. H., Jr. (1995). The life course paradigm: Social change and individual development. In P. Moen, G. H. Elder, & K. Luscher (Eds.), *Examining lives in context: Perspectives on the ecology of human development* (pp. 101–140). Washington, DC: American Psychological Association.

Ferriman, K., Lubinski, D., & Benbow, C. P. (2009). Work preferences, life values, and personal views of top math/science graduate students and the profoundly gifted. *Journal of Personality and Social Psychology, 97,* 517–532.

Gottfredson, L. S. (2005). Applying Gottfredson's theory of circumscription and compromise in career guidance and counseling. In S. D. Brown & R. W. Lent (Eds.), *Career development and counseling: Putting theory and research to work* (pp. 71–100). Hoboken, NJ: Wiley.

Gutek, B. A. (2001). Women and paid work. *Psychology of Women Quarterly, 25,* 379–393.

Halpern, D. F. (2005). Psychology at the intersection of work and family: Recommendations for employers, working families, and policymakers. *American Psychologist, 60,* 397–409.

Hoffman, B. J., & Woehr, D. J. (2006). A quantitative review of the relationship between person–environment fit and behavioral outcomes. *Journal of Vocational Behavior, 68,* 389–399.

Holland, J. (1997). *Making vocational choices: A theory of vocational and work environments.* Odessa, FL: Psychological Assessment Resources.

Kieffer, K. M., Schinka, J. A., & Curtiss, G. (2004). Person–environment congruence and personality domains in the prediction of job performance and work quality. *Journal of Counseling Psychology, 51,* 168–177.

Kirschmeyer, C. (2006). The different effects of family on objective career success across gender: A test of alternative explanations. *Journal of Vocational Behavior, 68*, 323–346.

Lent, R. W. (2004). Toward a unifying theoretical and practical perspective on well-being and psychosocial adjustment. *Journal of Counseling Psychology, 51*, 482–509.

Lent, R. W., & Brown, S. D. (2006). Integrating person and situation perspectives on work satisfaction: A social-cognitive view. *Journal of Vocational Behavior, 69*, 236–247.

Lerner, R. M. (2002). *Concepts and theories of human development* (3rd ed.). Mahwah, NJ: Erlbaum.

Little, B. R. (2000). Free traits and personal contexts: Expanding a social ecological model of well-being. In W. B. Walsh, K. H. Craik, & R. H. Price (Eds.), *Person–environment psychology: New directions and perspectives* (2nd ed., pp. 87–116). Mahwah, NJ: Erlbaum.

Magnusson, D. (1995). Individual development: A holistic, integrated model. In P. Moen, G. H. Elder, Jr., & K. Luscher (Eds.), *Examining lives in context: Perspectives on the ecology of human development* (pp. 19–60). Washington, DC: American Psychological Association.

Mayer, J. D. (2005). A tale of two visions: Can a new view of personality help integrate psychology? *American Psychologist, 60*, 294–307.

McAdams, D. P. (1995). What do we know when we know a person? *Journal of Personality, 63*, 365–396.

Medina, S., & Magnuson, S. (2009). Motherhood in the 21st century: Implications for counselors. *Journal of Counseling & Development, 87*, 90–96.

Moen, P., Elder, G. H., Jr., & Luscher, K. (Eds.). (1995). *Examining lives in context: Perspectives on the ecology of human development.* Washington, DC: American Psychological Association.

Nauta, M. M. (2010). The development, evolution, and status of Holland's theory of vocational personalities: Reflections and future directions for counseling psychology. *Journal of Counseling Psychology, 57*, 11–22.

Neufeld, J. E., Rasmussen, R. N., Lopez, S. J., Ryder, J. A., Magyar-Moe, J. L., Ford, A. I., . . . Bouwkamp, J. C. (2006). The engagement model of person environment interaction. *The Counseling Psychologist, 34*, 245–259.

O'Neil, J. M. (2008). Summarizing 25 years of research on men's gender role conflict using the Gender Role Conflict Scale. *The Counseling Psychologist, 36*, 358–445.

Piasentin, K. A., & Chapman, D. S. (2006). Subjective person–organization fit: Bridging the gap between conceptualization and measurement. *Journal of Organizational Behavior, 69*, 202–221.

Putney, N. M., & Bengtson, V. L. (2005). Family relations in changing times: A longitudinal study of five cohorts of women. *International Journal of Sociology and Social Policy, 25*, 92–119.

Roberts, B. W. (2007). Contextualizing personality psychology. *Journal of Personality, 75*, 1071–1081.

95

Roberts, B. W., & Robins, R. W. (2004). Person–environment fit and its implications for personality development: A longitudinal study. *Journal of Personality, 72*, 89–110.

Robinson-Wood, T. L. (2009). *The convergence of race, ethnicity, and gender: Multiple identities in counseling* (3rd ed.). Upper Saddle River, NJ: Pearson.

Rogler, L. H. (2002). Historical generations and psychology: The case of the Great Depression and World War II. *American Psychologist, 57*, 1013–1023.

Roisman, G. I., Masten, A. S., Coatsworth, J. D., & Tellegen, A. (2004). Salient and emerging developmental tasks in the transition to adulthood. *Child Development, 75*, 123–133.

Savickas, M. (2002). Career construction: A developmental theory of vocational behavior. In D. Brown & Associates (Eds.), *Career choice and development* (4th ed., pp. 149–205). San Francisco, CA: Jossey-Bass.

Savickas, M. L., Nota, L., Rossier, J., Dauwalder, J. P., Duarte, M. E., Guichard, J., . . . van Vianen, A. E. M. (2009). Life designing: A paradigm for career construction in the 21st century. *Journal of Vocational Behavior, 75*, 239–250.

Schneider, B., Smith, D. B., & Goldstein, H. W. (2000). Attraction–selection–attrition: Toward a person–environment psychology of organizations. In W. B. Walsh, K. H. Craik, & R. H. Price (Eds.), *Person–environment psychology: New directions and perspectives* (2nd ed., pp. 61–85). Mahwah, NJ: Erlbaum.

Silverstein, L. B., Auerbach, C. F., & Levant, R. F. (2002). Contemporary fathers reconstructing masculinity: Clinical implications of gender role strain. *Professional Psychology: Research and Practice, 33*, 361–369.

Smetana, J. G., Campione-Barr, N., & Metzger, A. (2006). Adolescent development in interpersonal and societal contexts. *Annual Review of Psychology, 57*, 255–284.

Spanierman, L. B., Todd, N. R., & Anderson, C. J. (2009). Psychosocial costs of racism to Whites: Understanding patterns among university students. *Journal of Counseling Psychology, 56*, 239–252.

Spokane, A. R., & Cruza-Guet, M. C. (2005). Holland's theory of vocational personalities in work environments. In S. D. Brown & R. W. Lent (Eds.), *Career development and counseling: Putting theory and research to work* (pp. 24–41). Hoboken, NJ: Wiley.

Steenbarger, B. N. (1991). All the world is not a stage: Emerging contextualist themes in counseling and development. *Journal of Counseling & Development, 70*, 288–296.

Stewart, A. J., & McDermott, C. (2004). Gender in psychology. *Annual Review of Psychology, 55*, 519–544.

Stroink, M. L. (2004). The conflicting standards dilemma and gender: A mediating model of its affective implications and coping styles. *Journal of Social Psychology, 144*, 273–292.

Super, D. E. (1980). The life-span, life-space approach to career development. *Journal of Vocational Behavior, 13*, 282–298.

96

Swanson, J. L., & Chu, S. P. (2000). Applications of person–environment psychology to the career development and vocational behavior of adolescents and adults. In W. E. Martin, Jr., & J. L. Swartz-Kulstad (Eds.), *Person–environment psychology and mental health: Assessment and intervention* (pp. 143–168). Mahwah, NJ: Erlbaum.

Tinsley, E. A. (2000). The congruence myth: An analysis of the efficacy of the person–environment fit model. *Journal of Vocational Behavior, 56,* 147–179.

Twenge, J. M. (2001). Changes in women's assertiveness in response to status and roles: A cross-temporal meta-analysis, 1931–1993. *Journal of Personality and Social Psychology, 81,* 133–143.

Walsh, W. B., Craik, K. H., & Price, R. H. (2000). Person–environment psychology: A summary and commentary. In W. B. Walsh, K. H. Craik, & R. H. Price (Eds.), *Person–environment psychology: New directions and perspectives* (2nd ed., pp. 297–326). Mahwah, NJ: Erlbaum.

Wapner, S., & Demick, J. (2000). Person-in–environment psychology: A holistic, developmental, systems-oriented perspective. In W. B. Walsh, K. H. Craik, & R. H. Price (Eds.), *Person–environment psychology: New directions and perspectives* (2nd ed., pp. 25–60). Mahwah, NJ: Erlbaum.

West, C., & Zimmerman, D. H. (1987). Doing gender. *Gender and Society, 1,* 125–151.

Young, R. A., Valach, L., & Collin, A. (1996). A contextual explanation of career. In D. Brown, L. Brooks, & Associates (Eds.), *Career choice and development* (pp. 477–511). San Francisco, CA: Jossey-Bass.

Behavior Is Meaningful

Ellen P. Cook

What is the meaning of life?

> In a "Zits" cartoon by Jim Borgman and Jerry Scott, one teen pensively notes that "There's something about life I just don't understand." His friend asks, "What is it?" His reply: "Exactly." (May 29, 2010)

> I was born in the best country in the world to two of the most loving parents anyone could have. I had married my childhood sweetheart and together we had three great kids. How could I rage at fate? How could I ask God for more?
> —Barbara Eckles, age 54, in her obituary (August 9, 2010)

> Life's but a walking shadow . . . a tale told by an idiot, full of sound and fury, signifying nothing.
> —Macbeth's soliloquy, Act 3, Scene 5, *Macbeth,*
> by William Shakespeare

There is no one answer to the question about the meaning of life. We humans are meaning-making creatures, trying to make sense of our world from the moment we are born until the day we die. Some of this meaning making pertains to the grander questions about life; most of it simply concerns the everyday series of events that become our lives. The process of thinking about life is meaning making.

Meaning making is crucial to individual well-being. What we believe is important to live for, our short-term and long-term aspirations, how we choose to spend our money and our time, the importance of family and other relationships, whether we believe in God and what this means for how we view our lives—all of these and many other central life concerns invoke meaning making. The world's great religions teach us that the universe does not orbit around us, and our highest meaning comes from finding our place alongside others. The media encourage us to believe that our rightful place is at the top of the ladder of material success and that we can reach it if we try. We assimilate and reject messages about what's worth doing day after day and learn to judge our own life experiences as successes or failures according to meanings distilled from what we have lived. At a time of human evolution when we are exposed to more possibilities for living life than ever before, we can flounder like aquarium goldfish unexpectedly deposited into the Pacific Ocean.

Most meaning making occurs without conscious reflection in the course of daily life events, unless something takes us by surprise. The sight of a preteen in a scout uniform at our front door gets us thinking about cookies rather than catastrophe; in wartime no parent of a soldier wants to see uniformed adults show up at the front door. Public restrooms do not provide instructions for use, an omission unnoticed by locals yet one that causes panic for some desperate international travelers. We know that an automated teller machine does not simply dispense money to anyone who asks (although as a parent of two teens, I have wondered when this awareness kicks in). These crucial life lessons about form and function are so much a part of everyday life that we often need to be reminded that not everyone shares what we know. Meanings express where we have been in life and how we find our way into the future.

In this chapter I explore the third basic proposition within the ecological perspective: Behavior is concerned with meaning. As I explain, meaning making is intimately involved with the other propositions within the ecological perspective about context and interaction. Although some contexts may affect people in similar ways (e.g., most human beings find 120-degree Fahrenheit weather to be too hot), our reactions to everyday life contexts are typically affected by how we personally view these contexts. An important determinant of person–environment interaction is how people perceive and understand what happens to them.

In this chapter I discuss important features of meaning making: different types of meaning making, the cultural foundation of meaning making, differences in *how* individuals make meaning (the process of meaning making), and how *what* we think about things influences our subsequent behavior (the content of meaning making). I also briefly describe how the pattern of our life choices over time may express some central themes or patterns, much as a story does (the narrative approach). Finally, I briefly discuss how the crushing experience of loss becomes a crisis of meaning making as the bereaved struggle to find ways to live without people or things crucial to their life's coherence. I begin with a brief review of some of the ways in which counseling approaches have addressed the importance of meaning making in people's lives.

What Is Meaning Making?

Meaning making is the aspect of the ecological perspective that is less immediately familiar to readers, yet in my experience it becomes a favorite part of it. Meaning making refers to what makes us unique as a species and what makes each of us unique from other humans with whom we share life. In this section I provide some background about how counselors have thought about meaning making, define meaning making with some everyday examples, and discuss how language serves as an essential building block to meaning making.

Background: Meaning Making and Counseling

Lightsey (2006) suggested that "counseling achieves some of its benefits via augmenting meaning" (p. 103). Indeed, meaning making has played a starring role in the behavior change process for decades. One of the most popular counseling approaches today is cognitive behavior therapy. Sue and Sue (2008) reviewed cognitive behavior theory and techniques in detail, including strategies based on classical and operant conditioning (learning) approaches, social learning, and cognitive behavior theory and counseling. In this last category they placed Albert Ellis's rational emotive behavior therapy and Aaron Beck's cognitive therapy, both common topics in counseling theory classes. These familiar approaches discuss how emotional distress can develop through meaning making gone awry, especially irrational beliefs that are inconsistent with logical conclusions, automatic thoughts that occur outside a person's awareness, and schemas that distort incoming information to fit underlying conclusions or categories about life. Cognitive–behavioral approaches, which are designed to change how clients perceive, understand, and respond to life events, are popular and well respected, and most counselors likely have some degree of expertise in them. Other recently developed counseling approaches (e.g., dialectical behavior therapy and motivational enhancement therapy) also emphasize that changing how people think about their problems is key to changing their lives in general (see Sue & Sue, 2008).

Insight-oriented approaches to counseling are also concerned with changing thinking patterns. With the help of the counselor, clients explore crucial past life events, express blocked feelings, and learn new meanings pertinent to themselves, others, and life experiences. For example, they might learn to think of themselves as survivors rather than victims, of their parents as deeply flawed but well intentioned rather than all powerful and always right, and of their lives as a courageous effort to make a valuable place for themselves in the world rather than a string of hopeless failures. These insights require a strong counseling alliance forged through empathy and fidelity, and some ability to tolerate painful emotions.

Still other counselors recognize humans primarily as seekers of meaning: Why are we here? What kind of life is worth living? Tragedies of the past century have illuminated humans' capacity for both engaging in unspeakable cruelty and affirming life's value in response to it. Viktor Frankl (1963), a survivor of the Nazi concentration camps, understood that finding answers to questions about the meaning of life could save lives. People who can find a reason to live in the face of the destruction of everything dear to them can find strength within themselves to survive. The loss or absence of meaning, however, can hasten death.

Constructivist theories bear the most similarity to the ecological perspective. Young and Collin (2004) defined *constructivism* as follows:

> Constructivism proposes that each individual mentally constructs the world of experience through cognitive processes . . . the world cannot be known directly, but rather by the construction imposed on it by the mind . . . Meaning is constructed in a social, historical, and cultural context, through action and discourse in which we form relationships and community. (pp. 375, 378)

Constructivist theorists (e.g., Hayes & Oppenheim, 1997) see people as truth seekers and answer makers in a world fraught with more questions than answers. Constructivist counselors do not focus on whether people arrive at the right answers to life's problems; rather, they are interested in how and why a person arrived at a particular solution and what implications it has for his or her future development. Constructivist counselors respect how people create their lives by how they interpret what happens to them, particularly in relationships with others.

All of these approaches (and more) have a place in the ecological perspective: Each one sheds light on how people make sense of their lives and how counselors can help them do so more effectively and satisfactorily. Because such counseling theories are part and parcel of counselors' professional expertise, I do not discuss them further in this chapter. Instead I focus on ideas that are less likely to be familiar to you yet are also helpful in developing a nuanced appreciation of the importance of meaning making in people's everyday lives.

Defining Meaning Making

Although meaning making has been discussed in the professional literature for decades, there is no simple consensus about how to define it. What first comes to mind is people's efforts to define the importance of their life as a whole, an ongoing search to discover what makes life worth living. Meaning making in this sense can indeed contribute to happiness and psychological health (see the review in Steger, Frazier, Oishi, & Kaler, 2006).

If meaning making were only about philosophizing, counselors might dismiss it as something most people don't have the time or the inclination to do very often and thus something not likely to matter much in people's everyday lives. In the ecological perspective we define *meaning making* more broadly than this as an eminently practical process whereby people perceive and try to understand everyday things in their lives. In this sense, meaning making refers to the thousands of times every day that people consciously or unconsciously transform the raw data of their senses into meaning. A rumble in the stomach is interpreted as hunger, too many beans, or an early warning sign of cancer. Which meaning you favor as an explanation can say volumes about how you understand the particulars of your life.

Meaning making is the most important tool that humans possess. In the words of Wilson (2009),

Human beings are the only species (as far as we know) that has the ability to reflect on itself and form metabeliefs about who we are, what happened to us in the past, and what is likely to happen in the future. (p. 387)

Meaning making accomplishes three essential tasks. First, it helps us *communicate* with others through a shared symbolic system we begin to learn in infancy. We have the unique capability to communicate a vast range of information about the physical world we share and the private world of our own needs, desires, thoughts, and feelings. Second, meaning making allows us to *understand*. We learn from others the significance of things. We learn the meaning of thunder, an upraised middle finger, and an engagement ring and also appropriate ways to respond to each of these things. Third, we gain some (albeit limited) ability to control our lives through our ability to *predict* what may happen. These adaptive qualities are consequences of our ability to make sense out of what would otherwise be a frightening mass of random phenomena. Consider the following examples drawn from real life.

A middle-aged man and his new wife move around the world to live with her family. He has lived overseas before but never in this new country; he cannot speak the language and knows little about the culture. Even though he can speak his native language on his new job and his wife patiently serves as a translator with his new extended family, he feels profoundly depressed and ashamed. He cannot even take a bus without her help.

On Halloween, a small child shrieks in terror at the scary monster lurking at the front door, calling her name. The monster removes his mask and reassuringly tells her, "It's Uncle Jim." Her tears subside as she says over and over, "It's Uncle Jim, Uncle Jim . . . "

A woman repeatedly consults with her doctor for answers about her baffling collection of symptoms. First he treats her with condescension, certain that she is merely seeking attention; later he becomes impatient with her and with himself because of his inability to treat her successfully. Finally, after consulting with colleagues, he is able to diagnose her with an incurable but not life-threatening disorder. Their doctor–patient relationship has a remarkable recovery.

In each of these situations, meanings hold the key to understanding the person's negative feelings and their eventual resolution. The new husband expects himself to adapt to an alien context without missing a step, minimizing the psychic costs of his overwhelming life transitions. The frightened child talks herself out of her terror by reminding herself of the reassuring truth about the monster's true identity. And the certainty provided by a label—a diagnosis—informs the patient about the steps she can take to manage her discomfort and allows the physician to resume the familiar role of authoritative expert with answers.

As we will see in this chapter, meaning making is essential in nearly every person–environment interaction. We make countless choices every day to respond to how we perceive and understand people, events, and features of our environment; to be consistent with life values or to reach goals; and to respond to nocturnal nightmares and daydreaming. Even how we utilize the data from our senses is affected by our meaning making. We may decide to tune out distractions at our local coffeehouse because we believe it is important to get our work done this afternoon. People sensitive to subtle forms of discrimination can perceive the subtle discrimination in vocal inflections in everyday conversations. A lonely person appraises every new acquaintance as possible dating material. How we interpret our interactions with others depends on the unconscious assumptions we make about strangers; our explanations for our friend's odd behavior based on previous experiences; a value to treat other people as we wish to be treated ourselves; our notions about polite behavior; or our expectations, projected outcomes, or long-term goals for the relationship. All of these examples refer to meaning making as we live it every day.

This emphasis on meaning making distinguishes the ecological perspective discussed in this book from other perspectives labeled as *ecological*. Meaning making is just as important as variable features of the participants, contexts, and interaction. How do people regard each other, the contexts in which they interact, and the nature of their interaction? The dimension of meaning making invites us to consider the incredible variability in human life and reminds us of the power humans uniquely have as a species to change the experiences of their lives from within. The fundamental building blocks for how meaning structures behavior involve language.

Language as a Building Block

Language is the fundamental building block in meaning making. Language permits humans a qualitatively different life than that experienced by our species' ancestors, a life with structured communities sharing rules, roles, communal and personal identities, and systems of beliefs about the nature of reality that grant us a sense of security and dignity. Experts are only now beginning to understand how language and the higher cognitive functions involved in social life depend on one another (see Fiedler, 2008). Through language, infants learn very early on that they are unique beings distinctive from others and capable of making things happen (Bandura, 2006). Language helps us develop from being a mass of undifferentiated needs and sensations to a human being capable of loving and being loved and of exerting some control in this frightening existence in which we find ourselves.

The dawning awareness early in life that interesting things in our environment are designated by a specific patterning of sounds or gestures allows us to communicate reliably with others. The miraculous nature of this awareness provides the climax to the story about Helen Keller, unable to speak, hear, or see from birth. Helen's realization that the finger movements drawn over and over in her palm by her dedicated teacher signified the *water* spilling over her hands suddenly transformed her life from one of frustration and isolation to one of endless possibilities for connecting with the world around her. This miracle of connecting meanings with physical sensations happens in the life of every child at a young age.

104

Very young children have a remarkable facility for learning language that is not present later in life, a facility that permits them to develop relationships with others at the very time that they are most dependent. Language development is crucial for intellectual, emotional, and social development. The utterances of "mama" and "dada" (or their cultural equivalents) certainly do reward exhausted caregivers at a time when they might be wondering just why they ever wanted children in the first place!

The particular language(s) we learn early in life shape our understanding of the world in unique ways. All languages permit people to describe personal thoughts, feelings, or objects within the environment. The symbols at the heart of languages can vary quite dramatically, as any budding linguist quickly learns. Characters can be unique to a language (e.g., Chinese) or shared across related languages (e.g., the Latin alphabet). Some languages use tonal, almost musical inflections to change the meaning of a word; in English, such inflections convey the speaker's feelings or intentions (e.g., say "I love you" three times, emphasizing a different word each time). Languages that share a similar grammatical structure with one's native language (e.g., English and French) can be easier to learn than those whose structures are not similar (e.g., English and Chinese).

In terms of meaning, the most basic way in which languages differ is with respect to vocabulary. Languages that have developed in a certain region of the world have words necessary to convey particulars about physical and sociocultural contexts that may not appear in a language that has evolved in another region. You may have heard that the Inuit people living in the Arctic regions have different words for *snow* to convey subtle distinctions in texture, density, and so on, distinctions important in their everyday lives. People living near the equator generally need to know about snow only for cross-cultural communication. With our world's shrinking borders, we English speakers have discovered that other languages have useful words that lack simple equivalents in English: *Mensch* in Yiddish, *joie de vivre* in French, and *Schadenfreude* in German are three of my favorites. The language we learn from the earliest days of life allows us to communicate about our lives with others yet constrains how and what we say in ways that we do not generally think about.

Beyond this basic language we share, we also learn certain specific vocabulary as part of group membership. Young people develop their own slang to demarcate their social reality. Any parent foolhardy enough to try using some of these words invites ridicule, as I know from personal experience. Urban gangs communicate on walls with symbols intentionally unintelligible to nonmembers. And professionals develop their own verbal shorthand to convey complex meanings succinctly. For example, if I were to inform a group of mental health counselors that a person was "borderline," my audience would be able to speculate with some accuracy about his relationship problems or behavior. Regardless of whether we agree that it is desirable to use such terminology, we do learn how to use it as part of our education (and other counseling specialties have their own language to learn).

105

Language is an extraordinarily important tool in meaning making, but it is only a tool. What is of greater concern to counselors are thoughts, feelings, hopes, and dreams—the psychological meanings that words are used to convey. I now consider the patterns that these meanings often take.

The Process of Making Distinctions and Its Consequences

Language succeeds as a means of communication because its rules and meanings are shared across people. Although regional variations in vocabulary and pronunciation exist, English speakers agree on the basics: *Key* refers to a tool that opens doors, and *pencil* is a writing implement. Language works because a group of people over time and across situations implicitly have agreed to accept that certain sounds grouped together carry specific meanings. Most interesting to counselors is how language is part of a meaning-making process that structures how we interact within our world. Language gains psychological resonance in how it allows us to evaluate, classify, compare, and predict our interactions within the world; the world around us structures patterns of meaning for us in turn.

From the first day of life, the human world around us imposes meaning on us. Experts on diversity generally agree that most differences attributable to biological sex and skin color are due not to genetic determinants of these physical distinctions (e.g., certain hormones or melanin in the skin) but to sociocultural classification based on these observable differences. Humans classify people into categories on the basis of these important criteria. This classification sets into motion a host of expectations, rewards and punishments for certain behaviors, self-fulfilling prophesies, and so on—a lifelong series of meaning-rich distinctions that shape a person's self-perceptions, others' perceptions of him or her, and interactions with others throughout life.

For example, one of the most important determinants of our life options is our biological sex. From the moment the doctor announces "It's a girl!" or "It's a boy!", people often expect us to behave in certain ways: to be interested in hunting or shoes, to prefer the color pink or blue, to plan on becoming a car mechanic or a secretary. Identifying *oneself* as either a boy or a girl is also linked to sex-typed behavior. It is not simply that others treat a child differently depending on biological sex; although this is certainly important, labeling oneself as male or female is an early step in a process leading to gender-typed behavior (Bussey & Bandura, 1999; Olson & Dweck, 2008). In a very real sense, we become what we perceive ourselves to be.

Biological sex is an obvious category for classifying people, but others categories also influence how we perceive and react to other people. Gender, race, sexual orientation, and age are the predominant cultural groups (Ponterotto, Casas, Suzuki, & Alexander, cited in Liu & Pope-Davis, 2004). Liu and Pope-Davis (2004) argued persuasively that social class also belongs on the list. We commonly have different expectations for the characteristics and behavior of people belonging to various categories in these classifications (e.g., lower class vs. upper class, older adults vs. middle-aged people).

This process of meaning making associated with various social categories involves stereotyping.

Stereotyping

Numerous sociocultural distinctions have the power to activate complex meaning-making processes: Without any personal knowledge of them, people may expect an elderly person to be asexual, a woman with Asian ancestry to be good at math, or a Muslim man to be personally acquainted with terrorists. These distinctions about the members of particular groups are cognitive shortcuts that help us understand and predict the behavior of groups of people for better or worse. Such cognitive shortcuts are commonly labeled *stereotypes,* or "qualities perceived to be associated with particular groups or categories of people" (Schneider, 2004, p. 24). In his extensive review of the research, Schneider (2004) explained how all human beings engage in stereotyping. Stereotypes are tools of meaning making crucial to understanding how people try to understand and predict the behavior of others.

Stereotypes can be about different things (e.g., gender stereotypes can pertain to one's career choice, hairstyle, and hobbies), and some can be easily changed with experience. For example, a person with limited culinary experience may believe that all seafood comes naturally breaded and shaped in flat rectangles, a stereotype quickly changed by a visit to a fine seafood restaurant. This stereotype about seafood is bound to be very different from the seafood stereotype held by a person from the Asian Pacific Rim! Some stereotypes do have a grain (or more) of truth to them. For example, elderly individuals may indeed engage in sexual activity less often than younger people (Hutchison, 2008). Unfortunately, stereotypes can be applied without thought to people who do not fit them: Some elderly individuals enjoy vigorous romance throughout their lives, and for others changes in medication, a new partner, and opportunities for privacy might prompt a dramatic resurrection of sorts.

According to Schneider (2004), the Big Three categories of stereotypes are gender, race, and age. As Schneider discussed them, stereotypes about gender, race, and age are important in most cultures, people generally do not choose their status within a category (with some exceptions), and others generally do not remember making classifications about people in these categories (i.e., classification is virtually automatic). Yet gender stereotypes have some unique features: Gender interactions occur nearly everywhere and for diverse purposes, a target of gender stereotyping is more likely than targets of other kinds of stereotyping to tolerate or even endorse the stereotypes, and gender stereotypes are both descriptive and prescriptive in intent (i.e., women "are" and "should be" certain things because of their female status). The gender stereotypes that we and others hold are therefore likely to influence our interactions every day whether we are aware of it or not.

All of us engage in stereotypic thinking every day, whether we think of baseball games as more exciting to watch than basketball (or vice versa), dormitory food as unhealthy and fattening, or residents of New York City as worldly. Many stereotypes are simply harmless shortcuts in our thinking processes, whose worst consequence is embarrassment when we discover how mistaken we might be. Yet stereotypes have received considerable attention in recent years because of how they can negatively impact how people treat members of certain groups. For example, social status, opportunities, and resources can be distributed according to gender and race. The stereotypes that concern us as counselors are those that lead us to judge certain groups and behave unfairly toward them. I now consider how difference becomes discrimination.

How Difference Becomes Discrimination

The human ability to perceive differences among us is a natural process crucial to the survival of our species; we need to be able to protect ourselves and our loved ones against threats from outsiders. Even today, children learn early on how to identify safe people (e.g., school personnel, police officers) and what to do if a threat is perceived. We continue to distinguish among people throughout life for reasons we cannot articulate but that are ingrained within our perceptual habits. Which individuals and groups we perceive as different, and the consequences of these perceptual distinctions for our behavior with others, are topics of critical importance in meaning making.

In the ecological perspective diversity issues develop through a fundamental meaning-making process. First, people everywhere distinguish among others on the basis of some criteria that are relevant within their sociocultural context: skin color, religion, biological sex, and so on. Second, these criteria also carry some evaluation or consequence, often implicit, of the person or group judged by the perceiver, and these evaluations can determine how the interpersonal interaction then proceeds. For example, because of a variety of social cues a perceiver might identify another person as gay and then evaluate that person according to the perceiver's meaning making. Alternatively, the perceiver in this example might conclude that this newly labeled gay person is an attractive potential date for a friend, brave for being honest in a conservative community (as long as he or she is not too gay), and/or simply immoral.

Stereotypes are commonly associated with *discrimination,* defined by Schneider (2004) as "the unjustified use of category information to make judgments about other people" (p. 29). The effects of stereotypes may be more subtle than the overt hostility that people may expect (see Schneider, 2004, for a detailed analysis). For example, members of certain groups may not receive the same opportunities at work that others do but may also receive excessively positive evaluations because others expect less from them than from their peers, a pattern labeled *the wow effect* (as in "Wow, that person just walked and chewed gum at the same time!"). Groups targeted with negative stereotypes may be favored initially because they are held to a lesser standard (e.g., "for a *woman,* she is not too bad"), but typically the evidence then required for competence is much higher (to become a manager, she then has to be much better than the rest; see Biernat, 2003, for a fascinating analysis about the complexity of stereotypes in everyday life).

Some stereotypes are positive in nature. For example, Asian Americans are expected to be a *model minority,* considered superior to members of other minority groups and successful because of how they purportedly actualize the American dream of success through hard work. Yet as explained by Yoo, Burrola, and Steger (2010), this model minority myth can cause considerable stress for Asian Americans: Who wants to be compared to an imaginary model irrelevant to one's personal gifts?

The inverse of being part of a model minority is being *stigmatized.* Major and O'Brien (2005) noted that

> people who are stigmatized have (or are believed to have) an attribute that marks them as different and leads them to be devalued in the eyes of others . . . Stigma is relationship- and context-specific; it does not reside in the person but in a social context. (p. 395)

Stigmatized individuals can be discriminated against in numerous domains (e.g., in the workplace and health care) based on multiple criteria: health status (e.g., being HIV positive), obesity, age, skin color, gender, and sexual orientation. Counselors need to pay particular attention to stigma associated with the labeling of mental illness (Overton & Medina, 2008).

How stigmatized individuals perceive their status and the threats inherent in particular situations will affect how they respond to their devalued status. Some individuals may attempt to hide their status (e.g., gay people may remain in the closet); some may calmly or defiantly proclaim their status (e.g., by marching in a gay rights' parade); and still others may simply stay away from certain situations (e.g., by calling in sick to the family reunion), concluding that their chances of acceptance are effectively zero. Some may feel threatened because the demands they perceive within the situation appear to exceed the coping resources they believe they have; others in the same situation may feel they have enough or more than enough resources to cope (Major & O'Brien, 2005).

Correcting misinformation and providing opportunities for people to interact in situations that underscore the humanity, strengths, and interdependence of people who appear different on the outside can help to correct what Major and O'Brien (2005) referred to as "the predicament of the stigmatized" (p. 412). Opportunities to work together on projects that make a difference to others (e.g., caring for a community garden that helps to feed families in need) can help to reframe each group as good hearted and full of useful skills. Counselors can enhance the resilience of stigmatized groups and individuals by addressing how they perceive and then respond to stressful situations.

Counselors need to be aware that some stereotypes and stigma may be invisible to us because of our own status in society. The issue of classism has recently come to light in this regard. Counselors commonly come from middle-class backgrounds and have limited personal experience with individuals from lower classes. In the United States, we are not comfortable acknowledging the existence of a class system associated with income and our own attitudes related to it. Counselors may share common negative attitudes about low-income people being lazy, promiscuous, uninterested in education or work, and uninvolved in their children's lives (e.g., Lott, 2001). Alternatively, counselors might conclude that the enormity of economic problems facing low-income people means that they cannot benefit from counseling, nor would they even be interested in it (cf. Smith, 2005). Both types of attitudes are based in the counselor's preconceptions, and neither may reflect the client's needs. Counselors also have "difficulty understanding how people may not choose to go to school, may choose to put effort into what we would perceive as menial work, and view work as a small component of life rather than a major focus" (Liu & Ali, 2005, p. 191). Liu and Ali (2005) asserted that counselors' difficulty understanding these choices can stem from a form of classism that sees upward achievement as a core life value and anyone who does not live by this value as lacking something crucial.

This discussion of stereotyping has focused on a level of meaning making associated with particular groups of individuals. We learn the contents of these stereotypes from our life experiences. Some stereotypes are formally taught in schools (e.g., past history textbook depictions of Native American peoples as unsocialized savages), whereas the content and intensity of other stereotypes can be the consequence of our own life experiences, which may counter learning from other sources (e.g., family members might have taught us to appreciate the rich ethnic heritage of Native American peoples). Schneider (2004) also noted that stereotypes do not inevitably lead to discriminatory behavior. For example, people may not support the career advancement of certain groups for reasons that have nothing to do with stereotypes about the group's members (e.g., they may have highly competitive feelings about any and all newcomers), or they may support a group's advancement despite holding negative stereotypes about its members (e.g., because their political beliefs advocate support for all minority groups). Yet two things are clear about stereotypes: All humans have them, and counselors need to be aware of theirs because of how these stereotypes might interfere with an accurate understanding of the unique individuals we desire to help. Schneider's analysis provides an extraordinarily detailed discussion of how these psychosocial interactions actually work, allowing us to consider the subtleties of various groups.

Although it appears that overt discrimination on the basis of stereotyping has diminished in recent years, stereotypes may still continue to operate on an unconscious level (Agars, 2004). In the case of gender-based discrimination, coworkers may forget to pass along critical information, exclude women from informal social gatherings (e.g., team sports, golfing weekends) where communication and trust are enhanced, or blame the women themselves rather than extenuating circumstances for performance difficulties. The effect of stereotypes on any one situation may be modest but can be cumulative over time. When added to other gender-related factors that affect women's employment patterns (e.g., family responsibilities, sexual harassment), "the end result is substantially fewer women in upper management" (pp. 107–108).

Schneider (2004) also emphasized that discriminatory behavior does not always follow from stereotypic thinking and that what appears to be discriminatory behavior may represent reasonable conclusions based on a target's own behavior. Racism and other negative attitudes that are more covert and hidden are more difficult for both the target and the perpetrator to detect. These more subtle forms of discrimination can be easily denied by onlookers but leave the target feeling angry and confused: Did what I think happened really happen? (Sue et al., 2007).

Vasquez (2007) made the startling assertion that because of how race and ethnicity are constructed in the United States, *everyone* probably has unintentional biases that lead to discriminatory behaviors that are hurtful to others. If we happen to be members of U.S. society's majority group (White, middle class, Judeo-Christian men), we are less likely to perceive discrimination when it occurs (Crosby, Iyer, & Sincharoen, 2006). We should also be aware that we might process information about others on two different levels: a logical, rule-based conscious level and an unconscious, automatic one that activates hidden stereotypes (Boysen, 2010). Our meaning making may affect our interactions with others in ways that do not fit with how we view ourselves as good counselors. Being especially alert in situations that could push our buttons or that are new to us can help us manage our behavior so that we are less likely to treat others unfairly because of how we make sense of the world.

Consider, for example, the academic performance of children in poor urban settings. When the performance of these children lags far behind that of their peers in the suburbs, it is common for counselors to blame children's lack of motivation and their parents' lack of interest. Yet what other factors might explain their difficulties? Perhaps an absence of previous success following one's efforts, children having to work to help support the family or babysit younger siblings, teachers' half-hearted efforts or lack of understanding, parents who do not know how to help, parents having to work multiple jobs for survival, inadequate funding for needed school facilities or supplies, the absence of relevant models for successful school behavior (see the review in Eccles & Wigfield, 2002).

It is certainly not a bad thing for counselors to be realistic in their expectations. However, citing lack of motivation as an all-encompassing explanation for a person's lack of investment in a particular area (e.g., school, career) might say more about ourselves as counselors than the people we are supposed to be helping. Counselors do not like to admit that certain situations are beyond their ability to change. Rather than admit we cannot help for whatever reason, it may be easier to blame the students (or their parents) for their lack of progress. When it seems that hope flies out the window as soon as we open our office doors, we need to look for creative ways to change what we *can* change.

This chapter has focused thus far on meaning making as influenced by specific variations in everyday life: Particular combinations of certain person characteristics, life contexts, and ways of understanding experiences (meaning making) viewed together can help explain why we behave in a particular situation. Now I step back to discern common patterns of meaning making across situations: how habits or themes implicit in individuals' meaning making across settings can contribute to stable patterns of behavior. I start with the most familiar form of pervasive meaning making: religious or spiritual meaning.

Pervasive Meaning Making: Religious and Spiritual Meanings

One of the most profound yet common varieties of meaning making concerns religious and spiritual beliefs and experiences. The subject matter of this meaning making is the role that human beings play in the grandest ecosystem of all, the universe: Who or what created human life, and why? How are we unique creatures to live out our few short years on planet Earth? Where do we turn for answers to unanswerable questions?

Until recently questions such as these were regarded as the province of faith communities, clergy, and philosophers, not professional counselors. Yet we have recently begun to acknowledge that meaning making that addresses these ultimate questions is crucial in people's everyday lives. The professional literature discussing religion/spirituality has expanded exponentially since the mid-1980s (Emmons & Paloutzian, 2003; Pargament, 2008). Counselors are now commonly expected either to develop expertise in helping clients explore this core of meaning at the heart of their lives or to recognize their own limitations by making referrals to other professionals better versed in the client's meaning-filled language.

The sacred texts of the world's great faith traditions date back thousands of years, but our understanding of the psychological dimensions of religion is very recent. *Religiousness,* defined as "a belief and meaning system that is stable over time and manifested across diverse situations" (Emmons & Paloutzian, 2003, p. 386), contributes to a person's wellness in a number of dimensions. Religiousness is associated with characteristics of gratitude, forgiveness, and humility. A religious orientation can also foster a strong sense of purpose, direction, and connectedness with others. These observations about the value of religiousness appear to hold across faith traditions (e.g., Islam, Judaism). Religious individuals would argue that this value is because humans find their fulfillment in God; others would point to the emotional and intellectual reassurances of having answers to life's unanswerable, frightening questions.

Religion has a special purpose in helping individuals cope with tragedies and difficulties in life. People have broad, global beliefs about the nature of life and more specific understandings about the purpose and meaning of certain life events. If specific events are inconsistent with broader life meanings—if something unexpected, out of time, or unimaginable happens—individuals must change how they perceive the meaning of life as a whole, the meaning of the specific life event, or both. Religion helps during the coping process by influencing how individuals see life in general or these specific events and by providing resources and strategies they can use in response to the crisis (Park, 2005). Solace during stressful times can come from the process of integrating the stressors with one's beliefs, values, and goals (Folkman & Moskowitz, 2004). This process comes more naturally when a person has a coherent view of life that is aligned with transcendent purposes and a community that will validate this view while providing personal and material support (e.g., hugs, meals, pastoral support). A strong faith tradition rooted within a supportive religious community can provide stories, symbols, structure, and companions that have withstood the test of time, elements that can gently position tragedy as a part, not the end, of a life worth living.

Other Examples of Pervasive Meaning Making

As members of a particular culture at a given point in history, we tend to share a worldview that underlies how and what we think about life (see Koltko-Rivera, 2004, for a discussion especially useful to researchers; see also the discussion about culture in Chapter 3). These worldviews can be influenced by the social complexity and demographic details of our communal lives (e.g., a densely populated urban setting vs. a rural farming region) and in turn can influence how we socialize our children (Greenfield, 2009). This shared foundation of meaning is generally discernible in the idiosyncratic life meanings that every person ultimately develops, although the foundation may be amended, rejected, or elaborated according to the person's efforts to make sense of life as it unfolds.

Over the course of their lives, people develop idiosyncratic patterns for interpreting a multitude of life events that channel how they subsequently respond to these events. People who agree with the musical *Annie*'s anthem that "the sun will come out tomorrow" endorse a general style of perceiving life that influences their ability to cope across a range of circumstances. Counselors today routinely look for such patterns of meaning making without necessarily labeling them as such—we might explore how one client tends to view people he does not know as untrustworthy or how another looks for clues to "God's will for her" in every ambiguous situation. As counselors we know that there is no way for us to tell how untrustworthy random strangers really are for him or whether God does indeed provide clues for this woman on a regular basis. We do know, however, that these patterns of meaning making affect these clients' daily lives in ways they can fruitfully explore with us. In this section I briefly sample some literature that illustrates some of the diverse ways in which people engage in patterns of meaning making across situations and over time. In a later section I discuss the process by which people make sense of their lives as a whole.

Everyday Explanations of Events

People are motivated to preserve central life meanings, because to question them might consequently challenge the very coherence and predictability that people seek through their meaning making. The desire to preserve important meanings can result in a type of mental gymnastics of puzzling contradictions, such as when a client attributes her dazzling career success to sheer luck but can readily see others' attributes and efforts. People may give themselves credit for positive life events but blame negative life events on factors outside their control, or the reverse is possible as well (e.g., Ho, Chu, & Yiu, 2008). Who gets the credit or blame for a manuscript rejected for publication, a failure on a licensure exam, or a promotion at work? Chances are that a person's characteristic explanation for these events recurs across situations and over time. Do we expect good things to happen, or do we routinely prepare ourselves for disappointment? Perpetual optimists do tend to be happier, although their optimism is often a bit unrealistic considering the realities of life, according to Baumeister (1991).

Similar to how counselors develop professional theories to help them understand why their clients behave the way they do, people in everyday life develop lay(person) theories to explain the behavior that they observe every day. Molden and Dweck (2006) described two basic types of lay theories about the self: the entity theory (in which people believe that human attributes such as personality characteristics are fixed and cannot be changed) and the incremental theory (which is based on a fundamental belief that a person can indeed change such basic attributes over time). Research has indicated that most people tend to endorse one of these theories, although both theories may be held in different aspects of the self (e.g., a person may believe that shyness but not intelligence can be changed), and the preference for a given theory is not strongly correlated with education, ability, or cognitive complexity.

It may not matter much whether you believe you like to sing in the shower because your parents sang to you in childhood or because musicality runs in your family. In the case of more crucial life issues though, it may matter very much indeed how you and others interpret your ability to change. You might assume, for instance, that your romantic partner cannot change messy behaviors because these habits reflect innate personality traits. If you believe that most or all irritating habits can be changed given the proper motivation and guidance, you are likely to approach a long-term commitment with a certain blithe optimism. If you are depressed, your underlying theory may prompt you either to respond with a renewed resolve to do something about your life or to admit defeat. Whether people's theories actually hold up in real life depends on a range of factors they may not be able to influence (e.g., another person's willingness to change or the presence of organizational skills).

Political Ideology

Another common yet fascinating difference in how people make sense out of the world is related to political ideology. Dating back to the French Revolution, discussions of political ideology have distinguished between conservative ("right-wing") supporters of the status quo and liberal ("left-wing") supporters of egalitarian social change. The simple description of self on a continuum from strongly liberal (left) to strongly conservative (right) has been linked to pervasive differences far beyond the election booth that encompass general views regarding tradition and social change (Jost, Nosek, & Gosling, 2008). Liberals tend to advocate social change in the direction of greater equality, whereas conservatives generally favor maintaining the status quo and a hierarchical social order. As Jost et al. (2008) concluded, liberals favor flexibility and progress, whereas conservatives support stability and tradition. Because of the impressive range of attitudinal and behavioral correlations their research demonstrated, Jost and his associates proposed that this political distinction actually reflects a pervasive structuring of people's meaning making that influences their thoughts, feelings, and behaviors concerning stability/change and equality/ inequality in general. Not surprisingly then, contextual influences ranging from threats (e.g., from terrorism) to exposure to novel experiences (e.g., via education or career) can impact one's ideology.

There appears to be an obvious connection between people's meaning making and their behavior, but the nature of this link in a particular person's life might not be as clear as we would expect. How people interpret life events can influence in many ways how they respond to them. People like to believe that their behavior is consistent with, and predictable from, their beliefs and values. We admire people who say what they mean and who follow up their assertions with actions, or who vote in the election booth and in the marketplace with their money in ways consistent with what is important to them. As any clergy member will tell you, what people say they believe and what they actually do can be miles apart. In the ecological perspective we remind ourselves to look for reasons to support a long shot as well as to bet on a sure thing. We teach our clients how to do so as well so that they can learn how to win their important races in the racetrack of life.

I next turn to *how* people do this thinking, or the process of meaning making. This topic has inspired thousands of research projects, classes in graduate school, and professional careers devoted to unraveling its complexities. My intent here is to inspire you to wonder how a client's cognitive gifts and habits might help to explain recurring patterns of thinking about his or her life.

The Process of Meaning Making

The process of meaning making refers to *how* individuals make meaning, or the variability across individuals in the cognitive process of perceiving and understanding phenomena. Processes people use to make decisions about romantic partners or new cars, memorize facts before an exam or lines in a play, draw conclusions about the guilt of a defendant in a trial or a candidate's promise as a politician—all of these and more differ partly because of what information we have at hand but also what we do cognitively to process information.

For example, two sisters recently discussed what new car the family should buy. One sister consulted online resources to learn about fossil fuel consumption, argued for certain luxury features, speculated how certain models would enhance family vacations, and (to preserve her social status) flatly refused to consider the possibility of driving her parents' first choices. The other sister suggested getting a car with four wheels, a roof, and a cup holder in the back seat. There are profound differences between these sisters in the complexity of the information they can process and the criteria they can use in making decisions. The *process* of their meaning making is decidedly different.

In discussing the process of meaning making, we refer to tools or strategies that human beings use when they think. Some processes are true of all conscious human beings; other processes can be developed to their fullest potential through training and education. We know, for example, that young humans rely on thinking processes based on data gathered by their senses (concrete thinking), and many humans, but not all, eventually develop the capacity to think about symbols created by other humans—a marvelous abstraction that is the sine qua non of formal education. Highly concrete individuals (such as the second sister in the car shopping example) may lead satisfying lives without thinking abstractly; if no humans thought abstractly, the world as we know it would cease to exist.

The most familiar category of differences in meaning-making processes is what we label *intelligence*. Americans typically think of intelligent people as possessing a vast array of factual information (e.g., contestants on the television program *Jeopardy!*) and interest in lifelong learning. Notions about intelligence are culturally specific, however. For example, in Asian countries humility, self-knowledge, and knowledge of external conditions are components of intelligence; in Kenya the ability to adapt to the environment is key (Sternberg & Grigorenko, 2004). Regardless of its form, interaction with the environment is required to develop and maintain intelligence throughout life.

Other personal qualities that affect meaning-making processes are professional expertise and wisdom. People who have developed expertise in professional fields can organize, retrieve, and evaluate information more effectively than others, see patterns (e.g., identify big ideas dominant in their field) inherent in disparate pieces of information, retrieve information relevant to a question, and consequently solve complicated problems in their discipline more effectively (e.g., Bransford, Brown, & Cocking, 1999). In a similar vein, people rich in wisdom are able to think about their own and others' thinking processes, avoid habitual thinking patterns, and frame solutions to problems that integrate opposing perspectives and are deeply insightful in their problem solving. In addition to these cognitive skills they have affective skills that permit them to be empathic and concerned with others (Hanna, Bemak, & Chung, 1999).

To some extent specific problem-solving capacities are honed within disciplines (e.g., how a scientist devises an innovative experiment vs. how an artist paints a masterpiece), but crucial thinking skills can apply across disciplines (e.g., the ability to communicate thoughts clearly via writing). Expert educators intentionally try to foster the broader thinking abilities useful across diverse life situations, a process of teaching and learning that goes beyond simple mastery of facts. Thus, it is probably not important whether you remember Latin verb conjugations (*amo, amas, amat* anyone?) or the details of photosynthesis, but effective instructors taught you how to think in ways you use today.

Researchers now understand that social and cognitive development processes are inextricably linked from early childhood. In particular, social-cognitive developmental theory and research (Olson & Dweck, 2008) focus on how developmental influences (e.g., parents' child-rearing practices) and outcomes (e.g., academic performance) in a child's life are connected by how the child processes and understands early life events. Olson and Dweck (2008) labeled this mental work the child does *mental representations and processes.* These complex social/cognitive developmental linkages can help to explain the diversity apparent across children's responses to similar life events. Olson and Dweck concluded that "mental representations play a central role in achievement motivation . . . how achievement motivation operates, how environments may foster it, and how interventions may change it" (p. 196). If one child labels academic difficulties as attributable to his or her innate incompetence and another labels them as manageable through personal effort and others' help, the long-term consequences for each child's life are not difficult to imagine.

Many counselors are familiar with stage or phase developmental approaches, which specify the tasks typically expected of individuals during a certain period of life (e.g., beginning a family in early adulthood) and qualities either needed to cope with, or developed as a consequence of coping successfully with, the developmental task (e.g., the quality of emotional intimacy needed for and developed in response to tasks of parenting). Eriksen (2006) described how constructive stage theories in general account for progressive changes in how individuals make meaning, changes that evolve as people respond to new environments that challenge customary ways of thinking (e.g., Kegan, 1982; Loevinger, 1976). In other words, the process of *how* people think about life changes such that they take increasing responsibility for how they make sense of the world. Their thinking about their lives becomes more flexible and complex and they become more tolerant of differences and able to resolve conflicts. These differences are not simply differences in the *quantity* of information processed, as in knowing more facts about life, but are *qualitative* differences, in that the manner in which life is understood is no longer the same. (Eriksen, 2006, provides a very readable overview of Kegan's fascinating yet dense theory, with examples of what might happen when family members' or counselor and client developmental levels do not match.)

Finally, one cognitive process variable that frequently appears in the counseling literature is *cognitive complexity,* or "the ability to absorb, integrate, and make use of multiple perspectives" (Granello, 2010, p. 92). Cognitively complex counselors may be more able to recognize, integrate, and work with a broad range of client information, including apparent inconsistencies (Lambie & Sias, 2009). Counselor trainees and practitioners appear to exhibit a range of cognitive complexity levels that may influence their ability to process complex social/cognitive information about their clients and the counseling relationship (cf. Lambie, Hagedorn, & Ieva, 2010; Welfare & Borders, 2010).

It is clear that people differ in both how and what they think about events in their own lives. Our cognitive patterns are crucial to our ability

117

to make sense of the world in which we live. However, some individuals, like plants, become rootbound—the structures that are meant to protect us become too small for us, choking our growth. By challenging familiar thinking patterns, counseling relationships can re-pot us in new cognitive patterns that allow us room to thrive once again.

Making Meaning About One's Life

So far I have focused on meaning making in everyday life: how people perceive and respond to the day-to-day events that make up our lives over time. If we think of weaving our lives on a cosmic loom, making meaning of our lives as a whole requires stepping back to look at the design that emerges over time; coming in close, we can see the design elements and colors that are added each day, elaborating the overall design. The grander design—how people make sense of their lives as a whole—is the life narrative. McAdams and Pals (2006) explained life narratives as follows:

> Beyond dispositional traits and characteristic adaptations, human lives vary with respect to the integrative life stories, or personal narratives, that individuals construct to make meaning and identity in the modern world . . . Narrative identity is . . . [the] story a person tries to "keep going"—an internalized and evolving narrative of the self that incorporates the reconstructed past and the imagined future into a more or less coherent whole in order to provide the person's life with some degree of unity, purpose, and meaning. (pp. 209–210)

All of us engage in this type of storytelling about ourselves. This process overlooks our inconsistencies in favor of an implicit integrity within ourselves; makes sense of our diverse, often baffling experiences; and allows us to make coherent decisions about our unfolding life paths. McAdams and Pals (2006) asserted that here culture exerts its greatest influence on us by providing the "menu of themes, images, and plots" (p. 211) we use to elaborate our presumably unique stories. The frameworks and values expressed in the stories (e.g., the valuing of redemption and generativity at midlife) might be anchored in our parent culture, but the details are poignantly our own (see also Cohen, 2006).

Counselors who adopt narrative approaches (e.g., Savickas, 2005) believe that throughout each of our lives, we enact key assumptions or plotlines that shape our life experiences, much as a skilled fiction writer develops a storyline from beginning to end. Our life patterns over time often express central themes that we strive to enact through the choices we make. In the words of Brown and Augusta-Scott (2007),

> We seek to make sense of our lives and experiences by ascribing meaning through stories . . . Stories do not simply represent us or mirror lived events—they constitute us, shaping our lives and our relationships . . . Stories organize, structure, and give meaning to events in our lives and help us make sense of our experiences. (p. ix)

Although these stories are profoundly personal, they are grounded in our relationships with the world around us. How we explain our lives to ourselves inevitably incorporates broad cultural assumptions about the roles we can play as actors within our life stories; we use the language, symbols, explanations, and relationships that constitute our social lives to communicate these critical life meanings.

Lafrance and Stoppard (2007) used these ideas to help explain women's experience of depression. Their interviews with women struggling with depression suggested the importance of cultural ideals: "practices of femininity" prescribing what it means to be a "good woman" (p. 26; emphasis in the original). These women articulated "stories of their daily lives consumed by domestic practices and governed by the needs of others" (p. 26). These women's cultural climate considered women to be suited by nature for seemingly endless caregiving. When they reached the limits of their resources, their physical and emotional exhaustion was compounded with self-blame for their inability to deal with daunting life demands that they presumed other women could handle. In this perspective healing requires depressed women to *restory* (italics Lafrance and Stoppard's) their lives through appreciating the power of ubiquitous cultural ideals about being a good woman and substituting more realistic and empowering ways to think about their lives.

Fundamental meanings have the power to constrain our lives in ways we do not perceive. A turning point in counseling relationships is when the client realizes that his or her familiar meaning making is not the only way to understand life and that changing core life meanings can open the door to a new life. To use a familiar adage, fish are not aware that they are swimming in water (my apologies to fish if I am mistaken). We humans are capable of knowing where we swim. We can choose other waters if the water around us is polluted; we can learn how to swim better in the water we have; some resilient humans are even amphibious, capable of living on—or in—all sorts of physical contexts! It is this very potential to become aware of the nature and relativity of our life's grounding that gives us hope for the future.

Meaning Making and Resilience

Coping begins with and proceeds through the process of meaning making. For example, a person first perceives a life situation as significant to her. The manner in which she then perceives features of the situation (catastrophic? irritating? mildly stressful?), its relevance for her important life goals, the resources she perceives she currently has or can access, and her likely success in handling the situation are all aspects of meaning making involved in coping (e.g., Folkman & Moskowitz, 2004; Lent, 2004). People who are generally successful at coping—resilient individuals—are concerned with finding meaningful purpose in life and believe that they can both learn from and at least partially influence events in their lives. They tend to view themselves very positively; contrary to what grandmother said, being "full of yourself" may not always be such a bad thing after all! Resilient people may also be skilled in avoiding thoughts about unpleasant events and may be able to exhibit positive emotions and laugh after adversity (Bonanno, 2004).

When a person must cope with life stressors that endure for some time, such as illness or caring for others, meaning making is literally life giving (Folkman & Moskowitz, 2004). We have all witnessed people drawing on extraordinary energy reserves out of sheer determination—a family member of mine danced at his daughter's wedding and hugged well wishers despite being in the last stage of excruciatingly painful metastatic bone cancer. For people in situations that require a different type of courage over time (e.g., raising a disabled child), finding some broader meaning in one's moment-to-moment sacrifices can determine whether they regard life with bitterness or equanimity, even gratitude. In our own ways all of us prevail during daunting circumstances simply because it is important to do so.

Meaning Making in Extremis: Living After Loss

Meaning making can help us endure the unendurable. How we view the tragedies of our lives can make all the difference between surviving and giving up. Consider the story of Jennifer Callahan and Mark Dittloff (2007), a couple eagerly awaiting the birth of their first child, Samantha Taylor Dittloff. Samantha died in utero while her parents sped to the hospital for her birth. On learning of her baby's death, Jennifer recounted, "I was suddenly aware of how pain can reach such an intolerable level that remission is unfathomable" (p. 548). She briefly considered suicide but "concluded that such an act would invalidate my daughter. Without me to remember her, it would be as if she had never existed. In that moment, a mother was born" (p. 548). Through this understanding she derived the strength to deliver her dead daughter in the hospital and to begin a motherhood with her daughter living in memory.

Jennifer's husband Mark also faced a crisis of meaning, but his was more philosophical in tone. Before this tragedy Mark "did not believe in losing; be it talent, wit, work ethic, or patience, I would find a way to win" (p. 550). As a result of their baby's death, Mark

> had lost something priceless and had been powerless to stop it from occurring, which created an existential crisis for me . . . Had I been perceiving situations wrongly my whole life? If I was not perceiving reality accurately, how could I trust myself to draw the right conclusions in the future? Suddenly, nothing that I had thought I knew was certain. (p. 550)

These parents instantly realized that the very foundation on which life was based had shifted forever and that they could never view themselves and their possibilities the same again. Through their unique experience of suffering, each partner eventually found his and her own way to integrate this traumatic experience into future family and professional life.

120

Sandler, Wolchik, and Ayers (2008) explained that bereavement disrupts familiar person–environment interactions and performance of roles. Over time bereaved individuals must learn new ways to satisfy their basic needs and engage in developmentally appropriate competencies, an adaptational process that is influenced by both personal and environmental factors. It will make a difference, of course, if a person's coping is complicated by factors such as preexisting psychological or substance abuse problems or perhaps having experienced considerable adversity in childhood (Neimeyer, Prigerson, & Davies, 2002).

How both children and adults eventually interpret the loss in the context of their lives thereafter is crucial. Especially for children, the loss of a beloved caregiver can snowball into continued family stressors and decisions (e.g., choices of peers) that complicate life immeasurably. Sandler et al. (2008) proposed the term *contextual resilience* to emphasize the interactional nature of this process. As Davis, Wohl, and Verberg (2007) noted, the process of posttraumatic growth appears to involve diverse types of appraisals of loss and corresponding meaning making. Some people lose a sense of the world as benevolent; others tend to focus on what meaning this event has for themselves and their lives. The same horrific loss (in Davis et al.'s study, a mine disaster) can be associated with "multiple paths to adjustment" (p. 710) as people struggle to rebuild a life worth living. Differences in how people process and make sense out of grief may also occur cross-culturally because of social relationship patterns, but here there are more questions than answers (e.g., Pressman & Bonanno, 2007). In general, living after a death requires struggling with wrenching questions of meaning that ultimately lead to a reconstructed self in a world that has lost its veneer of innocence.

For those who have experienced the loss of a beloved person, the crisis of meaning that can attend bereavement is a second, often unrecognized process of loss. Grieving individuals often question the meaning of tragedy: Why me? Why the people I love? How can I trust my God and hope in the future? In particular, unexpected crises—for example, a natural disaster or stillbirth—or those that occur out of their proper time—for example, becoming widowed before age 30—can be so wrenching that, in the words of one grieving individual, "it feels like a hole opened up in the universe and everything I love has fallen into it. I may never be able to walk around it" (personal correspondence). Experts on grief (e.g., Sandler et al., 2008) now teach that there is no one series of stages all grief-stricken people must navigate in order, no set time period distinguishing normal from abnormal grieving. The grieving process may be similar in certain ways across individuals, but the process of finding new meaning out of the incomprehensible is exquisitely personal.

To summarize briefly, when coping with grief after a terrible loss it is important to be able to make some sense of the loss, often in terms of philosophical or spiritual meaning (e.g., Keesee, Currier, & Neimeyer, 2008). It is not enough to simply search for meanings after trauma; people need to arrive at a new set of meanings about life (see Updegraff, Silver, & Holman, 2008, about meaning making after 9/11). Sandler et al. (2008)

advised counselors to "think of bereaved individuals as active agents who are aware of their experiences, capabilities and needs and who can benefit from support, information, guidance, and skill instruction to find ways to meet those needs" (pp. 68–69). Counselors willing to accompany clients as they reorient after life tragedies can help clients move ahead into a landscape of life whose contours have forever changed.

Summary

Meaning making is the process whereby humans perceive, understand, and predict what happens during their lives. It happens so frequently, so automatically that we take it for granted simply as the ways things are. Only when the process fails to work its magic—when we succumb to dementia perhaps, or if our autistic child seems to live in a universe we cannot begin to comprehend—do we appreciate how creative and stabilizing our meaning-making process is.

Meaning making is what makes our species unique and what makes each human different from every other. No one else exactly shares our exquisitely personal way of imposing sense on the billion random observations that make up everyday life. This process consists of content we have learned since birth—some of it common to others sharing our sociocultural context and some of it the private consequences of our moment-to-moment processing of life circumstances. Without knowing it we use habits of processing too. These habits, the how of meaning making, are composed of some combination of shared human capacities and of individual modes of processing rooted in our own genetic heritage and developed through progressively more complex life lessons. We do not cease to develop our meaning-making capacities until death. For some of us living a comfortingly familiar life, the changes over time may be relatively small. For others, who stretch their capacities through exposure to novel information and challenges to the limits of their ways of thinking about the world, progressive changes in meaning making can keep them intellectually, emotionally, and spiritually vital until the day they die.

Although challenges to meaning making nourish growth in how and what we think, some challenges can destroy the meaning-based framework that grants us security and confidence. Certain life traumas can leave us feeling bereft of navigational devices on a stormy sea, such as a previously inconceivable loss that leaves us in spiritual vertigo. Death in its finality can bereave us so completely—the death of a beloved being, to be sure, but also a private death of purpose, identity, order, or safety on a magnitude that leaves us a stranger in a strange land. To reestablish life on a sure footing we need to feel our way into a sadder but wiser view of life that understands loss as inevitable but potentially transformative. Some losses ultimately leave us surviving but not thriving; the psychic scars are simply too deep and wide. Counselors working with these individuals need to respect the gravity of such losses yet also need to remember that there is no timetable for recovering the loss of life's meaning, no predetermined sequence of stages to be mastered in due time. Human beings are capable of continuing life with all its impossible losses and all its unexpected joys, following their own process of grief and reaffirmation of hope once again.

Meaning making that attends profound loss represents an extreme form of the process that makes human life unique in Earth's ecosystem. As far as we know, humans are the only living beings capable of choosing to end life because we are no longer able to make any sense of it or choosing to leave our life context because it no longer nourishes us in a way that we view as crucial to life. The process of confrontation and healing occurs throughout life in mini-cycles of challenge and response, leaving us with an ever so slightly or significantly altered set of information, presumptions, hypotheses, and processes to use in confronting the next challenge. Our meaning making is more than thinking about life; it is *living* itself that continues even when all other activity has ceased (e.g., through dreaming during sleep). Some humans believe that this process continues beyond death itself.

The ecological perspective described in this book is unique from others in the literature because of the emphasis it places on meaning making. Ecological thinking in general relies on person–environment terminology and processes, emphasizing the unique products of this interaction. My coauthors and I believe that meaning making is more than simply something that happens after people interact with their environments. We believe that to understand people in context we must recognize meaning making as always operating in some capacity, because that is what human beings do. We are constantly in the process of perceiving and trying to make sense of what happens to us, and then we respond on the basis of this meaning making. Counselors who appreciate the power of meaning making can assist people to notice how they are making meaning and then make decisions about their lives with this understanding in mind.

Discussion Questions

- For the next few minutes, write down as many descriptors as you can for the following sentenced stems: "Men are . . . " "Women are . . . " How many of the descriptors in each set are positive, and how many are negative? How have these stereotypes of yours changed over time? What have you learned in formal education or personal study about the nature of these stereotypes? Compare your list with someone else's and look for similarities and differences.

- Spend some time thinking about your religious/spiritual development. How did your experiences early in life (e.g., in your family or with a faith-based community) affect your thinking today? Are you satisfied with your own development thus far, or do you need to work on clarifying and implementing your religious/spiritual beliefs and practices?

- Think back to a time when your meaning making was severely tested, whether through death or some other significant change (perhaps the divorce of your parents or the loss of a job you assumed you would always have). What helped you cope during this time? How do you think you were changed?

- Imagine that you are asked to be a commencement speaker at your alma mater. Your topic is "what I have learned about life since graduation." What are some important points you would want to cover? How did you learn these things over time?

References

Agars, M. D. (2004). Reconsidering the impact of gender stereotypes on the advancement of women in organizations. *Psychology of Women Quarterly, 28*, 103–111.

Bandura, A. (2006). Toward a psychology of human agency. *Perspectives on Psychological Science, 1*, 164–178.

Baumeister, R. E. (1991). *Meanings of life.* New York, NY: Guilford Press.

Biernat, M. (2003). Toward a broader view of social stereotyping. *American Psychologist, 58*, 1019–1027.

Bonanno, G. A. (2004). Loss, trauma, and human resilience: Have we underestimated the human capacity to thrive after extremely aversive events? *American Psychologist, 59*, 20–28.

Boysen, G. A. (2010). Integrating implicit bias into counselor education. *Counselor Education and Supervision, 49*, 210–226.

Bransford, J. D., Brown, A. L., & Cocking, R. R. (Eds.). (1999). *How people learn: Brain, mind, experience, and school.* Washington, DC: National Academies Press.

Brown, C., & Augusta-Scott, T. (Eds.). (2007). *Narrative therapy: Making meaning, making lives.* Thousand Oaks, CA: Sage.

Bussey, K., & Bandura, A. (1999). Social cognitive theory of gender development and differentiation. *Psychological Review, 106*, 676–713.

Callahan, J. L., & Dittloff, M. J. (2007). Through a glass darkly: Reflections on therapist transformations. *Professional Psychology: Research and Practice, 38*, 547–553.

Cohen, L. (2006). Remembrance of things past: Cultural process and practice in the analysis of career stories. *Journal of Vocational Behavior, 69*, 189–201.

Crosby, F. J., Iyer, A., & Sincharoen, S. (2006). Understanding affirmative action. *Annual Review of Psychology, 57*, 585–611.

Davis, C. G., Wohl, M. J., & Verberg, N. (2007). Profiles of posttraumatic growth following an unjust loss. *Death Studies, 31*, 693–712.

Eccles, J. S., & Wigfield, A. (2002). Motivational beliefs, values, and goals. *Annual Review of Psychology, 53*, 109–132.

Emmons, R. A., & Paloutzian, R. F. (2003). The psychology of religion. *Annual Review of Psychology, 54*, 377–402.

Eriksen, K. (2006). The constructive developmental theory of Robert Kegan. *The Family Journal, 14*, 290–298.

Fiedler, K. (2008). Language: A toolbox for sharing and influencing social reality. *Perspectives on Psychological Science, 3*, 38–47.

Folkman, S., & Moskowitz, J. T. (2004). Coping: Pitfalls and promise. *Annual Review of Psychology, 55*, 745–774.

Frankl, V. (1963). *Man's search for meaning.* New York, NY: Washington Square Press.

Granello, D. H. (2010). Cognitive complexity among practicing counselors: How thinking changes with experience. *Journal of Counseling & Development, 88*, 92–100.

Greenfield, P. M. (2009). Linking social change and developmental change: Shifting pathways of human development. *Developmental Psychology, 45*, 401–418.

Hanna, F. J., Bemak, F., & Chung, R. C. (1999). Toward a new paradigm for multicultural counseling. *Journal of Counseling & Development, 77*, 125–134.

Hayes, R. L., & Oppenheim, R. (1997). Constructivism: Reality is what you make it. In T. L. Sexton & B. L. Griffin (Eds.), *Constructivist thinking in counseling practice, research, and training* (pp. 19–40). New York, NY: Teachers College Press.

Ho, S. M. Y., Chu, K. W., & Yiu, J. (2008). The relationship between explanatory style and posttraumatic growth after bereavement in a non-clinical sample. *Death Studies, 32*, 461–478.

Hutchison, E. D. (2008). *Dimensions of human behavior: The changing life course.* Thousand Oaks, CA: Sage.

Jost, J. T., Nosek, B. A., & Gosling, S. D. (2008). Ideology: Its resurgence in social, personality, and political psychology. *Perspectives on Psychological Science, 3*, 126–136.

Keesee, N. J., Currier, J. M., & Neimeyer, R. A. (2008). Predictors of grief following the death of one's child: The contribution of finding meaning. *Journal of Clinical Psychology, 64*, 1145–1163.

Kegan, R. (1982). *The evolving self.* Cambridge, MA: Harvard University Press.

Koltko-Rivera, M. E. (2004). The psychology of worldviews. *Review of General Psychology, 8*, 1–56.

Lafrance, M. N., & Stoppard, J. M. (2007). Re-storying women's depression: A material-discursive approach. In C. Brown & T. Augusta-Scott (Eds.), *Narrative therapy: Making meaning, making lives* (pp. 23–37). Thousand Oaks, CA: Sage.

Lambie, G. W., Hagedorn, W. B., & Ieva, K. P. (2010). Social-cognitive development, ethical and legal knowledge, and ethnical decision making of counselor education students. *Counselor Education and Supervision, 49*, 228–246.

Lambie, G. W., & Sias, S. M. (2009). An integrative psychological developmental model of supervision for professional school counselors in training. *Journal of Counseling & Development, 87*, 349–356.

Lent, R. W. (2004). Toward a unifying theoretical and practical perspective on well-being and psychosocial adjustment. *Journal of Counseling Psychology, 51*, 482–509.

Lightsey, O. R. (2006). Resilience, meaning, and well-being. *The Counseling Psychologist, 34*, 96–107.

Liu, W. M., & Ali, S. R. (2005). Addressing social class and classism in vocational theory and practice: Extending the emancipator communitarian approach. *The Counseling Psychologist, 33,* 189–196.

Liu, W. M., & Pope-Davis, D. B. (2004). Understanding classism to effect personal change. In T. B. Smith (Ed.), *Practicing multiculturalism* (pp. 294–310). Boston, MA: Pearson.

Loevinger, J. (1976). *Ego development.* San Francisco, CA: Jossey-Bass.

Lott, B. (2001). Low-income parents and the public schools. *Journal of Social Issues, 57,* 247–259.

Major, B., & O'Brien, L. T. (2005). The social psychology of stigma. *Annual Review of Psychology, 56,* 393–421.

McAdams, D. P., & Pals, J. L. (2006). A new Big Five: Fundamental principles for an integrative science of personality. *American Psychologist, 61,* 204–217.

Molden, D. C., & Dweck, C. S. (2006). Finding "meaning" in psychology: A lay theories approach to self-regulation, social perception, and social development. *American Psychologist, 61,* 192–203.

Neimeyer, R. A., Prigerson, H. G., & Davies, B. (2002). Mourning and meaning. *American Behavioral Scientist, 46,* 235–251.

Olson, K. R., & Dweck, C. S. (2008). A blueprint for social cognitive development. *Perspectives on Psychological Science, 3,* 193–202.

Overton, S. L., & Medina, S. L. (2008). The stigma of mental illness. *Journal of Counseling & Development, 86,* 143–151.

Pargament, K. I. (2008). The sacred character of community life. *American Journal of Community Psychology, 41,* 22–34.

Park, C. L. (2005). Religion as a meaning-making framework in coping with life stress. *Journal of Social Issues, 61,* 707–729.

Pressman, D. L., & Bonanno, G. A. (2007). With whom do we grieve? Social and cultural determinants of grief processing in the United States and China. *Journal of Social and Personal Relationships, 24,* 729–746.

Sandler, I. W., Wolchik, S. A., & Ayers, T. S. (2008). Resilience rather than recovery: A contextual framework on adaptation following bereavement. *Death Studies, 32,* 59–73.

Savickas, M. L. (2005). The theory and practice of career construction. In S. D. Brown & R. W. Lent (Eds.), *Career development and counseling: Putting theory and research to work* (pp. 42–70). Hoboken, NJ: Wiley.

Schneider, D. J. (2004). *The psychology of stereotyping.* New York, NY: Guilford.

Smith, L. (2005). Psychotherapy, classism, and the poor: Conspicuous by their absence. *American Psychologist, 60,* 687–696.

Steger, M., Frazier, P., Oishi, S., & Kaler, M. (2006). The meaning in life questionnaire: Assessing the presence of and search for meaning in life. *Journal of Counseling Psychology, 53,* 80–93.

Sternberg, R. J., & Grigorenko, E. L. (2004). Why we need to explore development in its cultural context. *Merrill-Palmer Quarterly, 50,* 369–386.

Sue, D. W., Capodilupo, C. M., Torino, G. C., Bucceri, J. M., Holder, A. M. B., Nadal, K. L., & Esquilin, M. (2007). Racial microaggressions in everyday life: Implications for clinical practice. *American Psychologist, 62,* 271–286.

Sue, D., & Sue, D. M. (2008). *Foundations of counseling and psychotherapy: Evidence-based practices for a diverse society.* Hoboken, NJ: Wiley.

Updegraff, J. A., Silver, R., & Holman, E. A. (2008). Searching for and finding meaning in collective trauma: Results from a national longitudinal study of the 9/11 terrorist attacks. *Journal of Personality and Social Psychology, 95,* 709–722.

Vasquez, M. (2007). Cultural differences and the therapeutic alliance: An evidence-based alliance. *American Psychologist, 62,* 878–885.

Welfare, L. E., & Borders, L. D. (2010). Counselor cognitions: General and domain-specific complexity. *Counselor Education and Supervision, 49,* 162–178.

Wilson, T. D. (2009). Know thyself. *Perspectives on Psychological Science, 4,* 384–389.

Yoo, H. C., Burrola, K. S., & Steger, M. F. (2010). A preliminary report on a new measure. *Journal of Counseling Psychology, 57,* 114–127.

Young, R. A., & Collin, A. (2004). Introduction: Constructivism and social constructionism in the career field. *Journal of Vocational Behavior, 64,* 373–388.

Behavior Is Changeable

Ellen P. Cook and Susannah C. Coaston

Using the ecological perspective, counselors can help individuals and groups behave more effectively in the present and future by changing the person–environment interaction. This work proceeds through addressing relevant personal, contextual, interactional, or meaning-making concerns. The perspective also encourages counselors to help implement broader macrolevel changes through educational, consulting, and social justice initiatives. We begin this chapter on counseling practice with a scenario that may occur in counselors' offices everywhere.

Roberto anxiously asks his internship group for some new strategies to use with his client Juan. Juan is currently homeless and unemployed. He lives in his car but every day tries to see his three children, who live with his estranged wife. Roberto's efforts to help Juan get housing, food, employment, and medical assistance for his chronic ailments have run into one roadblock after another because of the economy. Juan is getting more and more frustrated and confesses that he has thought about using drugs and hurting someone, both problems he has had in the past. Juan wonders why he is working so hard to stay out of trouble—at least in jail he would have food and somebody to talk with. He feels depressed, isolated, and of "no worth to nobody," feelings that originated in his abusive childhood. Roberto's onsite supervisor feels stumped too, but Roberto hopes there is something else he can do to help.

Roberto's dilemma is played out in community agencies and counseling classrooms all over the country. Clients who request help from community agencies present with layer upon layer of challenges: poverty, difficult childhoods, difficult family lives, unemployment and little promise of change, substance abuse, relationship violence, anxiety and depression, and so on. Counselors who customarily refer environmental challenges to other agencies find that these agencies are grossly underfunded and overwhelmed. The gap between need and available assistance gets bigger every year. The burden often falls on the shoulders of newly trained, underpaid counselors and trainees like Roberto.

And what of the counseling process itself? Where to start? Past privations or present crises? Marital stress, job training, or identity confusion? No supportive friendships, functional illiteracy, or thinking patterns that lead to depression? Are counselors who focus on present stressors rather than past traumas being realistic or trying to put a Band-Aid on a deep wound?

If we could provide definitive answers to any of these questions, our own future career concerns would vanish forever in the wake of nonstop speaking engagements! All we can say definitively is that there *are no* simple definitive answers to these questions. Human behavior rarely has simple causes and corrections. We may desire to unravel and reweave the fabric of our clients' lives, but human lives tend to be messy, knotted creations with no clear beginning or ending point to the tangled spots.

The ecological perspective reminds us that we don't need to choose between attending to the past versus the present or to the environment versus the psyche. At any given time a person's life is a work in progress. In many situations all counselors can do—which is a great deal indeed—is to help a person behave more effectively in the present and future by changing the person–environment interaction. This work proceeds through addressing relevant personal, contextual, interactional, or meaning-making concerns. It may not be obvious where to begin, because these dimensions are inseparable. And just how a counselor thinks about the relevant concerns in a client's life depends on his or her own theoretical framework, values, skills, available resources, and so on—myriad factors that contribute to the uniqueness of the counseling process. No two counselors work in precisely the same way, and that diversity is a strength of our profession. The ecological perspective is intended to help counselors do what they already do well but to do so more consistently and effectively.

Professionals can use the ecological perspective in two ways. The concepts can stimulate new thinking about familiar parameters of a professional's existing conceptual base. For example, a counselor who utilizes a cognitive–behavioral approach might have fresh ideas about how clients' thinking patterns contribute to their life situations. In this example, the counselor maintains a cognitive–behavioral orientation but integrates aspects of the ecological perspective consistent with his or her current practice, consulting with other professionals as needed.

Alternatively, a counselor might wish to integrate ecological principles explicitly into his or her practice. In this case, the ecological terms and processes could serve as guiding principles in defining an integrative model for counseling practice. In this chapter we consider key applications of the ecological perspective that are likely to be helpful to counselors across theoretical orientations and client populations. But first we review some principles about human behavior discussed in previous chapters that are particularly salient to practicing counselors.

A Review of Basic Principles of the Ecological Perspective

The ecological perspective does not claim to provide a superior set of constructs, interventions, or recommendations for practice guaranteed to keep clients clamoring for your services. It is not meant to replace any theoretical approaches favored by counselors today. However, counselors who adopt the ecological perspective as a framework for practice do see that it offers some common denominators to unite diverse perspectives.

Just what is the nature of these common denominators? In earlier chapters it was suggested that certain themes regarding human behavior tend to recur in the professional literature and originate in a particular metaphor about human life: Life is an ecology featuring a unique, sentient organism who is dependent on and contributes to the myriad contexts surrounding him or her. These life contexts are both interpersonal (e.g., relationships) and impersonal (e.g., physical geography).

Consistent with a Western worldview, in the ecological perspective individuals are portrayed at the epicenter of a dynamic system represented by concentric circles, each level a type of systemic influence on their behavior (a subsystem within an overall ecosystem). These subsystems vary both in proximity to the person and according to the level of abstraction: from in-the-flesh, in-your-face daily relationships with others (microlevel) to the unseen but powerful sociocultural blueprints that grant form and function to our congregated social life (macrolevel). Behavior is described within the ecological perspective according to individual idiosyncrasies both inborn and learned over time, the life contexts at play within a person's ecosystem, and the unique synergy of the person interacting within the configuration of life contexts at a particular point of time.

Life is a series of meaning-filled interactions over time. Life is not a matter of internal psyche versus external influences but rather a fluid interplay in which we become people-in-relationship with our world, both inside and outside our skins. People produce their own development in terms of how they interact with others and various contexts throughout life.

What makes this ecological interaction different from that experienced by any other living creature is the human organism's ability to reflect on, understand, and consciously choose life events. We may never know for sure just why a person behaves as he or she does. All of us live with the uncertainties of existence by using our cognitive capacities to process, predict, and communicate about experience. It is this meaning-making process that makes human life so *human*.

The ecological perspective, then, encompasses a broad range of interventions flowing from its basic propositions about behavior: Behavior is both personal and contextual—interactional (P × E)—and meaningful.

Because person–environment (or context) interaction is an ongoing process subject to an array of influences, behavior can be dramatically changed by altering the personal, contextual, interactional, or meaning-making processes that all operate continuously within a person's life. Counselors and clients work collaboratively to help clients create new possibilities for their lives. Clients are experts on their lives; counselors are experts on behavior change strategies. Yet this change process is rarely simple to accomplish: We cannot change past events, and we have a limited ability to change the present. Even so, the counseling process can be truly transformative. The results of counseling can be strictly internal (e.g., a feeling of new hope for life after a wrenching loss) or visible (e.g., a loss of weight). Sometimes the process requires sequential steps, one new learning at a time. Counseling can be a process of planting seeds for changes that the counselor will never witness because they take time to blossom.

Research to determine the "best" counseling interventions for a given problem has been disappointing to counselors seeking simple solutions to client problems. The fact that a variety of strategies can be helpful does not mean that just *anything* will work. Instead counselors need to have a broad understanding of the range of person, contextual, interactional, and meaning-related factors that are likely to be operating within a client's life and of the possibilities for change appropriate for a given client. Implementing the ecological perspective requires an open mind, a healthy respect for the complexities of human behavior, and a good dose of humility.

In teaching counselors about the ecological perspective, we have found two metaphors to be useful. One pertains to the counseling relationship (counselors are tour guides) and one pertains to interventions (counselors use toolboxes).

1. *Tour guides:* Through the counseling process we as counselors accompany our clients on a journey of change that the clients wish to make. We know the terrain, what psychic gear our clients will need for the trip, and how to guide depending on how our clients wish to travel (e.g., do they want to get to the destination quickly or allow the trip to unfold in a leisurely manner?). We try in numerous ways to help our clients get the most from their journey by helping them appreciate the history of the area (i.e., engaging in an in-depth exploration of the past), for example, or perhaps inviting others to join us on the journey (i.e., through group work). We need to learn which ways of getting to their destination our clients can tolerate and how to map new destinations if the original travel plans do not work.

2. *Toolboxes:* No counselor can be an expert in every type of behavior or client that might appear in the course of his or her work. And yet as the old saying goes, if all you have is a hammer (one kind of counseling intervention), then everything looks like a nail (every client needs your hammer)! Instead competent counselors rely on a toolbox of knowledge and strategies consistent with the range of person–environment (P × E) interactions that characterize his or her scope of practice. In other words, hammers are still useful tools, but with some client building projects you might need to use screwdrivers or saws instead. Learning the ecological perspective can add some new tools to the box or suggest novel uses for familiar tools. (It's possible to use a scotch tape dispenser to hammer nails for picture hooks, but we wouldn't recommend it.)

Regardless of whether you like either of these metaphors, the ecological counseling perspective can help you recognize the diversity of clients' presenting problems and ways of understanding them, the complexity of the interactional influences that create or maintain these problems, and the usefulness of seeing more than one potential solution to these dilemmas.

Here are some examples of how counselors use ecological ideas, adapted from actual circumstances:

> Counselor A visits elderly people in their homes. She identifies which functional living skills they have, identifies the challenges their living environments pose for them, and helps them make decisions about the best life contexts for them. In planning her visits, she tries to imagine how it feels to be them, especially considering the many physical, social, and personal losses they have experienced. She often discusses with them what it feels like to grow older.

> Counselor B is a high school counselor in an urban setting. He is determined to use a variety of strategies to help his students succeed: study skills sessions, career counseling that focuses on heightening students' aspirations, parent groups strategizing how they can support their children, health classes that show teens the realities of caring for small children. He organizes consultations with social services agencies and local clergy to brainstorm ways they can collaborate to support local teens.

> Counselor C specializes in working with adult women who have problems with depression and eating disorders. She explores with her clients how sociocultural expectations for women, including multiple role demands and unrealistic models for attractiveness presented in the media, play a role in their concerns. She encourages her clients to develop their female support systems and to write new life scripts for themselves to affirm their own capacities and values.

> Counselor D helps individuals with developmental disabilities make the transition from high school to adult living. He assesses his clients' independent living skills, the type of jobs they might enjoy doing, and which types of living arrangements fit their personalities and needs. He especially enjoys thinking about how to get the most bang for the buck: how certain social programs might enhance both present friendships and future independent living, for example. He likes to think of his clients not as limited but as lifelong learners who can increase their independence and happiness throughout their lives with the proper type of support.

These counselors appreciate how multifaceted people's problems are, and in their own ways they are incorporating ideas about person–environment interaction and meaning making in their work. Which of these examples comes closest to fitting your present approach to counseling?

The discussion thus far about ecological counseling has described the client as a single person. One remarkable feature of the ecological perspective is that the locus of the change process can be various levels of the overall ecosystem beyond the individual, for example, the classroom in which a child's targeted behavior takes place or the local media that depict unrealistic body images for adolescents. Within the ecological perspective developmental or preventive interventions that target specific segments of the population can effectively plant seeds for change in years to come. And counselors who use these interventions value the skills of other experts. Referral and consultation have a place of honor within the ecological perspective toolbox. As counselors we need to know our limits and how to work with others whose expertise complements our own.

In this chapter we discuss features of the change process in more detail. We begin with a discussion of problem identification (including diagnosis), which is followed by description of ecologically oriented strategies that counselors might find useful. We close with some examples of how we ourselves have implemented the ecological perspective through consultation and program development projects.

Individual Counseling in the Ecological Perspective

One of the first questions counselors ask in any counseling process is, Why is the client seeking help? What will we be addressing in our work together? The level of the contextual system under consideration determines goal setting and the type of intervention used. Most counseling today focuses on helping individual clients explore, understand, and act within their lives as they experience them. With the ecological perspective, we recognize that counseling can also encompass a broader range of targets and interventions, as we discuss later in this chapter. In this section, we begin with some general guidelines that counselors can use to formulate problem identification in a way that facilitates goal setting and strategy selection. Then we discuss how formal diagnostic procedures can fit within an ecological perspective.

General Guidelines in Problem Identification

Regardless of their focus, ecologically based counseling goals and their associated strategies have the following features:

- They require collaborative work between the counselor and client.
- They have *ecological validity* regarding the client's life situation (see below for a definition).
- They are meaningful, plausible, and feasible to the client.
- They draw on and enhance the client's existing resources and opportunities within life contexts.
- They may specify changes to the environment instead of, or in addition to, changes in the client.
- They explicitly address challenges or barriers to change within the client and his or her contexts.
- They may change as the client's understanding changes.

A crucial criterion in ecological counseling is that goals and strategies have *ecological validity,* that is, that they fit the interactional realities of clients' lives as they experience them. For example, imagine that a new graduate student shares with her advisor that she feels disconnected with the program and wonders whether it is a good fit for her. The advisor listens sympathetically, then suggests that she hang out during weekdays at the program offices so that she can interact informally with other students and faculty. A good solution? Yes—for someone else. The student is a divorced mother who cares for her toddler and works part time; she simply has no time to spare during the week. Instead the student decides to sponsor a biweekly Saturday potluck lunch/playgroup with several other students who are parents of young children. They don't get any studying done but swap program information and ideas for projects while their little ones run through her apartment. Soon the parents are sitting together in class. Which solution had the greatest ecological validity for this student?

One direct way to begin problem identification, and to maximize ecological validity in the process, is to describe the presenting problem in terms of P × E interaction. A list of questions counselors might consider when developing a detailed ecological picture of a client's concerns is provided in Table 6.1.

Recall the case of Jamie, mentioned in Chapter 3 (and drawn from Conyne & Cook, 2004). Jamie was a young girl with developmental disabilities who was in trouble with the school authorities because of her disruptive behavior on the school bus. Jamie simply did not "fit" on the bus. School personnel immediately assumed that Jamie's disabilities (person factors) were to blame and that she did not have the capacity to change her behavior quickly enough to ensure the safety of other riders and herself (P × E interaction, coping). School personnel were ready to require that Jamie and her distraught parents find another form of transportation.

Luckily, her parents turned to an agency that provided behavioral support to people like Jamie. An experienced staff member rode the same bus as Jamie for a few days and talked with Jamie's parents. She learned that riding the bus was very important to Jamie (meaning making) and that Jamie was capable of exerting some control over her behavior given appropriate inducements (strengths, coping). Her parents were willing to enact any type of transportation plan necessary for Jamie's welfare (resources) but were hoping that Jamie could continue riding the bus because it was so important to her (values, parenting skills as resources). They also believed that Jamie was capable of change and that the agency could be very helpful in arriving at a solution (meaning making).

The staff member quickly saw that Jamie's misbehavior was influenced by lax disciplinary procedures on the bus, encouragement from other children to misbehave, and Jamie's loneliness because other children didn't befriend her (context, P × E interaction, diversity issue involving stigmatization). The staff member also knew from experience that children like Jamie face negative expectations every day regarding their ability to adapt their behavior and fit in in typical school situations (coping, P × E interaction, meaning making of others regarding disabilities). A multifaceted set of interventions eliminated the problem: better discipline on the bus to remove bad examples and encouragement to misbehave (context, P × E interaction),

135

Table 6.1

Questions to Consider in Developing an Ecological Analysis

What does the client state as the problem? What does the manner of communication (e.g., language, vocal inflection, choice of words) tell you?

Why does the client seem to feel that professional help is needed at this time? What solutions has he or she tried already?

How is the problem situated within the client's ecology (e.g., who, what, when, where)? And what does it mean to the client?

What events does the client believe are important in his or her life situation? Has anything changed in the client's life? What impact have these changes had on the client, on people who are important to the client, on the person–environment interaction, or on client meaning making?

Where does the client live out his or her life physically and interpersonally (i.e., where is the client's ecological niche)? Does this niche seem to provide for his or her needs successfully? How does everyday life feel to the client? Is he or she generally content, dissatisfied, or miserable?

What are the client's important interactions with people? Groups? Community or neighborhood? Larger systems? How do these interactions influence the client's life? What life roles connect the client to the world around him or her? What does the client feel he or she contributes to others?

What relevance might the concepts of fit or synergy have in the client's life?

What personal characteristics (e.g., body, traits) seem to be influential in the client's present life? In what ways is the client unique? How do the client's personal characteristics interact with one another or with contextual features to create unique circumstances?

How resilient does the client appear? How does he or she tend to cope with problems in general? What makes the current situation different or more challenging from others the client has encountered?

What life roles and identities appear salient to the client? To others in the client's life? What sociocultural stresses and strengths appear to be at work? What diversity issues contribute to the person's sense of self and interactions with others? How do these numerous aspects integrate to form a unique self?

What values are central in the client's life? What does the client feel is the meaning of everyday life? What formal value systems (e.g., religion, military training) play an important role in the client's everyday life?

What impact does time have on the client? How does he or she experience time every day (e.g., is there too little or too much of it, is it going by too quickly or too slowly)? Where does the person feel he or she is in the life cycle? How age appropriate does the person feel important life events or problems are?

What coping resources or challenges are operating in the client's everyday life? How does the client perceive the balance between resources and challenges?

What resources can the client draw on now to make changes? What challenges or barriers to change must be acknowledged and worked with?

What central life meanings are salient in the client's targeted concerns? How might central meanings have been challenged or destroyed by life events? Is the client looking to discover, affirm, or replace important meanings in his or her life? How might changes anticipated from counseling affect meaning making?

What can you tell about the client's thinking process that might affect your work together? For example, does the client appear to be especially intelligent, to be creative in describing people and life events, or to prefer black-and-white thinking patterns?

If your practice utilizes formal psychological diagnostic systems (e.g., the *Diagnostic and Statistical Manual of Mental Disorders*), which diagnosis best communicates the client's problem to other professionals? What other information must be added to depict the problem in its richness?

(Continued)

136

Table 6.1 *(Continued)*

Questions to Consider in Developing an Ecological Analysis

How should the problem statement or diagnosis be communicated to the client in a manner that helps him or her understand the problem (make meaning) and that empowers him or her in the change process?

How can the counseling relationship assist the client in making changes? How can you become a meaningful, trustworthy part of the client's life? How does your involvement change the system of interactions that characterize a client's life? What resources or challenges do you and your agency or setting bring to the process (e.g., personal skills, systems regulations)? How can other professionals or systems help now or in the future?

How can the change process be calibrated finely enough to achieve success yet be challenging enough to stimulate development?

How can you help the client prepare for future life challenges (e.g., anticipating a recurrence of the problem or strengthening the client's relationships to help him or her deal with new problems)? In particular, what life challenges might occur as a result of counseling?

discussions between Jamie's parents and school personnel about how to support each other more effectively in shaping Jamie's behavior (context, P × E interaction, resources), and a clever game that occupied Jamie's attention and facilitated positive interactions with other children on the bus (person factors, improved coping, P × E interaction). The school personnel also learned something about the needs and potential of children like Jamie (meaning making in the form of attitudes, school resources). Jamie successfully adapted to the bus situation and rode one throughout her school years.

This example illustrates how counselors might use ecological principles to enrich their work by drawing attention to contextual, interactional, and meaning-related aspects of clients' presenting problems. It is not necessary for counselors to ask every question listed in Table 6.1; it is likely that experienced counselors already ask most of these questions early in the counseling process. It is also likely, however, that some of these questions are not so routine, and counselors might find that asking them can produce interesting and useful information to explore. For example, what is the nature of the client's ecological niche, and how fulfilling are these parameters of daily life? How does the client perceive the physical context of his or her life? What important life values does he or she try to live by, and what other values get little attention in the pragmatic challenges of keeping daily life afloat? For many counselors today, a necessary activity in the early stages of the counseling process is developing a formal diagnosis. Diagnosis can fit within an ecological analysis, as we discuss next. Counselors might find it useful to make a list of frequently unexplored questions and ask themselves whether these omissions might have an impact on the comprehensiveness of their problem identification, their empathic appreciation of the challenges that their clients face, their rapport in the counseling relationship, their ideas for interventions, and ultimately the success of counseling in helping clients make life changes.

Experienced counselors know that the number of concerns explored in counseling is not crucial; what is important is being able to focus on concerns that are meaningful to clients and that can be addressed via feasible strategies. For some clients, simply having a caring person express an empathic understanding about their situation can be healing; other clients need specific ideas for how to alter relevant personal, contextual, meaningful, and/or interactional dynamics. Counselors who realize the multifaceted nature of typical client concerns and who consider a client's ability to change these dynamics from a number of different perspectives (e.g., skills training vs. cognitive restructuring) have more options for proposing strategies that best fit where the client is at this time of life.

Before moving on to strategies, we briefly discuss the issue of formal diagnosis.

The Question of Diagnosis

A reality of mental health counseling today is that counselors must utilize a standardized diagnostic system. Chapter 8 comprehensively reviews this system and how counselors might adapt it for use within an ecological counseling perspective. Unfortunately, these diagnoses quickly become accepted as just as real as the client's height and weight: He is schizophrenic, she is borderline.

Diagnoses rely on a "distinctive set of cultural categories, assumptions, and values" (Fabrega, 2004, p. 31) implicitly accepted by professionals to define the parameters of their work. Failure to account for the meaning making inherent in diagnostic work can compromise its validity (e.g., American Psychological Association, 2007; Cook, Warnke, & Dupuy, 1993; Eriksen & Kress, 2008; Ivey & Ivey, 1998; Kress, Eriksen, Rayle, & Ford, 2005; Zalaquett, Fuerth, Stein, Ivey, & Ivey, 2008). Some have argued that the diagnostic system does not adequately represent natural, expectable reactions to horrific life circumstances so that reactions to torture or rape, for example, are pathologized. In addition, some commonly experienced states, for example grief after becoming widowed, do not seem to fit anywhere. Some circumstances, for example, family distress that occurs from caring for a grandparent with dementia, may require one family member to be labeled with a disorder for the family to be served by an agency or covered by insurance. Current diagnostic procedures fail to recognize how social conditions contribute to life stress. Many everyday life dynamics, for example, experiencing repeated microaggressions (Sue et al., 2007) because of one's race or sex, are simply overlooked by the diagnostic codes. Finally, researchers have pointed out that even expert diagnosticians might disagree about appropriate diagnoses and may be subject to racial or gender biases (e.g., Schwartz & Feisthamel, 2009). Even a perfect diagnostic system has no laboratory tests or X-rays to lend support to our clinical hunches. Human judgment in all its amazing ability to integrate masses of data and its vulnerability to individual idiosyncrasies is the best and only tool we have.

Thus, during the diagnostic process it is crucial to be mindful about culture. Gielen, Fish, and Draguns (2004) noted that "what psychopathology is, how it is configured and handled in a community, and how best one may bring to bear resources of healing and restoration requires taking into consideration cultural systems of meaning and conventions about personal experiences and behavior" (p. 33). Smith, Spillane, and Annus (2006) concluded that it seems likely that some dysfunctions (e.g., uncontrolled psychosis) are universally recognized as dysfunctional. However, other practices widely agreed to be dysfunctional in Western culture (e.g., eating dead relatives) may be considered customary elsewhere (e.g., among the Fore peoples of Papua New Guinea). Some disorders appear in other cultures but not in U.S. culture (e.g., *koro,* or the fear some Chinese men experience that their penises are shrinking into their bodies, causing death). Individuals in other cultures may also experience and express problems common in the United States (e.g., affective disorders) but in very different ways. Smith et al. noted that cultures may evolve certain practices (e.g., slavery) for numerous negative reasons, including to dominate another group. Finally, it is possible that disorders that occur worldwide (e.g., anorexia nervosa) may be related to different causes or psychological dynamics according to the culture (Smith et al., 2006). In general, then, counselors need to know how common problems can be caused, expressed, and dealt with differently according to the culture of the client.

Within the ecological perspective formal diagnoses alone cannot represent the complex, interactive nature of clients' concerns. The diagnostic procedures used in the mental health system today fit best with the medical model (see Chapter 1), in which counselors are primarily concerned with identifying the deficits in a client's psychological functioning. Proponents of the ecological perspective assert that although some presenting problems might fit certain diagnoses perfectly, other client concerns fit poorly or not at all. How should counselors categorize a client's experience of having been brutally raped then further victimized by having had her experience dismissed by police as saying no but really meaning yes? How about the challenges of adjusting to civilian life after a year of combat in a war zone?

Another limitation of current diagnostic practices is a strictly pragmatic one: After assigning a diagnosis, a counselor may be no closer to knowing what to do next. A handful of diagnoses prompt certain specific actions to be taken by counselors; for example, a diagnosis of schizophrenia prompts a referral to the psychiatrist for medication evaluation. In the case of many other clients, a diagnosis may simply indicate more questions for the counselor to consider: Which professional literature or experts might the counselor need to consult regarding the client's form of depression? Which aspects of the client's life are precipitating stressors: a rebellious adolescent child, an unsuccessful job search, lifelong self-doubts, or chronic insomnia? Are these problems connected or unrelated?

Today mental health counselors typically have no choice whether to use these diagnostic classifications in their everyday work. These diagnostic procedures represent professional meaning making: a common language developed and disseminated by experts for describing clients. This meaning making has become required literacy within mental health professions, a complex language adopted by professionals throughout the world. Counselors do need to remember, however, that every language is necessarily limited by the cultural assumptions of the human world in which it originated. Counselors can appreciate that formal diagnostic systems are useful without assuming that diagnoses are all the information they need in planning the counseling change process. Counselors and other mental health professionals can supplement diagnostic codes with a nuanced, ecologically rich understanding of how a particular person experiences depression (or other diagnoses) in the context of his or her life and what this means to him or her at this time of life. Brown (2006) described her view of culturally rich diagnostic thinking as follows:

> After you describe the current distress, then you have got to stop and think about what informs that distress, what are the developmental factors informing the distress and accompanying coping strategies, what are the current and past issues of powerlessness and disempowerment, the current and past factors of social location, the possible biological vulnerabilities, and the strengths and competencies and talents that this person is bringing to the table. We diagnose the distress and dysfunction of the context in which this person lives . . . [The counselor must also ask,] How am I affecting, distorting, amplifying or obscuring the expression of any of these important issues by who I am and how I am with this person? (p. 19)

How well do your current diagnostic procedures fit with Brown's description? Do you agree that her recommendations are consistent with a more adequate, culturally valid assessment of client concerns? If not, which aspects, if any, of Brown's recommendations are worth following?

We turn next to a discussion of counseling goals and strategies. Because most counselors today think of counseling as remedial work with individuals, we focus first on these applications. Following this discussion, we consider how the ecological perspective can fit other purposes and settings.

Planning and Implementing the Change Process With Clients

Within the ecological perspective a broad range of interventions is useful depending on the goals set by the counselor and the client. Ideally goals have the following characteristics:

- They are plausible, feasible, and meaningful to the client.
- They are stated concisely in the client's own language.
- They use the language of interaction to depict problem situations.
- They are broken down into a series of moderately challenging but doable steps.
- They identify a level(s) within the client's ecosystem that is accessible to change.
- They explicitly recognize client strengths to be used and developed.
- They aim to increase coping strategies useful in future situations.
- They consider issues of maintaining change over time.

140

For counseling to be ecologically valid, the counselor and client need to work together in sharing information, formulating goals, and implementing change strategies consistent with the client's needs and preferences. For example, people with developmental disabilities such as Jamie may need a brief, clearly stated description of goals and strategies; other clients who are more comfortable with abstract thinking might be able to do remarkable work situated within a multifaceted analysis. Some anxious clients might welcome a step-by-step description of changes to be made over time (that is amended if necessary!); other anxious people might find this overwhelming and might be reassured by the prospect of the counselor introducing sequential steps in due time.

The language of metaphor or story can help convey these analyses succinctly and memorably, although its appropriateness depends on the client (Robert & Kelly, 2010). For example, in the case of a person whose flamboyant, expressive personality is neither understood nor appreciated by her introverted, studious family, the counselor might describe the children's story of *The Ugly Ducking*, about a gawky, funny-looking baby bird (a swan) who doesn't fit in with his peers (ducklings) but who eventually becomes a graceful, elegant creature in his own right. Alternatively, the counselor might describe how the client is like an exotic palm tree springing up on a rocky Maine coastline that will ultimately need another type of environment to flourish. The use of personalized, vivid language can make goals more real for a client.

Well-stated goals suggest appropriate strategies for change. Examples of counseling strategies consistent with the ecological perspective include the following:

- Enhancing physical wellness through exercise and diet
- Teaching study tips for high school and college students
- Applying cognitive interventions for depression
- Identifying problems with substance abuse
- Resolving home–career conflicts and other role conflicts through couples counseling
- Processing acute and longer term grief reactions, including various types of losses and corresponding life meaning concerns
- Identifying career strengths and job search strategies
- Assessing suicide risk
- Learning how to establish new friendships and social outlets
- Enhancing a sexual relationship through better communication
- Providing reentry support for war veterans
- Exploring racial or gender identity in the context of family history
- Clarifying career plans that implement central life values and narratives

All of these strategies can be expressed using theoretical terminology already familiar to counselors (e.g., family systems, cognitive–behavioral interventions). What makes the counseling process ecological in its ground-

141

ing is not the unique strategies used per se but how and why counselors do what they do.

Think back to Jamie, the girl with developmental disabilities. As Jamie grew up, she experienced times when she was noncompliant with familiar family routines and frightening periods when she would repeatedly hit her parents or babysitters. The same agency that helped Jamie ride the bus stepped in to help once more. Staff members arrived at Jamie's home before 6 a.m. so that they could secretly observe Jamie's morning habits and moods, and they returned after school for more observations.

These agency personnel provided Jamie's family with remarkably dedicated and expert assistance. They helped the family establish more effective daily care routines, and to help manage Jamie's violent episodes they provided some strategies for maintaining safe boundaries and helping Jamie regain self-control. Their interventions were ecological in many respects, based on careful observation of Jamie's behavior in her environment. Consistent with their respect for Jamie as an individual, they sought strategies that would be meaningful to her.

Another agency with a different mission, scope of practice, and personnel might devise a different yet equally ecological course of action for Jamie and her family. For example, Jamie's agency was dedicated to assisting people with developmental disabilities within their life situations. What might agencies without this expertise or ability to work with people in their natural environments do instead? Note that the staff did not spend much time exploring the reactions of family members to Jamie's violent outbursts and how they consequently thought about her as a family member, nor did they explore how other stresses in the family may have been contributing to Jamie's distress. These issues were beyond the scope of their agency. How might another agency have devised an ecologically sensitive intervention regarding these issues?

It is important to remember that what we are able to do as counselors has parameters defined by our own expertise, our agency's mission and clientele, and the structure of counseling as practiced there (e.g., home vs. agency based, short vs. long term). Counseling practice in the United States is enabled by an infrastructure that supports it culturally (e.g., through an awareness in the media about the need for counseling), educationally (e.g., through the presence of training programs in universities), and economically (e.g., through agencies that provide a living wage for counselors). (See Sells et al., 2007, for an eye-opening account of counseling in Honduras.) Counselors today face considerable work stress from ecological challenges that were not present a few short decades ago (e.g., documentation, reliance on outcome data, utilization rates; see the discussion in O'Connell & Mabry, 2004). An ecological perspective can help us distinguish between aspects of our work that we cannot change and other aspects that are a function of custom rather than necessity.

An example of a familiar but potentially changeable practice is counselors' tendency to think primarily in terms of direct service interventions with individual clients or small groups. The ecological perspective can suggest some exciting new possibilities for helping people.

Interventions Beyond a Remedial, Personal Process

It is human to imagine that one's familiar way of doing things is the best or only way to do it. This maxim applies to counselors and their professional practice as well. Counselors have become accustomed to considering their work as focused on helping individuals solve their personal problems. The fact that our professional wisdom can be used more broadly, for example, to prevent as well as to solve problems or to educate a community all at once, may not occur to us. But why *not* think more creatively about the counseling process? What might happen as a result?

Conceptualizing New Roles for Counselors

A groundbreaking framework for expanding counselors' thinking was provided in Morrill, Oetting, and Hurst's (1974) counselor functioning cube. The genius of the counselor functioning cube lies in how concisely and simply it reminds counselors that other options are indeed possible for making changes in people's lives.

Morrill and his associates (1974) proposed that counseling could be conceptualized in terms of three dimensions: targets (who or what?), purposes (why?), and methods (how?). Targets for counseling include (a) the individual, (b) the individual's primary groups (e.g., family), (c) the individual's associational groups (e.g., clubs), and (d) institutions or communities that affect the individual's behavior (e.g., the neighborhood). The purposes of counseling could be (a) remediation, (b) prevention, or (c) development. Finally, the target chosen for attention might be helped by (a) direct service (e.g., counseling with the target), (b) consultation and training (e.g., training other helpers), or (c) indirect interventions that use media (e.g., books or computer programs). Morrill and his associates emphasized the importance of assessment and evaluation regardless of how the intervention is designed.

In the terminology of the cube, counseling as typically practiced today is designed to help individuals (targets) remedy some life problem (purpose) using direct-service strategies (method). The simplest extension of the familiar one-on-one change process is remedial, direct-service work conducted within a group (change of target). Counselors in their professional training usually learn the basics of group work for three purposes: to change individual behavior with the help of powerful group interaction (e.g., to enable a group of individuals to help one another cope with substance abuse problems), to improve the interaction of an identified group (e.g., to enhance the effectiveness of a work team), or to use group work as a cost-effective modality for individual counseling (e.g., to allow members to take turns discussing their social interaction problems with the counselor). Group experts commonly believe that this last alternative fails to utilize the unique therapeutic qualities offered through group members' interaction with one another, but this option nevertheless remains a possibility.

With our apologies to cat lovers everywhere, the ecological perspective reminds counselors that there is more than one way to skin a cat: Counselors can do more than remedy identified problems through some form of direct service. For example, organizations can address problems experienced by their members through systemic strategies, such as educating members or developing programs to prevent commonly experienced concerns. The value of organizational consultation skills is increasingly obvious (e.g., Rapin, 2004). Counselors in recent years have begun to advocate for client groups by testifying on proposed legislative bills or lobbying for certain political candidates (or political institutions). Others have advised filmmakers who were developing television shows or movies on certain topics or have been interviewed on radio shows (impacting the media).

Are these appropriate roles for counselors? These roles are certainly consistent with our mission to alleviate human distress and are logical extensions of our conceptual understanding about the nature of human behavior. Unfortunately, these expanded roles do not fit how the job of counselor is currently conceptualized within the broader workplace (meaning making on the institutional level), so counselors typically are not granted the time or the salary for such activities. In the face of these challenges, many counselors think creatively about how to expand their reach—working with teachers to develop parent education programs, for example. Counselor education programs can also provide an ideal venue for experimenting with broadened role definitions. Students can learn how to advocate for causes and groups through lobbying and letter-writing campaigns. Students in program development or internship classes can consult with school personnel to design developmental programs for implementation. And a favorite based on personal experience: Faith-based organizations might enthusiastically welcome help in designing outreach programs that their members can implement on their own. Although changing the nature of counselors' daily jobs may be beyond our reach during a national economic crisis (context again), we can breathe new life into how we see our work today by thinking of new possibilities for service.

We conclude this overview about expanded interventions by briefly discussing environmental interventions, preventive counseling, and social change work. The latter two categories might be considered environmental interventions as well, but their ultimate intent shifts from remediation to reducing or eliminating distress before it occurs.

Environmental Interventions

When it comes to planning interventions, counselors routinely think about ways to change their clients' feelings, thinking, or behavior. Such person-centered strategies make good sense when some aspect of the way in which the client lives in his or her world is interfering with desirable life goals, or when the client is motivated to make changes in the ecosystem on his or her own. (There is a saying that if you want to make changes in the world, do so one person at a time, beginning with yourself.) There is another alternative: changing person–environment interactions by facilitating changes in the environment itself. Two questions are informative in an ecological analysis of any client or situation:

144

1. What level (e.g., personal, family, larger group) or type (remedial, developmental, preventive) of change seems most appropriate? Is a multistage change process possible or desirable?
2. What might the profession do to help groups of people like the client more effectively?

We advocate that counselors who use the ecological perspective should think more creatively about ways to change P × E interactions by changing a client's environment. Conyne and Cook (2004) outlined a range of change possibilities using the example of Heidi, an undergraduate student trying to cope with sexual harassment by one of her professors (let's call him Dr. Jerkyll). Conyne and Cook first outlined ways in which Heidi could change herself. Heidi could learn how to behave more assertively with Dr. Jerkyll, which would be a familiar and valuable person change strategy. Heidi could also change how she thinks about the context: She could learn about the dynamics of sexual harassment and about how Dr. Jerkyll's behavior is an abuse of power rather than a romantic overture. Or she could imagine Dr. Jerkyll dressed in outrageous costumes (fairy princess anyone?) to help her defuse her fear of him. She could strengthen her perception of herself as a resilient survivor by writing a column on the issue for the school newspaper. These interventions stress that Heidi is not to blame for the situation but that she is able to change troublesome aspects of her life by how she interacts with them.

Heidi could also try the following environmental interventions (adapted from Conyne & Cook, 2004):

1. Change her major or advisor. (Exit)
2. Choose only courses she knows are safe from harassment. (Encapsulate)
3. Join a campus support group for harassment. (Develop a niche)
4. File a grievance against Dr. Jerkyll. (Modify aspects of the environment)
5. Take Dr. Jerkyll's classes only in their online format. (Create a new setting)

These environmental strategies emphasize the fact that although responsibility for causing the problem may rest outside Heidi, she can behave differently in response to the problem. This emphasis is important to minimize feelings of powerlessness. When environmental causes for clients' problems exist, counselors need to empower clients to work on overcoming or transforming these conditions wherever possible (Vera, 2007).

Counselors should remember that clients may have different ideas about which aspects of their lives can truly be changed. One of the greatest sources of differences in perception is culture. For example, Heidi's culture may revere teachers. Thus, any strategies that involve directly confronting Dr. Jerkyll's behavior may feel inappropriate even though Heidi has no difficulty recognizing his behavior as problematic. For another example, consider that clients from a culture that honors the wishes of older family members regarding marriage partners and career choice may not agree with a counselor's view that choices contrary to elders' wishes are viable; such clients may consider estrangement from their families as intolerable. However, counselors should not assume without exploration that a client has certain perceptions because of his or her cultural identity (e.g., religion or ethnicity); individual meaning making is often more nuanced than we might expect. (Heidi might believe that Dr. Jerkyll's behavior has dishonored him and therefore that he does not deserve special consideration.) Consistent with the ecological perspective, counselors need to help clients explore what various options mean to them and help them develop alternatives that feel consistent with who and what they are as individuals.

Efforts to change the environment itself are not new in counseling. Proponents of gender, racial, or ethnic equality have long argued that the most justifiable strategy for dealing with an oppressive environment is to change the environment so that the oppression ceases. Alternatively, individuals can be empowered to recognize the oppression as injustice that they have personally experienced or observed and learn ways to deal with this oppression that affirm to the greatest extent possible their own or other targets' human dignity and self-determination (cf. Chronister, McWhirter, & Kerewsky, 2004; Watson, Collins, & Correia, 2004). Either strategy essentially changes the interaction between the person and the environment.

Preventive Counseling

Prevention expert Robert Conyne (2010) stated the basic rationale underlying preventive counseling interventions as follows: "Before-the-fact programs and everyday best practices can prevent negative conditions and outcomes from occurring or, at the least, lessen their duration and severity while they build and broaden competencies" (p. 5). Preventive counseling is a recent addition to mainstream counseling. Some of its roots as a counseling specialization lie decades ago in the work of college student personnel experts, who saw college students as an integral part of a campus-based ecology. By understanding students' developmental needs and the challenges they faced within the campus environment, campus personnel could intentionally enhance students' intellectual, social, and psychological development; prevent problems commonly experienced by students because of the unique person–environment interaction represented by campus life; and more effectively resolve student problems when they did occur. When coupled with insights about prevention culled from health professions, these early insights developed into the prevention specialty that has become increasingly important in counseling practice today.

Conyne (2004) defined *prevention* as follows:

> Prevention is a goal for both everyday life and for service delivery, through which people become empowered to interact effectively and appropriately within varying levels of systems (micro, meso, exo, and

macro) and in settings (individual, family, school, community, and work). Preventive application can yield a reduction in the occurrence of new cases of a problem, in the duration and severity of incipient problems, and it can promote strengths and optimal human functioning. (p. 25)

Prevention programs can decrease the incidence of new problems and lessen the duration and severity of existing problems. Conyne (2010) proposed that a change in incidence can be facilitated by a two-faceted process. First, prevention programs should attempt to decrease *deficits,* or a combination of environmental risks and stressors in physical, social, and cultural domains. Second, programs need to increase *strengths,* or protective factors on the personal, interpersonal, group, and systems levels. Both types of efforts are needed so that the proportion of deficits to strengths is changed in favor of more adaptive functioning.

Conyne (2010) also emphasized the fact that sets of deficits and strengths are multiplicative rather than additive in nature. That is, if an economically challenged person with a chronic illness and few interpersonal supports loses her home in a flood, the net experience of these challenges is much worse than simple addition would suggest. Conversely, a resilient person with close friends, financial resources, and skills for dealing with bureaucracies may appear to sail through life traumas. Counselors should consider how they can simultaneously challenge and support people as they interact within the various subsystems that make up the ecology of their lives. In so doing counselors may need to help the subsystems themselves (e.g., families, schools) to function more effectively and appropriately. Conyne (2010) emphasized the fact that counselors can work to assist people not only with diagnosed mental health problems but also with problems of everyday living, such as loneliness.

Ecologically oriented counselors understand that there is no way counselors can predict with any certainty whether and how people will develop certain problems in the future. This depends on which circumstances or contexts emerge and how people cocreate, interact with, and understand the happenings of their lives. Preventive interventions ultimately have to do with probabilities and the resources people need to cope with them. To design effective interventions, we need to have a clear understanding of the ecology of a group of people: their environment, history, and culture; the range of problems they experience as a group; their values, perceptions, and desires to change their lives. This respect for the idiosyncrasies of life is important whether a counselor is contemplating interventions 3 miles away or across the globe. In short, a broad, ecologically grounded respect for the target population is crucial for developing programs that are effective and valued by the community we aim to serve (Reese & Vera, 2007). Using community-based collaborative partnerships to engage key stakeholders communicates this fundamental respect and increases the likelihood that programs will be successful (Bond & Hauf, 2007).

Preventive counseling programs also typically focus on enhancing resilience. Prevention programs for children and youth have received particular attention in recent years (e.g., American Counseling Association, 2004; Weissberg & Kumpfer, 2003). Unfortunately, we cannot prevent problems like domestic violence in the same way that health care organizations can prevent malaria by distributing mosquito netting. What we can do is address the factors that make people vulnerable to remaining in violent relationships, such as women's economic dependence on men and men's emotional dependence on women (Bornstein, 2006).

Conyne's (2010) user-friendly manual for designing preventive counseling programs provides a concise yet detailed guide to planning and evaluating prevention programs of all shapes and sizes. His book provides examples of prevention programs, checklists, and timelines and a comprehensive list of Internet resources (e.g., www.strengtheningfamilies.org). This book is also a useful resource for anyone who is undertaking program development, preventive or otherwise.

Conyne (2010) acknowledged that social justice has been an ultimate goal of prevention programming from the very beginning. Prevention experts understand that every culture can exploit and oppress those who are defined as outside or less than other people. Effective prevention requires us to use our professional skills and convictions to acknowledge and confront social injustices.

Social Justice Work

All we ask is that you implement what's on paper.
—The Rev. Dr. Martin Luther King, Jr.
(cited in Wronka, 2008, p. xxxii)

The Universal Declaration of Human Rights adopted unanimously in 1948 by the newly formed General Assembly of the United Nations proclaims the rights of every human being to dignity; nondiscrimination; and a full range of civil, political, economic, social, and cultural rights. Wronka (2008) argued that the helping professions have committed themselves to creating a human rights culture that enhances the dignity and meets the basic needs of every human being.

Social justice work is a logical corollary of the ecological perspective. Counselors who implement the ecological perspective believe that human lives are interconnected and that we all bear some responsibility for looking out for the welfare of other humans. We believe that the course of people's lives is not predestined but is the product of P × E interactions and that human misery is often caused by contextual factors that can be changed (e.g., hunger, inadequate housing, preventable disease). We have a commitment to relieving human misery because of the mission of our profession but also because we have the knowledge, skills, and resources to make a real difference. By giving the best we have to offer—and the nature of these gifts will be different for each of us—collectively we can transform lives. It is an issue of justice and of taking seriously our own ability to do something meaningful in our own corner of the world.

According to Crethar, Rivera, and Nash (2008), social justice counseling initiatives involve concerns of equity and access—understanding how our social system perpetuates injustice among some and unearned privilege among others. When counselors intervene only at the microlevel and not to remedy systemic problems, they assert that they are complicit in perpetuating social injustice. As the mantra from the 1960s challenges us, do we want to be part of the problem or the solution?

This transformative work can take many forms. It can start with advocacy. Only in recent years has the counseling profession recognized the importance of advocacy; a model and competencies associated with advocacy are now available (Ratts & Hutchins, 2009; Toporek, Lewis, & Crethar, 2009). The framework stipulates three levels (client/student, school/community, and public), and each level has two domains (advocacy with or on behalf of an individual). A special section of the *Journal of Counseling & Development* offered specifics for conceptualizing and implementing social justice advocacy in a number of different formats (Goodman, 2009).

Any counselor can do advocacy work in some form. Counselors can teach clients to advocate for themselves. In Kiselica's (2004) words, "A crucial step to creating substantive healing for neglected and oppressed human beings is to help them to voice their concerns in a way that is empowering, self-directing, consciousness raising, and strength oriented" (p. 839).

Social justice work may also require us to stand up for the rights and needs of people who need voices supporting their own or who cannot speak up for themselves. Watson et al. (2004) referred to advocacy as assisting the oppressed and disenfranchised by arguing on behalf of them. Advocacy frequently occurs in the context of state and federal institutions. For example, we might lobby to expand the breadth and funding of mental health services or to increase funding and grants for innovative programming and research to improve the services we offer (Kiselica, 2004). Advocacy might also involve writing letters to politicians and community leaders regarding certain issues; testifying in the state (or perhaps national) legislature about a policy under consideration; participating in demonstrations to raise awareness about an issue; or speaking or writing in classes, conventions, newspapers, or professional journals to increase awareness and develop skills. Counselors can work toward change in children's lives by lobbying for better sick leave and vacation policies for parents, advocating for child care, working with schools to design after-school programs, or working within current systems in innumerable other ways (Vera & Shin, 2006).

There is plenty of work to do, but we may need to confront the possibility that this work is outside of our comfort zone. For example, the needs for advocacy within schools are legion, but school counselors may be reluctant to implement interventions that provoke discomfort and dissension. Bemak and Chung (2008) indict the *nice counselor syndrome*, experienced by counselors who may have a genuine concern for their students' welfare but whose "overarching concern to be perceived as being nice people, who promote acceptance, peace, and interpersonal harmony" (p. 374) effectively prevents them from taking actions that might be confrontational, provocative, or otherwise unpleasant to others. There is little question that we need to be able to work within the broad parameters of our work setting, but might our own discomfort keep us from trying something that could make a real difference to the people we serve? Might our inaction serve an unjust status quo when we could be doing something transformative instead? If you feel a bit uncomfortable about these questions, Bemak and Chung offer a long list of recommendations to support new adventures in advocacy.

We have focused on advocacy because of the new emphasis placed on it within the counseling profession and because counselors can easily engage in advocacy efforts beginning today if they wish to do so. (Write a letter! Call or e-mail someone!) Our hope is that someday enough counselors become involved in social justice initiatives that our profession is regarded as a formidable force for change.

The social justice movement in human services has generated a number of invaluable resources for describing the following: programs here and abroad, ethical dilemmas inherent in presuming to speak for another, applications to clinical practice, and so on (e.g., Aldarondo, 2007). Counselors in training will especially identify with Gerber's (2007) account of students wrestling with the limitations of current counseling practice today. We also particularly recommend Prilleltensky and Prilleltensky's (2006) guide to program development and social justice initiatives and Toporek, Gerstein, Fouad, Roysircar, and Israel (2006) for densely informative, thought-provoking discussions about counseling practice, program development, and research issues regarding social justice.

Implementing the Ecological Perspective in Counseling: Organizational Examples

The ecological perspective can encourage counselors to think of creative ways to facilitate change through existing organizations. In this section we discuss several projects developed with University of Cincinnati (UC) graduate students. These projects were all modest in scope but succeeded by using available organization and university resources during an economic downturn that taxed everyone's time, energy, and economic base.

Implementing Ecological Counseling as a Best Practices Model

When the ecological perspective described here was in the early stages of development, a fortuitous opportunity presented itself. The director of a comprehensive mental health center had read the first book on ecological counseling (Conyne & Cook, 2004) and believed it would be an ideal model for the agency's work. The agency was the primary provider of mental health services to county residents and had a stable, cohesive staff of counselors and social workers. For some years, the agency had operated with family therapy as its official model for practice, but this model increasingly felt like an unsatisfactory fit as the agency's scope of service continued to grow. The agency director made the courageous decision to pursue replacing the agency's official standard of practice with one that better corresponded with how staff actually did their work.

150

Thus began several years of ongoing collaboration between the agency and the UC (Ellen P. Cook and her doctoral students). The structure of the collaboration posed some unique opportunities. We could work directly with the agency staff in developing their ecological practice model. Senior administrators enthusiastically supported the rough framework of the ecological perspective as outlined in Conyne and Cook (2004) and could arrange necessary meetings and in-service training sessions. In many ways then, the context for the collaboration was ideal.

Yet there were also some considerable challenges. The agency was about an hour's drive from the university, so face-to-face meetings were less frequent than desired and required a considerable time commitment. There was also no funding to support the collaboration, so the UC team provided time, materials, and travel expenses free of charge to the agency on top of other professional commitments. The issue of resources waxed and waned in salience over the life of the project. Fortunately, I (Cook) was able to use the help of doctoral students in several professional seminars and internships. Some doctoral students (especially my coauthor Susannah Coaston) volunteered to continue with the project after the class phase was completed.

Our first step in the project was to develop a process for collaboration. Using Prilleltensky and Prilleltensky's (2006) model of program development to guide our thinking, we intentionally incorporated ecological principles into the collaborative process itself.

We *worked collaboratively,* recognizing the unique expertise of all parties involved. During class we used problem-based learning (Duch, Groh, & Allen, 2001) as a pedagogical framework to emphasize team problem solving rather than relying on the instructor to provide essential information. We spent a number of class sessions exploring conceptual connections between the Prilleltenskys' program development framework and the values and change processes that characterized the ecological perspective as we had come to understand it. In particular, we discussed the importance of affirming agency staff strengths, establishing an egalitarian and mutually respectful relationship among ourselves and with them, and developing skills consistent with their orientation to counseling practice (i.e., meaning making).

Students played an active role in staff trainings, on one occasion meeting with agency staff without me. As our work with the agency developed we discussed staff needs and reactions with the staff as a group and with the administrative staff on a session-by-session basis and also for longer range planning of our future work together. We also worked out a way for individual staff to discuss their perceptions directly with us rather than needing to go through their agency supervisors.

We also *clarified meaning making* about the counseling process. It was important to determine early on whether agency staff as a group and the UC team held similar ideas and values about the counseling process. In class and during an early training session all participants completed a mental mapping exercise in which they generated a list of characteristics that described the counseling process and then discussed themes that integrated the diverse descriptions. We determined that our perceptions of the counseling process were very similar and relied on shared language. We also asked agency staff what they hoped to gain from our work together, as both individual staff members and a treatment team, and framed these concerns in the language of the ecological perspective.

An important step was developing a detailed statement of best practices in ecological counseling endorsed by the staff. We refined a best practices list developed for preventive counseling (Hage et al., 2007) to represent the agency's own values. Staff members individually reviewed the list and discussed their reactions during a group meeting. This activity helped to clarify just how the ecological perspective reflected their own therapeutic models.

We also *identified resources and challenges* faced by the staff in their work. During an in-service staff training early in our work together we discussed the challenges they faced in their daily work because of the economic, political, and cultural features of the subsystems implicated in clients' concerns. Staff frankly shared their frustrations and discussed what they could and could not change through the counseling process. UC staff and students shared how ecological principles had helped them in their own work with clients. The metaphors of the counselors' toolbox and counseling as planting seeds for change in their clients' future lives were particularly helpful in framing possibilities for change.

One important challenge identified by the staff was the need to use ecologically consistent language in paperwork (e.g., intakes, diagnoses, and session notes). A senior staff member volunteered to fill out paperwork using her customary terminology. The staff discussed which language was already ecological in nature and how the conceptualizations and plans could be enhanced by incorporating new ecologically based ideas.

Finally, we *worked with idiosyncratic preferences and needs* for the services offered. The staff had a longstanding practice of scheduling in-service training and agency discussions during a certain time, which did not always fit well with UC team members' availability or ideas for our joint meetings. This predetermined schedule posed some challenges for UC team members, who traveled some distance and planned the sessions to fit the agency's availability and time frame. An enjoyable bonus was that agency staff also had a custom of sharing snacks or brown-bag lunches during this time, a practice that helped to enhance the general hospitality of these sessions.

Eventually, to the great delight of the agency director (and the UC team!), the agency's mental health board with little resistance accepted ecological counseling as the official mission and best practices model for the agency. The collaboration then continued with the agency's proposal of a grant to fund an ecologically based counseling program to decrease recidivism among parolees in the criminal justice system.

Collaborating With a Faith-Based Community

In addition to being a counselor educator, I (Cook) am a vocational deacon in the Episcopal Church, an order of clergy committed to facilitating service within the broader ecosystem containing the church at large. Because of my connections across graduate training and faith-based communities, I have become committed to exploring how counselors in general, and counselor education programs in particular, might work collaboratively with faith-based communities to address the some of the myriad challenges facing people today.

Several years ago I gave doctoral students in my professional seminar the challenge of helping a small church in the area identify an outreach project it could undertake to help the local community, a project that would meet a genuine need while utilizing the church's own resources and perceptions about outreach. The priest in charge also hoped to strengthen the congregation's presence in the area as an organization committed to the real-world needs of its community. The church was well established and financially secure because of past endowments but fairly small, with an aging congregation. Its members wanted to do something more hands-on than writing checks, as they had previously done, but had concerns about the physical challenges that many outreach projects seemed to present (e.g., purchasing supplies and staffing a food bank). The members also did not want to duplicate the efforts of other churches and social services agencies at a time when their local community was experiencing so many pressing economic and social difficulties.

At the beginning of the project the class focused on how churches within this denomination functioned as communities: the typical power structure, funding, decision making, independence from and connections with the broader structure of the denomination, the role of outreach in the congregation's functioning, and so on. We also discussed commonalities across faith-based communities (e.g., most denominations have a clergy member in charge) and areas of uniqueness (e.g., financial resources). Students were challenged to identify how their own life experiences had shaped their perceptions of faith-based communities in general. This learning phase was crucial to developing the plan of action with the church.

The team eventually identified important congregational stakeholders in addition to the priest in charge and determined the best ways to gather information about projects consistent with congregational structure and meaning making. We also identified demographic characteristics of the community based on census data and other reports. With other professionals in the area we discussed community needs and affiliated programs. Finally, we spent several seminars digesting all of this information about needs, resources, and the unique characteristics of our particular faith-based community, asking ourselves the following question: What programs might these congregants find most consistent with who they are and what they wanted to be in the future? An awareness of resources, challenges, and meaning making on multiple levels proved crucial in our eventual recommendations.

We finally developed a list of suggested programs, all fitting our evaluation of feasible and meaningful options. The congregation eventually implemented the option of adopting a local elementary school that labored under a daunting combination of limited resources and considerable life challenges that confronted the children (e.g., an usually high percentage of turnover because of foster home arrangements). Over the next few years, an ever-increasing number of congregants helped as they could, leading reading groups, buying school supplies for new students and rewards for teachers to distribute in class, and arranging holiday parties. Discussion with the priest some time later confirmed the class team's hypothesis about the importance of church members being able to draw on their self-perceptions as valued seniors who possessed money, time, and wisdom to support the young.

Teaching the Ecological Perspective at the UC

About 10 years ago, the counselor education program at the UC adopted the ecological perspective as the organizing vision of the program, and the faculty agreed to teach and implement the perspective however possible in classes, internships, research projects, and presentations. Much of this work has occurred via infusion into ongoing class discussions and supervision (see Chapter 12 for an example). We also require all doctoral students to take a year-long proseminar series that covers the ecological counseling perspective and culminates in a paper appropriate for publication in a professional journal. For the past several years graduate students have organized a 2-day local ecological counseling conference that offers a variety of sessions on theory and practice. A popular feature of the conference has been the poster presentations on ecological topics prepared by students specifically for this conference or adapted from class projects. As the ecological perspective has developed over time, regional and national presentations have also continued.

The more I (Cook) have learned about the ecological perspective, the more I am aware that our efforts have only scratched the surface of possibilities for reenvisioning the counseling process. Once we become aware how people's lives can change in more ways than we might think, we realize that the counseling profession is still in its infancy. What questions has our profession not even begun to answer? What areas of knowledge would you like to understand better (e.g., cultural anthropology, methods for assessing interpersonal interaction, community change processes)? How could you go about learning these things?

Summary

The ecological perspective suggests a way of understanding behavior that emphasizes commonalities across counseling approaches. Even apparently simple behavior can have complex determinants: individual idiosyncrasies both inborn and learned over time, the life contexts at play within a person's ecosystem, and the unique synergy of the person interacting within the configuration of life contexts at a particular point of time. Consistent with recognizing more abstract, distal causes in addition to more familiar proximal ones, the ecological perspective emphasizes sociocultural constructs (those blueprints for behavior that provide form and function to our shared social life) more than other theories tend to do.

Because person–environment (or contextual) interaction is an ongoing process, we can change people's behavior by focusing on the personal, contextual, interactional, or meaning-making processes that all operate continuously within a person's life. Rarely is there a single appropriate solution to the concerns targeted in counseling. The level of the contextual system under consideration determines goal setting and types of strategies. Ecologically based interventions have ecological validity regarding the client's life situation; are meaningful, plausible, and feasible to the client; draw on and enhance the client's existing resources and opportunities; explicitly address challenges or barriers to change within clients and contexts; and might specify changes to the environment instead of, or in addition to, changes in the client.

Understanding the multidimensionality of behavior encourages us to explore with our clients a variety of avenues for initiating a process of change in their lives. Career interventions can stimulate identity clarification in early adulthood; spiritual exploration can help strengthen the interpersonal resources available from joining a faith-based community. Encouraging parental involvement in a child's school can increase a parent's self-efficacy and assist a family in integrating into a new community. Understanding the value of cross-disciplinary collaboration can make it easier to admit our own limitations and decrease the professional isolation counselors often experience.

Counselors who endorse an ecological perspective tend to agree that change processes are not limited to helping individual clients make changes one person at a time. In recent years the counseling profession has advocated interventions at other contextual levels (e.g., school systems or communities) for purposes other than simply remedial ones (e.g., developmental or preventive purposes). We concur with social justice advocates that the most justifiable strategy for dealing with an oppressive environment is to change the environment itself so that the oppression ceases. We counselors have the professional resources to make a genuine difference in the world that we inhabit with our clients.

The cultural meaning making that explains the presence of, causes for, and appropriate treatments for psychological concerns also structures the policies and procedures that circumscribe our daily professional work. Some of us may not have the freedom to be truly inventive in how we address the interactive conditions that contribute to human misery. Some may be limited by personal meaning making or professional skills, and others may simply not view some types of interventions as the appropriate venue for their practice. Yet as a profession we have an obligation to continue to challenge ourselves to grow in our capacity to help those whose needs are marginalized or invisible in our society.

Discussion Questions

- Imagine that you are a classmate in Roberto's internship class (see the example at the beginning of this chapter). After reading this chapter, what suggestions do you have for how he might work with his client?
- Counseling is often taught as an individual or small-group process focused on the personal exploration of feelings and concerns. Other types of helping (e.g., prevention, consultation, and social justice initiatives) are taught as special topics skills. Do you agree with this emphasis? Why or why not?

- Many people experience psychological distress during the win-
ter holiday season. Using ideas from the ecological perspective,
discuss (a) possible factors that cause or contribute to this stress,
(b) counseling strategies to relieve this distress, and (c) strategies
to help an individual or group of individuals reduce or prevent
this distress during the next holiday season.
- Think of one social justice concern that you believe counselors
should become involved in changing. What have you done already, personally or professionally, to contribute to the needed
change effort? What else could you do now?

References

Aldarondo, E. (Ed.). (2007). *Advancing social justice through clinical practice.* Mahwah, NJ: Erlbaum.

American Counseling Association. (2004). [Special section on school vio-
lence]. *Journal of Counseling & Development, 82,* 259–312.

American Psychological Association. (2007). Guidelines for psychological
practice with girls and women. *American Psychologist, 62,* 949–979.

Bemak, F., & Chung, R. C. (2008). New professional roles and advocacy
strategies for school counselors: A multicultural/social justice perspective to move beyond the nice counselor syndrome. *Journal of Counseling
& Development, 86,* 372–383.

Bond, L. A., & Hauf, A. M. (2007). Community-based collaboration: An
overarching best practice in prevention. *The Counseling Psychologist, 35,*
567–575.

Bornstein, R. F. (2006). The complex relationship between dependency and
domestic violence: Converging psychological factors and social forces.
American Psychologist, 61, 595–606.

Brown, L. S. (2006). Still subversive after all these years: The relevance of
feminist therapy in the age of evidence-based practice. *Psychology of
Women Quarterly, 30,* 15–24.

Chronister, K. M., McWhirter, B. T., & Kerewsky, S. D. (2004). Counseling and ecological prevention practice. In R. K. Conyne & E. P. Cook
(Eds.), *Ecological counseling: An innovative approach to conceptualizing
person–environment interaction* (pp. 315–336). Alexandria, VA: American
Counseling Association.

Conyne, R. K. (2004). *Preventive counseling: Helping people to become empowered
in systems and settings.* New York, NY: Brunner-Routledge.

Conyne, R. K. (2010). *Prevention program development and evaluation:
An incidence reduction, culturally relevant approach.* Los Angeles,
CA: Sage.

Conyne, R. K., & Cook, E. P. (Eds.). (2004). *Ecological counseling: An innovative approach to conceptualizing person–environment interaction.* Alexandria,
VA: American Counseling Association.

Cook, E. P., Warnke, M., & Dupuy, P. (1993). Gender bias and the *DSM-III-
R. Counselor Education and Supervision, 32,* 311–322.

Crethar, H. C., Rivera, E. T., & Nash, S. (2008). In search of common threads: Linking multicultural, feminist, and social justice counseling paradigms. *Journal of Counseling & Development, 86,* 269–278.

Duch, B., Groh, S. E., & Allen, D. E. (2001). *The power of problem-based learning.* Sterling, VA: Stylus.

Eriksen, K., & Kress, V. E. (2008). Gender and diagnosis: Struggles and suggestions for counselors. *Journal of Counseling & Development, 86,* 152–162.

Fabrega, H. (2004). Culture and the origins of psychopathology. In U. P. Gielen, J. M. Fish, & J. G. Draguns (Eds.), *Handbook of culture, therapy, and healing* (pp. 15–35). Mahwah, NJ: Erlbaum.

Gerber, L. A. (2007). Social justice concerns and clinical practice. In E. Aldarondo (Ed.), *Advancing social justice through clinical practice* (pp. 43–61). Mahwah, NJ: Erlbaum.

Gielen, U. P., Fish, J. M., & Draguns, J. G. (Eds.). (2004). *Handbook of culture, therapy, and healing.* Mahwah, NJ: Erlbaum.

Goodman, J. (2009). Starfish, salmon, and whales: An introduction to the special section [Special section on advocacy competence]. *Journal of Counseling & Development, 87,* 259.

Hage, S. M., Romano, J. L., Conyne, R. K., Kenny, M., Matthews, C., Schwartz, J. P., & Waldo, M. (2007). Best practice guidelines on prevention practice, research, training, and social psychologists. *The Counseling Psychologist, 35,* 493–566.

Ivey, A. E., & Ivey, M. B. (1998). Reframing *DSM-IV:* Positive strategies from developmental counseling and therapy. *Journal of Counseling & Development, 76,* 334–350.

Kiselica, M. S. (2004). When duty calls: The implications of social justice work for policy, education, and practice in the mental health professions. *The Counseling Psychologist, 32,* 838–854.

Kress, V. E. W., Eriksen, K. P., Rayle, A. D., & Ford, S. J. W. (2005). The *DSM-IV-TR* and culture: Considerations for counselors. *Journal of Counseling & Development, 83,* 97–104.

Morrill, W. H., Oetting, E. R., & Hurst, J. (1974). Dimensions of counselor functioning. *Personnel and Guidance Journal, 52,* 354–359.

O'Connell, W., & Mabry, A. (2004). The ecology of community and agency counseling: An administrator's perspective. In R. K. Conyne & E. P. Cook (Eds.), *Ecological counseling: An innovative approach to conceptualizing person–environment interaction* (pp. 243–263). Alexandria, VA: American Counseling Association.

Prilleltensky, I., & Prilleltensky, O. (2006). *Promoting well-being: Linking personal, organizational, and community change.* Hoboken, NJ: Wiley.

Rapin, L. (2004). Ecological applications to organizational consultation. In R. K. Conyne & E. P. Cook (Eds.), *Ecological counseling: An innovative approach to conceptualizing person–environment interaction* (pp. 265–288). Alexandria, VA: American Counseling Association.

Ratts, M. J., & Hutchins, A. M. (2009). ACA Advocacy Competencies: Social justice advocacy at the client/student level. *Journal of Counseling & Development, 87,* 269–275.

Reese, L. E., & Vera, E. M. (2007). Culturally relevant prevention: The scientific and practical considerations of community based programs. *The Counseling Psychologist, 35,* 763–778.

Robert, T., & Kelly, V. A. (2010). Metaphor as an instrument for orchestrating change in counselor training and the counseling process. *Journal of Counseling & Development, 88,* 182–188.

Schwartz, R. C., & Feisthamel, K. P. (2009). Disproportionate diagnosis of mental disorders among African American versus European American clients: Implications for counseling theory, research, and practice. *Journal of Counseling & Development, 87,* 295–310.

Sells, J. N., Giordano, F. G., Bokar, L., Klein, J., Sierra, G. P., & Thume, B. (2007). The effect of Honduran counseling practices on the North American counseling profession: The power of poverty. *Journal of Counseling & Development, 85,* 431–439.

Smith, G. T., Spillane, N. S., & Annus, A. M. (2006). Implications of an emerging integration of universal and culturally specific psychologies. *Perspectives on Psychological Science, 1,* 211–233.

Sue, D. W., Capodilupo, C. M., Torino, G. C., Bucceri, J. M., Holder, A. M. B., Nadal, K. L., & Esquilin, M. (2007). Racial microaggressions in everyday life: Implications for clinical practice. *American Psychologist, 62,* 271–286.

Toporek, R. L., Gerstein, L. H., Fouad, N. A., Roysircar, G., & Israel, T. (Eds.). (2006). *Handbook for social justice in counseling psychology: Leadership, vision, and action.* Thousand Oaks, CA: Sage.

Toporek, R. L., Lewis, J. A., & Crethar, H. C. (2009). Promoting systemic change through the ACA Advocacy Competencies. *Journal of Counseling & Development, 87,* 260–268.

Vera, E. M. (2007). Culture, prevention, and the politics of disparities. *The Counseling Psychologist, 35,* 860–867.

Vera, E. M., & Shin, R. Q. (2006). Promoting strengths in a socially toxic world: Supporting resiliency with systemic interventions. *The Counseling Psychologist, 34,* 80–89.

Watson, A. L., Collins, R. L., & Correia, F. C. (2004). Advocacy and social action in the context of ecological counseling. In R. K. Conyne & E. P. Cook (Eds.), *Ecological counseling: An innovative approach to conceptualizing person–environment interaction* (pp. 289–313). Alexandria, VA: American Counseling Association.

Weissberg, R. P., & Kumpfer, K. L. (Eds.). (2003). Prevention that works for children [Special issue]. *American Psychologist, 58*(6/7).

Wronka, J. (2008). *Human rights and social justice: Social action and service for the helping and health professions.* Thousand Oaks, CA: Sage.

Zalaquett, C. P., Fuerth, K. M., Stein, C., Ivey, A. E., & Ivey, M. B. (2008). Reframing the *DSM-IV-TR* from a multicultural/social justice perspective. *Journal of Counseling & Development, 86,* 364–371.

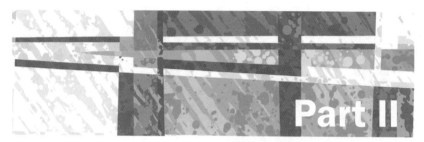

Part II
Applying the Ecological Perspective

In this section we explore whether the ideas explored in the first part of this book can really hold water: Are they helpful to counselors in the everyday contexts, interactions, and meaning-making processes that make up their professional work—and individual lives? I asked colleagues who are very knowledgeable about the ecological perspective and who represent a broad range of counseling expertise and interests to discuss the helpfulness of the ecological perspective in work built on questions rather than certainties. Does the ecological perspective offer anything of value? We believe that it does, and now it is time for you to decide for yourself.

Unfortunately, it was impossible to cover everything that we felt was important. We decided to focus on what we know best about certain topics and groups that characterize counselors' work today. There is no dedicated chapter on mental health counseling but considerable relevant discussion throughout the book, especially in Chapter 8 on assessment and diagnosis. The authors of this section agreed to be as specific as possible about which elements of the ecological perspective apply to their topics and to provide illuminating case examples. I close the book with an afterword that draws together the last few strands of meaning and turn over further development of the perspective to you. I am confident that even if you ultimately do not agree with our ideas, you will find that interacting with us in these pages affirms the value of what we all try to do.

Diversity From
the Ecological Perspective

Mei Tang and Huma Bashir

This chapter illustrates diversity in counseling through an analysis of the multifaceted nature of cultural identity, the intersectionality of multiple roles and life spaces, and the interaction of individuals with various contexts from the ecological perspective. We aim to provide an alternative framework for understanding diversity and for developing multicultural competency with ecological validity. Counselors working with diverse populations need to facilitate meaning-making processes with clients and empower clients to be change agents themselves.

Understanding diversity among clients and developing the cultural competence needed to effectively help clients of various backgrounds have been the focus of research and training in the counseling profession since the 1970s. Multiculturalism emerged as a fourth force in counseling several decades ago to respond to the increasing need for helping professionals in the United States to become competent in working with increasingly diverse populations (Pedersen, 1991). The understanding of diversity and its impact on the counseling process is evolving as the helping professions become more aware of the complexity and dynamics of diversity issues in human behavior and in the counseling process. As many scholars have argued, becoming aware of the limitations inherent in viewing human behavior solely on an individual level has significantly changed the mindsets of counselors and researchers, making them more cognizant of the multiple factors beyond individual characteristics that can potentially influence behavior (Ballou, Matsumoto, & Wagner, 2002).

OVER →

The ecological counseling approach (Conyne & Cook, 2004) explains human behavior from various levels of Bronfenbrenner's (1979) ecosystem and emphasizes the interactional dynamics of the multiple factors that influence human behavior. To build an effective therapeutic alliance, counselors must understand minority clients' cultural identity, because cultural identity is an inseparable part of the self. This chapter attempts to illustrate diversity in counseling through an analysis of cultural identity from the ecological perspective. Specifically, it reviews the multifaceted nature of cultural identity, the intersectionality of multiple roles and life spaces, and the interaction of individuals with the environment. Diversity is discussed in light of the ecological perspective to further an understanding of the complexity of cultural identity. The chapter ends with a discussion of the ecological approach to developing cultural competency for working with diverse populations. This discussion aims to provide an alternative framework for understanding diversity and developing multicultural competency with ecological validity.

Cultural Identity Development

Identity is developed in a cultural context, from the time we learn to hold a spoon to the time we have our first religious ceremony. Shared life experiences teach individuals the thoughts, values, and behaviors that they then incorporate into their personal identity. Cultural identity development is the process of seeking a sense of belonging. Belonging to a cultural group means accepting the beliefs and symbols of that group as having meaning and importance in a profoundly personal sense. According to Pedersen (2000), although people have just one cultural identity, many different salient identities presented by ethnographic, demographic, status, and affiliation groups help shape the formation of that identity.

Researchers have tried to understand cultural identity development from various perspectives, and many prominent models of cultural identity have been proposed. It was initially believed that the dominant majority group simply imposed a dominant culture on all minority groups. Early models presumed a movement toward the dominant culture as an appropriate adjustment for minorities. In recent years, many researchers have criticized the assumption of assimilation to the dominant culture as the only way of maintaining an appropriate cultural identity and have proposed many alternative cultural identity models.

Although it varies in its specific terms (e.g. Cross, 1991; Helms, 1990; Phinney, 1992), the linear model of cultural identity development generally depicts the process of identity development as occurring in sequential stages, from the absence of conscious awareness of one's cultural background to the personal integration of one's tradition into both internal and external views of the self. Transformation, the final stage, indicates that individuals have successfully resolved the inner struggle of doubting their self-worth and achieved a sense of personhood that includes their past, their current living environment, and their community. Self-worth is more internally secure rather than imposed by external standards or expectations.

162

The typology model, in contrast, considers cultural identity development in the form of several discrete statuses that result from one's encounter with two or more cultures—one's traditional culture and the mainstream culture. This model presumes that one can adapt to a new culture without losing contact with a traditional culture (D. Sue, Mak, & Sue, 1998). Biculturalism is seen as an ideal status that requires individuals to master or adapt well to both cultural norms. The undesirable status involves a lack of integration with either culture: Losing roots in one's traditional culture but not assimilating into the new culture, the individual becomes marginalized. Many new immigrants likely experience this at least temporarily soon after they immigrate.

If cultural identity involves encounters with two cultural experiences, then *acculturation* is a process by which individuals negotiate and adapt their experiences of being in two cultures. Berry (1980) stated that for the group caught between two cultures, two issues need to be resolved. One is the extent to which the individual or group members want to conserve their own cultural background as opposed to giving up their cultural traditions. The other is the extent to which the individual or group members want to interact with members of other groups in the larger society as opposed to turning away from these other groups. Berry's (1980, 2003) acculturation model proposed two intersecting dimensions that an individual would choose once he or she left the original cultural context (e.g., the home country) to live in the new culture (e.g., the host or receiving culture). One dimension is the acquisition of new culture, and the other is the retention of the heritage culture. Acquiring the new culture does not necessarily mean relinquishing the traditional culture; therefore, Integration of both is the healthier and more favorable acculturation process (high on both dimensions: high on acquiring new culture and high on retaining traditional culture). The other three categories are Assimilation (high on acquiring new culture and low on retaining traditional culture), Separation (low on acquiring new culture and high on retaining traditional culture) and Marginalization (low on acquiring new culture and low on retaining traditional culture).

Just like human development, cultural identity development is complex and does not happen in a linear manner (Pedersen, 2000). Humans go through change in a multidirectional rather than unidirectional process. As Pedersen (2000) argued, linear models do not incorporate the situational influences that occur in the developmental process. The typology and acculturation models seem to focus more on the outcome of encountering two cultures, and both view biculturalism as the ideal result. One of the criticisms of the bidimensional approach is its lack of empirical evidence for what makes a high versus low degree of culture (Rudmin, 2003). Rivera (2010) stated that Berry's (1980, 2003) model is limiting because acculturation is a complex and multifaceted process, as an individual's personal intention (e.g., relative or selective immigration), the environment in which acculturation takes place (e.g., an ethnically mixed vs. monoethnic community), and perceived discrimination could significantly influence the acculturation process. The high or low distinction for acquiring new culture and retaining traditional culture might involve many more delineated dimensions rather than a single integrated cultural dimension.

A multidimensional model presumes that one's cultural experience transitions along several dimensions at the same time with different degrees of adjustment on each dimension (Trimble, 2003). The recent literature supports this trend of viewing acculturation as multidimensional in both the nature of culture and the degree to which each cultural component is acquired. Schwartz, Unger, Zamboanga, and Szapocznik (2010) suggested that the construct of acculturation includes practice (or behavior), values (or value), and identification (or identity-based) acculturation. Individuals may change at a different pace for each aspect and not necessarily in the same direction. These researchers' broadened view of biculturalism proposes that synthesizing two cultures into a unique blend, rather than simply combining them, might be the preferred alternative for portraying biculturalism.

Cultural identity should be represented as multifaceted in nature because identity is developed though one's life experiences. This process involves personal traits, the interaction of personal traits with life contexts, and the way in which individuals make sense of themselves in these interactions (Robinson-Wood, 2009). As Rockquemore and Laszloffy (2003) claimed, multiple identities exist because they are developed through social interaction with others. Or in other words, "Cultural identity is constructed historically and socially within groups and is influenced by the contact with differences within those groups or differences between different groups" (Thomas & Schwarzbaum, 2006, p. 4). The development of cultural identity therefore is a relational and dynamic process.

Similarly, Pedersen (2000) stated that we become more aware of our cultural identity through contact with persons from other cultures who are different from ourselves, and we see ourselves in contrast with others. It is increasingly necessary to be aware of one's cultural identity when encountering members of a new or different culture (e.g., immigrants or members of the minority culture). Identity includes personal elements, such as one's name, physiological and physical features, and personal characteristics; social connections, which include one's family background, school friends, neighborhood communities, and work-related or family-related networks; and cultural connections, such as one's nationality and ethnicity (Pedersen, 2000).

In summary, cultural identity is multifaceted in nature because individuals shape their sense of identity through interactions with others who are different from themselves. Moreover, individuals not only react to their multidimensional cultural experiences but they try to make meaning of their experiences and the implications for their choice of behavior and identity. As argued by Schwartz et al. (2010), cultural identity is inherently subjective, meaning that it means different things to different individuals depending on the acculturative experiences they have had. The multidimensionality of acculturation and cultural identity therefore is not only about the construct itself but also about the sources of influences on one's cultural identity development. The key principles of the ecological counseling approach, namely that behavior is contextualized and that behavior involves meaning making, are helpful in analyzing the factors and sources that influence cultural identity.

Factors That Contribute to Cultural Identity

Many factors contribute to cultural identity: race, ethnicity, age, gender, sexuality, physical and mental ability, socioeconomic class, language development, and spirituality (see Atkinson, Morten, & Sue, 1998; D. W. Sue & Sue, 1999). Not only do multiple factors contribute to cultural identity development, but the process is multifaceted and intersectional (Unger, 2001). To better understand cultural identity in context we should examine the development of cultural identity from the ecological perspective.

Schwartz et al. (2010) argued that the goodness of fit between the embedded environment (e.g., the distal and proximal contexts) and one's acculturation orientation shapes the acculturation experiences one has. In other words, a mismatch could lead to acculturative stress. These stressors could be multiple (Rodriguez, Myers, Mira, Flores, & Garcia-Hernandez, 2002). One could be from the expectation and responses of the host or mainstream culture (e.g., immigration policy and reactions of the neighborhood to immigrants); another stressor could be from the traditional culture. For instance, studying a South Asian community in Britain, Goodwin and Cramer (2000) found that collectivist cultural values are held at all generational levels and maintained as much as possible because families in the community fear losing their cultural roots. As a result, second-generation South Asians in this community are cautious about engaging in relationships that might not fit with traditional cultural values. At the same time, these youths need to assimilate the new cultural values of the new world in order to survive and thrive.

The Influence of the Ecosystem on Cultural Identity

The ecological approach allows us to explore multiple influential factors discussed in the literature from various levels. According to Conyne and Cook (2004), one's choice of behavior is dependent on the interactions between individual characteristics and the environment. The ecological perspective argues that various levels of the ecosystem exercise their influence on individuals' cultural identity development in different ways. First of all, one's personal characteristics, such as physical and physiological makeup, personality, sex, age, cognitive ability, coping skills, and so on, could impact one's cultural identity development. Thomas and Schwarzbaum (2006) argued that cultural identity is person identity. Erikson (1963) also articulated that cultural identity is critical to understanding personality. According to the ecological perspective, cultural identity development is an ecological journey that everyone travels regardless of ethnicity, social class, spirituality, gender, or age. The ecology of a person's life is ever changing (Conyne & Cook, 2004). Thus, the process of exploring and defining one's cultural identity is fluid rather than occurring in fixed stages.

The second source of influence is diverse life contexts, which can be either proximal (immediate) or distal (see the earlier discussion). The proximal level is also referred to as the *microlevel* and *mesolevel*. At this level, people's family background, schooling experiences, and community all impact their growth and understanding who they are and what kind of behavior is expected of them (this cultural norm varies depending on the context). People learn from responses in each immediate context and develop their self-awareness and identities accordingly. For people whose cultural background is different from that of the dominant culture in society (e.g., ethnic minorities, immigrants), messages from family and schools may not always be the same because cultural values might be different in each context. This could leave children confused or conflicted. As a result, understanding the interplay of these seemingly contradictory messages in a single blended or synthesized value system could be a challenge for children.

The factors that influence one's cultural identity at the microlevel and mesolevel are greatly influenced by the broader cultural context, or exosystem and macrosystem. In other words, family and school influences are not isolated but are influenced by factors at the exolevel and macrolevel of the ecosystem. The cultural norms in the macrosystem for minority groups include at least two parts. One is the dominant cultural norm and the other is the cultural norm of the particular ethnic or racial group. In fact, cultural norms are not just based on ethnicity or race, but they can also be based on gender, religion, socioeconomic status, and so forth. If particular identities are shaped within particular contexts, it is important to bring those contexts into consideration to understand cultural identity.

One example of an exosystem-level influence on a person's cultural identity development is government policy related to minority groups and immigrants. When racial segregation was still the national policy in the United States, it was not possible for African Americans to interact with Whites as equals. So how would someone reach the integration stage as Helms (1990) discussed it? If the U.S. government were to impose English as the exclusive language, assimilation would inevitably become the dominant strategy for immigrants in order to gain education and employment. Thus, maintaining one's cultural tradition could be difficult because of the eventual loss of language skills.

Cultural norms and values that are endorsed by the larger society are macrolevel influences on cultural identity. People develop their identity by interacting directly with their immediate family members, their school and work colleagues, and people in other social networks (microlevel); however, all of these interactions are influenced by the cultural values at the macrolevel. For instance, when the larger society has a high expectation of assimilation and a low tolerance of being different, people often willingly or unwillingly make an effort to become one of the dominant group and as a result neglect their cultural heritage. At the macrolevel, in addition to cultural norms and values, historical context is an important factor that influences cultural identity development. Time is an essential although invisible part of a person's life context (Conyne & Cook, 2004).

166

The cohort effect, which refers to the idea that people experience the same macrolevel life events at the same time, certainly affects a person's value orientation and identity. Consider the terms the media use to depict various generations. From *Baby Boomer* to *Generation Y*, these terms are used to indicate that people within a cohort share some common characteristics because of their shared developmental experiences. The linkage between personality development and social events illustrates how the convergence of individual development and significant social changes can result in a strong "generational identity" (Unger, 2001). For example, people living in India under the British Empire may have developed a shared sense of oppression; Muslims living now as a minority in India may fear discrimination or racism and therefore live with a questionable identity of Indian-Muslim or Minority Indian.

In sum, people of minority groups can develop multiple identities through interactions with multidimensional cultural contexts. Guadalupe and Lum (2005) argued that counselors need to be aware that intrapersonal, interpersonal, environmental, social, cultural, and spiritual factors concurrently influence clients' lives and well-being. To help clients from various cultural backgrounds, counselors need to recognize not only the multifaceted nature of cultural identity but also the intersectionality of these multiple dimensions.

The Intersectionality of Multifaceted Cultural Identities

Not only do the various levels of a person's ecosystem influence the development of cultural identity, but different identities can emerge from the specific combination of one's cultural contexts (Unger, 2001). One cannot examine a particular identity, such as a racial, religious, or sexual identity, without also considering the impact of other overarching identities. For example, studies of racial identity often include both men and women but do not examine gender identity; similarly, studies of gender identity often include people of different ethnic backgrounds but do not examine the possibility that ethnic background is an important context shaping gender identity (Unger, 2001). Cultural identity is multifaceted and intersects with other aspects of identity. *Intersectionality* refers to the interaction of two or more roles or social statuses. For example, *Pakistani American woman* denotes a person as being not only Pakistani American but also a woman; this intersection of ethnic and gender roles could potentially be manifested in this woman's behavior. Her womanhood is or cannot be separated from her daily life experiences. She is always and everywhere circumscribed by race, ethnic background, and gender, and her experience cannot be wholly attributed to only one of these characteristics. Kurrie and Vo (2004) considered the interplay between religious and political identities among women and men of Hindu Indian background who had immigrated to the United States. Her work showed how gender and ethnicity are interwoven in the process of immigration and relocation.

Inman (2006) investigated the effects of education, level of religiosity, ethnic identity, racial identity statuses, and self-awareness on cultural value

167

conflict among first- and second-generation South Asian women. She found that cultural conflicts occurred in two areas, intimate relations and sex role expectations. This was because traditional practices in intimate relations (e.g., that intimate relationships can only occur within the context of marriage and that no premarital sex could occur) and traditional sex role expectations in South Asian culture (e.g., that women are to be selfless and to stay connected to the indigenous culture) were in direct opposition to Western cultural values. The same study also found that the intensity of cultural value conflict varied for different generations. First-generation South Asian women followed the linguistic, religious, and communal identities expected in the traditional culture; in contrast, second-generation women, who had been raised in the United States and who viewed themselves as Americans, more easily took a Western blended social position. The ultimate internalized racial identity would be more applicable to the U.S.-born South Asian Americans (second generation) than to the first generation, as the first generation did not adopt Western cultural values as readily as the second generation. The second generation, though more acculturated, might experience struggles with cultural conflicts (Inman, 2006). The literature suggests that a stronger ethnic obligation and greater involvement facilitates a stronger ego identity and greater collective self-esteem, thus enabling better coping with cultural conflicts (Sodowsky & Maestas, as cited in Inman, 2006).

The effect of the intersectionality of the various roles and contexts in one's ecosystem can also be illustrated by adolescents seeking religious identity (Balkin, Schlosser, & Levitt, 2009). In a study by Chaudhury and Miller (2008), Bangladeshi American Muslim adolescents tried to distinguish between their ethnic and religious identities by concluding that ethnic identity is assigned and inescapable whereas religious identity is asserted and more of a choice. They also formed their religious identity through both internal and external factors. These factors were open communication with family and loved ones, a support network of peers, safe havens, participation in ritualistic prayers, and a present time orientation versus a future life orientation (Chaudhury & Miller, 2008). The findings showed that these adolescents struggled with understanding both their Muslim side and their American side and with trying to strike a balance between these two components. Overlooking the complexity and intersectionality of the identities of these minority children could result in neglecting their needs. Other studies have found that many minority children do not have their needs met in foster home care because of a lack of understanding of the diverse needs of these children (Sewell, 2009).

Ethnic identity exploration is common in adolescence regardless of one's generational status or immigrant background. For the children of immigrants, the salience of ethnic identity may develop earlier, when children are socialized by their parents to understand their ethnic heritage while also being exposed to the majority culture in other contexts, such as in schools and among friends (Marks, Szalacha, Lamarre, Boyd, & Coll, 2007). Tuason, Taylor, Rollings, Harris, and Martin (2007) found that ethnic identity appeared to be different for Philippine-born versus U.S.-born Filipino Americans, even though both groups identified values such as family orientation, hospitality, politeness, and respect as Filipino characteristics and efficiency, punctuality, and expressiveness as American values. One's degree of inclination to be identified as American only or Filipino American may be an important distinction of whether the cultural identity is in favor of American or Filipino. It is important to note that identity differences within a group may be on a continuum. People's life experiences as members of a minority make their identity formation process a complex one. Finally, it is helpful to view their behavior in context and understand the meaning they have derived from their life experiences.

Diversity and the Ecological Perspective

People don't develop their identity and learn about behavior in a vacuum; instead, their psychological growth is based on their participation in social events and their interaction with others (Comstock et al., 2008). Hutchison (2008) argued that cultural identity results from a combination of the biological, psychological, physiological, physical, and spiritual selves interacting in life spaces. These life spaces (e.g., environments, societies, institutions, dyads, families, groups, formal organizations, communities, social movements) not only provide spaces in which people interact with others but also impact people's growth. Thus, a person's life space has a significant impact on his or her development of self-identity as well as cultural identity, values, and behaviors.

In the ecological counseling perspective these different life spaces correspond to the various levels of ecological systems in Bronfenbrenner's (1979) ecological circle. These layers of the ecological system have significant impacts on human development but not entirely independently; rather, each life space functions concurrently and interactively to influence individuals' behavior. In other words, people learn about culturally accepted behavior and values through their interactions with family members, peers and teachers in school settings, coworkers in organizations, and people in other social settings they encounter. However, these interactions are influenced by idiosyncratic family dynamics; the particular school climate in which the school policy and relationships among students, teachers, administrators, and parents emerge; and the broader organizational and state policies that influence these dynamics. Thus, multicultural differences are not only multidimensional but also relational in nature; each level of ecosystem is not isolated but interacts with others that make up a person's life space.

Viewing human behavior as the result of the interaction of person and environment is exactly what the ecological counseling approach emphasizes (see Conyne & Cook, 2004). As argued earlier, people cannot develop their identity without being in contact with others in their environment; diversity cannot be understood from one single perspective or one level of the ecosystem. For instance, the earlier literature on multiculturalism recognized between-group and within-group differences yet neglected the interacting nature of various ethnic groups in a society. Most often it is the interaction with other ethnic groups that makes the sociocultural context for individuals. In other words, groups are not isolated; instead, they coexist in a common society (macrolevel) in which many policies and regulations are the same. Therefore, colived experiences are very critical to understanding the dynamics of cultural impact on individuals. That said, we do not mean that individuals living in the same context will have the same life experiences. To the contrary, because the meaning-making process is different for each individual, two persons living in the same cultural context might have totally different feelings about their interaction with the environment. Ecological analysis and the meaning-making process would help counselors and clients understand better their individuality in relation to the various elements in the different levels of their ecosystems, including cultural context, as well as the interaction of each ecosystem.

Viewing diversity from the perspective of only one specific feature of a person's cultural background is hazardous because this neglects the interactive aspects of individuals' ecosystems. By focusing on merely one aspect, regardless of how comprehensive the list of cultural factors being considered is, counselors would lose sight of a client's true state of being as a dynamic, relational, and interactive creation. For example, the experiences of a female Muslim residing in a community in which 85% of the residents are Arab American are different from those of a female Muslim living in a community in which she is one of only five Muslim Arab Americans. A male Muslim living in the United States would encounter different reactions before and after the tragic bombing of the World Trade Center in New York on September 11, 2001. A middle-class African American girl growing up with both parents in the 1950s South would have very different educational and occupational experiences from one growing up in the 1990s in the inner city. In conceptualizing client issues, counselors must consider diversity issues as interactive and dynamic.

Similarly, mental health issues cannot be viewed separately from cultural factors because these factors may affect the definition and acceptance of mental health disorders. For instance, religious factors as well as other cultural factors can affect the diagnosis and treatment of mental health issues among Muslims (Hussain, 2009). The manifestation of certain emotional, cognitive, and behavior problems may be different in various cultures, even in different historical contexts. Thus, using one frame of reference (e.g., the *Diagnostic and Statistical Manual of Mental Disorders*) to evaluate mental health status may not work well for clients of different cultural backgrounds. For instance, having a dialogue with superpowers or natural forces (e.g., lightning, one particular star) might be a normal process of engaging in self-reflection in some cultural traditions; therefore, assuming that such a conversation is a form of hallucination can lead to misdiagnosis and ultimately maltreatment. Another example concerns career choice. Career development theories based on Western culture view career choice as an outlet for self-expression; however, for minorities in the United States, choosing a career may not be a completely individual choice.

170

In many cases, career choice is a compromise between individual interests and parental expectations (Tang, 2002), and career aspirations have a very strong relationship to minorities' acculturation level (Flores & O'Brien, 2002; Tang, Fouad, & Smith, 1999).

People from different cultures have different perceptions of self and others (Markus & Kitayama, 1991). Each person is simultaneously a unique self, a group self, and a universal self. The universal dimension of a person indicates that that person is like everyone else; the group dimension indicates that the person is like some others who share common characteristics; and the individual dimension indicates that the person is ultimately unique, a one-of-a-kind creation (Leong, 1996). We all share a universal human nature (e.g., the need to eat and sleep), and we identify with certain groups but not others (e.g., Hispanic Americans, licensed counselors in school settings); however, we each have a distinctive personality that cannot be replicated by another person. Depending on the context, people may emphasize one part of themselves over another. Having an awareness of these factors and the interplay of these factors in proximal and distal contexts is valuable for understanding clients' idiosyncratic personalities; this understanding can help us reach out to our clients wherever they are. One of the dangers of stereotyping is overemphasizing group characteristics and neglecting the individuality of the person. Ecological counseling advocates for meaning making as a tool in the counseling process because each individual has his or her own frames of reference to make sense of his or her environment, issues, and relationships. Counselors can facilitate this meaning-making process but cannot make meaning for clients. Each client must ultimately complete this process alone.

Appleby, Colon, and Hamilton (2001) argued that what is experienced as a stressful event depends on the interaction of many factors, including physiological, psychological, spiritual, social, and environmental ones. In the ecological counseling perspective the interaction among these factors at each level of the ecosystem (e.g., family dynamics, school environment, and political and economic situation) at a particular time plays a role in whether individuals experience an event as stressful. Consequently, what is perceived as stressful for one individual may not be so for another because the meaning derived from the same event is different for each individual. The interaction of each factor in the ecosystem shapes clients' experiences, subsequently impacting clients' behavior and their relationship with others. For example, siblings develop different behavior patterns and personalities even though they grow up in the same environment (e.g., family, school, community). From the ecological counseling perspective, the personal characteristics and living spaces might be similar for these siblings, but the interaction and intersection of the multiple factors in their life spaces may be different because their meaning-making processes are different.

Multicultural Competency and the Ecological Perspective

The multicultural counseling movement has significantly impacted counseling research, practice, and training (Arredondo, Rosen, Rice, Perez, &

171

ro, 2005; D'Andrea & Heckman, 2008). Multicultural awareness and competence are expected for all counselors according to the Association for Multicultural Counseling and Development's Multicultural Counseling Competencies (Arredondo et al., 1996). The challenge of becoming culturally competent lies in the fact that diversity is such an intricate, fluid, and multifaceted issue that simply having knowledge about all minority groups by itself is not sufficient. Every counselor must know how to make meaning of information about diverse groups and how to develop the appropriate skills to make the counseling process beneficial to clients from different cultural backgrounds; it is the meaning-making process in the counseling session itself that lends the best opportunity for counselors to become change agents for clients.

Counselors cannot habitually conceptualize clients' issues based on their familiar framework of reference, neglecting the complexity and uniqueness of individuals' concerns. Ballou et al. (2002) stated that encapsulated counselors are rigid in their thinking, reject alternatives, and may not be able to fully understand their diverse clients. Their encapsulated interventions may result in culturally conflicting and even oppressive counseling; therefore, counselors need to challenge their own thought patterns and be aware of their biases for the sake of fostering the well-being and development of culturally different clients. In other words, counselors need to meet clients where they are.

Being aware of the need to challenge one's own cultural views and values while working with diverse populations is important but not sufficient. As argued earlier, someone from a minority group may have complex feelings about his or her racial or ethnic identity because of his or her experiences growing up and the current contextual influences within his or her ecological system. Failing to address the cultural meanings of clients' life experiences is harmful (Thomas & Schwarzbaum, 2006). Put a different way, acknowledging the minority status of a client or his or her cultural concerns is just the first step. The counselor must then be able to incorporate the meaning of all of these factors into the counseling process. Clients will feel respected and valued, which is good, but they will not be helped effectively if the true meaning of their experiences as a minority and its relevance to their struggles is not recognized. This connection with clients must build on understanding, trust, and a solid working relationship. Gallardo and McNeill (2009) posited that addressing various dimensions of diversity can be a therapeutic factor that supports connection with clients. Minority clients can feel underserved even though counselors demonstrate respect, skill, and ethical behavior. If counselors focus on diversity issues without constructing an active and meaningful process for clients to make sense of their complete selves, clients certainly will feel that something is missing. For example, suppose a counselor focuses on addressing the struggle an adolescent has with her parents due to generational gaps. However, the counselor neglects the fact that the client is also a girl who immigrated with her parents at a young age, that she does not have many close friends because she has moved a lot for her parents' jobs, and that she cannot express her complex and uncertain emotions to her parents because she has not mastered her parents' native language. How would the counseling outcome be effective for this girl? Such a disconnection from elements of clients' life experiences would lead to the provision of inadequate service to clients who, as a result, would feel underserved. Multicultural counseling, as argued by Comstock et al. (2008), is relational and prepares counselors to transform the disconnections and related elements in clients' lives to provide more effective service.

In summary, it is common practice now after many years of advocacy and education to argue that counselors need to pay attention to the cultural backgrounds of clients to be able to help them effectively. Being aware of the importance of multiculturalism in counseling is widely accepted as a critical qualification of being a competent counselor. However, awareness per se is not sufficient to provide effective counseling. Connecting the various elements of individuals' life spaces to make the counseling process a meaningful one for clients is what multicultural competence should be. In other words, counselors need to explore an integrated viewpoint that incorporates various elements of individuals' ecological systems in order to more effectively help clients of diverse backgrounds. The ecological counseling approach is a metatheory (Conyne & Cook, 2004) and provides alternative views of diversity and multicultural counseling that integrate the multidimensional, intersectional, and interactive nature of diversity issues in counseling and their effects on human behavior.

Ecological Validity

Ecological validity refers to the appropriateness and feasibility of counseling strategies for the ecosystem of the client. In this sense, cultural appropriateness is equivalent to ecological validity, because the essence of culturally appropriate counseling approaches is using strategies that are accepted and that have been proven effective in the particular cultural context of the client. The phrase *one size fits all* is not applicable here; rather, it should be *one size does not fit all* (Pedersen, 2000). Counselors cannot make assumptions concerning the validity of any strategy until the client validates it. Because each individual is unique, ecologically valid counseling strategies are therefore individualized. In other words, multicultural competency needs to involve providing culturally appropriate counseling services that fit ecologically into the individual's ecosystem and that are appropriate and meaningful to the individual client. By examining similarities and differences within and across groups in identity issues, and by exploring multifaceted cultural identity, counselors can find the unique interplay of various dimensions for each client. This unique interplay of individual characteristics, group characteristics, and universal human nature forms the client's individuality. Moreover, this individuality is manifested contextually. When each of the dimensions of one's individuality is well supported in the environment or appropriately accommodated by the environment, ecological concordance occurs (Conyne & Cook, 2004). It becomes clear that an effective multicultural counseling process certainly addresses diversity

173

but not from a single focus. A multifaceted and contextualized diversity exists, requiring a broader and more integrated view of a client's cultural background.

Clients as Change Agents

In the ecological counseling perspective not only are counselors change agents, but clients themselves should be empowered to become change agents. In fact, the ACA (American Counseling Association) Advocacy Competencies (Lewis, Arnold, House, & Toporek, 2002) call for counselors to be change agents with and on behalf of their clients at all levels of the ecosystem. A counseling approach that neglects the active role clients can engage in in the counseling process and that treats individuals as passive receivers of social and political discourses would be oppressive (Ballou et al., 2002). The meaning-making process is critical to empowering clients to become active participants in the counseling process rather than purely receivers of the service; clients themselves can best make meaning of their interaction with environments. Zhuang Zi, an ancient Chinese philosopher, said, "If you are not a fish, how would you know the joy a fish has?" Similarly, counselors cannot take their clients' place in terms of life experiences; no matter how skilled counselors are, they cannot feel exactly the same way clients feel. Consequently, it is wise to assist clients in developing the awareness and skills needed to make sense of their environment. The counseling outcome will be more sustainable if clients themselves can become the change agent.

Ecological Analysis

Ecological analysis is a useful tool counselors can use to gain an accurate understanding of clients' issues. By analyzing the various layers of a person's ecological system, the counselor can draw on issues of multifaceted cultural identity, the sociopolitical context, the socioeconomic context, and the interaction of these factors to conceptualize problems and set goals with clients. Ecological analysis makes it possible for clients to be active participants and change agents because counselors need to work with clients to validate the meaning of these issues and to set goals. The first step in an ecological analysis is to ask clients questions pertaining to the basic facts about each of their ecosystems (e.g., personal background, family history, churches and communities). The second step is to facilitate a mapping process to help clients identify which resources/assets and barriers exist in their ecosystems for resolving their issues. Finally, counselors should analyze the sustainability of any strategies they have developed collaboratively with their clients by examining their ecological validity.

Summary

D'Andrea and Heckman (2008) discussed four accomplishments of the multicultural counseling movement: recognizing between-group differences and the broader impact of cultural backgrounds on human development and behavior, within-group differences and cultural identity development, the multidimensionality of human development, and standards competence. It is apparent that multicultural counseling has moved beyond simply recognizing the between-group differences needed to develop effective skills. Much literature has been produced on the subject of multicultural competency development (see Arredondo et al., 2005; Ponterotto, Casas, Suzuki, & Alexander, 2010). The Association for Multicultural Counseling and Development's Multicultural Counseling Competencies (D. W. Sue, Arredondo, & McDavis, 1992) is the most comprehensive and widely acknowledged guideline for developing multicultural competency. Although it is great that these standards are available to professionals, it is necessary to examine the ecological validity of these competency skills for different cultural groups.

Diversity in the ecological perspective is illustrated by intersectionality and the interaction of various roles and expectations in individuals' ecosystems. The roadmap to developing multicultural competency becomes clear if one uses the ecological approach to understand the multifaceted identity of clients, the intersectionality of their roles in various life spaces, and their interaction with their environment; to facilitate meaning-making processes with clients; and to empower clients to be change agents. Ecological validity is the ultimate criterion for evaluating the cultural appropriateness of counseling interventions.

Discussion Questions

- Why is it important to understand clients' cultural identity in order to help clients more effectively?
- Which ecological factors contribute to the multifaceted nature of cultural identity?
- How would you describe the intersectional nature of cultural diversity from the ecological counseling perspective?
- According to the ecological counseling perspective, what are the essential strategies counselors should use to help clients from diverse cultural backgrounds?

References

Appleby, G. A., Colon, E., & Hamilton, J. (Eds.). (2001). *Diversity, oppression, and social functioning.* Boston, MA: Allyn & Bacon.

Arredondo, P., Rosen, D. C., Rice, T., Perez, P., & Tovar-Gamero, Z. G. (2005). Multicultural counseling: A 10-year content analysis of the *Journal of Counseling and Development. Journal of Counseling & Development, 83,* 155–160.

Arredondo, P., Toporek, M. S., Brown, S., Jones, J., Locke, D. C., Sanchez, J., & Stadler, H. (1996). Operationalization of the Multicultural Counseling Competencies. *Journal of Multicultural Counseling and Development, 24,* 42–78.

Atkinson, D. R., Morten, G., & Sue, D. W. (1998). *Counseling American minorities* (5th ed.). New York, NY: McGraw-Hill.

Balkin, R. S., Schlosser, L. Z., & Levitt, D. H. (2009). Religious identity and cultural diversity: Exploring the relationship between religious identity, sexism, homophobia, and multicultural competences. *Journal of Counseling & Development, 87*, 420–427.

Ballou, M., Matsumoto, A., & Wagner, M. (2002). Toward feminist ecological theory of human nature: Theory building in response to real-world dynamics. In M. Ballou & L. S. Brown (Eds.), *Rethinking mental health and disorder: Feminist perspectives* (pp. 99–144). New York, NY: Guilford Press.

Berry, J. W. (1980). Acculturation as varieties of adaptation. In A. Padilla (Ed.), *Acculturation: Theory, models and some new findings to acculturation* (pp. 9–25). Boulder, CO: Westview Press.

Berry, J. W. (2003). Conceptual approaches to acculturation. In K. M. Chun, P. B. Organista, & G. Martin (Eds.), *Acculturation: Advances in theory, measurement, and applied research* (pp. 17–37). Washington, DC: American Psychological Association.

Bronfenbrenner, U. (1979). *The ecology of human development.* Cambridge, MA: Harvard University Press.

Chaudhury, S. R., & Miller, L. (2008). Religious identity formation among Bangladeshi American Muslim adolescents. *Journal of Adolescent Research, 23*, 383–410.

Comstock, D. L., Hammer, T. R., Strentzsch, J., Cannon, K., Parsons, J., & Custavo, S. (2008). Relational-cultural theory: A framework for bridging relational, multicultural, and social justice competencies. *Journal of Counseling & Development, 86*, 279–287.

Conyne, R. K., & Cook, E. P. (Eds.). (2004). *Ecological counseling: An innovative approach to conceptualizing person–environment interaction.* Alexandria, VA: American Counseling Association.

Cross, W. (1991). *Shades of Black: Diversity in African American identity.* Philadelphia, PA: Temple University Press.

D'Andrea, M., & Heckman, E. F. (2008). A 40-year review of multicultural counseling outcome research: Outlining future research agenda for the multicultural counseling movement. *Journal of Counseling & Development, 86*, 356–363.

Erikson, E. H. (1963). *Childhood and society.* New York, NY: Norton.

Flores, L. Y., & O'Brien, K. M. (2002). Using structural equation modeling to advance theory regarding the career orientation of Mexican adolescent women. *Journal of Counseling Psychology, 49*, 14–27.

Gallardo, M. E., & McNeill, B. W. (Eds.). (2009). *Intersection of multiple identities: A casebook of evidence-based practices with diverse populations.* New York, NY: Routledge.

Goodwin, R., & Cramer, D. (2000). Marriage and social support in a British-Asian community. *Journal of Community & Applied Social Psychology, 10*, 49–62.

Guadalupe, K. L., & Lum, D. (2005). *Multidimensional contextual practice: Diversity and transcendence.* Belmont, CA: Brookes/Cole.

Helms, J. E. (Ed.). (1990). *Black and White racial identity: Theory, research and practice.* Westport, CT: Greenwood Press.

Hussain, F. (2009). The mental health of Muslims in Britain. *International Journal of Mental Health, 38,* 21–36.

Hutchison, E. D. (2008). *Dimensions of human behavior: Person and environment* (3rd ed.). Thousand Oaks, CA: Sage.

Inman, A. (2006). South Asian women: Identities and conflicts. *Cultural Diversity and Ethnic Minority Psychology, 12,* 306–319.

Kurrie, R., & Vo, D. E. (2004). Who's in charge? Coparenting in South and Southeast Asian families. *Journal of Adult Development, 11,* 207–219.

Leong, F. T. L. (1996). Toward an integrative model for cross-cultural counseling and psychotherapy. *Applied and Preventive Psychology, 5,* 189–209.

Lewis, J. A., Arnold, M. S., House, R., & Toporek, R. L. (2002). *ACA advocacy competencies.* Retrieved from http://www.counseling.org/Resources/Competencies/Advocacy_Competencies.pdf

Marks, A. K., Szalacha, L. A., Lamarre, M., Boyd, M. J., & Coll, C. G. (2007). Emerging ethnic identity and interethnic group social preferences in middle childhood: Findings from the Children of Immigrants' Development in Context (CIDC) study. *International Journal of Behavioral Development, 31,* 501–513.

Markus, H. R., & Kitayama, S. (1991). Culture and the self: Implications for cognition, emotion, and motivation. *Psychological Review, 98,* 224–253.

Pedersen, P. B. (Ed.). (1991). Multiculturalism as a fourth force in counseling [Special issue]. *Journal of Counseling & Development, 70.*

Pedersen, P. (2000). *A handbook for developing multicultural awareness* (3rd ed.). Alexandria, VA: American Counseling Association.

Phinney, J. S. (1992). The Multigroup Ethnic Identity Measure: A new scale for use with diverse groups. *Journal of Adolescent Research, 7,* 156–176.

Ponterotto, J. G., Casas, J. M., Suzuki, L. A., & Alexander, C. M. (Eds.). (2010). *Handbook of multicultural counseling* (3rd ed.). Thousand Oaks, CA: Sage.

Rivera, L. M. (2010). Acculturation theories, measurement, and research. In J. G. Ponterotto, J. M. Casas, L. A. Suzuki, & C. M. Alexander (Eds.), *Handbook of multicultural counseling* (3rd ed., pp. 331–342). Thousand Oaks, CA: Sage.

Robinson-Wood, T. L. (2009). *The convergence of race, ethnicity, and gender* (3rd ed.). Columbus, OH: Pearson Education.

Rockquemore, K. A., & Laszloffy, T. A. (2003). Multiple realities: A relational narrative approach in therapy with Black–White mixed-race clients. *Family Relations, 52,* 119–128.

Rodriguez, N., Myers, H. F., Mira, C. B., Flores, T., & Garcia-Hernandez, L. (2002). Development of the Multidimensional Acculturative Stress Inventory for adults of Mexican origin. *Psychological Assessment, 14,* 451–461.

Rudmin, F. (2003). Review of acculturation: Advances in theory, measurement, and applied research. *Journal of Cross-Cultural Psychology, 34,* 751–753.

Schwartz, S. J., Unger, J. B., Zamboanga, B. L., & Szapocznik, J. (2010). Rethinking of concept of acculturation: Implications for theory and research. *American Psychologist, 65,* 237–251.

Sewell, H. (2009). *Working with ethnicity, race, and culture in mental health: A handbook for practitioners.* Philadelphia, PA: Jessica Kingsley.

Sue, D., Mak, D. W., & Sue, D. W. (1998). Ethnic identity. In L. C. Lee & N. W. S. Zane (Eds.), *The handbook of Asian American psychology* (pp. 289–323). Thousand Oaks, CA: Sage.

Sue, D. W., Arredondo, P., & McDavis, R. J. (1992). Multicultural counseling competencies and standards: A call to the profession. *Journal of Multicultural Counseling and Development, 20,* 64–88.

Sue, D. W., & Sue, D. (1999). *Counseling the culturally different* (3rd ed.). New York, NY: Wiley.

Tang, M. (2002). Comparison of African Americans, Americans, and Chinese in career aspiration. *Journal of Multicultural Counseling and Development, 30,* 124–134.

Tang, M., Fouad, N. A., & Smith, P. L. (1999). Asian Americans career choices: A path model to examine the factors influencing choices. *Journal of Vocational Behavior, 54,* 142–157.

Thomas, A. J., & Schwarzbaum, S. (2006). *Culture and identity: Life stories for counselors and therapists.* Thousand Oaks, CA: Sage.

Trimble, J. E. (2003). Introduction to social change and acculturation. In K. M. Chun, P. B. Organistra, & G. Martin (Eds.), *Acculturation: Advances in theory, measurement, and applied research* (pp. 3–13). Washington, DC: American Psychological Association.

Tuason, T. G., Taylor, A. R., Rollings, L., Harris, T., & Martin, C. (2007). On both sides of hyphen: Exploring the Filipino-American identity. *Journal of Counseling Psychology, 54,* 362–372.

Unger, R. K. (Ed.). (2001). *Handbook of the psychology of women and gender.* New York, NY: Wiley.

Assessment, Diagnosis, and Treatment Planning From the Ecological Perspective

F. Robert Wilson

Assessment, diagnosis, and treatment planning are the keys to a mental health professional's success in treatment delivery. From the ecological perspective, counselors consider what goes on inside the person, how the environment impinges on the person, how the person interacts with others, and how the person makes meaning of his or her inner and outer world experiences.

All clinicians, regardless of their discipline (e.g., counseling, social work, psychology, nursing, medicine) and work setting (e.g., schools, clinics, community mental health centers, hospitals, private practices), share common inner motivation and common environmental press. All are compelled by their inner sense of professionalism and also by external forces (e.g., state and federal law, professional codes of ethics) to acquire and to use both knowledge and skills wisely. All seek to know their clients thoroughly and to use sound clinical judgment in deciding the best course of action to take in serving them. All clinicians, regardless of their discipline, and proceeding from their theoretical framework of choice, seek to reduce their clients' distress, improve their performance in school or work environments, improve the quality of their interpersonal relationships, and reduce or eliminate their risk of incurring grave loss or harm. Some clinicians, especially those who adhere to the traditions of medicine and psychology, seek solutions within the client, making the assumption that client behavior is a function of personal characteristics and that therapeutic leverage can be gained through a focus on such within-person factors as biochemistry, cognitive

179

capacity, personality, knowledge, skills, attitudes, values, or conditioned responses. Other clinicians, especially those with a sociological bent, seek an explanation for the client's problems outside the personhood of the client and seek therapeutic leverage by focusing on changing environments (Conyne & Cook, 2004).

Ecological clinicians adopt a broad view of the determinants of behavior and of the sources of therapeutic leverage. Ecological clinicians believe that behavior is a function of persons' constant attempts to experience themselves as effective in their interactions with the people and things who make up their personal niches, or, as Willi (1999) said, "the totality of the relationships with animate and inanimate objects actually present in their surroundings" (p. 26). We create our personal niche by constantly and intensely negotiating with the people in our environment. As we negotiate to shape the niche about us, we are in turn shaped by the feedback we receive from our niche mates. Thus, it is the animate, human objects that are most critical; it is in our interactions with our human objects that we assess our reality and judge our effectiveness. In response to environmental feedback, we adapt our actions to improve our interactive effectiveness (Willi, 1999; Wilson, 2004).

Naturally, one's interactive effectiveness is bolstered or limited by one's personal characteristics; likewise, one's interactive effectiveness is bolstered or limited by the characteristics of one's environment and niche mates. Thus, ecological clinicians seek therapeutic leverage in the notion of *concordance*, or the fit between a person and his or her personal environmental niche (Conoley & Haynes, 1992; Conyne & Cook, 2004). With this broader perspective, a wide range of targets for assessment, problem identification and diagnosis, and intervention or treatment planning becomes available. Of course, ecological clinicians target the within-person attributes of the client. Obviously, they also target the coevolutionary interactions of couples and families. But ecologically grounded clinicians seek an even broader array of therapeutic targets that might include the associational groups (clubs, churches, organizations), institutional groups (educational settings, work settings), and communities (neighborhoods, cities, states) within which their clients live, work, and play (Conyne & Cook, 2004).

The purpose of this chapter is to describe how ecologically oriented clinicians use the core clinical processes of assessment, diagnosis, and intervention or treatment planning in deciding how to be of best service to their clients. Although the terms *assessment, diagnosis,* and *treatment planning* are drawn from the traditions of mental health counseling in community settings, parallels are drawn to the work of counselors in school settings.

A note about terminology: Throughout this chapter, the term *clinician* is used to refer to any and all members of the helping professions (e.g., school counselors, mental health counselors, social workers, pastoral counselors, psychiatric nurses, psychologists, psychiatrists). The notions of ecologically grounded clinical work are equally applicable within any of these helping disciplines. Also, gender-neutral pronouns are used throughout the chapter. However, clinical illustrations must of necessity involve characters who are gendered. Effort is made to vary the genders of the clinician and the client.

Assessment

Each time we greet a new student or client, we are faced with a very human puzzle: What do we do after we have said "hello" (Berne, 1972)? To solve this puzzle, we must successfully answer three core questions: Who are you (in relation to me)? Who am I (in relation to you)? and What shall we do together? The way we (clinician and client) choose to go about answering these questions will direct the course of our therapeutic relationship. Mental health counseling, arising as it does from the traditions of psychiatric and psychological science, has historically assumed that a client is a client because of problems that arise from within the person. Consequently, clinical interventions will involve marshalling the client's personal strengths to offset his or her personal limitations (Conyne & Cook, 2004; Wilson, 2004). Yet counseling as a whole also arises from another powerful tradition, the tradition of vocational and career counseling, which emphasizes the role of the environment and the goodness of fit between the person and the environment in which he or she is seeking interpersonal effectiveness (Parsons, 1909). Lewin (1936) first gave voice to a synergistic, ecological model: A person's behavior is a function of the pattern of interactions he or she has within his or her environment, or $B = f(P \times E)$. From the ecological perspective, the questions Who am I? and Who are you? are layered questions. To truly answer either one we must examine personal characteristics, both mine and yours; the characteristics of our respective environments; and the characteristic ways in which both you and I interact within our respective environments throughout the unfolding of our respective lives. Only then can we begin to guess what we shall do together and how we shall go about it.

An Ecological Framework for Assessing Health and Illness

Within the ecological framework it is assumed that mental health is best studied by assessing the person–environment fit (Banning, 1989; Wilson, 2004). To assess this fit the clinician must assess broadly, examining the client's intrapsychic sphere (particularly the constructs that form the basis of the client's intentions, plans, and actions), the client's ecological niche (particularly the people with whom the client interacts and the constructs that guide the client's intentions, plans, and actions), and the interactional sphere (the repeating patterns of interactions between the client and the client's niche mates; Willi, 1999; Wilson, 2004). From the ecological perspective health is construed as the degree to which one experiences interpersonal effectiveness within one's ecological niche (Lewin, 1936; Willi, 1999; Wilson, 2004).

The Person

Mental health assessment has historically assumed that intrapsychic factors are the most important determinants of a client's health, a view that can be modeled as $B = f(P)$. Encyclopedic works, such as the Buros Mental Measurements Yearbook (Plake & Impara, 2001) or the Maruish (1999) review of key mental health instruments, catalog a host of tools for assessing such intrapsychic features as cognitive capacity and attainment, mood and anxiety symptoms, and personality characteristics. The analysis of the person has been reified in the mental status examination (see Table 8.1).

The ecological view of health and illness recognizes that some problems, such as schizophrenia and mood disorders, may arise from a malfunction in the biological substrata. Other problems, such as eating disorders and substance use disorders, may arise from dysregulation of drive satisfaction and behavior. Still others are rooted in lifelong patterns of learning that lead to maladaptive personality traits: Antisocial personality disorder is a common outcome for children reared with chaotic disciplinary patterns by parents who may themselves evidence a criminal lifestyle (McHugh, 2002). What these problems of the person have in common is insensitivity to context. They are problems that tend to arise regardless of the social context in which the person finds himself or herself.

The Environment

Environmental assessment in mental health counseling has not kept pace with personological assessment. Grounded in the belief that behavior is a function of environmental forces, or B = f(E), environmental assessment has historically been the province of sociology, community psychology, and social work. Even though Axis IV of a *Diagnostic and Statistical Manual of Mental Disorders* (*DSM*)–based multiaxial diagnosis (American Psychiatric Association, 2000) addresses psychosocial and environmental problems, the findings of this environmental status examination are often not given much weight in many clinicians' diagnostic formulations and subsequent treatment plans. Ecologically grounded assessment, however, strives to obtain a comprehensive description of the daily contexts that make up an individual's life, including the objective qualities of the individual's ecological niche and his or her subjective perception of those qualities (Munger, 2000; Wilson, 2004).

Parallel to the notion of insensitivity to context mentioned in the discussion of person-based problems is the notion that some environments exert

Table 8.1

Elements of the Mental Health Status Examination: B = f(P)

Element	Examples
Appearance	Dress, grooming, identifying physical features
Behavior	Motor behavior, attitude toward examiner, eye contact
Speech	Rate, volume, tone, quality of speech
Mood and affect	Prevailing mood; range, stability, congruence of affect
Thought process	Degree and kind of thought disorganization
Thought content	Suicidality, violence potential, delusions, obsessions, phobias, cravings
Perception	Hallucinations, illusions
Cognitive capacity	Alertness, attention, concentration, memory, intelligence, fund of knowledge
Psychoactive substance use	Kind, quantity, frequency, effects of the use of prescribed and illicit substances
Insight and judgment	Degree of insight into origin and nature of problems, reasonableness of decisions

such potent toxic effects that people within the environment are negatively affected no matter how healthy they were when they entered the environment. For example, in *Stockholm Syndrome*, a paradoxical psychological reaction to being taken hostage, victims who have been put in danger against their will sometimes express strong positive feelings toward their captors and may even act in their captors' defense.

Therefore, a comprehensive evaluation of the environment includes the identification of both *nutrients* (e.g., jobs, housing, food sources, health care facilities, education and training facilities, social services, recreation sites, and friendly and supportive people) and debilitating *toxins* (e.g., poor air, dangerous housing, dangerous work sites, predatory people, neighborhood strife, civil unrest). A guide for conducting an evaluation of environmental status has been drawn from the *DSM-IV* Axis IV problem-focused list (American Psychiatric Association, 2000), Munger's (2000) list of core niche elements, and Bronfenbrenner's (1979) hierarchy of ecological contexts (see Table 8.2).

The Interaction Between Person and Environment

One's personal characteristics and the characteristics of one's ecological niche are the building blocks for a life, yet how do they combine as a life unfolds? In ecological assessment the interaction of the person with the elements and systems of the environment, B = f(P × E), is paramount (Bondurant-Utz, 1994; Horton & Bucy, 2000). Though not nearly so numerous, a variety of scales have been developed for assessing interactions among people. Notable examples include the Fundamental Interpersonal Relations Orientation scales (Schutz, 1958); the Interpersonal Check List (Leary, 1957); the Inventory of Interpersonal Problems (Horowitz, Rosenberg, Baer, Ureno, & Villasenor, 1988); and Hudson's series of instruments for assessing peer (1993), sibling (1997a, 1997c), and family (1997b) relationships. A rich description of the quality of a client's interactions within his or her ecosystem can be captured in genograms (Marlin, 1989) and ecomaps (WonderWare, n.d.) by coding life space patterns, what Lee (1985) described as individu-

Table 8.2

Elements of an Environmental Status Examination: B = f(E)

Microsystem—primary, face-to-face contacts
- Primary social group structure and function (family of origin, current family)
- Social niche membership (friendships, social groups)
- Neighborhood resources and toxins (housing, health care, schools)
- Employment opportunity

Exosystem—larger systems that affect the client
- Educational opportunity
- Medical care, psychological care, emotional care, spiritual care
- Legal involvement

Macrosystem—pervasive social forces
- Cultural, ethnic, religious considerations
- Neighborhood and community organization and governance
- Sociopolitical policies and dynamics

als' "characteristic ways of negotiating time, space, people, and activity in their day-to-day lives" (p. 624). A rich description of how a client interacts with his or her niche mates can be assembled by categorizing the client's relationship activities into a hierarchy of involvement ranging from little involvement and commitment (participating without interacting) to deep involvement and commitment (dyadic relationships with binding commitments). Willi's (1999) continuum of interpersonal patterns provides a scale for assessing a client's level of involvement with his or her niche mates (see Table 8.3). Qualitative questions such as the following should be a part of every clinician's repertoire for evaluating clients' interpersonal patterns: What is a typical day like for you? What is it like for you at work (or school)? What is it like to live in your neighborhood? What is it like for you when someone says, "I'll help you"?

An Ecologically Grounded Assessment of Meaning Making

Getting to know the personhood of the client, the client's ecological niche, and the interaction patterns typical of the relationship between the client and his or her niche mates provides critical information for clinicians to use in their professional determination of problems to be addressed in counseling. However, it is the manner in which we go about these activities that answers the opening question: What do we do after we say "hello"? Ecological clinicians construe counseling as an interactional process. Rather than viewing assessment as something a counselor does for and to a client, ecological clinicians view assessment as a process for assembling cocollected data and developing coconstructed meaning. Kleinke (1994) had further suggestions for assessment that are concordant with the ecological point of view.

Explain the Purpose of the Assessment and the Assessment Process to Be Followed

Ecological clinicians begin the assessment process by explaining its purpose and by suggesting how the assessment might be undertaken (Cormier & Cormier, 1991; Kleinke, 1994). By explaining one's ecologically grounded intent to assess within-person, environmental, and interpersonal material, the clinician introduces the client to the perspective that will be taken throughout the therapeutic endeavor. And by inviting the client to participate in shaping the process by which each of these spheres of data is explored, the ecological clinician sets the stage for cooperative, collaborative counseling

Table 8.3
Interactional Status: Hierarchy of Interpersonal Patterns: B = f(P x E)

Simple forms of interactions (participating without interacting)
Nonreciprocal interaction
Brief contacts without commitment
Reciprocal relationships without responsibility
Relationships with minimal personal closeness
Dyadic, coevolutionary relationships with binding commitments

interactions. Clients are likely to be more cooperative and spontaneous when the counselor structures the assessment experience accordingly. For example, a clinician could say the following:

> Our friends can be helpful to us because they know us. To be helpful to you, I need to know you too, but it would be good if I could get to know you more quickly than the way it usually happens with friend-ships. Suppose we start by talking about what things about you cause you to feel bad or worry and what things about you seem good and useful to you; what in the world around you is causing you problems and what you enjoy or count on; and what is good about the relation-ships you have with the people in your world and what feels bad or doesn't work very well. As we talk, I may ask questions to be sure I understand how things are with you. If you don't understand why I am asking about something, tell me and I will explain why I asked, and if I seem to be asking about things that don't seem very important or relevant to you, tell me and we can talk about it.

1 Define the Problem, Not Its Explanation

The ecologically oriented counselor works patiently to get the client's most elaborate description of his or her problems and strengths. Through his scientific study of languaging, Kelly (1963) taught that interpersonal effectiveness and health are in part a product of the degree to which we can describe our experience in multiple and contextually sensitive ways. Thus, ecological clinicians see that clients' problems and their inability to use their own strengths derive in part from failures in meaning making. A client's "stuckedness" is in part a failure to richly describe the *who, what, when, where,* and *how* of his or her experience and to focus instead on impoverished and perhaps misconstrued descriptions of *why.* Count-less clinical writers have warned us not to ask "Why are you angry with your [child, parent, teacher, employer]?" Rather, we are urged to ask the client "When do you get angry with ____? What is happening before you get angry? When do you first notice you are getting angry? When you feel angry, what do you do (or say)? What happens after you have done (or said) that? How do you feel after you have gotten angry and done what you did (said what you said)?" Our core question, whether we are working in school or community settings, should be this: In what way does the fit between the client and his or her environment fail to provide the nutrients needed for growth?

2 Separate the Fault for the Problem From the Responsibility for the Solution

When clients' problems derive mostly or solely from within-person causes, or $B = f(P)$, clients can often easily accept their role in the problem and their responsibility for solving it. For example, if a client suffers from attention-deficit/hyperactivity disorder, a disorder commonly thought to have clear biological origins, the clinician may explain to her that she has a chemical imbalance in her system and that with both pharmacological and behavioral treatment, she can gain control over her wandering attention and hyper-activity. However, when the client's problems result predominantly from environmental stressors, or B = f(E), or from the pattern of interactions the client has with his or her niche mates, or B = f(P × E), the client may feel defensive, arguing, "This isn't my fault! Why is it up to me to fix it?" Wise clinicians know that empathy is required to truly understand the client's sense of injustice and to gently help the client accept the inevitability of accepting responsibility for the solution to problems for which the client was not the sole cause (Stark, 1994).

3   *Explore the Meaning of the Problem to the Client*
Clients will want to talk about their view of the *why*. To help them explore the *why* in a deep way, look for the purpose or function the problem plays in the context of the client's life. Beyond problems based in what one has, what one does, or what one is, clients struggle with making meaning from their own lived experience and especially from such experiences as thwarted commitments, hopes, and aspirations (McHugh, 2006). Rather than asking "Why?" Kleinke (1994) suggested using Watzlawick's "What for?" question to explore the purpose the problem plays in the client's life. Another question that may stimulate deeper reflection is "Who would you be if you didn't have these problems?" Because any change precipitates more change, yet another option is to explore the price the client will have to pay for ridding himself or herself of the problems about which he or she complains: "If you were suddenly able to get rid of these problems, what else would you lose?" Even deeper, we may ask, "How do you explain all this to yourself?"

4   *Explore the Motivation for Presenting for Counseling*
Clinicians hope that the clients sitting in their office are there of their own free will, seeking to achieve a better fit between themselves and their ecological niches. Often this is not the case. The client we describe as a *mandated client* has many faces. Sometimes the client is remanded by the court or a probation officer in the legal system or the principal or teacher in the school system. Sometimes the mandate comes from a grandparent or parent in a family system or a spouse or partner in a romantic relationship. The question, as Kleinke (1994) might phrase it, is Who really wants the change?

After a thorough initial assessment of the client's inner problems and strengths, and the environmental factors and interpersonal processes that may support problem solution or that may maintain or exacerbate the problems, the counselor is ready to move toward problem formulation and diagnosis. As mentioned earlier, except for occasions when we work with a committed couple, with a family system (as in marriage and family therapy), or with a larger social organization (as in task group consultation or organizational or community development), we are typically working with a single client. Regardless of whether within-person processes or environmental forces are the cause of the problem, our interventions will likely be targeted toward things the client can change for himself or herself. As the counselor takes this step toward problem formulation and diagnosis, it is good for him or her to remember that the assessment–diagnosis–intervention planning process is an ongoing one. For example:

A recovering alcoholic with 3 years of sobriety requested treatment for chronic anxiety. The client, who during his drinking years had lived under bridges and on park benches, now had a room in a low-income, inner-city sheltering hotel. Since the onset of his drinking, he had always been a solitary drinker, and even in his recovery he found it difficult to be among other people. He worked for a nighttime cleaning crew in which he was not required to talk with others and spent the remainder of his waking hours in his room reading. He attended an inner-city meeting of Alcoholics Anonymous where he listened to other people tell their stories but rarely spoke. Diagnosed with social phobia, he was prescribed and responded modestly well to an antianxiety medication. A breakthrough occurred when his case manager found an opening for him to move to a church-sponsored retirement hotel located in a quiet, lower middle-class neighborhood. Several months after moving to his new residence, he reported that he noticed a change taking place. He said that when he was on the streets he had always been a man who walked at a military pace, avoiding eye contact and speaking to no one. He was surprised to find that now, in this quiet neighborhood, he was starting to take strolls and occasionally would catch himself chatting with folks who were sitting on their porches. He was also surprised that he was beginning to develop a friendship with a man in his building with whom he had common reading interests. Although he had always expressed pride in his ability to cope with life on the streets, now that he was living in a safer neighborhood he realized that his socially phobic behavior was a coping strategy he no longer needed. As a consequence, the clinician revised the client's diagnosis, and the treatment plan was modified to expand upon the client's new awareness.

Just as was true in this case, over the course of work with any client, clinicians should anticipate that as new assessment data become available, revisiting the diagnosis and revising the intervention plan may be required.

Diagnosis

Clinicians, regardless of their specialization, are in some sense of the word diagnosticians. From the Greek *diagignoskein*, diagnosing involves examining assessment data to discern, distinguish, and make meaning of the data. By tradition, clinicians, especially those who work within the health care professions, have concentrated on diagnosing problems that arise from within the person: $B = f(P)$. Each of the mental disorders classified in the standard taxonomic reference for the mental health profession, the *DSM-IV-TR* (American Psychiatric Association, 2000), is conceptualized as

a clinically significant behavioral or psychological syndrome or pattern that occurs *in an individual* and that is associated with present distress (e.g., a painful symptom) or disability (i.e., impairment in one or more important areas of functioning) or with a significantly increased risk of suffering death, pain, disability, or an important loss of freedom. (p. xxxi, emphasis added to highlight the exclusively within-person focus of traditional diagnosis)

However, not only health care clinicians are engaged in diagnostic activity. Like their colleagues in health care, school counselors engage in the assessment, discernment, and classification of student problems. Although under the American School Counselor Association (ASCA) National Model school counselors are cautioned against working with individual student cases in remedial therapeutic activities, they *are* directed to conduct assessments and determine whether individual students or student groups are experiencing problems with academic development, career development, or personal-social development (ASCA, 2009). These dimensions derive from a classificatory system based on the Missouri Diagnostic Classification Plan, a system that was proposed in the late 1950s and refined by a succession of researchers through the early to mid-1960s (Hurst & McKinley, 1988). Without stating it formally, the ASCA National Model does attend to the same sorts of causal factors delineated in the Missouri Diagnostic Classification Plan: lack of knowledge, skills, and attitudes necessary for effective learning in school and across the life span; lack of knowledge, skills, and attitudes necessary to investigate the world of work and make informed career decisions; and lack of knowledge, attitudes, and interpersonal skills necessary for respecting the self and others and managing interpersonal conflict with others. This system, although not formally tied to *DSM* diagnostics, serves a similar function and in fact attends to similar within-person issues.

The main strengths of classificatory systems such as the *DSM* are that they are empirically grounded, reliable, and useful. The *DSM-IV* was based on a three-stage empirical process to inform the revision process using systematic literature reviews, analysis of existing data sets, and design and implementation of fresh field trials. Consistent with findings from studies of the earlier *DSM-III* and *DSM-III-R*, field trial studies of diagnostic consistency over time and interclinician reliability under the *DSM-IV* show acceptable reliability of clinical diagnostic judgment. Finally, its utility was strengthened by the elimination of the rating for severity of psychosocial stressors (*DSM-IV*, Axis IV); the refinement in the scaling for judging adaptive functioning (*DSM-IV*, Axis V); and the demonstration that the two major international classifications for mental disorders, the *DSM-IV* and the *International Statistical Classification of Diseases and Related Health Problems* (10th ed.; ICD-10), have been successfully harmonized (Nathan, 1998). However, although the *DSM-IV* has been shown to be empirically grounded, reliable, and useful, it is far from ideal. Since the release of the *DSM-III*, the *DSM* system has been criticized for promoting a disease model of psychopathology, expanding the number and range of diagnoses, and adopting a definition of mental disorders that narrowly focuses the diagnostic process on within-person factors and simultaneously casts a very broad clinical net within which syndromes of even moderate severity may earn a diagnostic label. It has also been criticized for clinging to a categorical system when many believe a dimensional system might be more descriptive, especially for the highly comorbid personality disorders (Nathan, 1998).

When using the *DSM* system, ecologically grounded clinicians engage in pattern matching. In the *DSM* system, each disorder is described according to a list of criteria. Diagnosticians collect data about the client's complaints and symptoms and, based on experience, select a number of possible diagnoses for trial. The clinician compares the client's data to the diagnostic criteria for each of the diagnoses selected for trial to test for goodness of fit. The final diagnosis (or diagnoses) is the one (or ones) to which the client's data provides the best fit. The ecological perspective helps clinicians avoid the common but erroneous belief "that a classification of mental disorders classifies people, when actually what are being classified are disorders that people have" (American Psychiatric Association, 2000, p. xxxi). Ecological clinicians understand that diagnosing is not an act of labeling. A diagnosis does not does tell us what the client is. Rather, a diagnosis is more like a roadmap. It points the way to professional literature that can help us select or create a treatment plan that may be of help to the client. Thus, the core diagnostic question for any set of presenting problems, complaints, and symptoms is this: For which diagnosis or diagnoses do the client's presenting data (i.e., complaints, symptoms, problems) best fit the diagnostic criteria?

Perhaps the client's problems arise from context-insensitive, within-person dysfunction, such as chronic depressed or cycling mood, anxiety that arises suddenly and without obvious cause, or perceptual distortions such as hallucinations. We test this hypothesis by carefully comparing the client's data with various *DSM* criteria sets to determine which syndromes or disorders best fit the client data. Ecologically grounded clinicians, however, do not stop with this review of potential within-person problems.

Ecological clinicians are guided by Bronfenbrenner's (1979) description of the ecosystems that surround and impact a person's psychological life. Perhaps the client's problems arise from reasonably expected contextual responses to environmental forces within the client's *exosystem*, such as the effects of a parent's experiences in the work environment on the parent's interactions with children at home, the occurrence of natural or economic disaster, or the presence of environmental toxins or neighborhood predators (Bronfenbrenner, 1979; Willi, 1999; Wilson, 2004). Consider for example a client who reports that for the past 2 to 3 weeks she has been feeling depressed and has been sleeping all the time; has no energy; has no interest in food; cannot concentrate; and cannot even get herself to go to her music lessons, an activity that she historically has cherished. A diagnostician would have no trouble recognizing that she shows the signs of a within-person diagnosis of major depressive disorder. However, if on further inquiry the diagnostician learns that she is a single parent with dependent children, recently suffered the death of a close relative, recently lost a good job because of company downsizing, and because of the stagnant economy has not been able to land a job that meets her family's needs, the diagnostician might revise the diagnosis to the more environmentally driven diagnoses of bereavement arising from the close relative's death and adjustment disorder with depressed mood associated with her precarious economic circumstances.

Then again, perhaps the client's problems arise from influences within his or her *microsystem*—the ongoing pattern of reciprocal reinforcements that shape interpersonal expectations and behavior within the peer group,

189

school or work environment, and neighborhood. Microsystem influences are particularly powerful in the case of the coevolutionary pattern of relationships between parents and children and bonded couples or the *mesosystemic* contrasts between what is experienced in various settings: family, peer group, school, work, church (Bronfenbrenner, 1979; Willi, 1999; Wilson, 2004). Using depressed mood again as an example, if a diagnostician finds that a client presents the classic symptoms of major depressive disorder but only in the context of interacting with or talking about his interactions with his spouse, diagnostic caution is warranted. Suppose that when the client talks about his work life, the diagnostician finds him to be brighter and more animated, describing hopes and dreams and failures and successes in a realistic way. And suppose that when the client talks about his friendships, he reports maintaining friendships characterized by reciprocal support. Although such a contextually grounded depression as this client presents may evidence the same symptoms as the more context-insensitive, more biologically based major depressive disorder, the depressive symptomatology may be the result of learned helplessness related to marital interaction patterns rather than an endogenous major depressive disorder arising from internal, biological causes. Consider too how children's behavior may vary widely from context to context. For generations, parents have advised their children to avoid hanging around bad companions, knowing, at least at an intuitive level, how susceptible children are to learning from those they choose as models. In diagnosing misbehavior or emotional problems in children, the diagnostician is wise to collect information about the reinforcement patterns present in the various environments in which the child spends his or her time. The question with children is more often "Where and how did the child learn to act or feel this way?" rather than "What has gone wrong within the child that would lead to these actions or feelings?"

Across settings, clinicians work with diverse clients. Naturally, ecologically grounded clinicians are sensitive to gender and sexual preference differences among their clients. They also attend to the *macrosystemic* influence of the culture matrix surrounding the client, including socioeconomic status, ethnicity, and religious tradition (Bronfenbrenner, 1979). We know, for example, that the ways in which we experience and express disease (dis-ease) are influenced by our upbringing and the lessons taught by those closest to us: important adults in the schools we attended and our friends and their families. School counselors are all too familiar with how illness-affirming parents may reinforce a child's use of physical symptoms to avoid having to go to school and suffer being separated from the parents about whom the child is anxious. Mental health counselors likewise are challenged by the diverse ways in which mental illness is experienced by clients from different cultures. The *DSM* recognizes several forms of culturally bound disturbance, such as *latah* (a syndrome characterized by falling into a trance when startled and enacting repetitive verbal or physical behavior), that are specific to certain cultures and not to others. Thus in some cultures trance behavior may properly be described as a diagnosable syndrome, whereas in others trance behavior may be part of the culture's religious tradition and an integral part of religious observance.

While embracing their responsibility to diagnose problems that arise from within the child, adolescent, or adult, ecologically oriented clinicians attempt to determine the relative contributions of within-person assets, deficits, and pathology; environmental nutrients and toxins; or a mismatch between the person and his or her ecological niche (Banning & Kaiser, 1974; Hurst & McKinley, 1988; Lewin, 1936). Although a noxious environment does not appear to cause a diagnosable mental illness, the *diathesis–stress model* for the development of mental illness suggests that a person may inherit a susceptibility for a psychological disorder (the *diathesis*, or vulnerability), which may be prompted by the proper set of environmental stressors to erupt into an identifiable mental or emotional disorder. A companion theory, the reciprocal gene–environment theory, suggests that a person's vulnerability to a particular mental or emotional disorder may increase the likelihood that the person may seek out environments that provide the necessary stressful trigger. In both models the interactive effect of personal vulnerability and environmental stress is implicated. Studies of normal child development rest on the core assumption that the child was raised in a culturally standard environment. Kroll (1993) further argued that the diagnostic system for mental and emotional disorders rests on the same core assumption. "Once the childhood environment departs substantially from this broadly defined norm [the "average expectable environment"], in terms of neglect, abuse, violence, and unpredictability, than all assumptions about the orderly process of child development go out the window" (p. 75). Scarr (1992) drove the point home by saying, "Environments that fall outside of the species-normal range will not promote normal developmental patterns" (p. 5). Few current diagnoses (e.g., reactive attachment disorder, posttraumatic stress disorder, acute stress disorder) pay explicit attention to the impact of extraordinary environmental stressors, but clinicians can take such abnormal environments into account as they conduct their assessments, render diagnoses, and plan treatments.

As mentioned earlier, ecological clinicians view diagnoses as a roadmap to finding helpful treatments and work to minimize the negative effects of diagnoses being treated as client labels by remembering that diagnoses are categories of problems, not people. Furthermore, as Wright (1991) has suggested, clinicians try to attend equally to strengths and assets as to deficiencies and undermining characteristics, to environmental resources and opportunities as to environmental deprivations and toxins. They use person-first language to reinforce that a client may have a disorder or a noxious environment but that he or she is first and foremost a person who can change and who lives in an environmental niche that can also be changed. The use of "person-labeling" rather than "person-affirming" language can have a damaging effect on clients. Perhaps the most egregious example in modern times is the unfortunate portrayal of people who have borderline personality disorder. In all too many clinical settings, clients with borderline personality disorder may be viewed as difficult, noncompliant, impossibly needy people who may not even have a legitimate disorder and who are a drain on clinic resources (Kealy & Ogrodniczuk, 2010). In response to complaints about the difficulties a clinician might be having in working with a client diagnosed with borderline personality disorder, it is not uncommon to hear, "Well, what do you expect, she's a borderline!" Such pejorative attitudes have led in some cases to the rationing or withholding of services (Kealy & Ogrodniczuk, 2010). Blaming the supplicant for having problems a clinician does not know how to solve easily or comfortably is an understandable but thoroughly unprofessional response. Clinicians must strive to use currently available interventions to put the person before the disorder and to honor the person even though his or her problems may be dangerous, difficult, or intractable.

Ecological Perspectives on Diagnosis

From the ecological perspective, one may diagnose the nature of problems that arise from within the individual, or $B = f(P)$; problems that arise from the nature of the environment, or $B = f(E)$; and problems that arise from the interaction between the individual and the environment, or $B = f(P \times E)$.

Diagnosing Problems Arising From Within the Person

In the grand sense, diagnosing within-person problems is the act of making meaning of the rich flow of data emanating from within a person. Although the introduction of explicit behavioral criteria for mental and emotional disorders catalogued in the *DSM* may have improved diagnostic reliability, it may have done so at the cost of flattening the nuances of meaning available for understanding within a client's life story in service of fitting them into a diagnostic template. McHugh (2002) has advanced a metaclassification scheme for understanding within-person disorders, $B = f(P)$, that preserves nuanced explanation:

- *The Disease Perspective* ("What one has"). The first perspective is grounded in human biology. At the most fundamental level, disorders may arise from the biological substrata consisting of "an identifiable abnormality in structure or function of a bodily part" (McHugh, 2006, p. 182). Examples of disorders that arise from the biological substrata include brain disease (dementia); brain damage; perceptual disorders that involve illusions, hallucinations, delusions, or overvalued ideas; and fixed, persisting mood states.
- *The Dimensional Perspective* ("Who one is"). The second perspective is based in the notion of *constitutional vulnerability*—a weakness in cognitive power or instability of affective control that renders an individual vulnerable to distress and in need of psychological strengthening or hardening (McHugh, 2006). From the ecological perspective "who one is" may be construed even more broadly. The possession of visible characteristics that trigger hostile or predatory behavior on the part of others (e.g., physical deformity, skin color, biological sex) certainly is a permanent part of who one is and may increase one's vulnerability to stress.

- *The Behavioral Perspective* ("What one does"). The third perspective is grounded in body-based drives, both innate (e.g., hunger for food, craving for sexual stimulation) and acquired (e.g., craving for psychoactive drugs, craving for risk or high-stimulation activity). McHugh (2006) noted that individuals with disordered drive regulation require treatment "not because of what they have or who they are, but because of what they are doing and how they have become conditioned to doing it" (p. 58). Examples of disorders that arise from the behavioral perspective include alcoholism, drug addiction, the sexual paraphilias, and the eating disorders.

- *The Life Story Perspective* ("What one has encountered"). The final perspective is the existential perspective of the client's own meaning making. One's satisfaction with life depends in large measure on the meaning one makes from what one encounters. As Seligman (2006) has taught us, healthy people learn to construe life events in ways that promote optimism. When events frustrate one's wishes, hopes, aspirations, and dreams, unhealthy habits of thought—habits of viewing life's frustrations as being permanent, personal, and pervasive—lead to lives ruined not by the events themselves but by one's emotional reactions to these frustrations. In this case, people suffer because "they intended to do something—choose a job, sustain a marriage, succeed in college, relate to peers—and have suffered a number of unintended consequences: grief, isolation, demoralization, failure. They ask, 'Where am I going and why can't I get there?'" (McHugh, 2006, p. 174).

Diagnosing the Press of Client Environments

It is uncommon for clinicians to think about diagnosing environments, yet the opportunity is there for them to use the skills of diagnosis to determine whether a client's problems are initiated by, exacerbated by, or driven by environmental forces. This diagnosis will be based on assessment data, the enumeration and description of the quality and quantity of nutrients and the presence of stressors and toxins within the individual's niche environment. Because children are so responsive to environmental stimuli (having not yet established a relatively fixed personality), school counselors often observe how a child who disrupts one classroom may be a good citizen in another or how the problems a parent describes about a child at home do not arise when that same child is at school or at church. As individuals mature, they develop a more fixed set of personality characteristics that are less influenced by changes in the environment. Healthy adults maintain a sensitivity to context that allows them to adapt to changes in environmental demands. However, individuals who develop rigid, context-insensitive personality features may suffer from an inability to adapt to the changing demands within their environment.

Ecological clinicians in the schools can use observational techniques and functional analysis to describe the client's behavior; enumerate the

193

antecedents and consequences of the behavior; and hypothesize about the possible function of distressed feeling, interpersonal conflict, or dysfunctional or risky behavior in the child's attempts to achieve interactive effectiveness (O'Neill et al., 1997). When working in community settings, mental health clinicians may have only limited opportunities to engage in direct observation of their clients but can ask them to provide self-assessment data for diagnosing which environmental triggers and reinforcers play a role in their problems.

Without individualized functional analysis on which to base a diagnosis, ecological clinicians can fall back on some known truths about environments. In the language of Alcoholics Anonymous, some people, places, and things are nutritious (e.g., supporting life, promoting health) whereas others are toxic (e.g., undermining life, producing ill health). Some characteristics of social and occupational (including school) environments are often associated with stimulating or exacerbating distress or social-occupational impairment (e.g., unexpected change in routine or productivity standards, the receipt of critical feedback from others, a lack of personal attention or recognition). Sensory environments may also stimulate or exacerbate people's problems (e.g., extremes in or fluctuations of lighting, temperature, or noise; certain noises, tastes, or odors; disorganized or chaotic visual stimuli). Finally, the emotional environment may be a contributor or a cause of client's distress or dysfunction (e.g., high expressed emotion, intrusive questioning; witnessing or being a party to squabbling, bickering, arguing, devaluing, yelling, fighting, bullying, predation; cf. Alberto & Troutman, 1999). Environments such as these may be diagnosed as nonnutritious or toxic, warranting them to be changed if possible or avoided if not.

Diagnosing Patterns of Interpersonal Interaction

Throughout the assessment process, ecological clinicians seek to describe the reciprocal, interlocking patterns of interrelatedness between the individual and his or her key niche mates (the people with whom the individual has meaningful contact), especially those with whom the individual is involved in a bonded, committed, coevolutionary relationship. Hollis (2007) suggested that "a mature relationship is one in which each party assumes responsibility for her or his individuation, and supports the other in hers or his as well" (p. 99) and argued that when both parties are able to accept responsibility for themselves and support others' self-determination, the relationship is balanced and can tolerate lapses on the part of either party. Unbalanced relationships in which only one of the parties accepts responsibility for his or her individuation are rife with conflict and are unlikely to endure. Willi (1999) suggested three personal dilemmas (double approach–avoidance conflicts) that may interfere with interactive effectiveness:

- The dilemma of shying away from the risk of being hurt and suffering isolation, emptiness, and lack of acknowledgment versus entering into a relationship hoping for confirmation at the risk of being hurt

194

- The dilemma of clinging to the current level of dyadic interactive effectiveness at the risk of stable stagnation versus allowing change to occur in the relationship at the risk of diminished satisfaction
- The dilemma of selecting a partner who stimulates emotional intensity at the risk of a chaotic life versus selecting a partner who is stable and dependable at the risk of incurring boredom and stultification

Each of these double approach–avoidance conflicts describes polar opposites. At each end of the polarity is a desired reward and a feared consequence. To seek the upside at either end of the polarity one must bravely face the associated downside. This dimensional framework provides latitude for describing individuals who have achieved satisfactory balance between engagement versus self-protection, stability versus change, and stimulation versus quietude as well as those who have failed to achieve satisfactory resolution of these interpersonal dilemmas. Thus, Willi's polarities can be used as a dimensional framework for describing or diagnosing a client's historical approach in relating to niche mates.

With clients whose interpersonal relationships are filled with pain and suffering, other diagnostic schemes support interpersonal diagnosis. Nursing diagnoses for family functioning have been promulgated by the North American Nursing Diagnosis Association (2009–2011). These diagnoses include (a) family processes: dysfunctional, interrupted; (b) family coping: disabled, compromised; (c) parenting: impaired, at risk for being impaired; (d) caregiver role: strained, at risk for strain; (e) role performance: at risk for impaired parent–child attachment, conflictual, ineffective; (f) sexuality: dysfunctional, ineffective; and (g) social: social isolation, impaired social interaction, at risk for loneliness. Clinicians can use these categories to describe the nature of relationship problems clients may be experiencing.

An even more elaborate tool for describing dysfunctional interaction patterns has been developed by Eric Berne. In *Games People Play*, Berne (1996) presented a catalog of *games*—interactive patterns that, although seemingly ordinary, lead predictably to negative emotional payoffs. Berne's theory postulates that experiencing negative affects is to be preferred over feeling nothing at all; consequently, people who shy away from seeking or accepting the expression of positive affects may engage in games because they have a reliable emotional payoff potential. Berne's catalog of games can be used to categorize client behavior within an explanatory system that can teach clients the origin of their negative payoff interactions and that offers an alternative for client change.

Whatever nomenclature is used, the goal of interpersonal diagnosis is to describe the patterns of the interactional dance between the client and his or her niche mates that results in the client feeling distressed, diminished in school or occupational productivity, dissatisfied with his or her interpersonal effectiveness, or at greater risk for grave harm. An exploration of the client's interpersonal patterns may be facilitated by using Menninger's triangle of insight as a guide: (a) Explore the conditions under which these interpersonal patterns arise in the client's real-world relationships with niche mates, (b) explore the historical parental–familial origins of the diagnosed interactional patterns and dilemmas, and (c) explore the immediate consequences of the client's interpersonal style on how the client and clinician interrelate during their work together (Holmes, 1994; Menninger, 1958).

Intervention and Treatment Planning

For ecological clinicians, the value of the assessment–diagnosis–planning sequence is in its process, the development of a collaborative relationship between the client and counselor, and in its end product, the plan for "What we are going to do together (in the future)?" Planning an intervention or treatment, whether in school or the community, is a process that moves from broad goals to specific actions.

Goal Setting

Goal setting facilitates task accomplishment. This time-honored maxim, so well documented, has become part of our pool of common knowledge (Locke, Shaw, Saari, & Latham, 1981). For mental health clinicians and school counselors alike, goal setting is a key part of developing a consent agreement between the counselor and client that specifies what they will address in counseling and how they will do it. From the ecological point of view, goals may address change within the person, in the environment, or in the person's pattern of interaction with the environment. Although the outcome of interactions with all parts of the environment, both animate and inanimate, is important, of critical significance is the pattern of interpersonal negotiation that characterizes the client's interaction with his or her niche mates and by which the client evaluates his or her interactive effectiveness. Cook, Conyne, Savageau, and Tang (2004) have pointed out that best practice involves collaboration between counselor and client to identify goals and action steps that provide a challenge yet are sufficiently supported so as to be plausibly achievable.

Within-Person Goals

Drawing again on McHugh's (2006) framework for conceptualizing a client's within-person problems, I argue that clinicians work to help clients address problems that arise because of what they have (problems that arise from the biological substrata), who they are (problems that arise from the client's constitutional vulnerabilities), what they do (problems associated with what the client has been conditioned to do), and what they have encountered (problems associated with emotional reactions to environmental assaults or blockades). In concert with the core definition of mental illness (American Psychiatric Association, 2000), within-person goals can be conveniently divided into five basic goal groups:

- Alleviation of symptom distress (e.g., stabilization of mood, reduction in phobic anxiety)

196

- Reduction of social impairment (e.g., reduction of self-isolation, improvement in interpersonal skills, improvement in parenting skills, improvement in choice of niche mates)
- Reduction of school or occupational impairment (e.g., improvement in job or school attendance and performance, reduction in job or school rule infractions, improvement in career development skills)
- Reduction of risk of grave loss (e.g., reduction in self-mutilation or suicidality, reduction in violence ideation or violent behavior, reduction in thrill seeking or risky sexual behavior, reduction in dependence on addictive substances, prevention of relapse)
- Definition of and stabilization of sense of self (e.g., strengthening of self-definition and personal boundaries, increase in a sense of acceptance of oneself and strengthening of self-esteem)

Although school counselors may be unfamiliar with the *DSM*, the kinds of difficulties described in it are familiar topics of worry among parents of a school-age child and the child's teachers, counselors, and school administrators.

Environmental Goals

In addition to classic within-person goals, ecologically oriented clinicians also consider goals for niche improvement. Environmental goals focus on identifying nutrients and toxins within the person's current niche environment, broadening the person's niche to include missing nutrients, and redefining niche boundaries to eliminate toxic elements. No clearer example is found in the treatment literature than the two-pronged Alcoholics Anonymous admonition: Avoid people, places, and things that trigger your urge to drink; build a network of sober support. Ecosystem analysis (WonderWare, n.d.) can assist in identifying the supportive and unsupportive elements within a client's ecosystem and can be especially useful in finding who or what is missing. After mapping the people and social systems with whom the client regularly interacts and noting whether the interactions are supportive or unsupportive, or nutritious or toxic, simple questions like "What do you need that doesn't show up in this map?" and "What do you see here that you would be better off without?" can stimulate the setting of clear goals for environmental change.

Interpersonal Goals

Interpersonal interactive effectiveness is critical for one's sense of well-being. Interpersonal goals focus on how people interact with niche mates to get the nutrients they need and to avoid the toxins that may harm them. People shape and are shaped by their niche mates. As explained earlier, the ecological approach to counseling is focused on the interlocking interactions between people and their niche mates and on the coevolving development of people who live together (Willi, 1999). Schutz's (1958) tripartite guide for describing interpersonal behavior may be a useful framework for setting goals for improving interpersonal effectiveness. Schutz taught that people's interpersonal styles derive from three interpersonal needs—inclusion, control, and openness—and the differences between what a person wants from and offers to others.

- *Inclusion.* The interpersonal need for inclusion focuses on maintaining a satisfactory level of contact, interaction, and association with others with a comfortable balance of initiating and eliciting interactions (Doherty & Colangelo, 1984; Schutz, 1958, 1992). Happiness derives from a good match between inner need and niche resources. Clients whose unhappiness derives from being undersocial may set goals for increasing awareness of opportunities within their niche for inclusion by others, increasing interpersonal attractiveness, or increasing an assertive search for and initiation of contact with others. However, clients whose unhappiness derives from being oversocial may set goals for increasing internal boundary definition and developing assertive boundary maintenance skills.
- *Control.* The interpersonal need for control focuses on maintaining a satisfactory level of influence and power with a comfortable balance between controlling and being controlled by others (Doherty & Colangelo, 1984; Schutz, 1958, 1992). In Schutz's (1958, 1992) view, a healthy level of control involves wanting and accepting guidance from and offering leadership to others. As with inclusion issues, treatment goals may focus on within-person issues such as boundary awareness, management, and assertive boundary defense; environmental issues such as selecting niche mates with democratic rather than autocratic or abdicratic attitudes; and sharing control through democratic problem solving in coevolutionary couple and family relationships.
- *Openness.* Finally, the interpersonal need for openness (sometimes referred to as *affection*) focuses on maintaining a satisfactory level of personal and interpersonal openness with others while achieving a comfortable balance between privacy and confiding (Doherty & Colangelo, 1984; Schutz, 1958, 1992). Treatment goals may include developing an inner sense of acceptance of oneself that supports openness with others; selecting people for one's personal niche who are neither compulsively disclosing nor compulsively withholding; and developing an ongoing pattern of coevolutionary, interpersonal growth and development with a life partner.

Tools for Treatment Planning

Three tools—the problem list, the Ecologically Grounded Problem Guide (Wilson, 2010), and the Progress Evaluation Scales (PES; Ihilevich & Gleser, 1982)—have been developed to assist clinicians in developing intervention or treatment plans. Because of their simplicity and transparency, all are equally useful in school and community settings. Ecologically grounded clinicians plan treatments with their clients, not for them. Treatment planning is the final preparatory step in developing the working alliance necessary for the client to embrace the therapeutic work that lies ahead.

The Problem List

Perhaps the simplest tool for goal setting is the collaborative problem list. The clinician asks, "What brought you here to see me today?" and, as the client tells his or her story, the clinician notes the various problems the client is experiencing. Ecologically grounded counselors listen carefully for problems across the full ecological spectrum: intrapsychic problems, interpersonal problems with niche mates in both social and occupational spheres, and environmental problems. In concert with the ecological point of view, the client and clinician collaborate in the creation of this problem list. A detailed description of the problem list approach to treatment planning was provided by Woody, Detweiler-Bedell, Teachman, and O'Hearn (2003).

The Ecologically Grounded Problem Guide

The clinician can use a problem guide such as the Ecologically Grounded Problem Guide (Wilson, 2010; see Table 8.4) to support the development of the problem list. The Ecologically Grounded Problem Guide expands the key elements of diagnosis (American Psychiatric Association, 2000) by crossing them with the tripartite Lewinian ecological formulation (Lewin, 1936). It can serve as a clinician's personal prompt for helping clients to look broadly at their context-insensitive, intrapersonal problems; problems that are driven by the environment in which they live; and problems that arise from their interpersonal relations with others. The clinician can then sort the client's problems by *psychodiagnostic category* (painful symptom, social impairment, occupational impairment, risk of grave loss, environmental threat), *temporal triage category* (must be addressed immediately, can be delayed until immediate problems are solved, requires longer term treatment or can be delayed indefinitely), and *ecological structure* (intrapsychic, interpersonal, environmental) to support the development of an individualized treatment plan. Although the initial sorting and organizing may require the expert judgment of the clinician, subsequent discussion with the client may reveal additional information and will surely help to further the working alliance between the clinician and client.

The PES

Another excellent tool for engaging a client in the process of setting goals for counselling is the PES (Ihilevich & Gleser, 1982), which can be used as an initial tool for treatment planning and as a tool for follow-up evaluation of treatment outcomes. This assessment instrument features seven scales that address a broad range of disturbance that is typical of people with psychological problems. Selection of the scales was informed by both psychodynamic theory and comprehensive empirical evidence. The scales, listed by scale number, are as follows:

Table 8.4

Ecologically Grounded Problem Guide (Wilson, 2010)

Locus on Problem	P *Content Insensitive*	P × E *Content Responsive*	E *Content Driven*
Inner distress	Painful symptoms (e.g., mood dys-regulation, anxiety, psychosis, low self-esteem, hyperactivity)	Interpersonal disappointments, frustrated wishes, misinterpretations	Fear, hunger, dread (due to neglect, abuse, lack of nu-trients, presence of toxins)
Social distress	Lack of social skills	Conflict-ridden social relationships with family, friends	Loss or threatened loss of family, friends (due to sepa-ration, estrange-ment, illness, death)
Occupational distress (work, school)	Lack of work skills (attendance, performance) Poor work attitudes (compliance with policies/procedures)	Conflict-ridden relationships with work/school mates, supervisors/teachers	Loss of employment opportunity (due to plant closings, business failures or takeovers) Lack of educational opportunities
Risk of grave loss	Self-injurious behavior (suicidality, self-mutilation) Deteriorating health (due to poor nutri-tion choices, lack of physical exercise, medical problems, misuse of legal medications, poor sleep hygiene) Addiction (use of al-cohol or illicit drugs, unrestrained raging, unsafe or inappro-priate sex, gambling, thrill seeking)	Ongoing interactions with toxic or predatory people	Direct exposure to environmental toxins Attack by predators Direct exposure to occupational danger Lack of health care opportunities Direct exposure to triggers for addic-tive behavior

Note. Entries are meant to be examples of client problems, not an exhaustive listing. P = person; E = environment.

1. *Family Interaction:* quality of interpersonal relationships with family members (dependence–independence)
2. *Occupation (School–Job):* level of functioning in one's primary occupational role (productivity)
3. *Getting Along With Others:* ability to establish and maintain sat-isfying relationships outside the family unit (socialization)
4. *Feelings and Mood:* flexible expression and adaptive integration of feelings (affective modulation)
5. *Use of Free Time:* free use of inner and outer resources for play and enjoyment (sublimation)

6. *Problems:* the ability to deal effectively with life's daily problems (coping)
7. *Attitude Toward Self:* the balance of negative and positive attitudes expressed about the self (self-esteem)

Each item is rated on a 5-point scale anchored with descriptive phrases for each of the scale's values. For example, the Getting Along With Others scale consists of the following anchoring phrases: (1) "always fighting or destructive or always alone," (2) "seldom able to get along with others without quarreling or being destructive or is often alone," (3) "sometimes quarreling, but seldom destructive; difficulties making friends," (4) "gets along with others most of the time; has occasional friends," and (5) "gets along with others most of the time; has regular close friends" (Ihilevich & Gleser, 1982).

At intake, a client (child, adolescent, or adult) may be asked to rate his or her current level of functioning in each of the seven areas and then indicate the amount of change he or she wants (or could reasonably expect) to achieve in each of the areas by the next evaluation period (e.g., within the next 3 months). As a final step, the client may be asked to rank order the seven areas in terms of personal importance. A clinician can also make independent assessments and choices for desired change on a separate rating form. Comparing sheets can stimulate productive conversation about goals.

The PES method offers some unique advantages. The PES takes less than 10 minutes for clients to complete; clinicians typically complete their ratings even more quickly. Interrater reliability is quite good given the instrument's brevity. The scales are independent from one another and correlate well with other relevant rating scales. Furthermore, they differentiate healthy individuals from those with mental health disorders and discriminate among clinical populations with varying levels of disturbance. Finally, the PES scales are sensitive to changes over time in level of functioning. For additional information on the psychometrics of the PES, see Ihilevich, Gleser, Gritter, Kroman, and Watson (1982).

A key to success in goal setting and treatment planning is assessing the goodness of fit between the client and the plan (Rollnick, Mason, & Butler, 2000). Asking the client to rate the importance of achieving each proposed goal on a scale of 1 to 10, with 10 being the highest rating for importance, clarifies the client's investment in change. A low rating may suggest that the clinician has misunderstood the client's needs, that the goal may be a good goal but the timing is bad, or that other goals supersede this goal in the client's mind. A moderate rating can be explored by asking "What would have to happen to get your rating to move up in importance?" A high rating, say a 9 or 10, suggests that the goal is of sufficient value to the client to be worth pursuing. For highly valued goals, goodness of fit can be further assessed by asking how confident the client feels that he or she can succeed in making the desired change. Again, scaling the evaluation helps to make it concrete. Readiness to change, according to Rollnick and his associates (2000), is linked, though not perfectly, with importance more than with confidence. Knowing this, the ecologically oriented counselor can explore the advantages and disadvantages to keeping things as they are, raising the client's awareness of the possible benefits of and prices paid for not engaging the challenge of change.

Summary

Ecologically oriented clinicians use the core clinical processes of assessment, diagnosis, and intervention or treatment planning to build a solid therapeutic relationship with their clients as well as to meet their professional obligation to use sound clinical judgment in deciding the best course of action to take in the service of their clients. They strive to gather assessment data that help them know who their clients are in relation to themselves and to others. They use their clinical judgment to render an accurate diagnosis of their clients' intrapsychic, environmental, and interpersonal problems. Finally, they work in concert with their clients in a cooperative, collaborative, and joint search for ways to increase clients' sense of peace, joy, and freedom; to improve clients' school or work performance; to increase clients' interpersonal effectiveness among their niche mates; and to increase clients' sense of safety and security within their niche.

Discussion Questions

- In your own words, what is the ecological perspective on assessment, diagnosis, and treatment planning? How do these functions fit together?
- What is your niche? Take an inventory of the content of your own personal and professional niche. Evaluate your niche for the presence of people and institutions that provide nurturance and those that are toxic and predatory. What resources might you want to increase within your niche? How might your sense of personal effectiveness increase if certain elements were removed?
- Mental health clinicians are often required to complete a diagnostic assessment form (DAF) as part of the intake process. Using the DAF from your agency (or a sample DAF if you are not at a clinical placement), classify the sections of the DAF in terms of whether they emphasize personal, environmental, or interactional factors and evaluate the DAF for balance of coverage. What element(s) receive heavy coverage? What aspects of the person, his or her environment, and his or her patterns of interaction with others are slighted? What might you want to ask your clients about that is not covered in the DAF?
- If you are working in a clinical setting, examine the treatment plans you have created for several clients. Classify your planned interventions to see the degree to which you emphasize personal, environmental, or interactional changes. Do you make use of the full range of options available for treatment planning? What do you characteristically emphasize? What adjustments might you make in your treatment plans to make full use of your ecological understanding?

202

- Diagnosis of mental or emotional disorders focuses on conditions found within a person that yield a painful symptom, result in impaired social or occupational functioning, or increase an individual's risk of grave loss. What does the ecological perspective add to the *DSM*'s view of what is important to diagnose? How can you incorporate the broader ecological perspective on diagnosis into your clinical practice?
- Listen to your colleagues (e.g., fellow students, fellow clinicians). When they talk about their clinical work, what kind of language do they use? Does their discussion of clinical cases recognize the personal, environmental, and interactional factors in their clients' lives? If so, you are in an environment that embraces and reinforces your learning about the ecological perspective. If not, what can you do to find reinforcement for increasing your learning and adherence to the ecological perspective?

References

Alberto, P. C., & Troutman, A. C. (1999). *Applied behavior analysis for teachers* (5th ed.). Columbus, OH: Merrill.

American Psychiatric Association. (2000). *Diagnostic and statistical manual of mental disorders* (4th ed., text rev.). Washington, DC: Author.

American School Counselor Association. (2009). *The ASCA national model: A framework for school counseling programs.* Retrieved from http://www.schoolcounselor.org/files/Natl%20Model%20Exec%20 Summary_final.pdf

Banning, J. H. (1989). *Ecotherapy: A life space application of the ecological perspective.* Retrieved from http://campusecologist.org/cen/v7n3.htm

Banning, J. H., & Kaiser, L. (1974). An ecological perspective and model for campus design. *Personnel and Guidance Journal, 52,* 370–375.

Berne, E. (1972). *What do you say after you say hello? The psychology of human destiny.* New York, NY: Grove Press.

Berne, E. (1996). *Games people play: The basic handbook of transactional analysis.* New York, NY: Ballantine Books.

Bondurant-Utz, J. A. (1994). *A practical guide to infant and preschool assessment in special education.* Boston, MA: Allyn & Bacon.

Bronfenbrenner, U. (1979). *The ecology of human development.* Cambridge, MA: Harvard University Press.

Conoley, J., & Haynes, G. (1992). An ecological approach to intervention. In R. C. D'Amato & B. A. Rothlisberg (Eds.), *Psychological perspectives on intervention* (pp. 177–189). White Plains, NY: Longman.

Conyne, R. K., & Cook, E. P. (2004). Understanding persons within environments: An introduction to ecological counseling. In R. K. Conyne & E. P. Cook (Eds.), *Ecological counseling: An innovative approach to conceptualizing person–environment interaction* (pp. 3–35). Alexandria, VA: American Counseling Association.

Cook, E. P., Conyne, R. K., Savageau, C., & Tang, M. (2004). The process of ecological counseling. In R. K. Conyne & E. P. Cook (Eds.), *Ecological counseling: An innovative approach to conceptualizing person–environment interaction* (pp. 109–140). Alexandria, VA: American Counseling Association.

Cormier, W. H., & Cormier, L. S. (1991). *Interviewing strategies for helpers.* Pacific Grove, CA: Brooks/Cole.

Doherty, W. J., & Colangelo, N. (1984). The family FIRO model: A modest proposal for organizing family treatment. *Journal of Marital and Family Therapy, 10*(1), 19–29.

Hollis, J. (2007). *Why good people do bad things: Understanding our darker selves.* New York, NY: Gotham Books.

Holmes, J. (1994). Brief dynamic psychotherapy. *Advances in Psychiatric Treatment, 1*, 9–25. Retrieved from http://apt.rcpsych.org/cgi/reprint/1/1/9.pdf

Horowitz, L. M., Rosenberg, S. E., Baer, B. A., Ureno, G., & Villasenor, V. S. (1988). The Inventory of Interpersonal Problems: Psychometric properties and clinical applications. *Journal of Consulting and Clinical Psychology, 56*, 885–892.

Horton, C. B., & Bucy, J. E. (2000). Assessing adolescents: Ecological and person–environment fit perspectives. In W. E. Martin & J. L. Swartz-Kulstad (Eds.), *Person–environment psychology and mental health: Assessment and intervention* (pp. 39–57). Mahwah, NJ: Erlbaum.

Hudson, W. W. (1993). *Index of Peer Relations (IPR).* Retrieved from http://www.walmyr.com/perscales.html

Hudson, W. W. (1997a). *Index of Brother Relations (IBR).* Retrieved from http://www.walmyr.com/famscales.html

Hudson, W. W. (1997b). *Index of Family Relations (IFR).* Retrieved from http://www.walmyr.com/famscales.html

Hudson, W. W. (1997c). *Index of Sister Relations (ISR).* Retrieved from http://www.walmyr.com/famscales.html

Hurst, J. C., & McKinley, D. L. (1988). An ecological diagnostic classification plan. *Journal of Counseling & Development, 66*, 228–232.

Ihilevich, D., & Gleser, G. C. (1982). *Evaluating mental health programs: The Progress Evaluation Scales.* Lexington, MA: Lexington Books.

Ihilevich, D., Gleser, G. C., Gritter, G. W., Kroman, L. J., & Watson, A. S. (1982). The Progress Evaluation Scales: A system for assessing child and adolescent programs. *Professional Psychology, 13*, 470–478.

Kealy, D., & Ogrodniczuk, J. S. (2010). Marginalization of borderline personality disorder. *Journal of Psychiatric Practice, 16*, 145–154.

Kelly, G. (1963). *A theory of personality: The psychology of personal constructs.* New York, NY: Norton.

Kleinke, C. L. (1994). *Common principles of psychotherapy.* Pacific Grove, CA: Brooks/Cole.

Kroll, J. (1993). *PTSD/borderlines in therapy: Finding the balance.* New York, NY: Norton.

Leary, T. (1957). *Interpersonal diagnosis of personality: A functional theory and methodology for personality evaluation.* New York, NY: Ronald Press.

204

Lee, M. (1985). Life space structure: Explorations and speculations. *Human Relations, 38,* 623–642.

Lewin, K. (1936). *Principles of topological psychology.* New York, NY: McGraw-Hill.

Locke, E. A., Shaw, K. N., Saari, L. M., & Latham, G. P. (1981). Goal setting and task performance: 1969–1980. *Psychological Bulletin, 90,* 125–152.

Marlin, E. (1989). *Genograms: A new tool for exploring the personality, career, and love patterns you inherit.* Chicago, IL: Contemporary Books.

Maruish, M. E. (Ed.). (1999). *The use of psychological testing for treatment planning and outcome assessment* (2nd ed.). Hillsdale, NJ: Erlbaum.

McHugh, P. (2002). Classifying psychiatric disorders: An alternative approach. *Harvard Mental Health Letter, 19,* 7–8.

McHugh, P. (2006). *The mind has mountains: Reflections on society and psychiatry.* Baltimore, MD: Johns Hopkins University Press.

Menninger, K. (1958). *Theory of psychoanalytic technique.* New York, NY: Basic Books.

Munger, R. L. (Ed.). (2000). *Comprehensive needs-based assessment with adolescents.* Mahwah, NJ: Erlbaum.

Nathan, P. E. (1998). The *DSM-IV* and its antecedents: Enhancing syndromal diagnosis. In J. W. Barron (Ed.), *Making diagnosis meaningful: Enhancing evaluation and treatment of psychological disorders* (pp. 3–27). Washington, DC: American Psychological Association.

North American Nursing Diagnosis Association. (2009–2011). *Nursing diagnoses (NANDA): Accepted for use and research.* Retrieved from http://www.scribd.com/doc/15553980/NANDA-NURSING-DIAGNOSES-20092011

O'Neill, R. E., Horner, R. H., Albin, R. W., Sprague, J. R., Storey, K., & Newton, J. S. (1997). *Functional assessment and program development for problem behavior: A practical handbook* (2nd ed.). Pacific Grove, CA: Brooks/Cole.

Parsons, F. (1909). *Choosing a vocation.* Boston, MA: Houghton Mifflin.

Plake, B. S., & Impara, J. C. (Eds.). (2001). *The fourteenth mental measurements yearbook.* Lincoln, NE: Buros Institute of Mental Measurements.

Rollnick, S., Mason, P., & Butler, C. (2000). *Health behavior change: A guide for practitioners.* New York, NY: Churchill Livingstone.

Scarr, S. (1992). Developmental theories for the 1990s: Development and individual differences. *Child Development, 63,* 1–19.

Schutz, W. (1958). *FIRO: A three-variable theory of interpersonal relations.* New York, NY: Rinehart.

Schutz, W. (1992). Beyond FIRO-B—Three new theory-derived measures—Element B: Behavior, Element F: Feelings, Element S: Self. *Psychological Reports, 70,* 915–937.

Seligman, M. E. P. (2006). *Learned optimism: How to change your mind and your life.* New York, NY: Vintage.

Stark, M. (1994). *Working with resistance.* Northvale, NJ: Jason Aronson.

Willi, J. (1999). *Ecological psychotherapy.* Seattle, WA: Hogrefe & Huber.

Wilson, F. R. (2004). Ecological psychotherapy. In R. K. Conyne & E. P. Cook (Eds.), *Ecological counseling: An innovative approach to conceptualizing person–environment interaction* (pp. 143–170). Alexandria, VA: American Counseling Association.

Wilson, F. R. (2010). *Ecologically Grounded Problem Guide.* Unpublished guide.

WonderWare. (n.d.). Ecotivity (Version 3) [Computer software]. Silver Spring, MD: Author.

Woody, S. R., Detweiler-Bedell, J., Teachman, B. A., & O'Hearn, T. (2003). *Treatment planning in psychotherapy: Taking the guesswork out of clinical care.* New York, NY: Guilford Press.

Wright, B. A. (1991). Labeling: The need for greater person–environment individuation. In C. R. Snyder & D. R. Forsyth (Eds.), *Handbook of social and clinical psychology* (pp. 469–487). New York, NY: Pergamon.

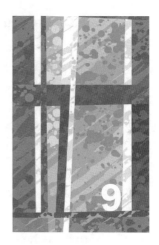

School Counseling

Jeri Crowell, Kerry E. Sebera, and Susannah C. Coaston

Utilizing the ecological counseling framework enables school counselors to be leaders, advocates, collaborators and team members who are able to transform a school environment by reducing barriers to academic success and helping to close the achievement gap for minority students. Students bring their own particular and unique context and academic experience, and teachers and counselors are charged with helping them improve the person–environment fit to achieve academic and personal success. Success is enhanced when meaning making is understood so that school counselors can support students by building resilience; identifying strengths, supports, and resources within the students and social system; and advocating for the students when necessary.

Schools as formal institutions of learning have changed significantly over the years, especially with the passage of the No Child Left Behind Act of 2001, which created sweeping change across the field of education. Schools have become progressively more complex collections of multiple and unique systems, including the distinctive cultures within individual classrooms, enclosed within their larger schools, nested within broad city or district systems, and accountable to greater state or national systems (e.g., the U.S. Department of Education). Individuals within the subsystems (be they students or school personnel) are influenced by their school's environment: Their person–environment interactions create the specific context through which they experience supports and challenges.

In this chapter we describe how ecological principles can be applied in the school setting. You will develop a better understanding of the systems that affect students, teachers, school counselors, and other school personnel through examples drawn from our work with children and in the schools.

Ecological Concepts

Ecological counseling emphasizes the interdependence between persons and environments, asserting that each influences the other. A systems model focuses on all elements of a situation, whereas an ecological perspective incorporates individuals' experiences within those systems. Both perspectives are derived from the ecological model developed by Bronfenbrenner (1979) and identify children within a microsystem that is composed of family, friends, school, and neighborhood. Children's interactions with any of the elements at the microsystem level create interrelationships of a mesosystem, such as children's relationships with adults in the community or parents' interactions with the school. The quality of these interrelationships influences children's behavior at home, in school, and in the neighborhood. Berns (2007) articulated that a school is also a microsystem on which influence is exerted by the exosystem through school or government policies, organizational authority, and the social relationships of parents and other adults. Although these exosystem influences do not directly involve the children, they impact their lives, such as when budget cuts limit the services of a school nurse to half time or less. Meanwhile, schools, children, and their families are increasingly influenced by ever-changing macrosystem factors such as politics, economics, and technology. Similarly, culture and ethnicity are macrosystem components reflected in the interactions of people and their environments, and they affect the ideology of everyday practices through individuals' perceptions of what it is to be a good student or what it means to be a patriotic citizen of the United States of America (Conyne & Cook, 2004). Finally, the chronosystem influences the entire model with the aspect of the historical time within which each person lives.

Context is the ecological principle that considers real, imagined, and symbolic circumstances of people's realities, or the people and events that form the unique environment within which each person exists (Conyne & Cook, 2004). Children who are involved in positive reciprocal interactions with their multiple levels of context are considered to thrive (Theokas et al., 2005). For example, Amanda lives in a suburb with her parents and younger brother. A high achiever academically, she participates in athletics and volunteers with her church group at a soup kitchen. Amanda has a close relationship with her extended family, is engaged in her community, and has an outlet for giving of her time and talents charitably. Not only has she developed positive relationships within multiple systems, but she reciprocates by contributing positively to her community.

The ongoing relationship between individuals and their contexts is dynamic in response to internal and external stimuli. External stimuli are provided to children by parents, teachers, schools, peers, and communities, whereas internal stimuli are unique to the individual and include the ecological principle of meaning making. The nature and quality of these interactions and subsequent relationships must be understood, as children seek to comprehend and determine significance for what happens within the family, school, and community environments (Crowell, 2007). As an illustration, Marc is a high school freshman whose single mother works overnight at a hospital. When his teacher expresses concern that Marc is alone all night, he shares how much he appreciates his mother taking on different shifts so that they can move into a safer apartment building and start saving for his college education. In this example, what might appear to be inadequate supervision or lack of parental involvement is perceived positively by Marc, who sees the benefits for himself and his future.

Schools are a natural milieu for understanding contextual influences on children's experiences of development, including race, sexual orientation, socioeconomic status, and culture and language. The context of the school setting is also referred to as *school environment* or *school climate*. K. M. Brown, Anfara, and Roney (2004) described *school climate* as the experience of the participants in a collective perception of behaviors in the school. Students from diverse backgrounds must learn to comprehend more than one set of norms, as rules and traditions at home may be quite different from those at school (Yeh, 2004). The dominant culture's values determine how school success is measured but may not be culturally relevant for all students.

The ability to maintain mental and emotional stability develops as the individual constantly responds to ecological challenges. Each person has a unique experience of the world, described as *person–environment fit* (Conyne & Cook, 2004). For example, Natalie is a third grader in a rural Appalachian community within 25 minutes of a large university. Ms. Mills, a school counseling intern from the local university, is placed at Natalie's school and presents a classroom guidance lesson on career exploration. Natalie shares with Ms. Mills that she would love to become a veterinarian but she cannot because she could never go to college. When Ms. Mills asks why Natalie believes she could never go to college, the child responds, "Because no one in my family has ever been to college and it costs a lot of money." Ms. Mills explains to Natalie that she, herself, is a first-generation college student, gives her some information about college, and discusses the possibility of scholarships to help with the cost. Ms. Mills is quite happy to have the opportunity to encourage Natalie's academic and career ambitions, so she is taken aback the next morning when she receives an angry note from Natalie's mother telling her "not to fill Natalie's head with crazy ideas about going to college." In this case, if Natalie learns not to value academic achievement and the pursuit of higher education, she will have a greater person–environment fit within her family and small community that does not value academic achievement. Although others in the broader community, including Ms. Mills and Natalie's teacher, may hold different values, how Natalie ultimately makes meaning of the environment will determine her path of personal and academic growth and development.

Challenges Faced in School Environments

School counselors must address the needs of students with a myriad of problems, such as physical and emotional issues, hunger, the effects of their own and their parents' substance abuse, lack of school supplies, and pressures to succeed. The American School Counselor Association (ASCA) recommends a school counselor–to–student ratio of 1:250 (ASCA, 2005). Unfortunately, ratios across the United States are much higher (Bemak, Murphy, & Kaffenberger, 2006; Paisley & McMahon, 2001), averaging 1:457 or more (U.S. Department of Education, 2009). School counselors find it difficult to attend to students effectively when they must be the primary counselor for so many (Musheno & Talbert, 2002). In addition, not all educators and administrators recognize the correlation between the existence of counselors in a school and the academic achievement of children.

With ongoing changes in the educational climate, school counselors are committed to improving their professional identities and roles (Perusse, Goodnough, Donegan, & Jones, 2004). ASCA (2005) developed the National Model to define the role of school counselors in supporting student learning and achievement. School counselors develop school–family–community partnerships to assist families and students in meeting students' increasing personal, social, academic, and career needs (Bryan & Holcomb-McCoy, 2007). Now more than ever, school counselors focus on being educational leaders who team with multiple stakeholders to improve the academic achievement of all students.

In the school setting, students and school personnel have unique resources that can allow them to achieve success in their environments. However, if the challenges become overwhelming, the result is more stress and an inability to cope with increased demands. Ecological concordance is experienced when the elements of challenge and support are in balance (Conyne & Cook, 2004). Individuals seek to maintain harmony by utilizing supports and strengths, such as when teachers, counselors, and other school personnel support one another and create positive interactions with their students even in the face of budget cuts and inadequate resources.

Urban schools are often described as challenging work environments for administrators, teachers, and staff (Bullough, 2001; Crowell, 2007; Prince, 2002; Quartz, 2003; Ringeisen, Henderson, & Hoagwood, 2003). School personnel in these settings deal on a daily basis with troubling issues, including a lack of resources, student performance that is below expectations, transportation issues, and shifting curriculum standards. External stressors beyond the school building include limited community support and social problems such as violence and racism (Brinson, Kottler, & Fisher, 2004). Many children arrive at school with difficult issues, such as insufficient support from parents, violence in their homes and neighborhoods, and problems resulting from parental substance abuse (Bullough, 2001; McEachern, Aluede, & Kenny, 2008; Quartz, 2003; Ringeisen et al., 2003). Some children do not arrive at school at all because of home environments in which they may care for an ill family member or be expected to work to assist the family financially.

A pressing issue faced by educators today is the recent emphasis on high-stakes testing and accountability. Governmental policies such as No Child Left Behind mandate that educators focus on outcomes-based learning to demonstrate academic achievement, primarily as measured

210

by proficiency tests. Classroom teachers are being held accountable for their students' test scores regardless of those students' given abilities and resources, which adds additional pressures to both the students and the teachers (McEachern et al., 2008). In addition to being accountable for their students' academic achievement, teachers are also regarded as "parental substitutes" (McEachern et al., 2008, p. 3), a role that includes all of the system dynamics of positively functioning or dysfunctional families. At times teachers are even described as "counselors" in their classrooms (Bullough, 2001; Crowell, 2007; Geltner & Leibforth, 2008), though they do not have the necessary training, knowledge, or skills to provide this service to their students. School counselors are often called on to assist and collaborate with teachers who find themselves confronted with situations for which they have not been trained, such as handling personal, social, and emotional issues with students and students' families.

Unfortunately, school counseling is not available at all in many schools because of budgetary restrictions. This means that school counselors are often absent from socioeconomically disadvantaged schools in rural, urban, or even suburban areas—schools where they may be needed the most. Comprehensive community interventions with children and families are particularly needed in impoverished communities. When school counselors are not available, it becomes the task of teachers and other community professionals to provide emotional support, opportunities for increased understanding and self-awareness, identification of personal strengths, and improved access to resources (O'Connor & McCartney, 2007).

The contexts of poverty and social problems expose individuals to stresses caused by health concerns and limited opportunities, which are often catalysts for school problems. The stress of economic disadvantages within the context of poverty can affect children's school functioning, such as through language and academic deficits and difficulties regulating emotions and attention (E. D. Brown & Low, 2008; Sirin & Rogers-Sirin, 2005). The degree of children's and adolescents' participation in violent activities correlates significantly with their socioeconomic status (Attar-Schwartz, 2009). Limited or nonexistent parental supervision also poses an increased risk for youths' involvement in community violence as both offenders and targets. Chaotic living conditions "limit opportunities for children to engage in predictable exchanges with the environment, and may engender helpless/hopeless responses to challenges" (E. D. Brown & Low, 2008, p. 920). Conditions such as residential noise and crowding, household instability, and lack of daily routine and structure can affect students' own regulatory resources—their ability to regulate emotions and attention (Evans, Green, & Serpell, 2005). Youth in these living environments often exhibit behavior problems that arise out of frustration and that can result in lower levels of achievement (O'Connor & McCartney, 2007).

Bronfenbrenner (1979) asserted that the most significant factors in fostering the positive or negative outcomes that put children at risk for school failure are social contexts, such as family and peer influences. For instance, E. D. Brown and Low (2008) described how marital conflict can

211

result in children's increased physiological and emotional sensitivity to other forms of conflict, such as school staff who yell in the classroom and hallways. Symptoms of emotional insecurity, sleep problems, and adjustment difficulties then appear in the school environment as poor academic and social interactions. School counselors and other personnel can serve as role models to ameliorate the negative effects of unhealthy interactions with those around them.

Although school personnel are important, parental involvement is paramount to student achievement. The amount of time parents interact with their children has been noted to be a positive resource for promoting academic and personal strengths (Kim, 2004; Van Horn, Bellis, & Snyder, 2001; Van Horn et al., 2009). Some parents find it difficult to be active participants in their children's school lives, even when they would like to be. Parents whose work begins before school opens and ends after school closes, or those who do not have reliable transportation, may struggle to be present at their children's school meetings and special school events or to volunteer in the classroom. Parents may not be involved for many reasons, including misperceptions about the educator's or school counselor's role as an authority figure (Fusick & Charkow Bordeau, 2004) or community suspicion about the goals of the education system's outreach and collaboration (Bryan & Holcomb-McCoy, 2007).

There are also many reasons why students may not be successful in school. Students in impoverished urban schools demonstrate an academic achievement gap, with lower success rates than those in more affluent areas (College Board, 1999; Education Trust, 1998; Gandara & Maxwell-Jolly, 1999). The fact that urban schools often have fewer educational opportunities and resources often results in a poor quality of education (Bemak, Chi-Ying, & Siroskey-Sabdo, 2005). High dropout rates can result from high student mobility, cultural misunderstandings, and negative stereotyping (Fusick & Charkow Bordeau, 2004; Mather & Adams, 2006). Teachers in troubled schools often resort to authoritarian teaching styles, which severely limits students' personal expression and academic performance (Fusick & Charkow Bordeau, 2004).

Similarly, rural educational systems often lack opportunities for the academic enrichment of their students. Academic skill gaps are predictable when children have been raised with a scarcity of resources. Financial disadvantage can create academic disadvantage. The Panel on High-Risk Youth (1993) identified the factors that can negatively influence youth development. These include

- lower proportions of family members with well-paying jobs;
- parents who are less likely to be married;
- parents with weak community ties, which negatively affects involvement in the school;
- lack of positive role models;
- lack of social institutions that support and encourage positive behaviors in children;

212

- residential and economic stratification, with poor allocation of resources to less affluent areas;
- health risks for children, particularly poor access to regular medical care;
- risk-taking behaviors more likely with urban children that lead to undesirable outcomes, such as teenage pregnancy;
- foster care issues, child abandonment, neglect and abuse; and
- crimes of violence and theft.

There are long-lasting consequences for youth with these types of contextual stressors. Herr (1999) asserted that children are particularly likely to carry over into adulthood stress from person–environment transactions in their youth.

Many professionals pathologize low-income families (Lott, 2001). Unfortunately such beliefs have serious consequences when they are translated through education professionals into disrespectful behaviors toward students and their families, such as negative and discouraging remarks or acts of ignoring and exclusionary behavior. Parents in a study by Lott (2001) "felt little control over their children's fate. When they went to school about problems, they were not confident that there would be acceptable resolutions" (p. 253). From these parents' perspectives, educators interpreted the parents' lack of communication and discouragement as lack of interest and apathy rather than helplessness and hopelessness. This parental discouragement and feeling of powerlessness was further transmitted to their children, who learned not to expect positive outcomes from their parents' interactions with their teachers or administrators. In contrast, students from families of high socioeconomic status perceived that their parents did have power and influence in their schools (Lott, 2001).

Professional School Counseling From the Ecological Perspective

From the beginning of the counseling profession, education has been thought to be the "key to social change" (O'Brien, 2001, p. 68). School counselors are ethically required to maintain an awareness of the social, political, or economic environmental changes in society in order to fulfill their role of advocating for all students (ASCA, 2005; Herr, 1999). O'Brien (2001) asserted that advocacy is the promotion of "equal access to resources for marginalized or less fortunate individuals in society" (p. 66). With the Transforming School Counseling Initiative, school counselors are committed to reducing barriers to academic success and closing the achievement gap between poor and minority youths and their more privileged peers (Perusse et al., 2004).

The ASCA National Model (ASCA, 2005) identifies four themes for the roles of school counselors: leadership, advocacy, collaboration and teaming, and systemic change within school transformation initiatives. Other aspects of these expanding roles include assessment and data-driven decision making in addition to direct counseling service to students and families.

School counselors can make an impact in their school in many arenas, such as classrooms, staff meetings, curriculum development teams, individualized educational program meetings, Parent–Teacher Association meetings, parent conferences, district-level consultation, student activities, and parent booster clubs. Interactions between one person and another cause change in both persons, demonstrating the reciprocal and interactional nature of ecological counseling (Conyne & Cook, 2004). Ecological school counseling is distinct in that its premise is contextualized help giving (Conyne & Cook, 2004). School counseling professionals who embrace the ecological perspective explore the reciprocal interactions of the multiple contexts in which their students live to implement strategies to best address their students' needs.

Case Example

In a qualitative study, Crowell (2007) explored one urban kindergarten through Grade 8 school in an impoverished community to understand the unique career fit of five teachers with students and families. The school was in a historic building but was situated in an area where events could not be held at night for safety reasons. The neighborhood was considered a high-crime area associated with drug trafficking, violence, and prostitution. School doors were always locked, and visitors were required to announce their arrival and purpose on an intercom to a staff member, who decided whether to allow them to enter. The school's interior colors were dark and the lighting was poor. This, in addition to noisy hallways and classrooms with hostile voices yelling, created a tense atmosphere. There was no playground, so recess was held on a paved parking area full of potholes. The median household income in the community was $15,500, and 81% of the students received free or reduced price lunches (U.S. Census Bureau, 2000). Community residents were predominantly African American but also included Appalachian families who were Caucasian and multiracial.

The school climate was described by all study participants as having a high level of noise and tension in the building, a lack of material resources, low teacher morale, and a lack of safety in the community (Crowell, 2007). School personnel used yelling as a behavior management strategy. Difficult students were reprimanded and isolated because central office policy did not permit principals to suspend or expel students from school grounds except under the most egregious circumstances. Teachers described the students as behaving disrespectfully and having highly emotional reactions, which resulted in time-consuming discipline issues for educators. When discipline problems arose, teachers felt compelled to engage students in a form of "counseling" to reestablish classroom order. For example, one teacher said he taught "people skills" so that students would learn that they must show respect for others in order to get along in the world. He coached students in using manners and common courtesy in interactions with peers and adults.

214

The organizational leadership had an influence on the environment at the school. The teachers interviewed in the study reported perceiving a lack of leadership from the school's principal. By all reports, the principal did not have good relationships with staff or families, and his personal life spilled over into his professional life, resulting in a lack of respect from his staff (Crowell, 2007). One teacher commented that the principal's own volatile personality contributed to the low morale in the school environment. Teachers seldom interacted during the day and remained alone in their classrooms or left the premises after students were dismissed.

Teachers perceived that students and their families were more focused on survival than on academic achievement and needed compassion for family predicaments. Families moved frequently because of financial concerns, seeking cheaper housing, better employment, and safer living conditions. Extended families often lived together, and children moved among family members to stay with those who were financially stable at any given time. Families often lacked survival needs such as water, electricity, and adequate food. Transportation was often a problem for families, as some smaller neighborhoods were cut off by major roadways and business districts and there were often no direct public transportation routes. Parents found it difficult or impossible to visit the school for parent–teacher conferences, volunteering, extracurricular activities, and so forth. Although it was positive that parents valued attendance and ensured that their children made it to school regularly, this was often the only type of involvement parents had in the educational system (Crowell, 2007).

When it was found that nearly 50% of the students in the area were not successfully progressing to high school, the central office moved to "redesign" the school (Crowell, 2007). Making sweeping changes in staffing, curricula, and school procedures is one way that districts attempt to remediate low-performing schools. As a result, all but four of the school's teachers were moved to other schools or relieved of their duties. This not only dismantled the students' sense of stability but also severed any established relationships parents and community members had with the school staff. For many families in chaotic living situations, relationships with school personnel are crucial because routine and predictability are often missing at home, and schools can provide children with a sense of stability, consistency, and order.

Although students often misbehaved, teachers also reported that students were eager for sincere relationships with caring adults and demonstrated resilience despite their difficulties. One sixth-grade teacher mentored two students, which included providing help with homework and occasional informal outings for a meal or a museum visit. Another teacher often stayed after school to organize his classroom and talk to students informally. He reported that he tried to help students learn self-discipline in order to be successful in life, not just in school. It also concerned him that his middle-school students talked about surviving in the present, not about following their dreams, thus seeming to lack a sense of the future. Students had learned to lower their expectations for the future to minimize disappointments (Crowell, 2007).

All five teachers in this study, however, created a positive learning environment by encouraging, listening, empowering, praising, and/or providing positive reinforcement to students. They watched for children to make good choices and affirmed positive behavior, as doing so empowers students to better control their reactions and teaches them that change is possible. Teachers longed to see the positive impact they made in students' lives resulting in learning and subsequent academic success. Teachers used various strategies to make their classrooms conducive to learning, such as the use of visual aids and motivational posters. Some used strong voice projection and direct eye contact, whereas others found giving specific directives about what to do to be a most effective strategy. All teachers confronted improper behaviors and asked students to make better choices. For example, one teacher knelt down to interact at the youngest students' eye level, offering her full attention to the child. All teachers used a mixture of formal and informal language, setting a relaxed tone in their classrooms. Yet as they explained new materials carefully and answered questions completely, they also projected the expectation that students take their education seriously (Crowell, 2007).

All five teachers in the study believed that students could overcome the challenges in the school environment with support from caring adults. Four of the five teachers had formed mentoring relationships with students. All of them reported a "mission" to work with students in urban schools. One teacher commented that suburban children would be educated regardless of the kinds of teachers they had because of the economic advantages and parental involvement they are assumed to have. She was frustrated with the lack of resources available to her urban students, such as computers in the home, Internet access, and transportation. Another teacher offered that he experienced multiple roles with his students, such as pseudotherapist, parent, clergyman, and advisor to children who were often parenting their own siblings.

The school did have a number of assets that helped the teachers and students meet the challenges they faced. There were positive collaborations with community agencies, including one that served a large number of homeless families in several schools. A community advisory board was created with teachers and community stakeholders, including two churches that worked closely with the students and their families. Teachers were persevering, resourceful, and caring and empathic toward students and their families. They also were experienced in working in this setting and used their creativity to improve the school's learning environment (Crowell, 2007).

Ecological Analysis

All people exist in an interconnected and interactional flow within their unique microsystem, relating with others and the environment. Children's relationships with their families, friends, and community members made up the mesosystem level of impact, at which the supports or challenges of those relationships either enhanced or detracted from the children's experiences. Exosystem influences included system changes, such as government funding cutbacks in mental health services for families in the area (Abrams, Theberge, & Karan, 2005). Macrosystem influences included political issues, such as government housing and education cuts, and cultural effects, such as the community's identity as an Appalachian community (Crowell, 2007).

Teachers utilized ecological principles in their work practices similar to those used by school counselors to do holistic assessments and interventions, "to know the student through interactions, with an understanding of the multiple contexts in which students live, and to what degree students experience fit and concordance" (Crowell, 2007, p. 133). Conyne and Cook (2004) defined *ecological concordance* as congruence and harmony, or "a state allowing for and encouraging growth . . . taking advantage of strengths and supports; a mutually beneficial interaction between person and environment" (p. 24). Thus, a teacher's ability to negotiate the setting effectively involved a complex interaction of job content, context, and personal satisfaction, which affected relationships with other teachers and with students.

Context was a primary ecological consideration in teachers' discussions about classroom strategies and their accommodating of children's different learning styles (Crowell, 2007). Contextual factors were noted not just in the physical school setting but also in classroom teaching and management styles. Teachers applied a variety of pedagogical methods and utilized realistic applications in the curriculum. Given the long waiting list for special education assessments, teachers chose to develop alternatives to provide the best possible learning methods for individual students rather than wait for learning disabilities to be diagnosed. Training on the culture of poverty (Payne, 2001) was offered throughout the school district, and teachers used this information to choose reading selections that worked better for their students than many of those provided in the curriculum. For example, a story about a little girl on a foreign holiday with an arctic wolf was replaced by one about a girl living with her grandmother on the outskirts of a large city. Many teachers described the standard curriculum as classist and biased toward middle-class values and experiences, which were unlike those of their students' families. Thus, the teachers described their classroom activities as responsive to students' needs (Crowell, 2007).

The most influential ecological principle in Crowell's (2007) study was meaning making, which is understood as the combination of a person's experiences, values, attitudes, goals, and purpose. The influence of meaning making was particularly noted in teachers describing a sense of personal reward and a "calling" to work with their students. Meaning was described by Young and Collin (2003) as "action and discourse in which we form relationships and community" (p. 378). Meaning for teachers was created through student and family interactions in which they connected at the personal level. At the mesosystem level, positive teacher–student and even teacher–family relationships can protect students from engaging in problem behaviors (Fusick & Charkow Bordeau, 2004; Patrick, Kaplan, & Ryan, 2007; Way, Reddy, & Rhodes, 2007).

Teachers showed their effectiveness in an urban environment by creating an atmosphere of mutual trust and respect for their students regardless of cultural identity. How they made meaning of the multidimensional aspects of their work determined their ability to thrive within the setting. Reflective teaching practices were utilized to discover any personal biases and to better align their teaching with the population they served. Several of the teachers emphasized knowing their students well in order to understand how they learned best. Students' environmental contexts were often considered in teacher–student interactions (Crowell, 2007). Years of experience had taught one teacher to avoid power struggles with students, recognizing that students may be looking for a sense of control at school because they believe they have no control in most other areas of their lives. Another teacher started the day by having students journal their feelings as a way to put aside the previous evening's events or events that had occurred on the way to school that morning.

Teachers demonstrated a considerable degree of awareness of students' external and internal challenges. The belief that teachers could positively impact students' lives beyond the classroom was heard through statements that students needed guidance and direction, self-discipline, and a sense of personal responsibility. At the mesosystem level, one teacher contacted parents with positive comments and not just with reports of misbehavior. The teacher recognized that parental involvement is often missing in the urban culture. Although some parents wanted to see their children achieve, several teachers reported that many parents did not seem to hold that value. Some parents even seemed to resent the fact that their children were achieving more than they had. Some parents who had had negative school experiences feared that their children would also fail and were not sure how to help them. Despite a lack of parental involvement, teachers repeatedly emphasized a strong desire for students to develop personal strengths, such as self-confidence and insight, curiosity about the world, and positive self-esteem (Crowell, 2007).

Emotionally supportive teachers contribute to an emotionally supportive and caring school environment, which has been linked to positive student development (Wang, 2009). *Healthy development* is "the presence of adaptive choices, happiness, optimism for the future, purpose, and meaningful relationships" (Theokas et al., 2005, p. 114). Students in an emotionally supportive and caring school are more likely to comply with teachers' expectations and to develop enhanced coping skills, better social competence, and more positive feelings about life (Wang, 2009). Stressing their sense of mission and their calling to the career of teaching, Crowell (2007) perceived the teachers in her study as serious, knowledgeable, and understanding professionals. Despite the school's detachment from the larger urban community, educators were resourceful in gaining local support from organizations to tie the community to the school. Community groups, including churches, fraternal organizations, local businesses, and a neighborhood center, assisted in the learning, growth, and development of the area's youths. Interventions targeted at the microsystem level included an increase in the number of mentoring relationships with individual students. At a broader system level, a local coalition provided a set of musical instruments for the school. Collaborative efforts increased the likelihood of impacting the immediate environment and influenced more than just one part of a complex systemic struggle.

School Counselor Interventions in School Environments

School counselors are trained to identify interventions that may include family, peers, and other community relationships significant to children's lives. D. Brown (2003) reported that the "personalized care children need is sometimes missing from students' homes . . . so that [need for] care must be met at school" (p. 279). With decreases in the number of mental health service providers, school counselors are at times the only professionals available to provide such services for some students and families, especially in rural communities (Abrams et al., 2005). Research in education indicates that student achievement would improve if additional efforts were made to ensure that classroom management was linked responsively to the home cultures of students from diverse backgrounds (M. R. Brown, 2007).

School counselors are also adept at training teachers and students in such skills as problem solving and decision making, group teamwork, and communication. These skills also assist teachers in collaborating with peers and other professionals on behalf of their students and in enhancing the ability of students in poverty to meet the challenges of their situations. Teachers' personal competence may be enhanced in these areas by collaboration with counselors in school settings. Counselors can team with teachers by collecting and assessing student data, advocating with community agencies for resources, and creating programming to provide support and learning opportunities for all students (ASCA, 2005).

Collaboration skills are essential for school counselors who must work in multiple systems to achieve student success. The ASCA National Model (ASCA, 2005) strives to achieve systemic change through collaboration, leadership, and advocacy. School counselors have a variety of roles in intervention, such as mediator, individual counselor, prevention specialist, group leader, advocate, and consultant. They must determine their course of action based on an assessment of the individuals involved and their environments. Modeling positive communication is an important strength that school counselors can use in assessment and interpretation (Geltner & Leibforth, 2008). A poignant example of this need for collaboration and differing roles for school counselors is that of Tommy and his family.

Tommy was a fourth-grade boy who was repeatedly sent home from school for head lice, who was in trouble for stealing at school, and who was also involved with Child Protective Services (CPS) because of reported neglect in the home. The teacher and principal reported a history of academic problems with Tommy, though his parents refused to allow him to be tested for special education services. The relationship between the school and the parents was tense, with each blaming the other for Tommy's academic and behavior problems. When a new school counselor started at the school, Tommy was almost immediately referred for counseling.

The school counselor began working with Tommy regularly, setting up a positive behavior plan and regular counseling sessions. Although building rapport and trust with Tommy was difficult, the school counselor slowly began to form a positive relationship with him.

By talking with his teachers and tracking specific details about Tommy's stealing, the counselor learned that the only things Tommy stole at school were school supplies and food. The school counselor was surprised that none of the school personnel had realized this. Tommy shared with the counselor that he often did not have school supplies or enough to eat when he was at home. Working with Tommy's teacher and his CPS caseworker, the school counselor had the teacher stock a drawer in her classroom with nourishing nonperishable food items and school supplies. Tommy was told that he could discreetly take what he needed from this drawer. Tommy did not steal at all after this drawer of needed supplies was provided.

In individual counseling sessions, Tommy revealed an extensive history of physical and psychological abuse, primarily by his father. As the oldest child, Tommy often tried to protect his mother from domestic violence and his younger siblings from their father's rage. Although incidents of suspected abuse were reported to CPS and referrals made for outside mental health and family counseling, the family did not follow through with counseling services. The school counselor continued to meet with Tommy regularly to process his feelings, discuss ways to keep himself safe at home, and help him learn strategies for managing his own behavior at school.

At the same time, the school counselor began trying to form a positive relationship with Tommy's parents. After initially introducing herself to them, she sent home positive notes and made phone calls to let them know when Tommy was having a great day. She worked with the CPS caseworker and local businesses to get transportation or a gas card donated for his parents so that they could attend school events. In time she was able to get Tommy's mother to agree to attend a parent support group at a local community center, though his father refused to participate. His mother seemed to learn and use the new parenting skills from the group and to benefit from the support of talking with other parents.

When school began the following year, the school counselor was disappointed to learn that Tommy was no longer enrolled at the school. When she checked with the CPS caseworker, she found out that the family had moved out of the county without notifying CPS. Unfortunately the school never knew what happened with Tommy after he moved, but the school counselor was hopeful that she had made a lasting positive difference in the lives of Tommy and his family.

In order for schools to make meaningful improvement, the current needs that affect students, schools, and community environments must be addressed (Holcomb-McCoy, 2005). Ringeisen et al. (2003) pointed out that educational systems must make student achievement, one of the four pillars of the No Child Left Behind Act, a priority. However, school districts must allocate limited resources to serve the needs of many children in many schools. Also, school personnel need to be culturally responsive to educate diverse youth (Locke, 2003).

220

Creating an environment that aids the learning process is just one task of school counselors. Wang (2009) stated that by preventing behavior and social difficulties, school professionals can improve school climate. Consequently, healthy school climates are goal oriented, with common values infused throughout the entire system, which ultimately improves student achievement. School-based interventions must be based on real-world assessments of resource needs in relation to resource availability. Engaging in ecological assessment enables school counselors to support students with interventions for problematic behaviors. For example, consider the case of Shyla, a high school student who is worrying about many things because of both personal factors (she believes she may be pregnant) and environmental factors (poor family support). Shyla talks back to her teacher after several requests for cooperation and is then removed from the class by the school resource officer and sent to the principal's office. Shyla's unemployed mother is called to the school, so she now also faces her mother's wrath. The principal calls in the school counselor and sets up a collaboration with the school social worker, who may be able to help provide resources for the family, and in-school support is provided by the counselor for Shyla's personal and school behavior issues. Though overly simplified, this scenario is not uncommon in high schools and demonstrates the value of collaborative evaluation and intervention within the school setting. It is a necessity for school professionals to consider intervention at both the individual and school levels (Abrams et al., 2005; Wang, 2009). The checklist in Figure 9.1 is one tool school counselors can use to attend to the many factors that influence their students.

Figure 9.1

Ecological Checklist for School Counselors (by Jerri Crowell)

I have considered:
- ____ students' gender, race, national origin, socioeconomic status, and education level.
- ____ any disability, including linguistic abilities and any physical, mental, or emotional handicaps.
- ____ family systems—the makeup of students' immediate families, relationships of family members to the community, and cultural influences.
- ____ students' social networks—their roles within the school setting and community, their level of support/influence, and the peer group influences that they exert on others.
- ____ the psychological, economic, and emotional impact on students of societal factors such as opportunity, safety, religious beliefs, and historical traditions.
- ____ ways in which students make meaning of their life experiences and environment—students' images of self and of self in context with their world (their worldviews).
- ____ the physical setting in which I work, including the availability of appropriate confidential meeting space and resources to enhance my counseling identity.
- ____ my own supervision and support resources.
- ____ the best practices and ethical codes of the American School Counselor Association and the American Counseling Association.

Summary

Applying ecological principles to a school environment makes perfect sense to school personnel who can see how influential the environment is on a student's academic success. In addition, understanding the role that meaning making has on each student's experience helps those who work in schools to understand why, for example, siblings may excel at different rates despite having the same home environment. Consideration of contextual factors in an ecological framework assists school counselors in identifying the focus of possible interventions and where interventions should be directed, whether it is the home, the school bus, the playground, the classroom, the lunchroom, or other environments.

School personnel face tremendously challenging issues, such as high-stakes testing, merit-based pay, reductions in school personnel, and sometimes little support and understanding from administrators. These issues can make the school environment tense for teachers and students alike. Students bring with them their own unique backgrounds and academic experience, and teachers and counselors are charged with helping them improve the person–environment fit to achieve academic and personal success. In Crowell's (2007) study it was apparent that teachers made significant efforts to understand their students' ecological niches to learn ways in which to teach them best. School counselors' roles are to remove barriers to achievement by building resilience; identifying strengths, supports, and resources within the student and social system; and advocating for the student when necessary.

As we saw in the example of Tommy, a collaborative, multidisciplinary team working from a strengths-based perspective can have a remarkable effect on a student's trajectory throughout his or her academic career and beyond. By utilizing outcome data, school counselors can justify time spent on social-emotional issues to reluctant teachers and administrators. The use of outcome data can have a greater influence throughout the district as others learn how effective a holistic approach can be. Engaging in an ecological assessment can help a team determine the individual needs of the students while also allowing the school counselor to utilize his or her preferred treatment modalities to improve person–environment fit.

The ecological model provides a framework for school counselors to determine risk factors and factors of resiliency that can be strengthened. Ungar (2004) stated that protective factors interact with risk factors in intricate relationships that are as unique and individual as each student and family. School counselors trained in ecological assessment are able to identify various risk and protective factors in order to conceptualize the person–environment fit of students, teachers, and others and recommend helpful interventions. Interventions that draw on family strengths and cultural awareness have demonstrated promising results in lowering risk factors and creating successful opportunities for at-risk children (Fusick & Charkow Bordeau, 2004). Alvord and Grados (2005) and other researchers who have engaged in resilience studies offer possibilities for "inoculating children against personal, familial, and environmental acute and chronic stressors" (Ungar, 2004, p. 343). Ecological school counselors are able to assist students in identifying sources of positive influence, which can help students boost their resiliency. Research has shown that adaptability, a sense of purpose, and at least one caring individual can make important differences in contributing to healthy growth (Abrams et al., 2005).

School counselors are able to identify student and environmental issues and create opportunities for school-based support programs. According to Katz (as cited in Condly, 2006), the vital ingredient for developing resiliency in children is creating meaningful opportunities. Dolan (2008) pointed to the context of family, school, and community, in which "turning points . . . enable the development of personal resolve in a child . . . and . . . children who are strong in themselves experience robust positive relationships in their family and . . . connect to their community are most likely to thrive" (p. 84).

Discussion Questions

- What are some possible influences on students that school counselors working from the ecological perspective might consider that school counselors who do not work from this perspective might not?
- What are some of the possible challenges of working from the ecological perspective as a school counselor? How could these challenges be addressed?
- How might school counselors collaborate with teachers to best address students' needs from the ecological perspective?
- How might school counselors also address the needs of their students and the needs of teachers and other school personnel to make positive changes in the school environment?

References

Abrams, K., Theberge, S. K., & Karan, O. C. (2005). Children and adolescents who are depressed: An ecological approach. *Professional School Counseling, 8,* 284–292.

Alvord, M. K., & Grados, J. J. (2005). Enhancing resilience in children: A proactive approach. *Professional Psychology: Research and Practice, 36*(3), 238–245.

American School Counselor Association. (2005). *The ASCA National Model: A framework for school counseling programs* (2nd ed.). Alexandria, VA: Author.

Attar-Schwartz, S. (2009). Peer sexual harassment victimization at school: The roles of student characteristics, cultural affiliation, and school factors. *American Journal of Orthopsychiatry, 79,* 407–420.

Bemak, F., Chi-Ying, R., & Siroskey-Sabdo, L. A. (2005). Empowerment groups for academic success: An innovative approach to prevent high school failure for at-risk, urban African American students. *Professional School Counseling, 8,* 377–389.

Bemak, F., Murphy, S., & Kaffenberger, C. J. (2006). School counseling leadership team: A statewide collaborative model to transform school counseling. *Professional School Counseling, 9,* 288–294.

Berns, R. M. (2007). *Child, family, school, community: Socialization and support* (7th ed.). Belmont, CA: Thomson Higher Education.

Brinson, J. A., Kottler, J. A., & Fisher, T. A. (2004). Cross-cultural conflict resolution in the schools: Some practical intervention strategies for counselors. *Journal of Counseling & Development, 82,* 294–301.

Bronfenbrenner, U. (1979). *The ecology of human development: Experiments by nature and design.* Cambridge, MA: Harvard University Press.

Brown, D. (2003). Urban teachers' use of culturally responsive management strategies. *Theory Into Practice, 42*(4), 277–282.

Brown, E. D., & Low, C. M. (2008). Chaotic living conditions and sleep problems associated with children's responses to academic challenge. *Journal of Family Psychology, 22,* 920–923.

Brown, K. M., Anfara, V. A., & Roney, K. (2004). Student achievement in high performing suburban middle schools and low performing, urban middle schools: Plausible explanations for the differences. *Education and Urban Society, 36,* 428–456.

Brown, M. R. (2007). Educating all students: Creating culturally responsive teachers, classrooms, and schools. *Intervention in School and Clinic, 43*(1), 57–62.

Bryan, J., & Holcomb-McCoy, C. (2007). An examination of school counselor involvement in school–family–community partnerships. *Professional School Counseling, 10,* 441–454.

Bullough, R. V. (2001). *Uncertain lives: Children of promise, teachers of hope.* New York, NY: Teachers College Press.

College Board. (1999). *Reaching the top: A report of the national task force on minority high achievement.* Retrieved from http://professionals.collegeboard.com/profdownload/pdf/reachingthe_3952.pdf

Condly, S. J. (2006). Resilience in children: A review of literature with implications for education. *Urban Education, 41*(3), 211–236. doi:1177/0042085906287902

Conyne, R. K., & Cook, E. P. (Eds.). (2004). *Ecological counseling: An innovative approach to conceptualizing person–environment interaction.* Alexandria, VA: American Counseling Association.

Crowell, J. L. (2007). *An exploration of urban teachers' work from an ecological perspective.* Unpublished doctoral dissertation, University of Cincinnati, OH. Retrieved from Proquest Dissertations and Theses database. (UMI No. AAT 3263052)

Dolan, P. (2008). Prospective possibilities for building resilience in children, their families and communities. *Child Care in Practice, 14*(1), 83–91.

Education Trust. (1998). *Education watch: The Education Trust state and national data book* (Vol. 2). Washington, DC: Author.

Evans, S. W., Green, A. L., & Serpell, Z. N. (2005). Community participation in the treatment development process using community development teams. *Journal of Clinical Child and Adolescent Psychology, 34,* 765–771.

Fusick, L., & Charkow Bordeau, W. (2004). Counseling at-risk Afro-American youth: An examination of contemporary issues and effective school-based strategies. *Professional School Counseling, 8,* 102–115.

Gandara, P., & Maxwell-Jolly, J. (1999). *Priming the pump: Strategies for increasing the achievement of underrepresented minority graduates.* Retrieved from http://professionals.collegeboard.com/profdownload/pdf/primingthep_3949.pdf

Geltner, J. A., & Leibforth, T. N. (2008). Advocacy in the IEP process: Strengths-based school counseling in action. *Professional School Counseling, 12,* 162–165.

Herr, E. L. (1999). *Counseling in a dynamic society: Contexts and practices for the 21st century* (2nd ed.). Alexandria, VA: American Counseling Association.

Holcomb-McCoy, C. (2005). Professional school counseling in urban settings: Introduction to special issue. *Professional School Counseling, 8,* 182–183.

Kim, H. J. (2004). Family resources and children's academic performance. *Children and Youth Services, 2,* 529–536. doi:10.1016/j.childyouth.2004.02.008

Locke, D. C. (2003). Improving the multicultural competence of educators. In P. B. Pedersen & J. C. Carey (Eds.), *Multicultural counseling in schools: A practical handbook* (2nd ed., pp. 171–189). Boston, MA: Allyn & Bacon.

Lott, B. (2001). Low-income parents and the public schools. *Journal of Social Issues, 57*(2), 247–259.

Mather, M., & Adams, D. (2006). *The risk of negative child outcomes in low-income families.* Retrieved from http://www.aecf.org/upload/PublicationFiles/DA3622H1234.pdf

McEachern, A. G., Aluede, O., & Kenny, M. C. (2008). Emotional abuse in the classroom: Implications and interventions for counselors. *Journal of Counseling & Development, 86,* 3–10.

Musheno, S., & Talbert, M. (2002). Transformed school counselor in action. *Theory Into Practice, 41*(3), 186–191.

No Child Left Behind Act of 2001, Pub. L. No. 107-110, 115 Stat. 1425, 20 U.S.C. §§ 6301 *et seq.*

O'Brien, K. (2001). The legacy of Parsons: Career counselors and vocational psychologists as agents of social change. *The Career Development Quarterly, 50,* 66–76.

O'Connor, E., & McCartney, K. (2007). Examining teacher–child relationships and achievement as part of an ecological model of development. *American Educational Research Journal, 44,* 340–369. doi:10.3102/0002831207302172

Paisley, P. O., & McMahon, H. G. (2001). School counseling for the 21st century: Challenges and opportunities. *Professional School Counseling, 5,* 106–115.

Panel on High-Risk Youth, National Research Council. (1993). *Losing generations: Adolescents in high-risk settings.* Washington, DC: National Academies Press.

Patrick, H., Kaplan, A., & Ryan, A. M. (2007). Early adolescents' perceptions of the classroom social environment, motivational beliefs, and engagement. *Journal of Educational Psychology, 99*(1), 83–98. doi:10.1037/0022-0663.99.1.83

Payne, R. K. (2001). *Framework for understanding poverty* (Rev. ed.). Highlands, TX: aha! Process.

Perusse, R., Goodnough, G. E., Donegan, J., & Jones, C. (2004). Perceptions of school counselors and school principals about the National Standards for School Counseling Programs and the Transforming School Counseling Initiative. *Professional School Counseling, 7*, 152–161.

Prince, C. D. (2002). Missing: Top staff in bottom schools: The challenge of attracting exemplary teachers to neediest schools. *School Administrator.* Retrieved from http://findarticles.com/cf_0/m0JSD/7_59/89927216/print.jhtml

Quartz, K. H. (2003). "Too angry to leave": Supporting new teachers' commitment to transform urban schools. *Journal of Teacher Education, 54*(2), 99–111.

Ringeisen, H., Henderson, K., & Hoagwood, K. (2003). Context matters: Schools and the "research to practice gap" in children's mental health. *School Psychology Review, 32*(2), 153–168.

Sirin, S. R., & Rogers-Sirin, L. (2005). Components of school engagement among African American adolescents. *Applied Developmental Science, 9*(1), 5–13.

Theokas, C., Almerigi, J. B., Lerner, R. M., Dowling, E. M., Benson, P. L., Scales, P. C., & von Eye, A. (2005). Conceptualizing and modeling individual and ecological asset components of thriving in early adolescence. *Journal of Early Adolescence, 25*(1), 113–143. doi:10.1177/0272431604272460

Ungar, M. (2004). A constructionist discourse on resilience: Multiple contexts, multiple realities among at-risk children and youth. *Youth and Society, 35*, 341–365.

U.S. Census Bureau. (2000). *Census of population and housing: Cincinnati, Ohio.* Retrieved from http://factfinder.census.gov/servlet/GCTTable?_bm=y&-geo_id=04000US39&-_box_head_nbr=GCT-PH1&-ds_name=DEC_2000_SF1_U&-format=ST-7

U.S. Department of Education. (2009). *Common Core of Data, National Institute for Educational Statistics—Public elementary and secondary school student enrollment and staff from the Common Core of Data: School year 2008–2009.* Washington, DC: Author.

Van Horn, M. L., Bellis, J. M., & Snyder, S. W. (2001). Family Resource Scale–Revised: Psychometrics and validation of a measure of family resources in a sample of low-income families. *Journal of Psychoeducational Assessment, 19*(1), 54–68. doi:10.1177/073428290101900104

Van Horn, M. L., Jaki, T., Masyn, K., Ramey, S. L., Smith, J. A., & Antaramian, A. (2009). Assessing differential effects: Applying regression mixture models to identify variations in the influence of family resources on academic achievement. *Developmental Psychology, 45*, 1298–1313.

Wang, M. T. (2009). School climate support for behavioral and psychological adjustment: Testing the mediating effect of social competence. *School Psychology Quarterly, 24*(4), 240–251. doi:10.1037/a007999

Way, N., Reddy, R., & Rhodes, J. (2007). Students' perceptions of school climate during the middle school years: Associations with trajectories of psychological and behavioral adjustment. *American Journal of Community Psychology, 40*(3/4), 194–213. doi:10.1007/s10464-007-9143-y

Yeh, C. J. (2004). Multicultural and contextual research and practice in school counseling. *The Counseling Psychologist, 32*(2), 278–285. doi:10.1177/0011000003261358

Young, R. A., & Collin, A. (2003). Introduction: Constructivism and social constructionism in the career field. *Journal of Vocational Behavior, 64*(3), 373–388. doi:10.1016/j.jvb.2003.12.005

Counseling in Context: Chemical Dependency and Substance Abuse Programs

*Albert L. Watson, Nzingha Dalila, Jill Gomez,
Greta Hochstetler Mayer, Steven W. Patrick,
and Michael D. Brubaker*

In previous chapters, the writers have shared their understanding of the complex ideology that supports ecological counseling. This transtheoretical model, like other dynamic approaches, works toward client empowerment with the hope or expectation of long-term behavior change. So how effective is this strength-based, client-centered approach with complex disorders such as substance abuse and addictions, which consist of biological, psychological, and environmental factors?

In 2007 it was estimated that the overall economic cost of illicit drug use in the United States was $193 billion dollars annually (Office of National Drug Control Policy, 2011). Although the U.S. population makes up only about 5% of the world population, it consumes approximately 60% of its illicit drugs (United Nations, 2005). Clearly the United States has a drug problem, and an innovative approach is vital. A Substance Abuse and Mental Health Services Administration (SAMHSA; 2010) study found that 21.8 million Americans aged 12 or older admit actively using illicit drugs. Surprisingly, this number comprises only about 9% of the American population in that age group (SAMHSA, 2010). Of the many drugs surveyed, Americans reported using marijuana most frequently (6.6% of respondents, or 16.7 million people), followed by cocaine (0.7%, 1.6 million), prescription drugs used nonmedically (2.8%, 7 million), and hallucinogens (0.5%, 1.3

million; SAMHSA, 2010). To put this in perspective, 9% of Americans are using 60% of the world's illicit drugs.

Notice that these studies do not include such legal drugs as alcohol and tobacco. In the United States alone, the estimated number of alcohol users is 119 million, roughly 70% of Americans aged 12 or older, and it has been estimated that nearly half of the U.S. population is either a current or past tobacco user (Sadock & Sadock, 2003). This reality put into better perspective when considered in terms of its cost. Alcohol is estimated to cost the health care community nearly $24.5 billion annually, whereas the total estimated cost of alcohol use exceeds $224 billion annually (these estimations include alcohol-related costs such as automobile accidents, crime, lost wages, etc.; Centers for Disease Control and Prevention, 2011). In comparison, smoking-related deaths cost the nation about $92 billion a year in lost productivity, and smoking-related health care costs total $75.5 billion, representing more than $167 billion annually (Armour, Woolery, & Malarcher, et al., 2005). Taken in context, the level and frequency of drug use is more than just an individual problem among users. A new approach is essential to address not only the issues connected to the complex web of problematic drug use but also the multitiered consequences of such use. We believe that an ecological approach to counseling is a comprehensive and effective approach for addressing substance abuse and addiction.

It is important to note that there are considerable differences of opinion among various professionals and cultures about the use of the terms *substance abuse, dependence,* and *addictions.* Substance abuse occurs when an individual uses a legal or illegal drug in excess of accepted standards (Doweiko, 2009). According to the *Diagnostic and Statistical Manual of Mental Disorders* (4th ed., text rev.; *DSM-IV-TR;* American Psychiatric Association, 2000) substance dependence is a chronic disease characterized by a variety of symptoms, including preoccupation with the drug, loss of control, a withdrawal syndrome, a change in tolerance, repeated efforts to reduce or stop use, and various social consequences. Future editions of the *DSM* are likely to include an entry for substance use disorders to describe a continuum between substance use and dependence. The term *addiction* is more commonly used than the word *dependence,* especially in 12-step programs (e.g., Alcoholics Anonymous [AA]), in which members will self-identify as addicts whether or not they meet the full *DSM* criteria for substance dependence. For our purposes in this chapter, the terms *substance dependence* and *addiction* are used interchangeably.

The purpose of this chapter is to describe an ecological approach to counseling to address substance abuse treatment and addiction. Our discussion begins with a brief review of traditional substance abuse approaches and the limitations of these methods. We address the role of context in addictions and the importance of considering clients' entire life spaces and their networks of persons and events when diagnosing, conceptualizing, and implementing interventions. Then we bring attention to meaning making because of the critical role it plays in recovery and rehabilitation.

230

Next we discuss special populations, in this case racial and ethnic minorities, to illustrate both the similar and unique characteristics of their drug experiences and, more important, to emphasize the utility of an ecological approach in serving these diverse populations. The flexibility of an ecological approach makes it useful for counseling with this population as well as with other disenfranchised groups (e.g., persons with disabilities, older adults, and gay men and lesbian women).

The final section discusses the need for evidence-based practice (EBP) and the contributions that an ecological assessment makes to EBP. Examples of ecologically oriented substance abuse programs are provided throughout the chapter.

Addiction: A Widespread Problem Poorly Addressed With Traditional Treatment Methods

Many individuals, including those working in the helping professions, fail to understand the prevalence of substance use disorders. The Centers for Disease Control and Prevention and the World Health Organization have jointly agreed on the seriousness of the drinking problem in the United States. They rate heavy alcohol consumption as the number 3 cause of preventable death in this country (National Institute on Alcohol Abuse and Alcoholism, 2009). Approximately 18 million Americans suffer from alcohol use disorders, yet only 7.1% of these individuals receive services for their excessive drinking (National Institute on Alcohol Abuse and Alcoholism, 2009).

To appreciate the experience of someone with an addiction one must consider how the disorder has been viewed over time and how this view impacts the affected population. Both religious and secular ideologies have shaped opinions about the causes of addictions and the services we should offer for those with addictive disorders. The roots of substance abuse treatment in the United States are grounded in the church. According to Peele (1995), the Puritans understood alcohol to be a blessing from God and embraced the substance as a healthy beverage. Other Protestants viewed alcohol and drug use as sinful habits, morally weak behavior that would likely ruin the family life of any person engaged in it. The temperance movement began in the 1850s as an effort to condemn excessive drinking (Kinney, 2008). This movement was instigated in an effort to secure rights for less fortunate Americans and to moderate the excessive consumption of alcohol, which was believed to be disrupting the lives of many families and individuals. These concepts or ideas fall under the umbrella of the *moral model* (Johnson, 2004). According to Johnson (2004), the moral model views addicted persons as weak-willed, immoral individuals who are not able to make meaningful decisions to run their own lives. Effects of the moral model, which came into being prior to the temperance movement, can still be seen in policy and public opinion today. This judgmental model is also one of many reasons why only 7.1% of individuals who need treatment actually receive services. Thus, it impedes America's treatment of the addicted population. Those with substance use problems often hide their excessive use and minimize the consequences, not seeking treatment, as doing so is considered a mark of weak willpower and low morals.

In the late 18th century several medical and human service professionals attempted to offer an explanation for the chaotic drinking patterns demonstrated by those who drank excessively. In 1785 an American medical practitioner, Benjamin Rush, offered one of the first writings to raise a disease model to explain the compulsive use of alcohol. Other professionals were also instrumental in identifying heavy alcohol consumption as a medical issue. In 1909 Jane Addams, an advocate and social worker, made public her view on heavy alcohol consumption, declaring that it was a disease (Van Wormer & Davis, 2008). Addams and her colleagues, working with immigrants and their families, witnessed the damaging impact of excessive alcohol consumption.

The disease model was better understood with the development of a movement called Alcoholics Anonymous. This organization allowed recovering persons to be heard clearly rather than to have medical practitioners and educators speak for them. Bill Wilson and Dr. Bob contributed substantially to the understanding of addiction by offering the 12-step program, which began in Akron, Ohio, in 1935 (Kinney, 2008). AA introduced language such as *powerlessness, divine guidance,* and *making amends* that allowed others who could not fully understand the addictive nature of this disease to grasp the problem more fully. Yet although the 12-step movement offered some insight into the experience of addicted individuals, it was only one piece of the complex puzzle of this baffling phenomenon. During this period in history alcoholism was still thought of as a disease. People with alcoholism were often institutionalized, much like those with mental illness (Van Wormer & Davis, 2008).

The 12-step movement placed greater emphasis on the disease model, and additional research in the field emerged. Jellinek's (1960a, 1960b) work is the foundation for most counselors' understanding of the disease model. He conducted research on male AA members and identified four stages of the progression of the disease: (a) prealcoholic, (b) prodromal, (c) crucial, and (d) chronic (Johnson, 2004). This research-based information provided the fuel needed to move the disease out of the closet and away from the moral model (Johnson, 2004).

As the emphasis shifted from the moral model to the disease model, the World Health Organization acknowledged alcoholism as an illness in 1956 and then as a disease in 1966 (Kinney, 2008). These acknowledgments triggered more money for research and increased public support, which resulted in improved treatment for alcoholics. These advancements are critical when one considers their influence on service development, research and training, and even personal perception and attitudes.

The passage of the Hughes Act in 1970 led to substantial funding for research for addiction studies through the creation of the National Institute on Alcohol Abuse and Alcoholism and the National Institute on Drug Abuse. Although money was directed toward research, funds were also made available by the federal government to open treatment centers across the United States (Van Wormer & Davis, 2008).

One might expect that the additional research and increased funding would advance efforts to more fully understand how to treat addictions more efficaciously. However, the very opposite has occurred. Society has addressed this problem much like any other medical problem—at the individual level, largely treating a cluster of symptoms within the patient. Because of advances in medical science we have an understanding of how to treat chronic illness, yet this disease is unique. Thanks to the declaration of addiction as a disease, and subsequent empirical studies, we have gained a better understanding of the complex nature of the biological, psychological, and environmental factors that contribute to it. Yet even with this framework, treatment is largely focused on the individual and his or her immediate social supports.

If we believe that addictive disorders have biological, psychological, and social roots, then we must treat the addicted individual from this same framework. We must examine the broader environmental and sociological factors that impact individuals and whole communities alike. These are complex layers that may take time to completely understand.

Systems theory is another important factor to understanding the addicted individual from an ecological perspective. Quite often a substance abuse counselor completes a diagnostic assessment in which his or her primary focus is the individual being assessed and that person's family. Counselors frequently fail to fully consider the wider system, such as the individual's friends and his or her work, school, or social environments. This might explain why a Treatment Episode Data Set report indicated that non-Hispanic Whites were more likely to successfully complete outpatient treatment than those from minority cultures (SAMHSA, Office of Applied Studies, 2009). Americans of European heritage are often less reliant on their broader supports and also experience fewer stressors related to cultural and racial oppression, such as job discrimination. These factors are often ignored in traditional assessments.

Individuals affected by addiction may become estranged from family members, experience job loss, and become detached from fulfilling activities and cultural events. The loss of fulfilling experiences may in turn prevent an individual from experiencing concordance. As counselors, we must offer contextualized help that is based on the meaning the client derives from his or her environmental interactions (family, job, culture).

This contextualized help requires us to identify that the client's problems are likely to have multiple causes. All too often in addiction counseling, we attribute the problem to the *denial* clients are experiencing in relation to their drinking or drugging behavior. We formulate answers to problems without fully grasping how individuals function within various systems. This superficial helping strategy fails to recognize the unique experiences individuals go through within the context of their environments.

As researchers and practitioners in the field of addiction studies have embraced the medical model, they have also developed intervention strategies that target individuals who are believed to have the disease. As previously mentioned, E. M. Jellinek identified the progression of alcoholism.

233

The *DSM-IV-TR* and the *International Statistical Classification of Diseases and Related Health Problems, Revision 10,* outline symptoms that allow professionals to diagnose substance disorders. All of these tools, although clinically useful, are of limited value when counselors fail to develop individualized, strength-based, person-centered treatment interventions.

It is interesting that many of the concepts of ecological counseling are compatible with those of the 12-step movement. On entering recovery, individuals are asked to consider changing the people, places, and things that have supported a using lifestyle. Indeed it is not only the individuals who must change but also their environments and the interactions between them and their environments. The recognition of the power of one's surroundings along with one's support systems is a major tenet of recovery as well as changing one's thinking, or meaning making.

In reviewing these issues of addiction we concur with Cook (2008) that every person's behavior can be understood within the multiple, intersecting contexts anchored by time and place as well as by the meanings that the individual assigns to these life events. As we develop an appreciation for the uniqueness of experiences, we need to offer individual treatment options that consider the unique experiences of individuals with the goal of empowering individuals to improve the quality of their life by changing themselves and the environment in which they live (Cook, 2008).

The Role of Context, Life Space, and the Person in Recovery: Interacting With Others

Examining the role of context in chemical dependency means exploring the interrelated conditions in which this diagnosis exists. The entirety of the context from which the chemically dependent client struggles to recover is his or her *life space.* From an ecological standpoint, this entire life space, the dynamic network of persons and events that creates the addicted individual's world, must be considered when conceptualizing, diagnosing, and developing intervention strategies (Danuta, 1981). For example, the situational conditions identified by the *DSM-IV-TR* are the psychosocial and environmental axes (or descriptors) of a person's presenting factors. These factors assist a counselor in formulating and conceptualizing all of the conditions that contribute to the person's presenting problem. These conditions provide indicators of which additional circumstances need to be addressed in order to help the client to successfully recover. Depending on his or her life space, a person may be exposed to conditions (e.g., genetic predisposition, neurobiological consequences of encounters with and combinations of interactions with specific substances) that result in the potential development of a biopsychosocial etiology of addiction. "The neurobiological and social consequences of these interactions produce a desirable (sought-after) shift that is a pre-morbid stage of the addiction . . . people teeter on a delicate balance that can shift them toward either more or less healthy behavior" (Shaffer et al., 2004, p. 368).

Therefore it is helpful to look at the etiology of chemical dependency as a brain disorder that both overlaps and is influenced by the set of ecological con-

234

texts as depicted in Bronfenbrenner's model of environmental realms (National Association of Alcoholism and Drug Abuse Counselors, 2009). Different factors within an addict's community (e.g., hereditary factors, traumatic events, and drug classes) can impact normal cerebral development. All of these relational situations can exacerbate addiction or interfere with recovery. It is in the dynamic spheres of the interconnected micro-, meso-, exo-, and macrosystems (Bronfenbrenner, 1981) where the addicted person's view of himself or herself and the world is formed, and this influences how and when a client progresses from experimentation to abuse, dependency, and recovery.

With Bronfenbrenner's fifth realm, the chronosystem, the concept of time, provides a deeper understanding of the client's life space. With regard to addiction, the concept of time can involve the age at which abuse began, the length of time engaged in abusing, the arrest in developmental milestones, or the number of unsuccessful recovery programs or engagements with the justice system. This added dimension changes the whole dynamic of the life space and the meaning that chemically dependent persons make of their disorder and recovery.

For individuals experiencing addiction, understanding the ecological system and the etiology of addiction can prove beneficial in placing their life spaces in context. Meaning making, however, redefines the context of a person's life space and helps to empower the recovering addict to see his or her history, behaviors, and relationships in a manner that creates purpose that spurs change and growth. Often an individual may choose to abuse mood-altering substances in an effort to self-medicate emotional or psychological disturbances, only to internalize feelings of shame or guilt as a result of the negative consequences that are often inherent in addictive behaviors. However, when an individual begins to see positive improvement in the quality of his or her life as a result of receiving therapeutic medication or therapy for the trauma he or she was abusing drugs or alcohol to escape, the chances of recovery are greatly improved.

Therefore, our discussion of the role of context includes an examination of the entire life space of the addicted individual. The role of context helps to clarify the ecological milieu from which the addition develops and is nurtured. Attention is devoted to the ways in which the life space interacts with the interconnected environments at various stages in the progression of the addiction. The discussion explores how these dynamics affect how the client makes meaning of these differing aspects of his or her life. In addition, examples are provided to exemplify how various organizations address addiction at each stage of the ecological model.

The Microsystem

The relationships and interactions that a person who is addicted maintains in his or her immediate surroundings include interchanges with family, significant others, the neighborhood, and school or the workplace. According to Bronfenbrenner (1981), these interactions result in bidirectional influences. The influences are bidirectional because the nature of the specific relationship will have an effect on the substance use of the addict and the substance use will have an effect on the relationship. Thus, these bidirectional influences create the context in which the presenting problem of the addicted client must be understood. An adolescent in a substance abuse program may admit his or her first use as one introduced by a parent or older sibling and thus may be resistant to identifying his or her behavior as a problem, despite academic or legal problems, because the adolescent may receive positive reinforcement for his or her continued substance use at home.

Pilkington (2007) used adolescents' narratives to underscore the importance of friendship groups in how these youth initiate drug use, which is consequently used to mediate collective mood changes. Marijuana use, for example, is often initially engaged in as a social event in which participants form a circle and pass a joint or a bowl around, experiencing feelings of warmth, acceptance, and understanding of one another. This analysis counters the traditional concept of adolescents becoming involved in drugs and alcohol out of a need to seek thrills and rebel against established norms. In this study Pilkington acknowledged the meaning making of adolescents.

Additional research counters the traditional notion of drug use by thrill-seeking youth (Crum, Storr, Ialongo, & Anthony, 2008). Crum et al. (2008) instead suggested that depressed mood is associated with drug abuse among youth of low socioeconomic status identified as being at risk of substance abuse due to the detrimental consequences of the quality of their lives (e.g., physical illness, lack of ability to obtain and manage their own resources, institutionalization, or death). The relationships between socioeconomic status, depressed mood, and increased alcohol use provide more evidence to support the importance of meaning making and the environment. The meaning making of the environment sets the stage for the development of cognitive and emotional conditions that result in many diagnosable mood and thought distortions, which in turn encourage drug use as a form of self-medication for these disorders. Van der Zwaluw et al. (2008) identified that the impact of problems in the home, such as drug use by parents and violence, contributes to an environment that moderates the progression of addictive behaviors in adolescents and young adults as they attempt to make meaning of an environment that feels out of control.

Located in Cincinnati, Ohio, the Center for Chemical Addiction Treatment, frequently referred to as the *CAT House,* is an excellent example of an addiction service that specifically addresses the individual and micro levels of intervention. Services offered at the CAT House range from medically monitored treatment (a person-level intervention) to family counseling, education, and prevention services. Services are geared toward helping the client at whichever level of treatment is needed. The CAT House is able to do this by providing a diverse array of services, helping clients and their families respond favorably to environmental stressors and equipping them with knowledge to make new meanings and prevent further use.

The Mesosytem

Bronfenbrenner (1999) described the *mesosystem* as the realm in which connections are made among the structures that make up and support the immediate community in which the addict lives (e.g., churches, schools, courts, housing). In addition to providing systems of support, these inter-connected structures may encourage perceptual distortions and emotional impairments (e.g., the denial of low-income housing or employment op-portunities to convicted addicts). In turn these system conditions can lead to bidirectional influences whereby individuals seek out mood-altering substances in order to cope with feelings of overwhelming systemic stress (e.g., not being able to support one's self or family, not being able to escape feelings of shame related to a lack of resources, being isolated from signifi-cant supports). Holder (2008) is an example of how systemic bidirectional influences can lead to substance use in the explanation of how location (e.g., public vs. private spaces) is evidenced in the proliferation of drugs and alcohol in certain neighborhoods due to economics or race. A study by Duncan et al. (2008) demonstrated a connection between environment and cannabis abuse and dependence among adolescent and young adult offspring of twins raised with different environmental factors (e.g., geo-graphic location, violence, childhood sexual abuse).

As individuals become trapped in a cycle of drug seeking to cope with and manage their deteriorating mesosystems, they become dependent on substances not just to change their moods but eventually just to feel normal. Harris, Fallot, and Berley (2005) found that women who received mental health and substance use treatment to recover from physical abuse, sexual abuse, and addiction returned to environments that further victimized and traumatized them, exacerbating the severity and entanglement of all of their disorders. This study exemplifies how co-occurring disorders of substance use and trauma become significantly more difficult to treat and frequently result in high incidents of relapse.

As attempts to cope with a broken mesosystem prove useless, the addicted person experiences neurological, physiological, psychological, and emotional disorders that become more acute as a result of the very environment from which he or she is struggling to escape. One qualitative study explored the factors that were a help and a hindrance to addicts' recovery (Palmer & Daniluk, 2007). Based on interviews with recovering addicts, the researchers identified significant relationships and resources in the community that either facilitated or impeded healing from addic-tion. For example, the loss of a spouse, partner, child, or family member was experienced by all participants as a serious setback to their recovery.

The Exosystem

When those who are chemically dependent finally move from contemplat-ing their addiction as being out of control to acting on a recovery plan, they often identify their association with groups as facilitative in their healing journeys, particularly when members of these groups do not use drugs or alcohol. Sharing their stories and lives in a supportive context with other addicts, often within AA or Narcotics Anonymous (NA) meetings, gave interviewees in one study the feeling of belonging to a group, sometimes for the first time in their lives (Hughes-Jones, 2009). This phenomenon of healing through a supportive self-help group is one example of the addict's interaction with his or her exosystem, or the structures (e.g., community-based resources) in which significant others in the addict's life are maintained. At the exosystem level, the recovering addict may not have direct access to the structure even while benefiting from the operation of the secondary organization (Berk, 2000). However, maintaining one's recovery is a long-term process that is facilitated by integrating one's recovery throughout one's life in a manner that is supported by the wider culture. In some cases, societal norms and practices interfere with an addiction recovery plan.

We can observe this level of intervention in the Positive Action program developed by Carol Allred. This program is designed to address a full range of problems experienced by students, including drug and alcohol abuse. This intervention, which is funded by the National Institute on Drug Abuse, seeks to change attitudes and promote positive behaviors within a whole community system that incorporates students, families, schools, and community leaders (Flay & Allred, 2003). In the classroom, students are taught about self-concept, positive actions, self-control, and productive personal interactions. This intervention is paired with a school climate packet designed to help principals and school administrators promote positive actions throughout the entire school. In turn parents are supplied with learning packets that offer family activities that complement the classroom modules. Additional interventions occur through local business leaders, including social services workers and local business executives, who are shown how to engage with the youths in ways that reinforce the idea of positive action throughout their communities. Although the children are often unaware of these connections, their lives can be greatly altered by this change in community climate.

The Macrosystem

The *macrosystem* refers to the cultural values, customs, and laws wherein the recovering addict makes meaning of his or her life (Berk, 2000). The macrosystem encompasses core beliefs about our identity and how the self, relationships, and the world aid us in making meaning and informing our behaviors. For example, there is evidence that aggressive policing practices result in higher utilization of shooting galleries and easily obtained injection equipment (Pollini et al., 2008). In a study of numerous U.S. metropolitan areas, the researchers found significant statistical evidence that higher levels of legal repressiveness were positively associated with HIV prevalence among injection drug users (Cruz et al., 2007). Even globalization is impacting illicit drug use. Evidence by Jirapramukpitak, Prince, and Harpham (2008) suggests that the urban migration of young rural Thai youth is characterized by stress and reduction in social networks. Furthermore, data from the same study support the argument that stress among the youth can increase the prevalence and progression of drug use and harmful drinking. Treatment interventions must take into account the values and norms of the culture and how societal principles and beliefs either enhance or hinder recovery.

One group that addresses macrolevel substance abuse issues is the Addiction Technology Transfer Center Network, a nationally organized program accessible globally through the World Wide Web. In the United States, this network is a multidisciplinary service that is available to professionals, students, policymakers, and educators. Regional substance abuse organizations use resources provided by the network to help providers build clinical skills, increase clinical competencies in new trends in the addiction community, and implement improved changes in their service delivery when new research and information become available. By translating recent research into practical guidelines for policymakers providers are able to play a significant role in the development of informed and up-to-date policies. The Addiction Technology Transfer Center Network focuses directly on the macrolevel of addiction treatment, providing new information, advocating for change, and connecting treatment providers across the United States.

The Chronosystem

The *chronosystem* refers to the dimension of time as it relates to a client's environment. Elements within the system can be external (such as how the passage of time affects relationships and organizations) or internal (such as a person's feeling of lost opportunities due to advancing age). How the client makes meaning of time in relation to these elements makes up his or her chronosystem.

There can be a contextual meaning to how the chronosystem influences the wider culture of society and addiction treatment. Historical and multigenerational life spaces affect both the stressors that increase the use of alcohol and other drugs and the variables involved in providing successful treatment interventions. The accumulation of stressors over time can exacerbate negative symptoms, including fixed distorted mood and cognitive responses, which may further impair relapse prevention and recovery.

One example of the interrelationship of the chronosystem and addictions treatment is the sustained recovery management model for communities of color. This model addresses how historical and cultural trauma that populations of color have experienced over time contributes to their substance use. Matching the experience of historical and cultural trauma with cooperative interventions by indigenous healers, institutions, and rituals has helped to create treatments that focus on building cultural and time-contextual recovery support services (White & Sanders, 2008).

Meaning Making

Meaning making is significant because it helps an addicted individual find purpose in the context of his or her life space. White, Laudet, and Becker (2006) conducted interviews with a number of recovering addicts to explore how they made meaning of their addiction and their future lives in recovery. They found that an addict's recovery process begins with making meaning of the disorder and continues throughout the recovery process. Such an individual creates a life absent of drugs and alcohol, a thriving, vibrant life with resolved old wounds and past regrets. Thus, recovery becomes the process of understanding the entirety of one's life—be it a childhood of abuse and poverty, a system of violence and injustice, or oppression and discrimination—and gaining some meaning and purpose in it for the future.

White et al. (2006) noted that throughout the stages of recovery the participants in their study were constantly in the process of providing new meanings for their values and personal goals. In short, they were crafting a new sense of self. Therefore the professional's role is to encourage the client's process of meaning making in a way that promotes the healing process and empowers the addict's confidence in his or her own ability to transcend contexts contrived from societal norms and values to create a self-directed life space full of awe, wonder, gratitude, and boundless potential.

Racial and Ethnic Issues in Substance Abuse Counseling

The brief discussion that follows highlights common experiences among racial/ethnic groups, specifically African Americans, Asian Americans, Native Americans/American Indians, and Hispanics/Latinos. We recognize and appreciate that the individuals we describe may have other identities (e.g., in terms of disability status, sexual orientation, age) that influence substance-related behaviors but that are not addressed here. The ecological perspective has been defined as "contextualized help-giving that is dependent on the meaning clients derive from their environmental interactions" (Conyne & Cook, 2004, p. 6). We believe that this ecological perspective is particularly appropriate in serving racial/ethnic minorities as well as other underserved populations.

We hold that an ecological perspective, specifically its attention to meaning making, is essential for clients whose symptomatic behavior entails routinely misrepresenting meaning (e.g., through denial and continual experiences of dysfunction due to their distortion of internal and external constraints and resources). For example, some addicted persons of color interpret their personal loss and lack of fulfillment as personal shortcomings. However, these losses may be the result of attempting to live and flourish in an environment that fails to acknowledge or support them because of their ethnicity.

The ecological perspective as applied to alcohol and drug treatment for minorities offers a unique benefit in that it acknowledges that structural factors (e.g., poverty, violence, discrimination) often play a very significant role in one's ability to define problems and access treatment, in the increasing availability of culturally appropriate treatment, and in other factors that are likely to influence both treatment outcomes and relapse prevention.

Straussner (2002) noted that most clients who abuse substances and enter treatment receive the same protocol regardless of their ethnicity. Until recently the counseling profession has not paid attention to differing worldviews, cultures, and diversity among clients. The imposition of treatment approaches (some of which may discredit a client's culture) and their ecological frame of reference can ultimately create resistance and disconnection from counselors and the overall treatment process (Sue & Sue, 2008).

Incidence and Prevalence

The incidence and prevalence of alcohol and other drug use, abuse, and addiction among African Americans, Asian Americans, Native Americans, Hispanics, and Whites varies. For instance, alcohol consumption is higher among Whites than African Americans (Harley, 2005; Straussner, 2002). Beatty (2003) compared alcohol consumption rates among Whites, Hispanics, and African Americans and found that Whites had a higher rate of consumption than both Hispanics and African Americans.

However, data also indicate that African Americans and Latinos, who make up 11% and 12% of the U.S. population, respectively, suffer from disproportionately high rates of negative drug-related consequences (Beatty, 2003). For example, African Americans and Latinos are disproportionately represented in drug abuse/dependence cases (16% and 15%, respectively), drug treatment programs (21% and 13%), drug-related incarceration rates (58% and 19%), and illicit drug use with HIV/AIDS (50% and 23%).

In considering the prevalence of the use of alcohol and other drugs by sex and race/ethnicity, Wallace et al. (2003) discovered that females consistently consumed fewer legal or illicit drugs (e.g., marijuana, cocaine, alcohol, tobacco) than men. However, females of color have unique substance abuse issues. Native American female adolescents account for more substance use, and Native American women account for more tobacco use. African American and Asian American girls are less likely than White girls to use licit or illicit drugs during early adolescence (Beatty, 2003). Foreign-born Latinas are less likely than U.S.-born Latinas to smoke. Among Asian American women, Japanese women smoke more than Chinese or Korean women. The majority of recent HIV/AIDS cases are among racial/ethnic minority women, with African American women representing more than 50% of those affected (Beatty, 2003; Beatty, Wetherington, Jones, & Roman, 2006).

There is even more discouraging evidence about the effects of substance misuse on girls (Johnston, O'Malley, Bachman, & Schulenberg, 2004). Girls are using tobacco, alcohol, illicit drugs, and controlled prescription drugs at rates that surpass those of boys. Once girls initiate use of these substances, they are more likely to become dependent on them and to have poorer treatment outcomes (Moochan & Schroeder, 2004; Rowe, Liddle, Greenbaum, & Henderson, 2004; Schinke, Di Noia, Schwinn, & Cole, 2006).

Girls also experience other negative consequences (e.g., poor nutrition, exposure to unprotected sex and sexually transmitted diseases, pregnancy, domestic violence) at disproportionate rates. Other factors associated with drug use among girls are weight control issues, unhealthy dating relationships, low self-esteem, and poor self-concept (Schinke et al., 2006). Family characteristics linked to female drug use are poor parental attachment, poor parental mentoring, and an unstructured home environment (Schinke et al., 2006).

Asian Americans and Pacific Islanders have historically reported lower rates of substance use and abuse than Whites; however, recent data reveal mixed results (Fong & Tsuang, 2007). Fong and Tsuang (2007) found that

Asian Americans and Pacific Islanders showed rates of substance abuse comparable to those of Whites. For example, among Vietnamese Americans the rate of substance abuse was very low, but for Japanese Americans substance use and abuse rates were comparable to those of Caucasians. The researchers also stated that methamphetamine abuse and dependence among Hawaiian and Pacific Islanders was very high, more than 3 times the rate observed in the general population.

Etiology or Cause(s) of Addiction

Loss of control is a major symptom associated with addiction. Loss of control due to the use of substances has been observed for thousands of years. A variety of theories of addiction were presented earlier in this chapter. A common feature of loss of control is that consumers cannot control their consumption once they have started consuming. Furthermore, they may intend and even make an effort to reduce their consumption but are unable to do so. For example, a drinker may stop at a local tavern to have one or two drinks but does not leave until he or she has consumed more than the intended amount.

Sociocultural theories contend that there are a variety of causes for drug use and misuse, both internal and external; thus, practitioners must have available a wide array of strategies for treating abuse and addiction. More precisely, substance abusers and addicts describe a variety of experiences, sometimes suggesting that the start of their problem is grounded in early childhood experiences. Yet other clients contend that loss of control occurred late in life as a reaction to cultural and societal factors. Morgan and Freeman (2009) asserted that historical trauma contributes to substance misuse among American Indians in Alaska. Finally, theory integration views addiction as a multidimensional process that requires multiple theories to explain.

Although any theory that is consistent, is robust, and reflects the cultural uniqueness of underserved racial/ethnic clients is worthy of consideration, sociocultural theories may be more culturally appropriate and therefore more useful for serving clients of color. These theories are sufficiently comprehensive to consider factors such as stressors, poverty, discrimination, and other cultural issues that are often associated with substance abuse and addictions. For example, substance-abusing Hispanics tend to show unique stressors related to immigration, acculturation, discrimination, language barriers, and disruptions of social support (Santisteban, Vega, & Suarez-Morales, 2006). Harley (2005) noted that the migration of African Americans from the South to northern urban areas trigged changes in their drinking patterns. Theories that incorporate both the individual and the environment, including the historical context and its impact, provide practitioners with resources and opportunities for unique treatment delivery.

Another benefit of sociocultural theories lies in their flexibility to address issues within the community. The abuse of substances brings about a variety of problems within minority communities. Illicit drug use is associated with higher levels of addiction, crime, and violence in African American communities and has contributed substantially to the HIV/AIDS crisis (Harley, 2005). What is interesting is that drug use is only slightly more prevalent in poor minority neighborhoods than more affluent communities. Drug distribution appears to be a major problem in disadvantaged neighborhoods.

In considering substance use in special populations, it is important not to assume that individuals from different racial/ethnic groups use substances for the same reason. The factors that contribute to the use and misuse of substances tend to vary across and within racial/ethnic groups. One factor, psychiatric disorders, has often been associated with the abuse of alcohol and other substances among Whites and has been assumed to play the same role for abusers in other groups as well. Yet compared to intrapsychic factors, sociocultural factors seem to impact more strongly Blacks addicted to cocaine (Barr, Farrell, Barnes, & Welte, 1993; Dembo, Williams, Wothke, & Schmeidler, 1994; Roberts, 2000). A recent study reported that although African Americans and Hispanics both experience disadvantages (e.g., poverty and discrimination), such potential protective factors as ethnic identification and religious participation may explain the lower lifetime risk of psychiatric disorders in these groups (Breslau et al., 2006; Sharma & Kanekar, 2008).

Limitations of the Use of Traditional Programs With Clients of Color

According to the National Treatment Center (1997), 93% of 400 privately funded inpatient and outpatient treatment programs surveyed based their practice on the 12-step program, which was developed by and based on the experiences of White men. Furthermore, 83% of these programs stated that they held AA meetings on site. Yet minority substance users differ in their motivations for using, their patterns of use, the substances they use, and their service utilization patterns (Fong & Tsuang, 2007; Roberts, 2000; Walton, Blow, & Booth, 2001). Thus, even decades ago Bell (1990) identified the need to present culturally appropriate services to clients of diverse backgrounds.

Research on alcohol-related issues has often involved only White males while ignoring factors associated with race, ethnicity, and culture (Caetano, Clark, & Tam, 1998). Treatment programs are designed, implemented, maintained, and evaluated by individuals with varying levels of cultural competence. Castro, Proescholdbell, Abeita, and Rodriguez (1999) outlined five levels of cultural competence: (a) cultural destruction, (b) cultural incapacity, (c) cultural blindness, (d) cultural competence, and (e) cultural proficiency. Less culturally competent practitioners differ from culturally competent practitioners in various ways. Culturally competent practitioners are more apt to respond to issues unique to the individual as well as address issues in a more culturally appropriate manner. For example, competent counselors serving Latino clients might explore ways of engaging corrective factors such as family or church because both are important among many Latinos. They also recognize that group-related issues are not necessarily pertinent to other groups. Racism and sexism are important in the lives of clients of color and women but probably not pertinent in the treatment of other groups of clients.

Beatty (2003) suggested that there are few overall differences in drug use by race or ethnicity. However, the consequences of drug use and addiction tend to be more serious among racial and ethnic minority populations than among Whites. African Americans often suffer from higher rates of health problems than Whites. Harley (2005) noted that drug addiction is probably the primary social and mental health problem in the Black community. Some researchers (e.g., Walton et al., 2001) have also found that women and racial/ethnic minorities appear to enter treatment with unique and different needs. Hispanics often cannot access treatment because of a lack of health insurance, a lack of cultural and linguistic support services, and the imposition of rigid treatment schedules and procedures.

Historical trauma has been explored as an explanation for the onset of mental health problems (Leary, 2005) and specific addiction issues among African Americans. The manner in which alcohol was used to control African Americans during slavery, coupled with contemporary circumstances (e.g., poverty, racism, oppression), increases the risk of alcoholism among Blacks. Many Blacks enter treatment with scant family support and find it difficult to adjust to a predominantly White treatment system (Beatty, 2003). African American women often enter treatment with limited financial resources (Walton et al., 2001). Substance abuse among Native Americans and American Indians in Alaska (Morgan & Freeman, 2009) and Canadian aboriginal clans (Jiwa, Kelly, & Pierre-Hansen, 2008) is viewed as a community illness rooted in historic trauma. Morgan and Freeman (2009) reported that the best clinicians' efforts to resolve the social and physical ills that have plagued the Alaskan people since their occupation have been inadequate.

The communities in which underserved drug abusers and addicts reside frequently face unique circumstances. Consumers in African American communities are disproportionately targeted by the alcohol industry and advertising agencies, both of which utilize well-researched strategies that are oriented toward Blacks (e.g., the use of African American language, culture, music, and role models). To make matters worse, many neighborhood stores sell alcohol, thereby making it readily available (Harley, 2005). Even more costly to disadvantaged neighborhoods than drug abuse and addiction is the transformation of neighborhoods into drug distribution centers for surrounding communities. Each disadvantaged neighborhood becomes the victim of its own drug abuse and acts as a base for criminal drug markets to serve neighboring communities (Saxe et al., 2001). Microlevel interventions targeted at individual clients (e.g., counseling, incarceration) fail to have any effect on macrolevel issues (e.g., sustained drug markets, disadvantaged communities).

In 1972 President Richard Nixon declared victory in the war against crime (Winslow, 2000), and in the 1980s the Reagan Administration launched the war on drugs. These initiatives were implemented for the express purpose of protecting poor minority communities from drug abuse and addiction and from the violence associated with the illegal drug trade. Some critics have noted that what actually has been waged is a war against the under-class. The racial disparity in the enforcement of drug laws is one example of unfair treatment. Esona and Shelden (2005) reported that people of color are more likely than Whites to be stopped and searched for drugs and to be convicted when caught with drugs and that on average they receive harsher sentences than Whites for similar charges. Fellner and Vinck (2008) reviewed National Corrections Reporting Program data for 2003 from 34 states. Findings revealed that (a) African Americans made up 53.5% of all persons entering prison because of drug convictions, (b) African American males were 10.1 times more likely than Whites to enter prison for drug of-fenses, (c) African American women were 4.8 times more likely than White women to enter prison for drug offenses, and (d) African American men were 11.8 times more likely than White men to enter prison for drug offenses.

An Ecological Approach to Counseling Addicted Clients of Color

Brunswick (1999) indicated that drug abuse and addiction occurs within multiple embedded systems: the individual, microsystem, mesosystem, exosystem, and macrosystem. Unfortunately, much of the psychosocial research on drugs has been restricted to an intraindividual perspective. As the intraindividual perspective is continually affected by other ecological systems, it remains continually in flux. For instance, the cocaine purchased on an urban corner and its price (microlevel) is driven by the availability and quantity of the drug (exolevel) and various factors such as general economics and the political climate (macrolevel). Any analysis that fails to consider multiple-level results is incomplete. Interventions based on an incomplete or inadequate analysis of the problem are very likely to lead to undesirable outcomes.

As indicated previously, drug abuse and addiction, as well as treatments for abuse and addiction, are often efforts to discover personal meaning. Interventions that both incorporate an environmental/contextual perspective and assist individuals in gaining personal meaning are especially effica-cious. White et al. (2006) offered some valuable resources for discovering the meanings of addiction and recovery. They raised the following ques-tions: (a) Why and how did this happen? (b) What does it mean to have this problem? (c) How did I come to escape the problem? (d) What action is needed to sustain my recovery? and (e) How does this problem affect the future of my life? As clients discern the answers to these questions, they rewrite their personal stories.

Although an awareness of meaning and purpose is necessary for clients to thrive (Frankl, 1959), clients also need wholesome personal relationships, personal growth, successes, altruism, creativity, religion, and a legacy (Proehl, 2007). These needs are often compromised by the addiction itself, mental illness, and other challenges. Saint Mary's Center in Oakland, Cali-fornia, offers a treatment approach for aging persons with mental illness and addiction (many of whom are homeless) that purports to help clients achieve meaning in their lives. Not only do clients improve their function (i.e., improve at the microlevel), but as recovery progresses they assume other roles such as advocate, fundraiser, and so on. Advocates seek to secure the human rights of low-income and homeless seniors in downtown and West Oakland.

Beatty (2003) offered recommendations for providing culturally appropriate drug abuse treatment to women of color. Several recommendations seem appropriate for treating other underserved populations. First, practitioners can benefit from foundation training to become culturally competent and proficient in recognizing both risks and strengths. Second, counselors should modify or revise traditional interventions to be culturally appropriate for clients. Third, practitioners should address the unique consequences associated with client characteristics (e.g., the fact that poor minorities are more likely than Whites to be involved with various systems such as unemployment, criminal justice, etc.). Fourth, practitioners must be aware of the increased potential risks associated with serving disenfranchised populations, such as feeling overwhelmed, feeling unappreciated, and experiencing burnout. Fifth, practitioners must learn to avoid confusing or misinterpreting behavior as resistance or noncompliance when it is something different (e.g., adaptive behavior to a racist environment). Sixth, practitioners must respond to the racial, ethnic, and cultural characteristics of each client without stereotyping. Seventh, practitioners must understand what is needed at both the individual (micro) level and the structural (macro) level to effect long-term change. Beatty's recommendations for culturally appropriate drug treatment are a valuable contribution to the ecological perspective.

EBP

Several types of EBP are ecologically based and offer counselors the framework to decide how best to intervene based on an individual's unique experiences. Client advocacy and consumer movements, competition for financial resources, and quality research have fueled the demand for EBP in the field of substance abuse (Eliason, 2007; Haug, Shopshire, Tajima, Gruber, & Guydish, 2008). Substance abuse programs and professionals need to demonstrate quality outcomes to be accountable to their clients, local communities, accrediting bodies, various stakeholders, and funding organizations. According to a recent descriptive study, 83% of professionals in the field reported using some form of EBP in the past year (Haug et al., 2008). Though the divide between research evidence and real-world applications continues to narrow, many authors have suggested that this gap still blocks the implementation of effective practices in the community, a particular concern for ecologically minded counselors who deal with underserved populations (Center for Substance Abuse Treatment, 2000; Eliason, 2007; Haug et al., 2008; Institute of Medicine, 1998; Simpson, 2002). Leaders in the field advocate for financial and workforce development incentives, including accessible training and recognition, the development of cross-system quality outcomes, and the forging of consensus in terminology (Eliason, 2007) to advance the EBP movement (Center for Substance Abuse Treatment, 2000; Institute of Medicine, 1998).

According to Eliason (2007), the goal of EBP is to improve outcomes of substance abuse treatment. Moreover, Eliason has advocated for cultural competency in terms of ethnicity, class, gender, and sexual orientation to improve the effectiveness and relevance of EBP for minority populations. Although efforts to investigate the relevance of EBP for minority populations are under way, there are no well-established practices at this time (Huey & Polo, 2008). Thus, the ecological counselor is encouraged to be responsive to ethnic and other minority statuses as well as to act as an advocate for underserved populations and conduct further research to promote treatment advances in the field.

Because a thorough assessment of the presenting problem and contributing factors is paramount to selecting appropriate treatment practices, the next section reviews the principles of ecological assessment. Following this, one EBP, multisystemic therapy (MST), is discussed.

Ecological Assessment

A comprehensive ecological assessment helps tailor treatment to the needs and strengths of individuals with chemical dependency problems. The assessment should target the necessary level of care as well as the selection of the most appropriate EBP to fit the personal characteristics of the person within his or her culture, life space (i.e., objective and subjective elements over time), spirituality, and meaning-making processes (Conyne & Cook, 2004). Accreditation, licensing, and reimbursement requirements also affect the quality of an assessment, a discussion that is beyond the scope of this chapter. Many forms of EBP have corresponding assessments and require a formal *DSM-IV-TR* (American Psychiatric Association, 2000) diagnosis. Moreover, the treatment population (e.g., adolescent, pregnant woman, African American man), the setting and level of care (e.g., criminal justice system, drug detoxification and drug treatment center), as well as the type of substance abuse (e.g., alcohol, opioid, polysubstance) contribute to the selection of assessment protocols.

An ecological assessment begins with determining the client's unique presenting situation, treatment needs, a thorough history of his or her past and present substance use (e.g., illicit, over-the-counter, prescription, and legal drugs), as well as an evaluation of its severity (Dziegielewski, 2005). Diagnostic information also reveals the methods of ingestion, the age of onset of the disorder, and the dates of past substance abuse treatments, including support groups attended (e.g., AA, NA). Informal support networks should also be explored, such as client involvement and relationships with members of faith-based, volunteer, and other community groups. Further areas of evaluation need to incorporate the client's medical and nutritional history and present health status, including sexually transmitted infections; infectious diseases; physical/medical traumas; and high-risk behaviors such as

247

intravenous use, unsafe sex, and risk of suicide (Dziegielewski, 2005; Kleber et al., 2007). It is recommended that the practitioner use objective blood, breath, or urine screens to assess the types of substances used and other laboratory tests as needed to determine the presence of other co-occurring conditions (Kleber et al., 2007). Furthermore, collateral information must be gathered from loved ones (Dziegielewski, 2005; Kleber et al., 2007). In addition, the client's past and current mental health functioning must be assessed, especially the cohesiveness of his or her relationships with peers, family, and significant others, whose perspectives on the client's substance abuse and his or her social functioning may inform the interventions (Conyne & Cook, 2004).

Other areas for evaluation include the kinds of interpersonal coping strategies utilized, family histories, and the effects of substance abuse on other systems (e.g., finances, housing, employment, child care, school performance, grades; Dziegielewski, 2005). The identification of client strengths and resources is necessary to the development of a collaborative, individualized treatment plan. Strengths and resources consist of positive and effective coping behaviors (i.e., skills and attitudes that help negotiate person–environment interactions; Cook, 2008) such as resiliency, self-esteem, and spirituality. Community and cultural supports, motivations for treatment, and meanings derived from such support are other examples of client resources (Conyne & Cook, 2004). In addition, the client's personal theory of change (i.e., the client's belief about how to improve a problem situation), events that have prompted the need for immediate change, and meaning derived from various life experiences and events are ecological constructs relevant to assessment and treatment selection (Conyne & Cook, 2004). Finally, the personal, interpersonal, and contextual barriers that may impede the client's change process at present and in the future need to be considered at the onset of and throughout the course of treatment.

MST

MST, which is listed in the National Registry of Evidence-Based Programs and Practices (SAMHSA, 2009), is a treatment practice consistent with the ecological perspective. MST reportedly has the potential to be a culturally competent practice (Huey & Polo, 2008). Huey and Polo (2008) categorized MST as probably efficacious for treating conduct disorders in African American youth and mixed/comorbid problems in multiracial Hawaiian youth (i.e., Mixed Asian/Caucasian/Pacific Islander). They found MST to be possibly efficacious for treating substance use and suicidality in African American youth.

In general Huey and Polo (2008) described how EBP may be applied to ethnic minorities. One way is to maintain the EBP in its prescribed form and apply only culturally responsive elements or modifications discussed in the treatment manual (Huey & Polo, 2008). That is, the counselor can be taught specific ways for tailoring treatment in response to culture-specific needs as they arise. However, culture-specific examples of client needs and corresponding interventions are seldom identified, which complicates fidelity and replication. Similarly, MST involves treating minority youth at the onset of therapy no differently than majority youth until culture-specific barriers (e.g., language, intergenerational conflict) or opportunities (e.g., a treatment team representative of client population) arise (Huey & Polo, 2008). At this point, attention to minority status or cultural factors is warranted. Defining outcomes in ethnically diverse ways is another area for improvement for EBP (Huey & Polo, 2008; Kleber et al., 2007). Overall, current research points to poorer outcomes for ethnic and racial minorities in traditional substance abuse treatment programs, which may be due in part to socioeconomic inequalities (Kleber et al., 2007).

MST most clearly exemplifies an ecological approach to substance abuse treatment. This home-based intervention, which serves youth ages 12–17, occurs within the life context of the youth, offering the youth and his or her family convenient and comfortable counseling at home (rather than in an office). The risk and protective factors for youth substance abuse are conceptualized within Bronfenbrenner's (1979) framework of addressing the individual youth within his or her family, peer, school, and community contexts.

For example, individual youth risk variables for substance abuse involve interest in criminal behavior, low self-esteem, low social conformity, genetic vulnerability, and positive drug and alcohol expectancies (e.g., teens expect a positive outcome, like increased relaxation, as a result of smoking marijuana, thereby increasing their perception of relaxation following drug use). Common family factors are high conflict and ineffective discipline, scant warmth, and parental substance use. Peer association with those who use substances and few positive peer influences add to the risk for substance abuse development. Moreover, lack of success in school and low commitment to succeed are contributing risk factors. Neighborhoods with high rates of crime and other forms of disorganization tend to be associated with risk factors for adolescent substance use problems (Sheidow & Henggeler, 2005).

The basic goal of MST is to build family resiliency to effectively manage serious problems presented by the family's youth. Master's-level counselors work in teams, with each counselor working with four to six families at a time. Counselors are available to families 24 hours a day, 7 days a week, and each team is supervised closely to encourage fidelity to the model (Sheidow & Henggeler, 2005). The counselors identify resources and strengths available within each family. During the assessment process, the counselors' goal is to apply the family's strengths to change those characteristics of the youth's ecology that are linked with substance use and related problematic behaviors. In addition, counselors identify barriers to treatment success rather than perceive clients as fostering resistance.

MST is centered on nine treatment principles (Henggeler, Schoenwald, Borduin, Rowland, & Cunningham, 1998). The first is finding the fit determined during assessments administered throughout the treatment period. These assessments provide information on how the identified problems fit within the broader context. A counselor's careful monitoring of this dynamic person-in-environment fit allows for ongoing interactions among family members and the client. Another principle, the use of positive and strength-focused interventions, utilizes strengths within the youth's system as "levers for change" (Henggeler et al., 1998, p. 28). The next principle promotes responsibility among family members across multiple contexts. Therapeutic contacts are present-focused and action-oriented to target specific problems or desired outcomes. Interventions also focus on sequences of behavior among family members within multiple systems believed to maintain the identified problems. Likewise, interventions are developmentally appropriate for the youth and family members. Another principle, continuous effort, requires all family members to work toward collaborative goals on a daily or weekly basis. The next tenet, evaluation and accountability, expects counselors to participate in ongoing evaluation from multiple perspectives and to be held accountable for overcoming barriers and achieving outcomes. Finally, interventions promote treatment generalizability and long-term sustainability for change through empowering caregivers to address multiple needs of family members across multiple contexts (Sheidow & Henggeler, 2005).

A number of studies have confirmed effectiveness of MST for treating delinquent youth who have substance abuse disorders (Henggeler et al., 1991; Henggeler, Clingempeel, Brondino, & Pickrel, 2002; Henggeler, Pickrel, Brondino, & Crouch, 1996). Given the problematic substance abuse of parents, which interfered with treatment success, the cognitive–behavioral treatment approach of contingency management was added in subsequent studies with success (Henggeler et al., 1999; Henggeler et al., 2006; Swenson, Henggeler, Taylor, & Addison, 2005). Family therapy in general is a recommended practice for treating substance abuse disorders, including those involving marijuana and alcohol (Kleber et al., 2007).

Consider the case of Jeff as an example of MST in practice. Jeff is a 16-year-old biracial male living in a low-income housing project. He was recently released from the juvenile detention center and referred for intensive home-based services to address his criminal behavior and substance abuse. Jeff had previously been referred to counseling services but did not successfully complete the program. His mother is unable to take time off work to attend counseling with him. The MST counseling allows the family to access services that are not otherwise accessible. The therapist becomes involved with the client, family, and community by engaging them in the natural environment. The counselor works around the caregiver's work schedule as well as school schedules.

Jeff's most recent legal charge involved theft. Jeff began smoking pot 3 years ago with neighborhood kids and recently hooked up with his biological father, who got high with Jeff and introduced him to criminal behavior. Jeff's mother and father were never legally married, and his father left the home shortly after Jeff was born.

As the MST counselor worked to engage Jeff and his mother, it became clear that Jeff and his mother had a very close relationship. The counselor also became involved in Jeff's schooling and was successful in getting him back into the classroom. Jeff had been engaged early on in learning but had become distracted once his mother picked up a sec-

250

ond job. That loss of time together seemed instrumental in Jeff engaging with peers who were less focused on academics and more involved in criminal behavior.

As the counselor and the family established goals, it became clear that Jeff needed support and structure from his mother as well as his extended family members. Initial treatment goals included the following:

- To decrease the level of conflict within the home
- To improve Jeff's school attendance and grades
- To eliminate Jeff's substance use and contacts with his father unless the father agreed to attend family counseling sessions
- To empower Jeff's mom to provide clear boundaries for Jeff and to discipline him based on established rules
- To increase Jeff's refusal skills and help him engage in more prosocial behaviors

The counselor engaged this family through her presence. She stepped in and offered homework assistance until Jeff's problem-solving skills increased. The counselor observed Jeff's mom withdraw as Jeff confronted the structure his mom was providing. The counselor then coached the mom on how to implement the communication skills practiced in the counseling sessions. As the family system became stronger, reliance on the counselor for support decreased. The family became involved with extended family, church, and friends again. These relationships helped solidify the changes the family had made as a result of the counseling.

Future ecological studies are warranted to systematically incorporate the exploration of client meaning making and cultural competency within EBP. It is hoped that as progress is made in determining practices that maximize optimal treatment outcomes for underserved and majority populations, concomitant ineffective and potentially harmful practices (e.g., confrontation, breaking down denial) will be eliminated (Eliason, 2007).

Summary

The purpose of this chapter was to relate the ecological approach to counseling persons for substance abuse or addiction. The following important points were discussed:

- Approximately 18 million Americans suffer from alcohol use disorders, yet only 7.1% of these individuals receive services.
- Although Americans make up 5% of the world population, they consume 60% of the world's illicit drugs
- Shame and blame among individuals and families continue to function as barriers to treatment. Because of shame and blame, substance abusers often choose not to seek treatment.
- Many approaches to drug treatment are limited because although factors at multiple levels (micro-, meso-, eco-, macro-,

chronolevels) contribute to abuse and addiction, interventions are typically restricted to the micro- and mesolevels.

- Meaning making helps individuals find a purpose in their lives, and many involved in the field believe that it is valuable for initiating and maintaining recovery.
- An ecological perspective can help counselors develop cultural competence for working with marginalized clients and use EBP to improve substance abuse treatment for all clients.
- There is a pressing need for ongoing research into various facets of the ecological perspective. These studies will further illuminate the cultural competence of substance abuse professionals and increase knowledge about EBP and substance abuse treatment.

Discussion Questions

- Compare and contrast an ecological perspective versus traditional psychotherapeutic or self-help group approaches for the treatment of drug addiction.
- What knowledge and skills are required by addiction professionals and mental health professionals to facilitate multitiered interventions like the Positive Action program described in this chapter?

References

American Psychiatric Association. (2000). *Diagnostic and statistical manual of mental disorders* (4th ed., text rev.). Washington, DC: Author.

Amour, B. S., Woolery, T., Malarcher, A., et al. (2005). Annual smoking-attributable mortality, years of potential life lost, and productivity losses—United States, 1997–2001. *Center forDisease Control and Prevention Morbidity and Mortality Weekly Report (July 1, 2005), 54*(25), 625–628.

Barr, K. E., Farrell, M. R., Barnes, G. M., & Welte, J. W. (1993). Race, class, and gender differences in substance abuse: Evidence of middle-class/underclass polarization among Black males. *Social Problems, 40,* 314–327.

Beatty, L. A. (2003). Changing their minds: Drug abuse and addiction in Black women. In D. Brown & V. Keith (Eds.), *In and out of our right minds: The mental health of African American women* (pp. 59–79). New York, NY: Columbia University Press.

Beatty, L. A., Wetherington, C. L., Jones, D. J., & Roman, A. B. (2006). Substance use and abuse by girls and women. In J. Worrel & C. Goodheart (Eds.), *Handbook of girls' and women's psychological health: Gender and well-being across the life span* (pp. 113–121). New York, NY: Oxford University Press.

Bell, P. (1990). *Chemical dependency and the African American: Counseling strategies and community issues.* Center City, MN: Hazelden.

Berk, L. E. (2000). *Development through the life span* (2nd ed.). Boston, MA: Pearson/Allyn & Bacon.

Breslau, J., Aguilar-Gaxiola, S., Kendler, K. S., Su, M., Williams, D., & Kessler, R. C. (2006). Specifying race-ethnic differences in risk for psychiatric disorder in a USA national sample. *Psychological Medicine, 36,* 57–68.

Bronfenbrenner, U. (1979). *The ecology of human development.* Cambridge, MA: Harvard University Press.

Bronfenbrenner, U. (1981). *The ecology of human development.* Cambridge, MA: Harvard University Press.

Bronfenbrenner, U. (1999). Environments in developmental perspective: Theoretical and operational models. In S. Friedman & T. Wachs (Eds.), *Measuring environment across the life span: Emerging methods and concepts* (pp. 3–28). Washington, DC: American Psychological Association.

Brunswick, A. F. (1999). Structural strain: An ecological paradigm for studying African American drug use. In M. De La Rosa, B. Segal, & R. Lopez (Eds.), *Conducting drug abuse research within minority populations: Advances and issues* (pp. 5–19). Binghamton, NY: Haworth Press.

Caetano, R., Clark, C. L., & Tam, T. (1998). Alcohol consumption among racial/ethnic minorities: Theories and research. *Alcohol Health and Research, 22*(4), 233–238.

Castro, F. G., Proescholdbell, R., Abeita, L., & Rodriguez, D. (1999). Ethnic and cultural minority groups. In B. S. McCrady & E. E. Epstein (Eds.), *Addiction: A comprehensive guidebook for practitioners* (pp. 499–528). Oxford, England: Oxford University Press.

Centers for Disease Control and Prevention Online Newsroom (2011). *CDC reports excessive alcohol consumption cost the U.S. $224 billion in 2006.* Retrieved from http://www.cdc.gov/media/release/2011/p1017_alcohol_consumption.html

Center for Substance Abuse Treatment. (2000). *Changing the conversation: The National Treatment Plan Initiative.* Rockville, MD: U.S. Department of Health and Human Services, Substance Abuse and Mental Health Services Administration.

Conyne, R. K., & Cook, E. P. (2004). *Ecological counseling: An innovative approach to conceptualizing person–environment interaction.* Alexandria, VA: American Counseling Association.

Cook, E. (2008). *Draft of best practice guidelines for ecological counseling at FSC.* Unpublished manuscript, University of Cincinnati, OH.

Crum, R. M., Storr, C. L., Ialongo, N., & Anthony, J. C. (2008). Is depressed mood in childhood associated with an increased risk for initiation of alcohol use during early adolescence? *Addictive Behavior, 33*(1), 24–40.

Cruz, M., Mantsios, A., Ramos, R., Case, P., Brouwer, K., Ramos, M., . . . Strathder, S. (2007). A qualitative exploration of gender in the context of injection drug use in two U.S.–Mexico border cities. *AIDS and Behavior, 11*, 253–262.

Danuta, M. (1981). Life space ecological model of family treatment. *International Journal of Family Psychiatry, 2*(1–2), 75–94.

Dembo, R., Williams, L., Wothke, W., & Schmeidler, J. (1994). The relationships among family problems, friends' troubled behavior, and high risk youths' alcohol/other drug use and delinquent behavior: A longitudinal study. *International Journal of the Addictions, 29*, 1419–1442.

253

Doweiko, H. E. (2009). *Concepts of chemical dependency* (7th ed.). Belmont, CA: Brooks/Cole Cengage Learning.

Duncan, A. E., Sartor, C. E., Scherrer, J. F., Grant, J. D., Heath, A. C., Nelson, E. C., . . . Bucholz, K. K. (2008). The association between cannabis abuse and dependence and childhood physical and sexual abuse: Evidence from an offspring of twins design. *Addiction, 103*(1), 78–79.

Dziegielewski, S. F. (2005). *Understanding substance addictions: Assessment and interventions.* Chicago, IL: Lyceum Books.

Eliason, M. J. (2007). *Improving substance abuse treatment: An introduction to the evidence-based practice movement.* Los Angeles, CA: Sage.

Esona, D., & Shelden, R. G. (2005). *Racial disparities and the drug war.* Retrieved from http://www.cjcj.org/files/racial_disparities.pdf

Fellner, J., & Vinck, P. (2008). *Targeting Blacks: Drug law enforcement and race in the United States.* New York, NY: Human Rights Watch.

Flay, B. R., & Allred, C. G. (2003). Long term effects of the Positive Action program. *American Journal of Health Behavior, 27*(Suppl. 1), S6–S21.

Fong, T. W., & Tsuang, J. (2007). Asian Americans, addiction, and barriers to treatment. *Psychiatry, 4*, 51–58.

Frankl, V. E. (1959). *Man's search for meaning.* Boston, MA: Beacon Press.

Harley, D. A. (2005). African Americans and substance abuse. In D. A. Harley & J. M. Dillard (Eds.), *Contemporary mental health issues among African Americans* (pp. 119–131). Alexandria, VA: American Counseling Association.

Harris, M., Fallot, R. D., & Berley, R. W. (2005). Qualitative interviews on substance abuse and prevention among female trauma survivors. *Psychiatric Services, 56*, 1292–1296.

Haug, N. A., Shopshire, M., Tajima, B., Gruber, V., & Guydish, J. (2008). Adoption of evidence-based practices among substance abuse treatment providers. *Journal of Drug Education, 38*(2), 181–192.

Henggeler, S. W., Borduin, C. M., Melton, G. B., Mann, B. J., Smith, L., Hall, J. A., . . . Fucci, B. R. (1991). Effects of multisystemic therapy on drug use and abuse in serious juvenile offenders: A progress report from two outcome studies. *Family Dynamics of Addiction Quarterly, 1*, 40–51.

Henggeler, S. W., Clingempeel, W. G., Brondino, M. J., & Pickrel, S. G. (2002). Four-year follow-up of multisystemic therapy with substance abusing and dependent juvenile offenders. *Journal of the American Academy of Child and Adolescent Psychiatry, 4*, 868–874.

Henggeler, S. W., Halliday-Boykinds, C. A., Cunningham, P. B., Randall, J., Shapiro, S. B., & Chapman, J. E. (2006). Juvenile drug court: Enhancing outcomes by integrating evidence-based treatments. *Journal of Consulting and Clinical Psychology, 74*, 42–54.

Henggeler, S. W., Pickrel, S. G., Brondino, M. J., & Crouch, J. L. (1996). Eliminating (almost) treatment dropout of substance abusing or dependent delinquents through home-based multisystemic therapy. *American Journal of Psychiatry, 753*, 427–428.

Henggeler, S. W., Rowland, M. R., Randall, J., Ward, D., Pickrel, S. G., Cunningham, P. B., . . . Santos, A. B. (1999). Home-based multisystemic therapy as an alternative to the hospitalization of youth in psychiatric crisis: Clinical outcomes. *Journal of the American Academy of Child and Adolescent Psychiatry, 38,* 1331–1339.

Henggeler, S. W., Schoenwald, S. K., Borduin, C. M., Rowland, M. D., & Cunningham, P. B. (1998). *Multisystemic treatment of antisocial behavior in children and adolescents.* New York, NY: Guilford Press.

Holder, H. D. (2008). Alcohol and violence: A complex nexus of drinking environment and drinking pattern. *Addiction, 103*(1), 78–79.

Huey, S., & Polo, A. (2008). Evidence-based psychological treatments for ethnic minority youth: A review and meta-analysis. *Journal of Clinical Child and Adolescent Psychology, 37,* 262–301.

Hughes-Jones, M. (2009). *Women's recovery in the eating disorders: Exploring the role of perceived mutuality in close relationships and social support satisfaction.* Retrieved from https://circle.ubc.ca/bitstream/handle/2429/7145/ubcspringhuhes-jonesmegan.pdf?sequence=1

Institute of Medicine. (1998). *Bridging the gap between practice and research: Forging partnerships with community-based drug and alcohol treatment.* Washington, DC: Author.

Jellinek, E. M. (1960a). Alcoholism, a genus and some of its species. *Canadian Medical Association Journal, 83,* 1341–1345.

Jellinek, E. M. (1960b). *The disease concept of alcoholism.* Highland Park, NJ: Hillhouse Press.

Jirapramukpitak, T., Prince, M., & Harpham, T. (2008). Rural–urban migration, illicit drug use and hazardous/harmful drinking in young Thai population. *Addiction, 103*(1), 91–100.

Jiwa, F. L., Kelly, C., & Pierre-Hansen, N. (2008). Healing the community to heal the individual: Literature review of aboriginal community-based alcohol and substance abuse programs. *Canadian Family Physicians, 54,* 1–7.

Johnson, J. L. (2004). *Fundamentals of substance abuse practice.* Belmont, CA: Brooks/Cole.

Johnston, L. D., O'Malley, P. M., Bachman, J. G., & Schulenberg, J. E. (2004). *Monitoring the future, national results on adolescent drug use: Overview of key findings, 2003* (National Institutes of Health Publication No. 04-5506). Bethesda, MD: National Institute on Drug Abuse.

Kinney, J. (2008). *Loosening the grip: A handbook of alcohol information* (9th ed.). Boston, MA: McGraw-Hill.

Kleber, H. D., Weiss, R. D., Anton, R. F., George, T. P., Greenfield, S. F., Kosten, T. R., . . . Woods, S. M. (2007). Treatment of patients with substance use disorders (2nd ed.). *American Journal of Psychiatry, 164*(4), 5–123.

Leary, J. (2005). *Post traumatic slave syndrome: America's legacy of enduring injury and healing.* Baltimore, MD: Uptown Press.

Moochan, E. T., & Schroeder, J. R. (2004). Quick attempts among African American teenage smokers seeking treatment: Gender differences. *Preventive Medicine, 39,* 1180–1186.

Morgan, R., & Freeman, L. (2009). The healing of our people: Substance abuse and historical trauma. *Substance Use & Misuse, 44*(1), 84–98.

National Association of Alcoholism and Drug Abuse Counselors. (2009). *Principles of drug addiction treatment: A research-based guide* (2nd ed.; National Institutes of Health Publication No. 09-4180). Retrieved from http://www.nida.nih.gov/PDF/PODAT/PODAT.pdf

National Institute on Alcohol Abuse and Alcoholism. (2009). *Alcohol across the lifespan. Strategic plan 2009-2014*. Retrieved from http://infodoc.inserm.fr/pnr/alcool.nsf/ViewAllDocumentsByUNID/74CB404B5CCFE808C12574AD0030E8E8/$File/StrategicPlan.pdf?OpenElement

National Treatment Center. (1997). *National Treatment Center Study, Summary report: A comprehensive report detailing findings from on-site interviews at 450 alcohol and drug addiction treatment programs nationwide*. Retrieved from http://ntcs.uga.edu/reports/NTCS%20summary%20reports/NTCS%20Report%20No.%201.pdf

Office of National Drug Control Policy. (2011). Study shows illicit drug use cost U.S. economy more than $193 billion. *ONDCP Update, 5*(2), p. 1.

Palmer, R. S., & Daniluk, J. C. (2007). The perceived role of others in facilitating or impeding healing from substance abuse. *Canadian Journal of Counseling, 41*(4), 199–212.

Peele, S. (1995). *The diseasing of America*. Lexington, MA: Lexington Books. (Original work published 1989)

Pilkington, H. (2007). Beyond peer pressure: Rethinking drug use and "youth culture." *International Journal of Drug Policy, 18*(3), 213–224.

Pollini, R. A., Brouwer, K. C., Lozada, R. M., Ramos, R., Cruz, M. F., Magis-Rodriguez, C., . . . Stranthdee, S. A. (2008). Syringe possession arrests are associated with receptive syringe sharing in two Mexico–US border cities. *Addiction, 103*(1), 101–108.

Proehl, R. L. (2007). Social justice, respect, and meaning-making: Keys to working with the homeless elder population. *Health and Social Work, 32*(4), 301–307.

Roberts, A. (2000). Psychiatric comorbidity and African American illicit substance abusers: Evidence of differential etiology. *Clinical Psychology Review, 20*, 667–677.

Rowe, C., Liddle, H. A., Greenbaum, P., & Henderson, C. (2004). Impact of psychiatric comorbidity on treatment of adolescent drug abusers. *Journal of Substance Abuse Treatment, 26*(2), 129–140.

Sadock, B. J., & Sadock, V. A. (2003). *Kaplan and Sadock's synopsis of psychiatry: Behavioral sciences/clinical psychiatry* (9th ed.). New York, NY: Lippincott, Williams & Wilkins.

Santisteban, D., Vega, R. R., & Suarez-Morales, L. (2006). Utilizing findings to help understand and bridge the research and practice gap in treatment of substance abuse disorders in Hispanic populations. *Drug and Alcohol Dependence, 84*, 94–101.

Saxe, L., Kadushin, C., Beveridge, A., Livert, D., Tighe, E., Rindskopf, D., . . . Brodsky, A. (2001). The visibility of illicit drugs: Implications for community based drug control strategies. *American Journal of Public Health, 91*, 1987–1994.

Schinke, S., Di Noia, J., Schwinn, T., & Cole, K. (2006). Drug abuse risk and protective factors among Black urban adolescent girls: A group-randomized trial of computer-delivered mother–daughter intervention. *Psychology of Addictive Behaviors, 20,* 496–500.

Shaffer, H. J., LaPant, D. A., LaBrie, R. A., Kidman, R. C., Donato, A. N., & Stanton, M. V. (2004). Toward a syndrome model of addiction: Multiple expressions, common etiology. *Harvard Review of Psychiatry, 12,* 367–374.

Sharma, M. J., & Kanekar, A. (2008). Substance abuse in minorities. *Journal of Alcohol and Drug Education, 52*(3), 3–8.

Sheidow, A. J., & Henggeler, S. W. (2005). Community-based treatments. In K. Heilbrun, N. E. Sevin Goldstein, & R. Redding (Eds.), *Juvenile delinquency* (pp. 257–281). New York, NY: Oxford University Press.

Simpson, D. D. (2002). A conceptual framework for transferring research to practice. *Journal of Substance Abuse Treatment, 22*(4), 171–182.

Straussner, S. L. (2002). Ethnic, culture, and substance abuse. *Counselor, 3*(6), 34–37.

Substance Abuse and Mental Health Services Administration. (2009). *National registry of evidence-based programs and practices.* Retrieved from http://www.samhsa.gov/newsroom/advisories/0912171412.aspx

Substance Abuse and Mental Health Services Administration. (2010). *Results from the 2009 National Survey on Drug Use and Health: Volume I. Summary of national findings.* Retrieved from http://www.drugabusestatistics.samhsa.gov/NSDUH/2k9NSDUH/2k9ResultsP.pdf

Substance Abuse and Mental Health Services Administration, Office of Applied Studies. (2009). *Treatment Episode Data Set (TEDS) highlights—2007 national admissions to substance abuse treatment services.* DASIS Series: S45, (U.S. Department of Health and Human Services Publication No. [SMA] 09-4360). Rockville, MD.

Sue, D. W., & Sue, D. (2008). *Counseling the culturally diverse: Theory and practice* (5th ed.). Hoboken, NJ: Wiley.

Swenson, C., Henggeler, S. W., Taylor, I. S., & Addison, O. W. (2005). *Multisystemic therapy and neighborhood partnerships: Reducing adolescent violence and substance abuse.* New York, NY: Guilford Press.

United Nations. (2005). *2005 world drug report. Volume I: Analysis.* Retrieved from http://www.unodc.org/pdf/WDR_2005/volume_1_web.pdf

Van der Zwaluw, C. S., Scholte, R. H., Vermulst, A. A., Buitelarr, J., Verkes, R. J., & Engels, R. C. (2008). The crown of love: Intimate relations and alcohol use in adolescence. *European Child Adolescent Psychiatry, 18,* 407–417.

Van Wormer, K., & Davis, D. (2008). *Addiction treatment: A strengths based perspective.* Belmont, CA: Brooks/Cole.

Wallace, J. M., Bachman, J. G., O'Malley, P. M., Schulenberg, J. E., Cooper, S. M., & Johnston, L. D. (2003). Gender and ethnic differences in smoking, drinking and illicit drug use among American 8th, 10th and 12th grade students, 1976–2000. Addiction, 98(2), 225–234.

Walton, M. A., Blow, F. C., & Booth, B. M. (2001). Diversity in relapse prevention needs: Gender and race comparisons among substance abuse treatment patients. *American Journal of Drug and Alcohol Abuse, 27*(2), 225–240.

White, W. L., Laudet, A. B., & Becker, J. B. (2006). Life meaning and purpose in addiction recovery: The counselor can help clients identify meaning that fits their value system. *Addiction Professional, 4*(4), 18–23.

White, W. L., & Sanders, M. (2008). Recovery management and people of color: Redesigning addiction treatment for historically disempowered communities. *Alcoholism Treatment Quarterly, 26*(3), 365–395.

Winslow, G. (2000). Capital crimes: The political economy of crime in America. *Monthly Review, 52*(6), 38–53.

Working With Faith-Based
Communities in Ecological Counseling

Joseph A. Stewart-Sicking and Wairimu Wanjau Mutai

Faith-based communities (FBCs) are important members of local communities and are often central in clients' lives, making them key actors in both preventive and clinical counseling. Given the immense diversity of these communities and the often limited experience that counselors have with working with them, ecologically minded counselors can benefit from tools for conceptualizing these social systems and their interactions with other systems in clients' lives. Counselors should consider the internal dynamics of FBCs, their capabilities for providing care, their relationships to their neighborhoods, and aspects of person–environment fit between them and clients. This multilevel perspective can help counselors forge productive partnerships with these organizations and determine ethically and spiritually sensitive ways to discuss them with clients.

Since the mid-1990s, there has been a widely documented explosion of interest in the topics of spirituality and religion in counseling. Counseling programs are beginning to see these areas as important domains of counselor preparation, supported by competency lists developed by divisions of the American Counseling Association that note that working with indigenous spiritual and religious resources is essential to competent counselor practice (see Arredondo et al., 1996; Association for Spiritual, Ethical, and Religious Values in Counseling, n.d.). Although there has been much work in these areas, it sits in uneasy tension with a tradition stretching back to William James (1902/1997) that tends to see religion as "feelings, acts, and experiences of individual men in their solitude" (p. 42). Recently this style of

259

thinking can be seen in the relative prominence of spirituality over religion in discussions of counseling. As a result, counselors do not usually receive training in how to approach issues of spirituality and religion beyond the microsystem, and this dearth of knowledge is exacerbated by the over-representation of spiritual seekers among those who provide counseling (Pargament, 2007; Shafranske, 1996; Stewart-Sicking, 2002). Thus, not only do counselors tend to focus on microsystemic issues of individual spirituality, but many also have little firsthand experience in how FBCs work at higher levels in the ecosystem. This chapter considers religious and spiritual issues through an overarching ecological perspective that provides an understanding of FBCs as social institutions, their capacities for promoting well-being and development, the contextual and internal systemic issues they face, strategies for working with these communities as a counselor, and ways clients' FBCs can be explored in individual or family counseling.

FBCs as Social Institutions

What do a storefront chapel and a downtown cathedral have in common? How do they help promote wellness and care for their members? In answering these questions, this chapter explores the social dynamics of FBCs, those communities whose primary reason for existing is to help members pursue together a way of life informed by a mutual commitment to a faith tradition. We have chosen the term *faith-based communities* (FBCs) instead of *religious organizations* for two reasons: (a) It avoids the thorny issue of defining *religion*, which is continually contested across the social sciences; and (b) its broader connotations more accurately reflect the pluralism of belief that characterizes America. In this pluralism of belief, the established order of "Protestant, Catholic, Jew" (Herberg, 1983) has broken down to make room for a variety of groups that meet the definition of pursuing a way of life together informed by mutual faith but that may not fit into the traditional denominational or religious hierarchy (e.g., communities that practice meditation on a regular basis or para-church organizations such as "new monastic" houses). Although the relative newness of these communities means that most of the research and theory used in this chapter about faith-based organizations derives from studies of more traditional religious organizations, it is hoped that these reflections will be useful heuristics for working with a variety of faith-based organizations.

America's Landscape of Faith

Denominations and Faith Traditions

When talking of FBCs, we often turn first to the language of *denominations,* those formalized organizations to which local FBCs belong—Episcopalian, Catholic, Baptist, Reform Jew. Though these formal structures are salient in circumstances such as scandals or schism, in which individual members are especially concerned about organizational image or values, denominations are a distal influence on clients' lives. Denominational structures form part of clients' exosystems, and the most important influence from these organizations is often not their formal actions and declarations but the ways in which these labels are a brand marking a particular way of doing religious practices. In fact, the most useful way to think of denominations is probably as closer to traditions of wisdom (Bass, 2004) than to the local office of the national corporation. Thus, counselors considering learning about different FBCs would be better off learning about the cultural identity conveyed by denominational identity and focusing their knowledge of organizational dynamics to those that impact congregational life. For FBCs, denominational identity is more of a cultural marker, identifying the particular style of the religious tradition being followed. Thus, although not every FBC is a member of a formal denomination, all FBCs draw on some style of practicing spirituality. Moreover, multiple denominational organizations can arise from a single style of spiritual practice—for instance, Lutheranism in the United States has three primary denominations: the Evangelical Lutheran Church in America, The Lutheran Church—Missouri Synod, and the Wisconsin Evangelical Lutheran Synod. In each of these denominations, the Lutheran style of Christianity is interpreted slightly differently.

For these reasons, counselors would do well to begin their approach to FBCs through a multicultural lens. In addition to consulting the many resources written for therapists exploring the cultures of different religious groups (e.g., Richards & Bergin, 2000), counselors should learn from a skilled insider the nuances of those groups with whom they will regularly work. In fact, attending local congregational events can be an excellent way for a counselor to be introduced these cultures, not to mention a powerful way to build contacts and connections for working with clients.

De Facto Congregationalism

For a variety of historical and sociological reasons, the basic unit for understanding American faith-based organizations is not the denomination but the *congregation,* a "body of people who regularly gather to worship at a particular place" (Wind & Lewis, 1994, p. 1). Congregations have their roots in Christianity and Judaism, but they have proven particularly successful for propagating religious ideas across America to the extent that even faith traditions with very different norms of organization (e.g., Buddhism) have come to assume a congregational form in the United States (Warner, 1994). The congregational structure creates an ecological niche that has several unique features: (a) Members are expected to have regular, face-to-face contact with one another; (b) the congregation provides another primary space outside the household for developing social relationships and thus is a strong mesosystemic force; (c) the congregation's primary purpose is formational: to help members cultivate ethical and spiritual ideals through repeated engagement with the practices of a faith tradition; (d) the congregation possesses a unique mix of cultural, economic, and social capital that come from the pooled resources of its members and its own link to its tradition; and (e) even when the congregation is part of a larger denominational structure, it tends to be experienced as independent of these structures (Bass, 2004) except under special circumstances.

261

Although the congregational structure of American religion does not include those individuals who negotiate their own spiritual identities through piecing together several faith traditions or the rapidly expanding group of Americans who report no spiritual or religious affiliation whatsoever (16.2% of Americans, including agnostics, atheists, and those who report endorsing "none of the above" religion on surveys; Pew Forum on Religion & Public Life, 2008), congregations remain the dominant feature of American religion. For this reason, the field of congregational studies offers several insights into FBCs that can inform ecological counseling practice.

The Role of FBCs in Providing Care for the Needy

Counselors are most likely to encounter FBCs in their role as providers of care to clients and communities. Acts of care are deeply embedded in faith traditions, and they constitute a key aspect of the meaning making of FBCs regardless of their religion. For this reason FBCs of all types continue to have a key role in the social services system. They do so at many levels, mobilizing individuals to help one another, providing congregational services, and organizing regionally and nationally to combine resources and fund agencies and hospitals.

In the United States, the early 2000s highlighted the importance of FBCs with a major push for them to increase their work among the poor (Kissane, 2007; Wuthnow & Evans, 2002). However, there has been considerable debate over whether FBCs can effectively provide services, especially those seen as critical in moving welfare recipients toward self-sufficiency (Kissane, 2007; Twombly, 2002). A landmark study by Chaves (2004) found that congregations tended to focus more on cultural activities such as worship, religious education, and the arts and less on social services and politics. Furthermore, the social services provided by FBCs to the needy were not only few but also short term and fleeting (peripheral) in nature, and most congregations were too small and lacked the sophistication required to implement social welfare programs.

In contrast, a study of congregations in Philadelphia by Cnaan, Boddie, McGrew, and Kang (2006) found that congregations did provide a substantial amount of social services to the needy and others around them. Ammerman's (2005) research supports these findings, showing that FBCs offered multiple services aimed in many directions with the goal of caring for the needy. Although there are many ways to bridge these two seemingly contradictory findings, at the simplest level they suggest that counselors need to be aware that FBCs are both actively involved in caring for the needy and not equivalent to larger scale social welfare organizations.

So what do FBCs do to care for their communities? The two most common ways FBCs help the needy are by feeding the hungry (mainly nonmembers, through food pantries, soup kitchens, and so on) and caring for children and youth (mainly those of members; Chaves, 2004; Cnaan et al., 2006). They are also involved in service, advocacy and development, education and culture (Ammerman, 2005).

Because of the stigma attached to the welfare system, people are more open to receiving informal care from FBCs than formal care (Cnaan et al., 2006). This informal care includes self-help and mutual aid provided by both the leaders and members of FBCs through church gatherings or activities (e.g., picnics or neighborhood clean-up days). At these gatherings, important connections are made that can help meet community needs. Informal help is also provided via counseling, social action, the provision of technical skills such as financial counseling or legal assistance, and social care such as hospital visits or transportation for seniors.

In addition to this emergency help, congregations offer many types of services. Wuthnow and Evans (2002) identified several such social services, including

- neighborhood projects (such as mobilizing for volunteer work or sponsoring or participating in food, clothing, housing, homeless, or health programs);
- education (including having a school, hosting an academic speaker, sponsoring a mentoring program, and giving money to an educational institution);
- religion (including holding meetings to learn about another religion or participating in joint worship with another congregation of a different religious tradition or of a different racial or ethnic makeup);
- culture (including hiring singers or musicians to sing at a worship service, holding classes to discuss a book other than the Bible, and permitting outside groups to use or rent the building for various needs);
- community services (including discussing race relations in society and conducting an assessment of community needs); and
- politics (including hosting events to discuss politics, getting people registered to vote, and distributing voter guidelines).

The provision of these services creates a wide array of opportunities through which counselors can partner with the FBCs.

Although FBCs often provide emergency care, few congregations provide advocacy and development. In American religious circles, politically concerned groups are mostly found in African American churches, mainline Protestant churches, and Catholic parishes with more than 300 regular attendees (Ammerman, 2005). Congregations fear overinvolvement because of the risk of losing their tax-exempt status if they are perceived as beginning to sound partisan. However, many congregations are politically and economically active, having action groups and educating or mobilizing members on an ad hoc basis. Most activism is channeled through larger outside coalitions or agencies, though some congregations have developed community economic development projects to address poverty through income generation (Ammerman, 2005; Reese & Clamp, n.d.).

Many FBCs work with multiple minority groups and special populations. These institutions have set the stage for culturally specific help—such as indigenous forms of healing—to be given (Yeh, Hunter, Madan-Bahel, Chiang, & Arora, 2004). And for counselors, these congregations can become important partners for reaching these populations. Many minority groups and immigrants tend to be more collectivist in nature. They are also less likely than Caucasians to seek professional mental health services (Zhang, Snowden, & Sue, 1998). Many prefer to seek help from informal care sources such as clergy, traditional healers, family, and friends (Yeh & Wang, 2000). Many congregations run by and for minority groups are able to address cultural values, class values, as well as language variables (Sue & Sue, 1999) that are key to being able to provide care for these groups.

A prominent example comes from the African American church, which was the only place to find mutual aid and support in the pre–Civil Rights era. As a result the church became a major means for education, organization, and leadership (Cnaan et al., 2006). These congregations are generally more active in social service provision than Caucasian churches, especially in specific activities geared to the poorest and neediest members of society (Cnaan et al., 2006). It is interesting to note that in 2005 the most active group in terms of service provision, regardless of congregation size or budget, was the African American church—27% of churches were involved at some level (Ammerman, 2005).

Many African American congregations work to revitalize neighborhoods (Cnaan et al., 2006; Thomas & Blake, 1996). Generally these congregations tend to be situated in areas of high need, and services target more than just the African American congregations. They are responsive to the needs of poor people, people with addictions, and people with disabilities (Cnaan et al., 2006). Furthermore, they bear the load of meeting needs that many consider to be the responsibility of the government. When these needs are unmet in Black neighborhoods, Black churches and mosques get involved to support their members and neighbors (Cnaan et al., 2006). Black congregations have historically acted as political agents and been actively involved in fighting against economic and social injustice (Cnaan et al., 2006; Sunnemark, 2003). Blacks are generally very spiritual as a culture and have relied on this spirituality to thrive. Cnaan et al. (2006) speculated that if a process of secularization happened in this community, there would be a major disruption in the status quo for this population.

Another important population to consider is Latino/as. Latinos make up the largest minority group in the United States, but they are also very diverse (and multiethnic, with at least 22 countries of origin represented); they have multiple in-group differences and no unifying experience (Cnaan et al., 2006). Religion is a major source of identity for this group, creating social cohesiveness and social organization (Cnaan et al., 2006). The resources Latino/a congregations provide include legal assistance, financial assistance for rent, advice for dealing with problems in the neighborhood, and kind words in desperate moments (Menjivar, 2002).

Latino/a congregations tend to be less involved in social service provision than others, especially when it comes to intervening with youths, older adults, and sick individuals. Cnaan et al. (2006) posited that this may be because many of these tasks are already carried out by the extended family. Furthermore, although they are less engaged than other congregations in programs for the poor (e.g., food pantries), they are more engaged in homeless shelters, which may be an unfolding issue in this population.

This overview of congregations within two minority groups in the United States does not imply that there is no cross-assistance among groups. The literature is replete with examples of many congregations that reach across racial and other differences to provide services to those who need them most, and real-life examples abound in neighborhoods all across the United States.

The services FBCs provide present a platform for counselors to partner with them in service provision. FBCs are an important referral point for clients who may be in need. It behooves counselors to explore which services are provided by their local FBCs, as they could serve as referral sources for one another.

Contextual Issues Facing FBCs as Social Institutions

How can counselors connect with FBCs to promote the well-being of their clients and communities? To take an ecological approach to FBCs, counselors must be willing to examine the influences on them beyond the microsystem level. Congregational studies have identified several contextual or mesosystemic influences on FBCs that can inform counseling.

Congregations and Their Communities

Although one might assume that congregations mirror the communities in which they are located, this is very often not the case. Given the religious free market in the United States, congregations often draw from several zip codes, some far from their location. However, congregations are not insulated from the dynamics of their surrounding communities—negotiating these dynamics is often a key determinant of how congregational culture is created. In a study of how community change affects a congregation, sociologist Nancy Ammerman (1997) found four common patterns of response: (a) redefining itself by opening up to the new demographics of the community; (b) moving to a new location that better reflects its existing demographics; (c) becoming a niche church that specializes in some sort of worship, ministry, or practice; and (d) resisting change and slowly dwindling and closing. These dynamics must be kept in mind when counselors interact with FBCs—it is quite possible that the church down the road in an inner-city, predominantly African American neighborhood is a predominantly White niche church with many gay members. This diversity brings with it unique strengths (not all congregations in materially impoverished communities may be materially impoverished) and challenges (not all congregations in a given community will have similar demographics).

Varieties of Religious Presence

Another key feature of how FBCs interact with their community can be seen in the ways in which they put their faith into action in those communities. Roozen, McKinney, and Carroll (1984) conducted a landmark study of congregational mission in public life based on data from several Jewish and Christian congregations from across the denominational spectrum in Hartford, Connecticut. Their analysis identified a two-dimensional typology that locates congregations on worldliness and focus.

Civic congregations are this-worldly and membership centered. Like the chapel on the village green, they are concerned with public issues and see the congregation as an appropriate place for having education and civic discussion but not politics. There is little expectation that the congregation will take coordinated action on civic issues; instead, members are left to their own consciences to decide what to do without interference or guidance from congregational leaders. These congregations tend to be uncomfortable with challenging the status quo when doing so would be seen as partisan.

Activist congregations are this-worldly and publicly proactive. They are concerned with establishing God's reign in the here and now and believe that this is the central work of the congregation. Therefore, such congregations are comfortable critiquing society and making community concerns their own. In this type of congregation clergy are expected to be involved in community action and to be able to articulate a strong social vision. Members are educated to move from prayer into taking action and confronting injustice.

Sanctuary congregations are otherworldly and membership centered. They see their role as providing a place to step out of the trials and challenges of daily life and be uplifted. This otherworldly focus unites members through a common view of liturgy, morality, or common heritage. Although society is seen as flawed, it is to be honored as God's creation; efforts to change society are not highlighted. There is little optimism regarding the efficacy of social action, and people are counseled to be patient and endure until the consummation of God's plan.

Evangelistic congregations are otherworldly and publicly proactive. Although focused on the world to come, they are nonetheless concerned with bringing others into the fellowship of believers. Individual morality is stressed, but there are also active programs for sharing one's faith in public life and bringing others to salvation.

As Roozen et al.'s (1984) typology shows, the mission orientation of a congregation can be crucial in determining its interactions with clients, both as individuals and at higher levels of the ecosystem. For instance, consider the many ways that counselors could partner with FBCs with this knowledge in mind: Civic congregations are likely excellent places for doing psychoeducation but may shirk from more aggressive prevention programs based in client advocacy. Activist congregations seem like natural partners for counselors, but these shared goals should not be confused for purely secular motives on their part, and counselors should be careful not to hijack God for their own service. Sanctuary congregations can be places of great spiritual and psychological refreshment for clients, but they may not have much time or energy for systematic engagement with counselors. Evangelistic congregations are often very involved in their communities, which leads them into contact with counselors, but partnerships will need to negotiate the difficult topic of proselytizing.

FBCs as Microsystems

Because they are involved in the most intimate and central facets of their members' lives, FBCs are often more like extended family systems than bureaucratic ones. However, as congregations grow, this balance of family-like and corporate-like begins to change. For the purposes of size analysis, congregations are often grouped into four categories based on the number of members: family, pastoral, program, and corporate (Rothauge, 1983).

Family congregations (0–50 functioning members) function like a single-celled organism. Power is held by the patriarchs or matriarchs of that family, who have an extended history with the congregation. Newcomers are met by gatekeepers who either adopt them into the family or keep them at bay, depending on the respect shown to the family heritage. The clergyperson is not the central power but more like a family chaplain.

Pastoral congregations (50–150 functioning members) tend to have inner and outer circles of membership centered on the clergyperson. The congregation's life is not very structured but open and organic, often depending on the charisma of the clergyperson. There is an expectation that everyone will know everyone else and see everyone on a regular basis.

The transition to a *program* congregation (150–350 functioning members) tends to be quite difficult, as the organic and intimate nature of the pastoral congregation becomes less tenable with more members. To make this transition, the congregation will need to become more democratic, relying less on the clergy for things to happen and seeing the clergy as enabling and administrating programs, which become more standard and routine. In this type of congregation, elected lay leaders run much of the program and take responsibility for the life of the church.

The largest congregational size (350+ functioning members) is called *corporate* because of its complexity and its developed bureaucratic management style. The clergy in this system tend to function as the chief executive officers and division heads of the congregation, often with the head clergyperson having achieved somewhat legendary status among the congregation. Because of its resources, the corporate congregation can provide programming for all types of people, and much of its work and ministry is done in small groups, which become members' primary ways of socializing.

As these categories show, the ways in which counselors can partner with congregations will be influenced to a large extent by the size of the congregation. Although many counselors might assume that it is the clergy who hold the center of power, this is not the case in family and program congregations. In congregations of this size, it may in fact be more useful to partner with key lay leaders. This would not be the case for pastoral congregations; here things usually happen solely because of the clergyperson's leadership. In a corporate congregation, counselors are not likely to

267

get much access to the lead clergyperson but might work better with an associate. Similarly, formal, ongoing programming suitable to some sorts of prevention work tends to materialize only at congregations of the program size and larger. Therefore, it is important for counselors to consider the size of a congregation when considering systemic interventions or partnerships.

Working With FBCs for Prevention and Advocacy

Who Are the Leaders?

Although the congregational structure of American religion often necessitates some formal leader, there are wide differences across FBCs in the role and nature of leadership. Some traditions, such as the Society of Friends (Quakers), do not have clergy in the traditional sense, though there are elders (who maintain the order of meetings), pastoral visitors, and some individuals with special spiritual gifts who may be recorded as ministers (Friends United Meeting, 2006). On the other end of the continuum are such traditions as Roman Catholicism, Eastern Orthodoxy, and Anglicanism, who see ordination as a sacrament that effects an ontological change in the being of the person being ordained, setting him or her apart from the laity. These theological variations can be important for counselors to consider, but it is often more important to understand who does what in an FBC.

Although theologies of ordination vary, there are two primary variations of official leadership in American congregations. First there is the *professional* model of congregational leadership common among most Jews, Catholics, mainline Protestants, and first-career clergy from Evangelical and African American traditions in which the leader (whether called *pastor, priest, elder,* or *rabbi*) has undergone formal education and mentorship in the craft of leadership in the congregational setting. These leaders tend to work full time and often have some formal preparation in how to care for those in their community. Second there is the *bivocational* model of leadership more common among second-career clergy in Evangelical and African American traditions (Carroll, 2006) in which the congregational leaders often have less formalized training and instead have been chosen as leaders because of some special gift. Many of these leaders work full-time jobs in other occupations and therefore have less time than full-time ministers to spend on the work of the congregation.

In addition to these two models of formal leadership there has been a great increase among some groups (e.g., Roman Catholics) in using lay professionals for specialized tasks in congregational ministry, such as pastoral care. Moreover, immigrant groups such as Muslims, Sikhs, and Hindus also have their own models of leadership, which tend to be more formal than the bivocational model but do not fit into an American professional model. As this variation indicates, counselors would do well to move beyond the simple assumption that all FBCs have a full-time, professional pastor. Instead counselors can engage a wide range of gifts and models of leadership to promote well-being among their clients. Moreover, it is important to consider that many leaders of FBCs are no longer associated with a single congregation; as congregations dwindle in size, it is increasingly common for a single leader to be associated with multiple congregations.

Principles for Working Effectively With FBCs

Research has shown that there are strained relationships between counselors and religious leaders, especially African Americans and conservative Protestants. As one study (McMinn, Aikins, & Lish, 2003) found, this strain is due to a constellation of related factors: (a) Mental health practitioners overrepresent a spiritual but not religious worldview and therefore are unfamiliar with or skeptical of more conventionally religious worldviews; (b) mental health practitioners have used their theories for a theological critique of some religious worldviews; (c) values conflicts, although infrequent, are especially potent in undermining relationships with religious leaders; and (d) mental health practitioners tend to see leaders of FBCs as having no pertinent complementary expertise for helping clients, an attitude that these leaders pick up on. While McMinn et al.'s (2003) interpretations give the impression that counselors are willfully disrespectful toward leaders of FBCs, it may be more an issue of ignorance than malice. As this chapter has demonstrated, many facets of the lives of FBCs make them unique and difficult to understand at first glance, especially for counselors who come from a different cultural location. Therefore, the first step in working effectively with FBCs and their leaders is to gather knowledge about these communities, approaching them with a spirit of openness and appreciation.

With this foundation in knowledge, several other principles emerge for working with FBCs.

Work for Parsimony in Interaction

Since its inception, the ecological approach has stressed *parsimony*, the smallest intervention that will produce ecological concordance with the fewest unintended consequences on the ecosystem (Cook, Conyne, Savageau, & Tang, 2003). This principle is key to interacting with FBCs. Counselors should use their knowledge of the size and leadership training system of an FBC to identify whom to involve and what level of intervention to consider. For instance, a corporate congregation might have an associate minister for pastoral care who would be interested in hosting a multisession series on parenting, whereas a pastoral congregation with a bivocational minister might prefer to receive handouts for referrals or booklets on the same topic.

Forge Commonality in Mission

Counselors and FBCs do not need to share every aspect of their worldviews to be able to collaborate (McMinn et al., 2003; Stewart-Sicking, 2008). Instead counselors should look for common goals that all parties can pursue without having to sacrifice core convictions. An understanding of the variety of religious presence can be very useful in allowing a counselor to identify areas of common mission and those places in which there is likely to be friction. Where there are multiple orientations toward religious presence in a group (e.g., a group of local congregations), counselors should be aware of potential conflicts and also of the division of labor. A civic congregation might be the best location for a community forum on homelessness and mental illness, whereas a neighboring activist congregation might be open to sponsoring a walk for the homeless. By forging a common mission, counselors can avoid theological arguments and bring a diverse group of partners to the table to work on shared problems without any of them feeling resentful.

Respect Differences in Mission and Values

In any community-based partnership, there will be differences in mission and values, whether it is the community policing unit clashing with advocates for the mentally ill or two congregations arguing about the best response to increased drug use in the community. While focusing on a common mission counselors should also build an environment in which differences in mission and values are respected and not allowed to veto productive collaboration. As pastoral counseling students are often reminded, suffering is not the time for theological critique, and this basic principle should guide counselors in their work with FBCs. Instead counselors should foster open and respectful communication with FBCs that focuses on their shared mission.

Build on Assets

As we discussed earlier in this chapter, congregations have a unique set of assets that they can bring to ecological partnerships. One way to capitalize on these assets is to utilize asset-based community development. The asset-based approach to community development assumes that even in marginalized communities, every person has talents, skills, and gifts important to a community and that "each time individuals use these abilities, the community in which they live is strengthened and these people feel a sense of empowerment" (Beaulieu, 2002, p. 5). Thus, strong communities are places where local talents and resources are connected to one another and used (Kretzmann, McKnight, Dobrowolski, & Puntenne, 2005). Each entity within an ecosystem has its own set of assets: people, expertise, social power, networks, financial assets, space, equipment, and cultural assets (cf. Kretzmann et al., 2005). For FBCs, these assets may not be immediately apparent: for instance, niche congregations might have financial and social resources outside of the communities in which they are housed. By assessing the unique assets of FBCs and connecting them to community needs, counselors can play a central role in creating a more resilient community.

Example: The Fairmount Provider Group

All of these principles can be seen at work in the following example from the work of an ecologically minded pastoral counselor (Anno, n.d.).

North Fairmount is a materially impoverished urban neighborhood in Cincinnati, Ohio. Its residents include older German and Italian immigrants from the 1930s, new Latino/a immigrants, African Americans, and, most recently, refugees from the genocide in Burundi. To bring residents together with community service providers and congregations, the counselor hosted a block party for the neighborhood in which helpers and residents could make first-person contact and form relationships. This party led to the development of the Fairmount Provider Group, a group that has been meeting monthly for more than 4 years to network, advocate, and support one another. Participants include social services workers and leaders from a wide variety of congregations ranging across the size, cultural, and theological spectrums. Over the years they have found common areas of mission and partnership: advocating for better funding for programs to combat childhood hunger; and providing wraparound services for the Burundian refugees, including health care, mental health care, English classes, and spiritual care. In their work together, each group brings its own unique assets and commitments in service to the broader shared goals and has built a sense of mutual respect and appreciation. For instance, one congregation has a large unoccupied school building that it has opened to community use, another hosts Alcoholics Anonymous and Narcotics Anonymous groups, and a third is actively involved in petitioning city government.

The Fairmount Provider Group has not limited its work solely to secular pursuits. Those who are interested meet as a small group before the monthly meeting to pray for the needs of the community. On the National Day of Prayer, members of FBCs come together in a prayer caravan to circle the neighborhood in prayer, with a different church leader praying at a dozen locations—schools, recreation centers, food pantries, senior housing—and then they come together for food and fellowship. The counselors and other health professionals from secular organizations are not expected to take part in shared spiritual activities, but they honor it as an important asset to the community.

In this example, we can see how potent the combination of asset building, respectful communication, shared mission, and parsimonious interaction can be. The Fairmount Provider Group has targeted goals that allow its members to share in its mission while honoring their own understandings of public ministry. It has remained open to the core convictions of congregations as communities of prayer. It has learned to be open to different participation in different aspects of mission. And it has helped connect community resources across different organizations.

Implications of FBCs for Counseling Individuals and Families

Although FBCs can be very valuable partners for systemic interventions such as prevention and advocacy, many counselors encounter them more regularly as characters in the stories their clients bring to therapy. Understanding FBCs allows counselors to understand these aspects of their clients' lives more effectively and to evaluate how these organizations foster or hinder the concordance between person and environment that is at the heart of ecological assessment and intervention.

A well-established body of research in counseling, psychology, sociology, and public health has established the many ways in which religion and spirituality are linked to health (for a summary, see, e.g., Koenig, 2005), and counseling has increasingly seen spirituality as the fundamental characteristic of wellness (Myers & Sweeney, 2008). Among other benefits, participation in a faith community supports mental health through providing social support, training in healthy practices such as forgiveness and gratitude, a reservoir of positive emotions, a sense of meaning, and specific religious forms of coping. In fact, religious forms of coping have been shown to confer even greater benefits among those with limited resources (Pargament, 2007). It is not surprising therefore that many clients find participation in FBCs to be central to their well-being and a core resource for their coping.

If this is the case, why not strongly encourage all clients interested in doing so to participate in FBCs that match their own values and culture? Unfortunately, although religion and spirituality can be important resources for health, research has also shown several problems that can result from a poor fit between a person and FBC. Counselors should pay attention to these potential issues just as much as they look for ways in which FBCs can foster well-being.

In his extensive research on spiritual coping, Pargament (2007) suggested three ways in which clients' spiritual pathways (such as participation in an FBC) can be a poor fit with their broader development. The first problem is that clients may choose spiritual groups or practices that are incapable of leading them to their goals. Spiritual extremism or perfectionism, often reinforced by one's community, can promote self-defeating criticism of oneself or others that can paralyze one's development. In counseling, this may manifest in many ways (e.g., clients constantly needing to verify that the counselor is "orthodox," constant scrupulosity over the morality of one's actions or attitudes, or a lack of openness to potential sources of wisdom). Conversely, individuals can engage in spiritual hypocrisy, participating in spiritual communities for extrinsic goals such as social approval or currying God's favor. In not bringing one's authentic self to the spiritual life, one is unlikely to make the kind of sacrifices or efforts needed to reap its benefit, leading to a sense of incongruence in this core aspect of oneself. Clients in this situation are less likely to be able to use spiritual coping methods well, and they may also have difficulty articulating and connecting to their deepest values and identity.

A second problem of fit can emerge when clients choose spiritual pathways that do not match the kind of problems they are encountering (Pargament, 2007), a phenomenon others have named "spiritual bypass" (Cashwell & Young, 2011). Clients can approach a problem in a hyperspiritualized manner, using spiritual language to avoid addressing difficult psychological issues or relying on passive spiritual coping strategies that avoid the difficulty of taking one's own action. Certain problems cannot be solved solely through prayer; or perhaps more accurately, the prayerful way to approach some problems also includes some action. This preference for spiritualized language can manifest itself in the culture of some FBCs as "church speak," a set of stock language for problems or invocation of scriptures that is not in itself a problem but that can mask the specifics of a client's life in ways that require the skilled counselor to move beyond this kind of language.

A third problem of fit can occur when a client does not match the spiritual community in which he or she participates. In this case, the congregational typologies discussed earlier can be useful. For instance, a client whose spirituality has a strong social justice component might be frustrated by the way in which a sanctuary congregation avoids dealing with social issues. An introverted client who belongs to a pastoral congregation may find the lack of chances for anonymity stressful. In situations such as these, in which the person–environment fit with an FBC is a problem, the counselor might give thought to having clients evaluate their participation in these communities and how it fits their own personality, social needs, spiritual needs, and core values. Clients can be reminded of the diversity of FBCs. However, counselors should realize that individuals' and families' attachments to a particular FBC can be deeply rooted, even across generations, and that it may not be beneficial to change them: perhaps one was married there, or family is buried there, or one's ancestors built the building, or one had a spiritual awakening there under the old pastor. Both a lack of fit with a spiritual environment and the loss of that environment can lead to spiritual struggles, which are accompanied by particularly intense emotions. Counselors need to be prudent in working with clients to decide whether they need to change environments, change the environment they are in, or supplement this environment through another.

Example: A "Returner"

James is a 41-year-old client of European descent who came to counseling struggling with symptoms of anxiety and depression. Having recently been made an executive at his urban planning firm, he was surprised at how little this mattered to him. Instead he found himself questioning just what contributions he has really made in his life and whether life itself really has any purpose. That feeling of emptiness scared him and led to even more anxiety. He said that although he didn't feel like he could be old enough to be at midlife, he thought that he was probably undergoing some sort of midlife crisis, and he thought that counseling would be a good way to work this issue out.

After working with his counselor from an existentialist perspective, James has begun to see his questions in more spiritual terms. He has begun reading books on spirituality, mostly from a Buddhist perspective, which he has appreciated, but as he has been reading he has been thinking more and more about Christian spirituality, which both attracts and repulses him.

James was raised in a family-size, conservative Christian congregation in a suburban area, and he has fond memories of his close group of friends there growing up. For much of his childhood he loved church—the singing; the community; the way in which he had a whole group of surrogate grandparents, aunts, and cousins. But as James reached adolescence his identity as a gay man began to crystallize for him. His church had not made a big deal about human sexuality when he was younger, but when James came out to his parents at 15 they sent him to the pastor, who was kind but disapproving, urging James to keep praying for strength and not

273

to give into temptation. Almost worse, the pastor seemed at pains to forget the whole incident happened, and the church seemed to be in denial of James's true identity.

After that meeting James began to drift away from church, slowly at first but then dramatically in his senior year in high school, when he stopped attending. As he went through college and matured in the coming out process he began to identify many ways in which his church community had subtly harmed him—perhaps unintentionally—through its blindness to his presence as a gay man and the inescapable atmosphere of judgment that he experienced. So throughout his adult life James was a spiritual person, especially through interest in the arts, but he had little desire to join a religious community.

In therapy James has said that he wants to consider going to church again. He has a friend who is involved in a congregation open to and affirming of lesbian, gay, bisexual, transgender, and queer persons, and he has decided to take the plunge and attend a worship service. After attending James is encouraged. He found the worship inspiring and the community welcoming. But it was all a little big for him—four times the size of his old church—and the focus on social justice issues was unlike the church he had grown up with, which was much more of a sanctuary from the world.

In working with James the counselor has the opportunity to explore with him the ways in which participation in an FBC might be healthy for him. However, the question of fit is multidimensional, involving the congregation's openness to him as a gay man but also its worship style, size, and attitudes toward social involvement. If James wishes to get more involved with this FBC the counselor cannot merely assume that it seems like a tolerant place with many resources and thus will be unambiguously helpful. It is in this way in which an ecological approach provides additional routes for exploration compared to a more person-centered approach. The counselor may indeed help the client draw on new coping and forms of social support from this community, but issues of fit, which are closely related to issues of meaning and spiritual identity, will also come into play. Knowing some basic information about the ways in which FBCs can differ will allow the counselor to engage in more fruitful conversations and consider the ways in which this involvement can foster ecological concordance.

Summary

This chapter reflects the challenge of the ecological approach more generally: With more complex knowledge come more complex choices. FBCs are critical partners in the counseling field, and the ecological approach illuminates many new ways that they might be engaged in common mission with counselors. But FBCs are also very complicated social organisms in their own right. Engaging them calls for sensitivity, prudence, and a willingness to learn. To this end, this chapter has tried to approach FBCs from four perspectives: how they function as systems, how they are able to provide care, how counselors might interact with them to produce mutually enriching partnerships, and how they are an element of person–environment fit. But this outline is only a start. Just as it is important for counselors to move from generic knowledge about cultural diversity to more specific knowledge of the cultures of their clients, it is important for counselors to move from general knowledge about FBCs to specific and personal knowledge of the FBCs with whom they will partner and in which their clients are involved. And when counselors make the effort to cultivate this personal and connected knowledge, they are likely to find themselves much better prepared to help clients create meaning, pursue well-being, and work for justice.

Discussion Questions

- Which characteristics of FBCs most surprise you as a counselor? How might these characteristics change how you approach working with FBCs?
- In what ways would you be able to tap into the resources of FBCs in your capacity as a counselor-trainee at the different ecosystem levels? Is this any different from the way you perceive yourself to be able utilize these resources once licensed?
- How can you encourage FBCs to increase their partnerships with mental health providers to better meet their congregants' needs without compromising their values? In a similar vein, how can you encourage community agencies to partner with FBCs to meet their client needs without violating their values (e.g., separation of church and state)?
- Which aspects of a client's involvement in an FBC are ethical and appropriate for a counselor to explore? Should a counselor ever encourage membership in an FBC? Should a counselor ever discourage membership?
- *Role play.* Consider the following situation: A counselor at a junior high school has become alarmed at the increase in truancy and disciplinary problems among students from a nearby neighborhood and has been invited by the leaders of a large church in that community to speak to its parenting group about the issue. Before the meeting the counselor and the pastor thought that it might be interesting to talk to other religious leaders from the neighborhood to see whether they might like to be included. Form small groups and assign parts to five members: the counselor; the pastor of the large activist church partnering with the counselor; a bivocational pastor of a family-size, evangelistic congregation; a pastor from a pastoral-size sanctuary congregation; and the lead pastor from a corporate-size civic church. For 15 minutes role-play the discussion about what to do at the presentation and beyond in the community in a fishbowl style in front of the other students in the group. After this discussion, debrief for 15 minutes to discuss which dynamics helped and hindered the work of the counselor and of each pastor.

Recommended Readings

Cnaan, R., Boddie, S. C., McGrew, C. C., & Kang, J. J. (2006). *The other Philadelphia story*. Philadelphia: University of Pennsylvania Press.

Kretzmann, J., McKnight, J., Dobrowolski, S., & Puntenne, D. (2005). *Discovering community power: A guide to mobilizing local assets and your organization's capacity*. Retrieved from http://www.abcdinstitute.org/docs/kelloggabcd.pdf

Roozen, D., McKinney, W., & Carroll, J. (1984). *Varieties of religious presence: Mission in public life*. New York, NY: Pilgrim Press.

References

Ammerman, N. T. (1997). *Congregation and community*. New Brunswick, NJ: Rutgers University Press.

Ammerman, N. T. (2005). *Pillars of faith: American congregations and their partners*. Berkley: University of California Press.

Anno, A. (n.d.). *Community as client: How working with the community brings about positive change in individuals and neighborhoods*. Retrieved from http://aces.lfchosting.com/wp-content/uploads/2010/11/Community_As_Client_Angela_Anno.pdf

Arredondo, P., Toporek, M. S., Brown, S., Jones, J., Locke, D. C., Sanchez, J., & Stadler, H. (1996). Operationalization of the multicultural counseling competencies. *Journal of Multicultural Counseling and Development, 24*, 42–78.

Association for Spiritual, Ethical, and Religious Values in Counseling. (n.d.). *Guidelines for integrating spirituality into counseling*. Retrieved from http://www.aservic.org/resources/spiritual-competencies/

Bass, D. B. (2004). *The practicing congregation: Imagining a new old church*. Herndon, VA: Alban Institute.

Beaulieu, L. J. (2002). *Mapping the assets of your community: A key component for building local capacity*. Retrieved from the Southern Rural Development Center website: http://www.srdc.msstate.edu/publications/archive/227.htm

Carroll, J. (2006). *God's potters: Pastoral leadership and the shaping of congregations*. Grand Rapids, MI: Eerdmans.

Cashwell, C. S., & Young, J. S. (2011). *Integrating spirituality and religion into counseling: A guide to competent practice* (2nd ed.). Alexandria, VA: American Counseling Association.

Chaves, M. (2004). *Congregations in America*. Cambridge, MA: Harvard University Press.

Cnaan, R., Boddie, S. C., McGrew, C. C., & Kang, J. J. (2006). *The other Philadelphia story*. Philadelphia: University of Pennsylvania Press.

Cook, E. P., Conyne, R. K., Savageau, C., & Tang, M. (2003). The process of ecological counseling. In R. K. Conyne & E. P. Cook (Eds.), *Ecological counseling: An innovative approach to conceptualizing person–environment interaction* (pp. 109–140). Alexandria, VA: American Counseling Association.

Friends United Meeting. (2006). *Do Friends have pastors?* Retrieved from http://www.fum.org/FAQs.htm#pastors

Herberg, W. (1983). *Protestant–Catholic–Jew: An essay in American religious sociology.* Chicago, IL: University of Chicago Press.

James, W. (1997). *The varieties of religious experience.* New York, NY: Touchstone. (Original work published 1902)

Kissane, R. J. (2007). How do faith-based organizations compare to secular providers? Nonprofit directors' and poor women's assessments of FBOs. *Journal of Poverty, 11*(4), 91–115.

Koenig, H. G. (2005). *Faith and mental health: Religious resources for healing.* Philadelphia, PA: Templeton Foundation Press.

Kretzmann, J., McKnight, J., Dobrowolski, S., & Puntenne, D. (2005). *Discovering community power: A guide to mobilizing local assets and your organization's capacity.* Retrieved from http://www.abcdinstitute.org/docs/kelloggabcd.pdf

McMinn, M. A., Aikins, D. C., & Lish, R. A. (2003). Basic and advanced competence in collaborating with clergy. *Professional Psychology: Research and Practice, 34,* 197–202.

Menjivar, C. (2002). Religion and immigration in comparative perspective: Catholic and evangelical Salvadorans in San Francisco, Washington, D.C., and Phoenix. *Sociology of Religion, 64,* 21–45.

Myers, J., & Sweeney, T. (2008). Wellness counseling: The evidence base for practice. *Journal of Counseling & Development, 86,* 482–493.

Pargament, K. I. (2007). *Spiritually integrated psychotherapy: Understanding and addressing the sacred.* New York, NY: Guilford Press.

Pew Forum on Religion & Public Life. (2008, February). *U.S. religious landscape survey, religious affiliation: Diverse and dynamic.* Retrieved from http://religions.pewforum.org/pdf/report-religious-landscape-study-full.pdf

Reese, T. D., & Clamp, C. A. (n.d.). *Faith-based community economic development: Principles and practices.* Boston, MA: Federal Reserve Bank of Boston.

Richards, P. S., & Bergin, A. E. (Eds.). (2000). *Handbook of psychotherapy and religious diversity.* Washington, DC: American Psychological Association.

Roozen, D., McKinney, W., & Carroll, J. (1984). *Varieties of religious presence: Mission in public life.* New York, NY: Pilgrim Press.

Rothauge, A. (1983). *Sizing up a congregation for new member ministry.* New York, NY: Episcopal Church Center.

Shafranske, E. P. (1996). Religious beliefs, affiliations, and practices of clinical psychologists. In E. P. Shafranske (Ed.), *Religion and the clinical practice of psychology* (pp. 149–164). Washington, DC: American Psychological Association.

Stewart-Sicking, J. A. (2002). *Measures of religious orientation among counselors with a positive spiritual identity who differ in religious culture* (Unpublished doctoral dissertation). University of Cincinnati, OH.

Stewart-Sicking, J. A. (2008). Virtues, values, and the good life: Alasdair MacIntyre's virtue ethics and its implications for counseling. *Counseling and Values, 52,* 156–172.

Sue, D. W., & Sue, D. (1999). *Counseling the culturally different: Theory and practice* (3rd ed.). New York, NY: Wiley.

Sunnemark, F. (2003). *Ring out freedom! The voice of Martin Luther King, Jr. and the making of the civil rights movement.* New York, NY: Cambridge University Press.

277

Thomas, J. M., & Blake, R. N., Jr. (1996). Faith-based community development and African-American neighborhoods. In W. D. Keating, N. Krumholz, & P. Star (Eds.), *Revitalizing urban neighborhoods* (pp. 131–143). Lawrence: University Press of Kansas.

Twombly, E. C. (2002). Religious versus secular human service organizations: Implications for public policy. *Social Science Quarterly, 83*, 947–961.

Warner, R. S. (1994). The place of the congregation in the contemporary American religious configuration. In J. P. Wind & J. W. Lewis (Eds.), *American congregations: Vol. 2. New perspectives in the study of congregations* (pp. 54–99). Chicago, IL: University of Chicago Press.

Wind, J. P., & Lewis, J. W. (1994). Introduction. In J. P. Wind & J. W. Lewis (Eds.), *American congregations: Vol. 1. Portraits of twelve religious communities* (pp. 1–22). Chicago, IL: University of Chicago Press.

Wuthnow, R., & Evans, J. H. (2002). *The quiet hand of God: Faith based activism and the public role of mainline Protestantism.* Berkley: University of California Press.

Yeh, C. J., Hunter, C. D., Madan-Bahel, A., Chiang, L., & Arora, A. K. (2004). Indigenous and interdependent perspectives of healing: Implications for counseling and research. *Journal of Counseling & Development, 82*, 410–419.

Yeh, C., & Wang, Y. W. (2000). Asian American coping attitudes, sources, and practices: Implications for indigenous counseling strategies. *Journal of College Student Development, 41*, 94–103.

Zhang, A. Y., Snowden, L. R., & Sue, S. (1998). Differences between Asian and White Americans' help-seeking patterns in the Los Angeles area. *Journal of Community Psychology, 26*, 317–326.

Counseling in Context: Counselor Training

Michelle Flaum Hall and Geoffrey G. Yager

This chapter provides a basis for understanding our approach to teaching ecological counseling. Intellectual, emotional, and behavioral flexibility is crucial to the most effective work of an ecological counselor. A plan for achieving these aims is addressed through numerous examples and a potential measurement tool.

This chapter addresses the process of training new counselors to pay close attention to ecological principles in their work with clients. The job of a counselor educator requires creating a learning environment conducive to the development of counseling trainees who will be competent in delivering counseling services. When we as counselor educators are invested in the importance of the ecological perspective, we have the additional expectation that graduates will practice in ecologically sensitive ways. This sensitivity will be reflected in their client conceptualizations and interventions, reflecting each client's unique context. Ecological training will also be evidenced in graduates' self-understanding and continued development. When counselor educators teach from an ecological perspective, they attend to the bidirectional interaction process of the student, dealing with how the student both shapes and is shaped by the training environment. Teaching students to appreciate proximal processes such as individual differences, contextual influences, multiple causation, meaning making, and diversity issues is certainly important for *any* counselor educator. Nonetheless, ecological counselor educators consider these issues essential building blocks that aid their efforts to increase the cognitive complexity of our students.

In this chapter we outline two developmentally appropriate approaches to graduate-level counselor training that focus on increasing students' ecological sensitivity for both self and client: conceptual training with concrete case study analysis and skill training using a self-rating instrument, the Communication Habits Assessment. We begin with our assumptions about ecological counseling and training. Although we acknowledge that we likely make many more, perhaps less obvious, assumptions in our training on a daily basis, these six beliefs give us a place to start.

Assumption 1

Because they must pay close attention to the developmental level of the counseling student, counselor educators should ensure that the presentation of a concept or skill matches the cognitive complexity and developmental level of their students (Granello, 2010; Perry, 1970). Thus, we begin our introduction of ecological principles by stating that at its core, ecological counseling involves a simple, uncomplicated idea: There is *more* to a client's problems and concerns than what goes on within the person and within that person's interpersonal interactions. This basic assumption has been enumerated many times in this text as well as in other resources on ecological counseling (e.g., Conyne & Cook, 2004). Each human being is the product of a complex set of contributing factors, including (but not limited to) intrapersonal characteristics, physical health, intellect, geographic location, gender, race, religion and spirituality, education, and social interactions.

Assumption 2

Ecological counseling *can* be presented in a way that makes it more difficult to comprehend than is necessary. Imagine for a moment that you are a new counseling student in a program with an ecological orientation. During your training you are encouraged to internalize a view of counseling that incorporates the following concepts: microsystems, mesosystems, exosystems, macrosystems, proximal and distal relationships, meaning making, interdependence, concordance, personal niche, reciprocal interaction, and constructivism. Without a doubt, we could take each of these conceptual terms and define them straightforwardly. We could give examples and discuss these concepts until each is understood clearly. Once their meaning is familiar, each of these words will provide a helpful framework on which to build an understanding of ecological counseling. But at least initially, a new counseling trainee will likely be completely unaware of the meaning and application of any of these concepts; they will most likely seem foreign and difficult to comprehend, especially given the student's lack of real-world counseling experience. In fact, if a new student's reaction to this relatively long list of unfamiliar terms is similar to our own, the list may well *initially* engender considerable discomfort and intellectual stress. Although we are not suggesting that intellectual stress is always negative, we do believe that it is best to consider the developmental level of the student when determining how best to introduce concepts. For the graduate-level counseling student, this often means *beginning* with a concrete and more readily understood presentation of ideas. It is our sense that in the area of counseling skills training, many master's students tend to overwhelm themselves with internal directives (e.g., "I *must* make sure that I attend, empathize, summarize, challenge, reflect...").Adding additional ecological conceptualization at this beginning point in the students' learning may in fact prove counterproductive by adding to the potential internal confusion. As students advance in knowledge and in skills, they can integrate ecological concepts, principles, and terminology of much greater complexity.

Assumption 3

Although it is valuable to introduce the term *ecological counseling* directly to beginning counseling students, it is certainly possible to introduce the important concepts contained within the ecological approach without explicitly using the term. In fact, many excellent ecological counselors have no idea that the work they do is ecological in nature. This seems like a minor and unimportant observation, but if it aids a student's acceptance of the ecological approach to refrain initially from giving it a label, we are more than happy to do so.

Assumption 4

When training beginning counselors, we find it helpful to introduce the bidirectional interaction process and proximal processes that shape behavior by expanding Lewin's (1936) formula, in which behavior is a function of the interaction between the person and the environment, into three correlated formulas:

$B = f(P \times E)$ for behaviors
$C = f(P \times E)$ for cognitions
$A = f(P \times E)$ for affect

Lewin's (1936) intention, of course, was to include cognitions and affect as subcategories of behavior, but the application of the formula seems easier when divided into the three components. Given the trilogy inherent in our work (i.e., a focus on thoughts, feelings, and behaviors), it makes sense to give each category separate yet equal attention when conceptualizing and intervening with clients (and with counseling students). In addition, as students begin to apply ecological sensitivity to their own development, it can help to examine the components separately before moving into more complex phases of training later in their programs.

Assumption 5

We believe that an ecological understanding applies equally well to the counselor as it does to the client. For example, Lewin's (1936) formula $B = f(P \times E)$, in which behavior is a function of the interaction between the person and the environment, can be used to understand the beginning counselor just as it helps to conceptualize the client. Students do not learn counseling skills in a vacuum: They bring with them their personal styles of communication, their core issues, their life histories, their emotional triggers, their biases, and a wide variety of additional important influences. In other words, the students' proximal influences shape their interactions with clients (and vice versa). Just as we can list a wide variety of person and environmental factors for clients, we should also attend to the person and environmental factors characteristic of our students. Such is the bidirectional nature of the process of counseling: The counselor's context is a complex interaction of influences, as is the client's. We see it as crucial that trainees increase their ecological sensitivity and learn how to apply self-awareness to enhance skill development. Thus, we present both sides of the therapeutic coin in this chapter: understanding *both* the client *and* the counselor through the same ecological lens.

Assumption 6

Unless the circumstances are particularly unusual, the best (and fastest) way to communicate an ecological counseling approach to new trainees is through the introduction and discussion of concrete client examples, including those of the counselor's own clients. These examples are presented most effectively within a group discussion context. People usually learn most quickly from applications that are presented and discussed with others.

Ecological Counselor Training

Building Ecological Sensitivity Through Meaning Making

In this chapter we provide a set of examples that should be useful in training counselors. Given our previously stated assumption that graduate counseling students often begin programs with relatively simplistic cognitions about the practice of counseling, we often use case illustrations to elucidate concepts from the ecological perspective. We believe that it is critical that counselor educators match instructional methods to the developmental level of their students. Although doctoral-level counseling students will most likely possess the cognitive complexity necessary to entertain immediately the more pedantic elements of the ecological perspective (Granello, 2010), we believe that master's-level students initially benefit from being exposed to more concrete examples.

To illustrate the need to begin concretely with new counseling students, we present the following case based on a class interaction experienced by the first author of this chapter (Hall). This case provides an excellent example of using ecological thinking in a learning setting. It describes the belief of many typical beginning counseling students about the role of the counselor. In this case, the beginning student held the simplistic belief that a counselor's job is to give advice and to tell his or her client what to do. In many ways, this case exemplifies one of the first lessons we teach and directly impacts students' meaning making regarding the role of the counselor in work with clients.

Case Study: Advice Giving

One night in class I had an interesting conversation with my students. It was early in the term, and most of the students in this beginning counseling skills class had just begun their programs.

On this particular night, I was introducing the role of the counselor and how our personal qualities and communication habits influence our relationships with clients as well as our effectiveness in counseling. At one point in the conversation about "unhelpful communication habits" the topic of advice giving came up. One student asked, "Why is advice giving considered unhelpful? If I were paying hard-earned money to see a counselor, I would want him or her to *tell me what to do* to *fix* my problem."

Recognizing a teachable moment, I proceeded to ask her a series of questions, hoping that our exchange would be fruitful for class learning.

"Good question," I began. "Maybe I can give you a scenario that will help you answer that question for yourselves. First of all, can we all agree that *advice* is *contextual?*"

"What do you mean by *contextual?*" someone asked.

"I mean that the advice you give to someone is based on your own life experiences, perspectives, worldviews, values . . . your *context*. In other words, there is no sacred Advice Manual that counselors consult when working with clients."

The students agreed.

"So if there is no one right piece of advice, or one way to *fix* the problem, then the advice that you give is just *one out of many* ways to solve the problem, right?"

"Right."

"Do you think that it is safe to assume that the clients who come to you for counseling will be different from you in many ways?"

"Yes," the class responded.

"Okay, so you will be seeing clients who are possibly of a different gender, age, race, sociopolitical affiliation, religious affiliation, et cetera. In other words, they come from different *contexts*." I could see some students begin to nod their heads in understanding.

I continued, "If I were to hear a client's story and make the assumption that I have the answers to solve his or her problems, I would be discounting the context in which my client lives and from which my client makes decisions. Furthermore, if I simply tell my client what to do, I would be assuming responsibility for the outcome, and my advice may or may not be what this particular client needs at this particular moment in time."

At that point another student chimed in: "And if we tell our clients what to do, who is to say that they will not come to us every time they need to make a decision . . . this doesn't seem very empowering!"

"Exactly," I mused, "which is another reason to pay attention to the habit of advice giving. This is an example of a communication habit that

283

you bring from your own development, or context, into the counseling relationship. The particular habit of advice giving, if overused or used incorrectly, could end up disempowering your clients. Advice giving in your personal context is different. Many of you likely receive calls from friends and family for 'advice.' You may be known in your circle as being wise and giving excellent advice. These are people whose contexts you know well, and these are also people, I would guess, who call you often when they have an issue with which they need help. They *depend* on you for your advice as well as for your listening ear. Because the counseling relationship is different from your relationships with family, friends, and significant others, the implications for advice giving will be different. One old adage that will serve you well as counselors is this: Give a man a fish, he eats for a day. Teach a man to fish, and . . ."

"We know . . . he eats for a lifetime."

"Exactly."

Discussion of the Case

Beginning students often equate helping with advice giving or problem solving. We believe it is important to dispel this belief early in students' counseling careers. In our view, counseling skills involve more than just the skills themselves (e.g., active listening, challenging, problem solving). Counselors use their skills to gain a better understanding of the unique context of their clients (Wilson, 2004; Yager, 2004). Knowing clients within context allows counselors to *communicate* understanding more meaningfully to clients. Counseling skills can also provide counselors with valuable inner dialogues about their own context; their thoughts, feelings, and reactions to their clients; and their personal reactions to the counseling experience.

Similar to many who have come before us (Carkhuff, 1969; Crowley & Ivey, 1976), we believe that a counselor's basic skills lay the foundation on which good counseling relationships are built. Indeed, scholars have conducted hundreds of studies on the impact of particular characteristics of the counselor or his or her context on a particular variable of counseling. Some examples include the effects of student development level on empathy skills (Lyons & Hazler, 2002), active listening on self-efficacy (Levitt, 2001), program accreditation on counselor self-efficacy (Tang et al., 2004), demographic characteristics on perceived empathy (Crutchfield, Baltimore, Felfeli, & Worth, 2000), and counselor likeability/physical attractiveness on perceived counselor competence (Flaum, 2008). These studies make up a tiny sample of the countless explorations of how the counselor—as a person in context—influences the therapeutic relationship. Because studies have demonstrated the relative influence of counselor qualities and skills on the effectiveness of counseling (see Strong, 1968, for more on counselor influence), it seems critical to gather baseline data on counseling students with respect to many of the qualities and skills thought to promote effectiveness in counselors (Carkhuff, 2000). To be effectual in learning basic counseling skills, counseling students must make the effort to become aware of any problematic issues or communication habits that can hinder their ability to both communicate effectively as counselors and understand the contexts of their clients. Therapeutic decisions will then be informed by the counselor's awareness of his or her own internal dialogue.

Building Ecological Sensitivity Through Self-Assessment

Generally speaking, beginning counseling students increase cognitive complexity following basic skills training (Duys & Hedstrom, 2000). In order to maximize the development of basic skills, we consider it helpful for students to gain self-awareness of the proximal processes that impact *their own* learning of counseling skills. Because counseling students must learn how to incorporate new skills and concepts into current ways of conceptualizing and communicating, it is important that they understand the covariations of communication habits across settings (Carter & Hall, 2008), thus increasing their ecological sensitivity. Many beginning students are new to the helping profession, and it can therefore be beneficial to provide opportunities for exploring variations in behavior across personal and professional settings. Like so many other competencies in the counseling profession, building basic competencies in counseling skills requires that we start with self-awareness. To aid counseling students in building self-awareness of these covariations across personal and professional settings, Flaum (2009) developed the Communication Habits Assessment (see Figure 12.1). This instrument, based on beginning counseling skills texts by Chen and Giblin (2002) and Davis, Paleg, and Fanning (2004), provides the beginning student with an opportunity to review present thinking, emotion, and behavior necessary for learning counseling skills. Following a brief assessment, the student is directly encouraged to design plans to address improvements in each area of communication in which self-ratings are below "sometimes." The use of this instrument and the development of plans for improvement have led to remarkably successful learning efforts in our students. Often simply raising students' awareness of unhelpful communication habits is sufficient for improvement to occur. If change efforts run into difficulties, a discussion with the student's faculty advisor or the counseling skills instructor seems to provide the needed incentive (and expertise) to aid the student in dealing with effective revisions and changes in the plan.

Building Ecological Sensitivity Through Case Illustrations

To clarify our thoughts on teaching ecological counseling, we provide two case illustrations. For each we initially describe the client and give a brief description of the client's concerns. These descriptions are similar to the client overviews that one might expect to receive during a case consultation meeting in an agency or educational institution. Following the client description we provide the counselor's conceptualization of the client. Next we include a set of questions that, when addressed by a group of counseling students, would likely stimulate an active discussion leading to a better ecological understanding of the client and the counselor. Then we have written a very brief ecological conceptualization of the client.

285

Figure 12.1

Communication Habits Assessment—Counselor Form

Before you begin learning specific counseling skills, it is helpful to assess your natural interpersonal communication skills, as well as any problematic habits. In this class, you will work not only to learn new counseling skills, but also to minimize unhelpful habits. Why do both? Think of it as smoothing out any chipped paint before applying a fresh coat!

1 = *Never do this skill* (i.e. never in any situation and/or setting)
2 = *Rarely do this skill* (i.e. often not in any situation or setting)
3 = *Sometimes do this skill* (i.e. depends on the situation and/or setting)
4 = *Usually do this skill* (i.e. in many situations and/or settings)
5 = *Always do this skill* (i.e. consistently in situation and in setting)

When completing the assessment, place an O for your skill level in the PROFESSIONAL setting or place an X for your skill level in the PERSONAL setting.

Skill	Always 5	Usually 4	Sometimes 3	Rarely 2	Never 1
COGNITION (Thinking)					
Express ideas logically					
Think abstractly					
Understand and use metaphor					
Consider multiple perspectives					
Recognize patterns in behavior					
Can tolerate ambiguity					
Possess self-insight					
Maintain focus while listening					
EMOTION (Feeling)					
Perceive the mood of others					
Comfortable talking about emotions					
Sense tension in a conversation (self)					
Sense tension in a conversation (others)					
Experience full range of emotion (with awareness)					
Regulate emotion					
Feel what others feel when in conversation					
Label emotions when felt					
Notice others' non-verbal expressions of emotion					
Notice non-verbal emotional expression in self					
Feel comfortable with others' emotional expression					
Feel comfortable with own emotional expression					

(Continued)

Figure 12.1 *(Continued)*

Communication Habits Assessment—Counselor Form

Skill	Always 5	Usually 4	Sometimes 3	Rarely 2	Never 1
BEHAVIOR (Doing)					
Maintain appropriate eye contact					
Use a friendly tone of voice					
Maintain an open posture					
Communicate sense of humor					
Show non-verbal interest (leaning in, head nodding)					
Mirror others' body language					
Mirror others' tone, volume, rate of speech					
Have a warm smile					
Allow for silence in conversation					
Use non-offensive language					
Am respectful of differences					
Discuss disagreements rationally					
Speak concisely (avoid rambling and "fluff")					
Avoid using fillers (um, uh, like)					
Avoid using judgmental statements					
Avoid advice giving					
Avoid circumscribing (talking in circles, making the same point over and over)					
Avoid need to solve problems quickly					
Avoid interrupting others					
Avoid talking too fast					
Avoid monopolizing conversation					
Avoid using monotone voice					
Avoid overuse of slang					
Avoid fidgeting behaviors					

Note. From Flaum, M. E. (2009). *The Communication Habits Assessment.* Unpublished manuscript.

Finally, we wrap up by focusing on the ecology of the counselor as we offer suggestions for dealing most effectively with potential counselor blocks.

William and Anissa

William, a first-year master's student, is seeing Anissa, a White, 14-year-old, eighth-grade girl in a local public school. Anissa, by all reports, is a bright girl who nearly failed last year. She is currently doing very poorly in all of her core classes. An only child, Anissa has been refusing to do her schoolwork, frustrating both her parents and her teachers. Anissa typically arrives late to her classes; refuses to dress properly for gym; and insists on wearing an all-black wardrobe with black lipstick, eye shadow, and nail polish and multiple ear piercings.

Anissa initially told William that she wanted to get along better with her teachers. She believed that one major hassle for her was that "the teachers are prejudiced against me because I dress in black and wear studded jewelry. I think they believe I worship Satan." Although she indicated that she has never been too much into any kind of worship, Anissa acknowledged that she thinks it is fun that some of the kids at school are scared of her, thinking she might be a member of a satanic cult. She really likes rap music and heavy metal and has plans to become a heavy metal rock star. Although Anissa has a guitar, she does not know how to play.

A fine student in elementary school, Anissa began to be sick often and miss school regularly in the seventh grade. Medical evaluation eventually led to a diagnosis of aplastic anemia, a condition in which the body produces lower counts of all three blood cell types: red blood cells, white blood cells, and platelets. Anissa spent several weeks in the hospital for treatment, including blood transfusions and eventually a bone marrow transplant. Despite missing a great deal of school she was promoted to eighth grade because of her excellent scores on the school-administered IQ test. She doesn't want to be left in middle school at the end of the year, and she knows she'll need to improve her grades to be able to start next year at the high school. Nonetheless, she views her school assignments as pointless.

Clearly Anissa went through an extremely scary time medically during the past year, and she simultaneously witnessed her parents' extreme fear and anxiety. While going through the medical crisis, she talked about her condition and her emotions only superficially with her mom and dad. She did not discuss these issues at all with anyone else.

Her dad drives Anissa to school daily, and her mom is constantly in touch with both the school counselor and many of Anissa's teachers. Recently Anissa loaned William one of her favorite heavy metal CDs, which contained a great deal of profanity and direct sexual references. William reports that although Anissa may not know it herself, her teachers find her very likeable, with a good sense of humor. They have reported that Anissa appears to have the unique ability to be able to laugh at herself. Teachers have expressed a willingness to go out of their way to help Anissa succeed.

William's Conceptualization

Anissa is interested in making a statement to school personnel through her outrageous dress and behavior. She is desperately seeking attention and enjoys the reactions of others to the bizarre things she does. Anissa has the desire to shock and surprise others, including me as her new counselor. She does not care about her schoolwork, and she has overprotective parents who have effectively reinforced her past acting-out behavior and who likely collude with Anissa by giving in when she refuses to complete class assignments.

Possible Discussion Questions

1. Could William's hypotheses about Anissa and her behavior be accurate?
2. What, if anything, is William's conceptualization missing?
3. What additional information does William need to make an assessment of Anissa's concerns?
4. What is the possible impact of overlooking certain areas of Anissa's experience?
5. If you were William's supervisor, how would you encourage him to add additional possibilities to his perspectives on Anissa?

An Ecological Conceptualization of Anissa

As we imply in the preceding questions, we view Anissa within her own environmental context. Yes, she may be seeking attention, just as William has indicated. However, an ecological understanding goes beyond this simple truth to ask "Why is it that Anissa is acting in an attention-seeking manner?" or "How does she avoid doing her assignments?" William's statement implies that she is being a willful young adult who has refused to cooperate and who demands inappropriate attention.

From an ecological perspective, we see Anissa as a 14-year-old child who has experienced what most certainly was a very scary and traumatic medical crisis. In this context, we might view her avoidance of homework and her attention seeking very differently. Although she has successfully completed her treatment and returned to school, she has "been through hell" during her illness. She feels overwhelmed and behind at school, perhaps inadequate to complete her school assignments. Her parents, rather than being *over*protective, could be seen as being appropriately caring in their close monitoring of her as she returns to school.

William's conceptualization focuses on Anissa's unusual dress and behavior without placing that behavior within the context of what may well be a very scared child who has missed significant time with her peer group. Anissa is likely seeking attention from others (e.g., other students, teachers, and even William) because she felt exceptionally lonely and alone during her hospitalization. Having others react negatively to Goth clothing, black lipstick and nails, and piercings is probably very rewarding. It may *only* be clothing, but others are *noticing* and *caring* about her! Our understanding of the *context* of Anissa's life directly helps us understand her emotions (e.g., isolated, separate, lonely, scared, overwhelmed, stupid), her cognitions (e.g., "People will only 'see me' if I'm really unusual," "I so want others to connect with me," "Maybe if I don't do my homework, the teachers won't see how stupid I am"), and her behaviors (e.g., wearing black clothing, listening to sexually themed songs, refusing to complete assignments).

To be truly ecological, our conceptualization would of course need to be flexible to accommodate additional relevant contextual information as it is presented. For example, we initially are hypothesizing that much of the behavior that is creating a problem for Anissa at school is tied to her fear

289

and isolation. It is possible that these ideas may need to be totally revised if, in our counseling, we find that Anissa has no apparent anxiety and enjoys the companionship of numerous friends who wear the same type of clothing. It is important to note that our ecological understanding of the client is always evolving as we gain more knowledge of the ecological context of the client. It is in fact this openness to new information that is perhaps one of the primary differences between William's conceptualization and our own.

An Ecological Conceptualization of William

In order to put William into *his* ecological context, we would need to talk with him about his lifestyle, earlier learning experiences, and beliefs. In this assessment let us assume that we have reviewed some of his life history. We have found out that William is a 28-year-old who grew up in a military family with an older brother and a younger sister. As the middle child, it was very important for William to blend in to nearly every situation and not to attract attention to himself. The attention was always directed to his siblings, and that was fine with young William. He is an active member of a local fundamentalist church, and his favorite music has always been country. He is a very caring individual who donates a significant portion of his income to charitable causes.

Clearly, as we talk more extensively with William, there would be even more complexity to our description of his personal, ecological context as a counselor. Additional information would deepen our understanding, but even the short description above would suggest that the interaction and communication between William and Anissa would certainly be affected by the background and experiences of each person. William's conservative family background, his birth order, his present religious preferences, his gender, and his age all add to his worldview that subsequently influences his conceptual understanding of Anissa and her concerns. In William's conceptualization of Anissa we have a summary of his *cognitions* related to this counseling contact. How have all of the various ecological influences in his life (see Figure 12.1) impacted William's *emotions and behaviors?* The answers to this would be assessable through our conversations in supervision. The conceptualization hints that he may be reacting emotionally by feeling discounted, ignored, hurt, and angry because people in his life experience don't typically act the way Anissa is acting. Our hope is that William's relatively negative cognitions and emotions will *not* directly impact how he interacts with Anissa. Nonetheless, it is likely that he is more distant and aloof with Anissa than he may be with other clients.

Can we as counselor educators help William to broaden his perceptions of Anissa? The answer to that question is a resounding "Yes." Our job is to provide the stimulus to extend William's awareness of other potential understandings, explanations, emotional reactions, and, ultimately, counseling behaviors. We must start with awareness because changes in cognitions, emotions, and behaviors only occur after one recognizes a reason to change. The Communication Habits Assessment (see Figure 12.1) provides a useful adjunct to supervisory exploration in creating the needed counselor awareness.

290

Vicky and Delaney

Vicky is a first-year counseling trainee who is working with a 34-year-old African American client, Delaney. Delaney had been in counseling for 4 years, and she recently had to change counselors because her former counselor became ill. Delaney was quite upset that she could no longer see her first counselor because she strongly believed that the counselor had come to know her extremely well. Delaney had trusted her with much that she'd never talked to anyone about previously. Despite her reservations about seeing a new counselor, Delaney came into the first session and, although crying throughout, self-disclosed a great deal of information relative to her distress.

Delaney and her twin sister had grown up with an alcoholic mother. Delaney had been abused as a child, both physically and sexually by some of her mom's boyfriends. As a child Delaney had been extremely nervous, often rocking herself to sleep. Her family did not acknowledge Delaney's nervousness, and there is no way to know if they were even aware of how panicked she often felt.

As an adult Delaney has repeatedly found herself in abusive relationships with men. Her most recent boyfriend engaged in several other sexual relationships even while he was living with Delaney. Although he'd been absent for a year, he recently returned to her, asking to renew their relationship. She is unsure about whether she wants to allow him back into her life because she still feels a great deal of betrayal and hurt about his leaving the last time.

Delaney stated to Vicky that she tries to arrange her schedule to leave the house only early in the morning when there aren't too many people out. She doesn't like being out on the streets for fear of what people might be likely to do to her. She has trouble sleeping, and she often stays up late praying. She reported that she feels most at peace when she is praying with her bible.

Delaney has a very limited support system. She feels that people misunderstand her and misjudge her. Her mother, who is now abstinent, and her twin sister tell her to "snap out" of her depression and simply "go out and do things." Delaney has an 8-year-old daughter from an earlier marriage to a man who was both addicted to crack and psychologically abusive. Her child was in fact conceived when her boyfriend (later to be her husband) raped her while she was sleeping.

Vicky's Conceptualization

Delaney is extremely depressed and is likely in a major depressive episode. With symptoms of posttraumatic stress disorder such as flashbacks and impaired sleep, she is wrestling with ongoing difficulties that make everyday life difficult. She has low self-esteem and continues to be very anxious, likely exhibiting the criteria necessary to be classified as agoraphobic. She is stuck in an increasingly difficult emotional state that will be extremely hard to alter.

291

Possible Discussion Questions

1. How helpful is Vicky's conceptualization of Delaney?
2. Does this conceptualization represent a good synopsis of what we know from the brief case description?
3. As you talk with Vicky she reports a desire to focus on accomplishing a full five-axis diagnosis according to the *Diagnostic and Statistical Manual of Mental Disorders*, but her discussion with you only addresses Axis I (Clinical Syndromes) and Axis II (Developmental Disorders and Personality Disorders). How does Vicky's choice of focus relate to ecological counseling?
4. What else might be added to Vicky's conceptualization to strengthen our understanding of Delaney and her history?
5. What is the possible impact of overlooking certain areas of Delaney's life, environment, and experience?
6. If you were Vicky's supervisor, how would you encourage her to add additional possibilities to her perspectives on Delaney?

An Ecological Conceptualization of Delaney

We view Delaney within an ecological perspective that is not as restrictive as that presented by Vicky. Vicky sees Delaney as being in what might be a nearly irreversible condition. It is of course possible that such a dire prognostication may be true, but an ecological conceptualization, which examines a wide variety of additional contextual contributors to Delaney's distress, cannot be so narrow.

Delaney has experienced an incredibly difficult life, *and* she recently experienced one more major trauma when her previous counselor could no longer work with her. Growing up in an alcoholic family and living through sexual abuse as a youngster are major life traumas. Given her long history of anxiety that has been downplayed and ignored, it seems likely that Delaney has learned to internalize a great deal of her personal emotional distress: She is constantly panicked and on edge. Religion has been Delaney's solace among repeated disappointments and traumas, and the strength of her religious beliefs may prove extremely helpful to later work that she will undertake with her counselor.

As often occurs concurrently among people who have experienced early childhood sexual abuse, Delaney appears to have very low self-esteem: She has cognitively accepted that her own inadequacies have been the cause of her emotional and behavior problems. Dysfunctional and abusive personal relationships appear to be characteristic of Delaney's present environment, and the behaviors that have led to these relationships may well be a function of her beliefs about herself. Although Vicky is likely correct in diagnosing that Delaney is depressed, there is so much more to the life context defining Delaney that the depression seems only a minor part of a more complete understanding.

An Ecological Conceptualization of Vicky

Perhaps in talking with Vicky we find that she is very uncomfortable with ambiguity. Growing up as the only child in a high-achieving family, Vicky learned to have specific, clear goals and to move forward directly to achieve those goals. Sitting back and waiting for clarity to evolve into making decisions is a skill foreign to Vicky's experience. She is a very intelligent and concerned individual who can often help focus a group of colleagues to meaningful and worthwhile accomplishments.

As was true in the earlier case description, there is much more to Vicky than this quick review. Nonetheless, even with this limited ecological context of Vicky as a counselor we perceive that she might want to wrap up Delaney's concerns and worries into a clear, concrete, and finalized conceptual package. She may wish to have specific strategies to implement to help Delaney improve her life and feel better. If Vicky tends to be anxious in the face of vague direction and ambiguity, her behavior in her interactions and communications with Delaney may be pushier and less accepting. Vicky's desire to find solutions and quickly explain things runs counter to Delaney's fears, confusions, and lack of clarity.

As counselor educators and supervisors we will want to broaden Vicky's ability to deal with uncertainty while seeing Delaney. We need to provide the stimulus to extend Vicky's awareness and understanding of Delaney by asking the type of questions outlined in "Possible Discussion Questions."

Summary

We hope that these case descriptions and discussions provide a basis for understanding our approach to teaching ecological counseling. Counselors who are learning to develop an ecological counseling perspective need to be flexible and open to a wide variety of environmental influences in their clients and in themselves. This intellectual, emotional, and behavioral elasticity is crucial to providing the best in client care. The steps to encourage the changes needed to become an ecological counselor are normally straightforward: (a) The counselor educator (or supervisor) needs to promote awareness; (b) alternative hypotheses, feelings, and actions must be introduced; (c) potential plans for change and improvement need to be discussed with the counselor (these plans may have been initially addressed in the Communication Habits Assessment; see Figure 12.1); and (d) the counselor educator must, in an ongoing manner, review and evaluate the counselor's progress in implementing the plan.

The training we have accomplished with our students has been exceptionally gratifying. *Emotionally* speaking we have reveled in the excitement of student explorations above and beyond the immediately obvious intrapersonal influences. *Intellectually* speaking we have found ourselves convinced of the relevance of identifying the ecological context of both the client and counselor. *Behaviorally* speaking we have moved to implement the breadth of ecological counseling into academic as well as clinical coursework. And, as you likely already know, all of reactions described here are a direct product of the interaction of many factors in our own environmental experience. We, too, are a complex fit within our own ecological niche!

Discussion Questions

As with any new skill or way of knowing, we believe that the best way to understand the application of the ecological principles of conceptualization, assessment, and intervention with both clients and beginning counselors is to practice. Considering the complexity inherent in the person–environment interaction for one person, it makes sense that the complexity can increase exponentially when we begin to examine the interaction between two people, such as with the counselor–client interaction. To help students practice applying their understanding of proximal processes and results from the Communication Habits Assessment (Flaum, 2009), consider the following activities:

- Either alone or in small groups, choose one person factor (e.g., gender) and think about how counselor–client similarity or difference with respect to this factor could influence the counseling relationship (see Cook, 1990).
- How might similarities in this factor impact the counselor's and client's cognitions, behaviors, and affect? What about differences?
- How could the counselor best address this, either in session or in supervision?
- Take the Communication Habits Assessment, answering the items based on your professional setting.
- On which habits did you score yourself below a 3?
- What do you believe would be the possible implications of this for your counseling relationships?
- Take the Communication Habits Assessment again, but this time answer from the personal context (i.e., based on your habits with your significant other, friends, or family).
- On which items did you score differently?
- How do you believe the difference in context affects your scores?
- How could you apply this insight to your continual development as a counselor?
- Explore ecological contexts as they relate to relationships by viewing one of the following films: *Harold and Maude* (1971), *The Shawshank Redemption* (1994), *Good Will Hunting* (1997), *Finding Forrester* (2000), *Reign Over Me* (2007), or *The Soloist* (2009).
- What is the central relationship depicted in this film?
- How would you conceptualize the ecological contexts of each member of the relationship?
- What are some key similarities and differences with respect to the ecological contexts of these characters?
- How do the characters adapt or use factors of their ecological contexts to build the relationship? How do some factors hinder the relationship?

294

References

Carkhuff, R. R. (1969). Critical variables in effective counselor training. *Journal of Counseling Psychology, 16,* 238–245.

Carkhuff, R. (2000). *The art of helping in the 21st century.* Amherst, MA: HRD Press.

Carter, J., & Hall, J. (2008). Individual differences in the accuracy of detecting social covariations: Ecological sensitivity. *Journal of Research in Personality, 42,* 439–455.

Chen, M., & Giblin, N. (2002). *Individual counseling: Skills and techniques.* Denver, CO: Love.

Conyne, R. K., & Cook, E. P. (Eds.). (2004). *Ecological counseling: An innovative approach to conceptualizing person–environment interaction.* Alexandria, VA: American Counseling Association.

Cook, E. P. (1990). Gender and psychological distress. *Journal of Counseling & Development, 68,* 371–375.

Crowley, T. J., & Ivey, A. E. (1976). Dimensions of effective interpersonal communications: Specifying behavioral components. *Journal of Counseling Psychology, 23,* 267–271.

Crutchfield, L., Baltimore, M., Felfeli, M., & Worth, S. (2000). Empathic responding skills across counselor education training tracks: A comparison study. *Journal of Humanistic Counseling, Education and Development, 38*(3), 162–169.

Davis, M., Paleg, K., & Fanning, P. (2004). *The messages workbook.* Oakland, CA: New Harbinger Press.

Duys, D. K., & Hedstrom, S. M. (2000). Basic counselor skill training and cognitive complexity. *Counselor Education and Supervision, 40,* 8–18.

Flaum, M. E. (2008). *The effects of likeability and attractiveness on perceptions of the competency of counselors committing ethical violations.* Retrieved from http://www.ohiolink.edu/etd/view.cgi?acc_num=ucin1211918450

Flaum, M. E. (2009). *The Communication Habits Assessment.* Unpublished manuscript.

Granello, D. H. (2010). Cognitive complexity among practicing counselors: How thinking changes with experience. *Journal of Counseling & Development, 88,* 92–100.

Levitt, D. H. (2001). Active listening and counselor self-efficacy: Emphasis on one microskill in beginning counselor training. *The Clinical Supervisor, 20*(2), 101–115.

Lewin, K. (1936). *Principles of topological psychology.* New York, NY: McGraw-Hill.

Lyons, C., & Hazler, R. J. (2002). The influence of student developmental level on improving counselor student empathy. *Counselor Education and Supervision, 42,* 119–130.

Perry, W. G. (1970). *Forms of intellectual and ethical development in the college years.* New York, NY: Holt, Rinehart & Winston.

Strong, S. (1968). Counseling: An interpersonal influence process. *Journal of Counseling Psychology, 15*(3), 215–224.

Tang, M., Addison, K. D., LaSure-Bryant, D., Norman, R., O'Connell, W., & Stewart-Sicking, J. A. (2004). Factors that influence self-efficacy of counseling students: An exploratory study. *Counselor Education and Supervision, 44,* 70–80.

Wilson, F. R. (2004). Ecological psychotherapy. In R. Conyne & E. Cook (Eds.), *Ecological counseling: An innovative approach to conceptualizing person–environment interaction* (pp. 143–170). Alexandria, VA: American Counseling Association.

Yager, G. G. (2004). Training and supervision. In R. Conyne & E. Cook (Eds.), *Ecological counseling: An innovative approach to conceptualizing person–environment interaction* (pp. 171–193). Alexandria, VA: American Counseling Association.

Afterword

I hope that my fellow authors and I have convinced you of the value of the ecological perspective in thinking about human behavior. As I clarified at the beginning of the book, we did not intend to present a brand new theory. It is more of a metatheoretical perspective that provides terminology and relationships among ideas that you can apply across diverse theories. That is, you could conceivably discuss humanistic, cognitive–behavioral, or reality therapy approaches using ecological principles and terms to describe ideas from each theory with respect to their personal, contextual, interactional, and meaningful nature. (That task might make an interesting essay exam question for a theories class.)

The term *ecological* has also been used for some time by researchers and practitioners to explore how people are interactional beings whose well-being is more affected by life contexts than we usually recognize. In recent years ecological language has most often been used by three groups of professionals: (a) intervention specialists working with children, an age group particularly vulnerable to the influences of their family, school, and community contexts; (b) community experts who have always viewed humans as beings-in-context but who have had little interest in understanding how any one person lives out his or her life; and (c) professionals advocating for preventive and social justice interventions, often group-level conceptualizations intended to eradicate the macrolevel factors that promote the systemic distress and disempowerment of people. In my experience social workers introduced to the ecological perspective typically claim that they have been implementing it all along and assert that it's about time that counselors catch up with them.

It *is* about time that counselors stop thinking about people as troubled psyches on legs (or wheels, crutches, etc.) and begin to think more about people as beings-in-interaction involving a host of factors. For example, imagine that the following descriptions characterized one woman:

- Personal characteristics—an innate talent for writing that has never been recognized and developed; cooking skills and a fiery temper both learned from observing a parent; a perception that she is unattractive to potential dates because of an unusually gawky adolescence
- Contextual systems and levels—relationships maintained over time and across distance that define her location in the world at large (family of origin); a series of domiciles, some feeling like home, others a bad fit; a move from a city apartment to a suburban development after marriage
- Interactions—no job opportunities for a career that she loves, and a family dependent on the income from a career she hates; being the only artistic type in a family of rational problem solvers; intersectional identities and ambivalent reactions from others stemming from her status as an Orthodox Jew and a Southern woman
- Meaning making—life values that stress both concern for others and materialism, upward job mobility versus unselfish giving; viewing herself as Native American because a great-grandparent lived on a reservation

What types of life problems might this woman be vulnerable to developing? What resources and challenges does she have in her life?

Although the ecological perspective is not exactly new, the model as presented here in this book is not the same type of ecology discussed by others. The most significant change in focus is the emphasis on meaning making. For example, home is the physical address where one lives, but it is also more: whether it fits one's dreams for a home or represents a fall from grace occasioned by the loss of a job or is simply a place to sleep between activities. People of color are certainly subjected to macro- and microaggressions; however, one person of color may be oblivious to all but the most egregious acts of discrimination, whereas his best friend may perceive discrimination where none has occurred. Meaning making defines the possibilities a person sees available in life as a whole, for better or worse. One former client thought that science careers were not an option because of her lack of aptitude: On an achievement test she scored only at the 93rd percentile in science rather than the 99th percentile, as she did in all other subjects! The meaning of life, in its trivial daily manifestations and the questions we ask at the brink of our endurance, always rests in the heart and mind and spirit of the person.

To use the ecological perspective in counseling, one should ideally have a broad understanding of human behavior and the counseling change process; curiosity, tolerance for ambiguity, respect for clients' knowledge about life, and an open mind are crucial. Because most people's problems are determined by many factors, there is rarely one correct goal or one best strategy. Professional wisdom is a matter of being able to see themes within a client's life and to quickly sort through possible change strategies to select something that fits the client's needs and comfort zone. We never stop learning these things.

Counselors also need to remember that our sense of rightness about interventions implicates our own meaning making, both professional and personal. We use some interventions because they fit with (frequently unarticulated) notions about the change process in addition to systematic knowledge about how to change people's lives effectively. Given the breadth of topics covered in this book, it is very likely that some offer new areas to explore with clients: What do our clients hope to get out of life? Who do they aspire to be, and why? What is their ecological niche like, and how do they wish it were different? How did people know them in high school, and what happened to that emergent person? How do they feel about growing older? There are many ways to discern how our clients see themselves in the context of the world around them and many, many ways that they can develop new skills, affirm life values, learn to interact more effectively, and make more satisfying choices starting from where they are now. The same is true for us as counselors!

In particular, people are interactional creatures who often find their greatest satisfactions through relationships with others. One aspect of this interaction worth exploring in counseling is the range and meaningfulness of relationships from the client's perspective and ways to enrich them consistent with the client's resources and challenges. Religious traditions also teach us that people find fulfillment in service to others. Such service, again defined in terms meaningful to the client and actualized in forms that fit his or her life (e.g., giving money to charity, volunteering, engaging in activism), can serve as a life-giving antidote to the often toxic focus on material success and personal achievement in our culture. I know from personal experience that membership in a faith-based community can be a powerful source of life meaning and supportive relationships, although these communities can be just as dysfunctional as any other type of community! Counselors can certainly encourage clients to consider whether such communities might be helpful to them and whether particular options are a good fit for them.

The ecological perspective also strongly encourages counselors who are accustomed to defining counseling as direct service with individuals to stretch their own professional parameters. This recommendation is a bit ironic in that one of the unique contributions of ecological counseling as developed in this book is its application to just this familiar version of counseling practice (as opposed to community development or prevention, for example). We have hoped to coax you into thinking of new directions beyond the remedial, direct service we know and love. In particular, preventive and social justice initiatives are logical avenues to pursue, as the counseling profession has officially recognized in publications, statements about competencies (e.g., advocacy), convention themes, and so on. What might we do collectively and individually to change conditions of our shared world that distress and oppress others? How might we train new professionals to conceptualize concerns more broadly than we were taught some time ago and empower clients to confront the unjust realities of their lives? How might we unwittingly sustain these systemic injustices by personalizing the causes of clients' pain rather than recognizing their contextual or interactional nature? Who or what is served by how we conceptualize our work?

Finally, the literature supporting the ecological perspective encourages a far more complex view of diversity issues than has been characteristic of recent years. Diversity related to gender, race, ethnicity, and other variables is not the property of an individual but an interactional process that begins in sociocultural categorizations of people, is elaborated through systems of meaning and personal and group interactions, and ends in considerable heterogeneity within these categories. Consequently, although people of a culture can agree about the traditional stereotypes of womanhood, there is incredible variability among women as a group in how they live out their lives as women.

What this means for us as counselors is that we need to be careful in making statements like "Women are . . ." or "African Americans are . . ." We will probably be mistaken if we assume that any member of such a classification will closely fit a summary listing of characteristics developed for the group in general. Clients might find it helpful to discuss how such lists do *not* describe their own lives very accurately: How has your own life permitted you to develop your own version of being a woman/person of color/etc.? How meaningful and satisfying has this unique version been for you? Considering that you are still a person in process of becoming, how might you like to change things in the future?

The implications for researchers are more challenging. Categories of gender and race are generally not meaningful as independent variables unless there are some conceptual reasons to expect differences between groups. For example, it makes sense to compare men's and women's career plans vis-à-vis some aspect of their family roles because evidence suggests that the sexes do differ with respect to life plans. Far too often, however, researchers compare men and women just to see whether they might differ on something serendipitous. The researcher is then typically stumped to explain the results of such proverbial fishing expeditions in any meaningful fashion. Far more meaningful studies come from researchers' efforts to consider what about the interactional nature of gender might produce differences between men and women and how each sex might differ because of gender dynamics as well. Helms, Jernigan, and Mascher (2005) were much more bluntly critical about research on race: Because there is no general consensus on what defines racial groups, researchers who use racial categories for comparison are using "factitious" (p. 27) categories that serve as "conceptually vacuous correlates of other variables" (p. 32)! In short, researchers interested in studying diversity need to be well educated about what their categorization of interest actually means and which research questions are meaningful to ask based on professional knowledge today.

If you find yourself questioning some things about professional work that you formerly took for granted, we have succeeded in stretching your professional boundaries. The fundamental things still apply: Clients ask for our help to change their lives. We can help only if we are open to understanding reality as they experience and understand it and if we can communicate our compassion and respect for them. Let me close with a story told by Kagan (2003):

> There is a fable of a king who asked his wisest advisors to reduce to one word the knowledge contained in all of the volumes in the palace's library. After years of work, the scholars brought the king a piece of paper on which was written the single word "maybe." (p. 20)

Maybe a certain set of ideas or research findings can explain a client's behavior, and maybe it cannot. Maybe you have learned something from the ecological perspective that is worth using; if not, I hope the process of engaging these ideas has clarified what does work for you and why. There are many ways to be an ethical, effective professional. I hope that you have considered what that means to you personally and as part of a profession of helpers and that you feel some renewed excitement about doing work that at its core is genuinely life affirming.

References

Helms, J. E., Jernigan, M., & Mascher, J. (2005). The meaning of race in psychology and how to change it: A methodological perspective. *American Psychologist, 60,* 27–36.

Kagan, J. (2003). Biology, context, and developmental inquiry. *Annual Review of Psychology, 54,* 1–23.

Index

Figures and tables are indicated by f and t following page numbers. Alphabetization is letter-by-letter (e.g., "Ecologically Grounded Problem Guide" precedes "Ecological niche").

Courage, 21
Craik, K. H., 70
Cramer, D., 165
Crethar, H. C., 148
Crowell, Jeri, 10, 207, 214, 217–218, 221*f*
Crum, R. M., 236
Cues, 51, 108
Culture. *See also* Diversity
    changing person–environment
        interactions and, 145–146
    cultural identity development,
        162–167
    culturally related behavior, 7
    deep cultural meaning, 54
    defined, 53
    diagnosis and, 190–191
    diagnostic process to be mindful of,
        138–139
    factors that contribute to cultural
        identity, 165
    intersectionality of multifaceted
        cultural identities, 167–169

D

Dalila, Nzingha, 229
D'Andrea, M., 174
Davino, K. M., 50
Davis, C. G., 121
Davis, M., 285
Deep cultural meaning, 54
Deficits, 147, 191
DelVecchio, W. F., 17
Demick, J., 72
Depression, 57, 119, 189, 190, 236, 273
Detweiler-Bedell, J., 199
Development. *See* Human development
Developmental niche, 48, 180
Diagnosis, 10, 187–196
    in ecological perspective, 138–140,
        192–196
    environmental assessment and,
        182–183, 193–194
    of patterns of interpersonal interaction,
        194–196
    problems arising from within the
        person, 192–193
*Diagnostic and Statistical Manual of
    Mental Disorders* (3rd ed.; *DSM-III* and
    DSM-III-R), 188

*Diagnostic and Statistical Manual of
    Mental Disorders* (4th ed., text rev.;
    DSM-IV-TR), 182, 183, 187–189, 192,
    197, 230, 234, 247
Dialectical behavior therapy, 101
Diathesis-stress model, 191
Dimensional perspective, 192
Discordance, 8, 75
Discrimination, 108–112. *See also*
    Racism
    environmental factors, 39
Disease perspective, 192
Disorder vs. order, 51
Distal contexts, 44, 165, 166, 171
Distancing, 58
Dittloff, Mark, 120
Diversity, 161–178
    Big Five personality traits across,
        17
    in chemical dependency and substance
        abuse programs, 240–246
    child-rearing practices and, 47
    consistency vs. authenticity and, 24
    cultural identity development,
        162–167
    culturally related behavior, 7
    ecological perspective and, 169–171
    factors that contribute to cultural
        identity, 165
    family obligations and, 46
    happiness and, 21
    influence of ecosystem on cultural
        identity, 165–167
    intelligence and, 116
    interactional behavior and, 89–91
    intersectionality of multifaceted
        cultural identities, 167–169
    MST as culturally competent
        practice, 248–249
    multicultural competency, 171–174
    power and, 58
    in religious congregations, 265
    school personnel and, 220
    social support and, 47
    sociocultural classification in
        determining, 106
    stereotypes based on race, 107
    wellness and, 22
Divine guidance, 232
Dolan, P., 223
Domestic violence, 149, 220

Double approach-avoidance conflicts, 194–195
Draguns, J. G., 138
Drinking problem. *See* Chemical dependency and substance abuse programs
Drive regulation, disordered, 193
Dropout rates, 212
Drug abuse programs. *See* Chemical dependency and substance abuse programs
DSM. See Diagnostic and Statistical Manual of Mental Disorders
Duckworth, A. L., 23
Duncan, A. E., 237
Dweck, C. S., 114, 117
Dyadic relationships, 43
Dysfunctions, diagnosis of. *See* Diagnosis

E

Eastern vs. Western cultures, 54
EBP (Evidence-based practice), 246–248
Eckles, Barbara, 99
Ecological analysis, 174
Ecological concordance, 217
Ecologically Grounded Problem Guide, 198–199, 200*t*
Ecological niche, 18, 48–50, 180, 184, 186
Ecological perspective, 6–9
  as best practices model, 150–152
  collaborating with faith-based community, 152–154
  in counselor training, 280–281
  defined, 6, 208
  drug abuse and addiction counseling, 245–246
  fundamental propositions of, 6, 131–134
  goals of, 8–9, 297
  individual counseling, 134–142
    diagnosis, 138–140
    planning and implementing change process with clients, 140–142
    problem identification, 134–138, 136–137*t*
  interactions and, 70
  interventions beyond remedial, personal process, 143–150
    environmental interventions, 144–146
    new roles of counselors, 143–144

preventive counseling, 146–148
social justice, 148–150
teaching at UC, 154
meaning making and, 104, 131
metaphor of ecology as basis for, 4–6
organizational approach, 150–154
origins of, 38–39
school counseling from, 213–214
Ecological validity, 134–135, 173–174
Ecomaps, 183
Ecosystem, defined, 5
Education
  of counselors. *See* Counselor training
  poverty and, 57
  rural schools, 212
  school as microsystem, 208
  school children counseling. *See* School counseling
  urban schools, 210, 212, 214–218
Edwards, John, 84
Ego identity, 168
Ego resiliency, 23
Eliason, M. J., 247
Ellis, Albert, 101
Embedded contexts, 44
Emotional insecurity, 212
Empathy skills, 284
Entity theory, 114
Environment
  behavior understood within, 6–7, 39
  defined, 38, 70
  diagnosis and environmental assessment, 182–183, 193–194
  drug and alcohol use linked to, 237
  oppressive environment, 146
  person–environment interactions, 6–7, 69–77, 130, 144–146. *See also* P × E formula
  school environment or climate, 209, 214
  traits interacting with, 17–19
  treatment goals for, 197
Environmental status examination, 183, 183*t*
Episcopal priests, balance of private life with priesthood, 25
Erickson, M., 23

Gender (*Continued*)
  "doing gender," 89
  drug use and, 241
  gendered self, 27–30, 106
  home–career conflicts, 87–89
  masculinity ideology, 89
  personality-work environment
    match and, 73
  self-esteem and, 26
  stereotypes, 107, 110
Generational effects, 82–83, 167
Generation Y, 167
Genetics, 14–15
Genograms, 183
Gerber, L. A., 150
Gerstein, L. H., 150
Giblin, N., 285
Gielen, U. P., 138
Gilbert, L. A., 28
Gleser, G. C., 201
Globalization, 27, 59–60, 238
Goals and planning of treatment,
  196–198
Goals of ecological counseling, 8–9
Goldstein, H. W., 72
Gomez, Jill, 229
Goodness of fit, 69, 72–74, 165, 201
Goodwin, R., 165
Gottfredson, L. S., 17–18, 74
Grados, J. J., 222
Gratitude, 21
Greenfield, P. M., 54
Grieving, 120–122
Grit, 23
Gritter, G. W., 201
Group counseling, 143
Group interactions, 45, 46
Guadalupe, K. L., 167

H

Hall, Michelle Flaum, 10, 279
Hamilton, J., 171
Happiness and psychological wellness,
  20–22, 102, 198
Harkness, S., 47
Harley, D. A., 242, 244
Harpham, T., 238
Harris, M., 237
Harris, T., 168
Haslam, S. A., 14

Health, ecological framework for, 181–184
Healthy development, 218
Heckman, E. F., 174
Helms, J. E., 166, 300
Herr, E. L., 213
High-stakes testing, 210–211
Hipp, J. A., 59
Hispanics
  religious congregations of, 264–265
  substance abuse counseling for, 240–242
HIV/AIDS, 238, 243
Holder, H. D., 237
Holistic assessments and interventions,
  217
Holland, J., 73, 75
Hollensbe, E. C., 25
Hollis, J., 194
Home–career conflicts, 87–89
Homeless individuals, 129
Horney, M. J., 14
Hudson's series of relationship assess-
  ment instruments, 183
Huey, S., 248
Hughes Act of 1970, 232
Human development, 77–83
  ecology of, 77–78
  healthy development, 218
  language development, 104–106
  P x E interaction and, 78–80
  stage/phase developmental
    approaches, 117
Humanity, 21
Human rights advocates, 39
Hurst, J., 143
Hutchison, E. D., 45, 169
Hypocrisy, 272

I

Identity development
  personal identity, 24
  place identity, 41
  self-identity and self-esteem, 24–26
  sociocultural identity, 26–27
Ihilevich, D., 201
Inclusion, 198
Incremental theory, 114
Individual counseling
  in ecological perspective, 134–142
  in faith-based communities,
    271–274

Q

Qualitative differences in knowing about life, 117
Quintana, S. M., 27

R

Racial and ethnic issues. *See* Culture; Diversity; Stereotyping; *specific racial or ethnic group*
Racism, 111, 244
Rader, J., 28
Rashid, T., 21
Reactive attachment disorder, 191
Reciprocal gene-environment theory, 191
Referral, 134
Regional substance abuse organizations, 239
Religion. *See also* Faith-based communities (FBCs); Spirituality
    addictions, view of, 231
    diagnosis and, 190
    meaning making and, 112–113
    mental health issues and, 170
Religiousness, defined, 112
Relocation, 41, 49
Resilience, 22–24
    children living in poverty and, 56
    culturally based, 23
    defined, 22
    ego resiliency, 23
    grit, 23
    intimate, mutual relationships and, 47
    meaning making and, 119–120
    MST building, 249
    preventive counseling and, 147–148
    of stigmatized groups, 109
    struggling with adversity and, 80
Respect for differences, 270
Restorying, 119
Ringeisen, H., 220
Rivera, E. T., 148
Rivera, L. M., 163
Roberts, B. W., 17, 85, 86
Robinson-Wood, T. L., 89
Rockquemore, K. A., 164
Rodriguez, D., 243
Roles in everyday life, 85–87
Rollings, L., 168
Rollnick, S., 201

Roney, K., 209
Roozen, D., 266
Ross, C. E., 51
Roysircar, G., 150
Runnerstrom, M. G., 59
Rural schools, 212

S

Saegert, S., 56
Saint Mary's Center (Oakland, California), 245–246
Salience, 44
Sanctuary congregations, 266
Sandler, I. W., 121
Savageau, C., 196
Savickas, M. L., 24, 87
Scarr, S., 191
Schaller, M., 53
Schneider, B., 72
Schneider, D. J., 107, 108, 110, 111
School counseling, 10, 207–227. *See also* Education
    advocacy and, 149
    assessment and diagnosis, 187–188, 190, 193–194
    case example, 214–216
    challenges in, 209–213
    comparison of Asian and U.S. schools, 52
    ecological analysis, 216–219
    ecological checklist for, 221, 221*f*
    ecological concepts, 208–209
    ecological perspective, 213–214
    interventions in school environments, 219–221
    school as microsystem, 208
School environment or climate, 209, 214
Schutz, W., 197–198
Schwartz, S. J., 164, 165
Schwarzbaum, S., 165
Scott, Jerry, 99
Sebera, Kerry E., 10, 207
Seidman, E., 52
Self, 45, 114, 171
Self-assessment by counselor, 285
Self-efficacy, 26
Self-esteem, 24–26, 76, 197, 218
Self-identity, 24–26
Self-satisfaction, 21
Self-views, 24–25, 197

315

T